The Cambridge Companion to Gilbert and Sullivan

Memorable melodies and fanciful worlds – the comic operas of
Gilbert and Sullivan remain as popular today as when they were first
performed. This *Companion* provides a timely guide to the history
and development of the collaboration between the two men, including
a fresh examination of the many myths and half-truths surrounding
their relationship. Written by an international team of specialists, the
volume features a personal account from film director Mike Leigh on
his connection with the Savoy operas and the creation of his film
Topsy-Turvy. Starting with the early history of the operatic stage in
Britain, the *Companion* places the operas in their theatrical and musical
context, investigating the amateur performing tradition, providing new
perspectives on the famous patter songs and analysing their dramatic
and operatic potential. Perfect for enthusiasts, performers and students
of Gilbert and Sullivan's enduring work, the book examines their legacy
and looks forward to the future.

David Eden is a former Chairman of the Sir Arthur Sullivan Society
and is currently editor of its *Magazine*.

Meinhard Saremba is a freelance author, translator and broadcaster.

The Cambridge Companion to

GILBERT AND SULLIVAN

. . . .

EDITED BY
David Eden and Meinhard Saremba

CAMBRIDGE
UNIVERSITY PRESS

CAMBRIDGE UNIVERSITY PRESS
Cambridge, New York, Melbourne, Madrid, Cape Town, Singapore, São Paulo, Delhi

Cambridge University Press
The Edinburgh Building, Cambridge CB2 8RU, UK

Published in the United States of America by Cambridge University Press, New York

www.cambridge.org
Information on this title: www.cambridge.org/9780521716598

© Cambridge University Press 2009

First published 2009

Printed in the United Kingdom at the University Press, Cambridge

A catalogue record for this publication is available from the British Library

Library of Congress Cataloguing in Publication data

The Cambridge Companion to Gilbert and Sullivan / edited by David Eden, Meinhard Saremba.
    p.   cm.
Includes bibliographical references and index.
ISBN 978-0-521-88849-3
1. Sullivan, Arthur, Sir, 1842–1900. Operas.   2. Gilbert, W. S. (William Schwenck), 1836–1911 –
Criticism and interpretation.   I. Eden, David, 1942–   II. Saremba, Meinhard, 1960–   III. Title.
ML410.S95C35   2009
782.1'20922 – dc22   2009022104

ISBN 978-0-521-88849-3 hardback
ISBN 978-0-521-71659-8 paperback

Contents

Illustrations

Frontispiece A: Arthur Sullivan 1842–1900. Photo courtesy of Sir Arthur Sullivan Society.

Frontispiece B: W. S. Gilbert 1836–1911. Photo courtesy of Sir Arthur Sullivan Society.

1 The Tower Furnishing Company's advertisement. *Kensington and Hammersmith Reporter*, January 1888. [*page* 16]

2 Rebecca defies the Templar in Sullivan's *Ivanhoe*. Unidentified contemporary periodical. [18]

3 Mechanised characters in Gilbert's *Mountebanks*: Hamlet and Ophelia as clockwork dummies. Unidentified contemporary periodical. [21]

4 Two great men fail to convince: *Jane Annie* by J. M. Barrie and Arthur Conan Doyle. *The Queen*, 20 May 1893. [25]

5 *In Re His Majesty*: Sir Arthur to Sir Alexander – 'Not such child's play as you thought, is it, Mackenzie?' *The Entr'acte*, 6 March 1897. [30]

6 Sullivan the musician: conducting the Leeds Festival. *Illustrated London News* (23 October 1886), p. 421. [46]

7 James Gillray: *The March on the Bank* 1787. Private collection. [54]

8 A contemporary take on *Ruddygore*: *Moonshine*, 12 February 1887. [56]

9 *The Oak and the Reed*: illustration by Thomas Bewick to Aesop's *Fables*, 1818. [93]

10 Charles Mathews as Mephistopheles in F. C. Burnand's *Faust and Marguerite*: caricature by W. S. Gilbert. *Fun*, 23 July 1864. [100]

11 Stately home opera: *Haddon Hall*. *Illustrated Sporting and Dramatic News*, 8 October 1892. [111]

12 Rosemary Joshua, Anne Collins and Anne-Marie Owens in the ENO production of *Princess Ida* (1992). Courtesy of English National Opera. Photo credit: Michael Le Poer Trench. [130]

13 The Fairies have the stage to themselves in *Iolanthe*. Courtesy of Carl Rosa Opera 2008. Photo credit: Ralph Rapley. [144]

14 Jim Broadbent and Allan Corduner as Gilbert and Sullivan in *Topsy-Turvy*, directed by Mike Leigh, 1999. Courtesy of Thin Man Films. Photographer Simon Mein © October Films, October Films/Photofest. [158]

15 *Topsy-Turvy* (directed by Mike Leigh, 1999): first night of *The Mikado*. Central figures, from left to right: Allan Corduner (as Sir Arthur Sullivan), Timothy Spall (as Richard Temple/The Mikado) and Jim Broadbent (as W. S. Gilbert). Courtesy of Thin Man Films. Photographer Simon Mein © October Films, October Films/Photofest. [175]

Note. While the editors have made every effort, it has not always been possible to identify the ownership of copyright, if any, in Victorian periodicals and other works of similar date.

Contributors

Michael Beckerman is Professor of Music in New York, co-founder and president of the Czechoslovak Music Society and director of the Center for Interdisciplinary Studies in Music (CISM). His major publications include books on Janáček and Dvořák.

Ian Bradley has sung Gilbert and Sullivan on the QE2 in mid-Atlantic, with the widow of a British Prime Minister in Oxford Town Hall, with an Anglican bishop on the sacred island of Iona, live on BBC Radio 4 accompanied by Donald Swann and Rolf Harris, in a cellar in Philadelphia and from the pulpits of several churches. A Vice-President of the Sullivan Society and Honorary Life President of the St Andrews University Gilbert and Sullivan Society with whom he has sung several principal bass roles, he is the author of the *Complete Annotated Gilbert and Sullivan* and *Oh Joy! Oh Rapture! The Enduring Phenomenon of Gilbert and Sullivan* as well as over thirty other books on less compelling subjects. He is also Reader in Practical Theology in the School of Divinity and Honorary Church of Scotland chaplain at the University of St Andrews and Associate Minister of the Parish Church of the Holy Trinity, St Andrews. He broadcasts frequently on BBC Radio 4.

Horst Dölvers is a retired professor of English Literature at Technische Universität Berlin. He has published on a wide range of subjects including the Vøluspa, an Eddic poem written in Old Norse, Robert Louis Stevenson's narrative art, Walt Whitman's poems as set to music by British composers between 1880 and 1920, and deconstructive positions in literary theory. In 1994, he brought out a monograph on a Victorian picture book, Walter Crane's *The Baby's Own Aesop*. This he expanded, in 1997, into a study of English fables and parables of the nineteenth century and their illustrations. In 1999, he published a monograph on Jonathan Swift's friend, Dr Thomas Sheridan, and the dunces of Dublin. Since then, he has written about Hubert Parry and Frederick Delius.

David Eden, acknowledged Sullivan scholar, is a founder member of the Sir Arthur Sullivan Society. He has been editor of the Sullivan Society *Magazine* since its inception, and he has been chairman for a number of years. His publications include *Gilbert and Sullivan: The Creative Conflict* (1986); *W. S. Gilbert: Appearance and Reality* (2003) and *Sullivan's Ivanhoe* (2007). He has also written and edited specialist studies of works by Sullivan: *The Chieftain, The Gondoliers, The Grand Duke, Princess Ida, Haddon Hall, Ivanhoe, King Arthur, The Mikado, Ruddigore, The Yeomen of the Guard* and others. In addition, he has written sleeve notes for several recordings of Sullivan's works.

Laura Kasson Fiss has an AB in English and Music (Vassar College, Poughkeepsie, NY) and an MA in Text and Book (University of Birmingham, England). She is currently a doctoral student at Indiana University in the English department, with a minor in Victorian Studies. She has presented papers on Charlotte Brontë's reading and the work of language in vocal pedagogy, as well as Gilbert and Sullivan. Her research interests include Victorian humour, sound and affect.

David Russell Hulme, musicologist at the University of Aberystwyth (Wales) and conductor, has a life-long association with the Savoy operas. He completed a PhD based on a study of Sullivan's autograph full scores, has published widely on English opera and has conducted the works of Sullivan and Gilbert worldwide for the Carl-Rosa Opera Company.

Raymond Knapp is Professor of Musicology at the University of California, Los Angeles, and author of *The American Musical and the Formation of National Identity*, winner of the George Jean Nathan Award for Dramatic Criticism. He has also published books on Brahms and Mahler.

James Brooks Kuykendall is Chair of the Music Department at Erskine College in South Carolina; his PhD dissertation on a ceremonial style in English music won the Donald J. Grout award from Cornell University in 2005. He was the Charterhouse Ralph Vaughan Williams Research Fellow in 2003, and has edited two volumes of William Walton's orchestral works for the new critical edition published by Oxford University Press.

Mike Leigh, is the director of *Topsy-Turvy*, *Secrets and Lies* and many other well-known films.

William Parry, Savoy opera expert and enthusiast, has been Treasurer of the Sir Arthur Sullivan Society for a number of years. He has published articles and sleeve notes, mainly on Sullivan's non-operatic works.

Stephanie Pitts is a Senior Lecturer in Music and Director of Undergraduate Studies at the University of Sheffield. She is the holder of a Senate Award for Teaching Excellence, and was recently awarded a HEFCE grant to lead the redesigning of the distance learning MA in Psychology for Musicians and the introduction of a new MA in Music Psychology in Education. She is the author of *A Century of Change in Music Education* (2000) and *Valuing Musical Participation* (2005) – and has published widely in journals and edited volumes.

Jana Polianovskaia, Russian musicologist and pianist, graduated from the piano and the theory and composition faculties of the St Petersburg State Conservatory. She now lives in Leipzig. She has lectured and published on the reception of Gilbert and Sullivan in Russia.

Meinhard Saremba, German writer, translator and lecturer, is the author of *Arthur Sullivan: Ein Komponistenleben im viktorianischen England* (1993), *Elgar, Britten & Co.: Eine Geschichte der britischen Musik in zwölf Portraits* (1994), *Leoš Janáček: Zeit, Leben, Werk, Wirkung* (2001) and *Fortunas Narren* (2007). He also contributed to books on Janáček, Tippett and German–British musical relationships, magazines, *Pipers Enzyklopädie des Musiktheaters*, *Metzlers Komponistenlexikon* and *Die Musik in Geschichte und Gegenwart* (*MGG*).

Richard Silverman, American musicologist and composer, has degrees in music from Brooklyn College and the University of North Carolina. He completed a doctoral thesis entitled 'The Contrapuntal Style of Hector Berlioz'. He has published widely in books and magazines on French and British music. Silverman's own musical compositions include a string seranade, four tone poems and three string quartets.

Benedict Taylor is currently an Alexander von Humboldt Research Fellow at the Humboldt University, Berlin. He studied earlier in Britain, Germany and the US, and has published articles on Beethoven, Mendelssohn, Berg, Barber and musical aesthetics in such journals as *19th-Century Music* and *The Journal of Musicology*. His research concentrates on the notion of musical temporality and subjectivity in the nineteenth and twentieth centuries; he has also written intermittently on the music of Arthur Sullivan.

Martin T. Yates, musicologist and conductor, began his life-long love of Sullivan's music as a teenager and sang his first role, the Major-General in *The Pirates of Penzance*, as a boy soprano. Singing, producing and conducting the works of Sullivan has been the core of his musical life since then and especially bringing to the stage some of the lesser known operas such as *Haddon Hall*, *The Beauty Stone*, *The Chieftain* and *The Rose of Persia*.

Preface

Almost a century after the deaths of Sullivan and Gilbert and fifty years after the expiry of the copyright in their work a new look at the collaboration of these two brilliant men is imperative. By taking a fundamentally musical approach this volume makes use of the latest developments in research and offers fresh insights which will open new perspectives and inspire future research, exciting investigation and thrilling performances.

This book is a work of inter-disciplinary research which adds up to a deeper understanding of the place of the Savoy operas in the wider operatic context. The first part throws light on the historic, artistic and cultural background, putting the achievements of Sullivan and Gilbert into perspective. Part II focuses on relevant aspects and details of the operas. The third part covers the reception, educational and practical aspects of the operas, the perception in countries other than England and Part IV looks at the laborious process of rediscovering the originals of the Savoy operas and provides an outlook on future perspectives.

In order to remove the accumulated burden from the plot and score, we must be able to link the past to the present, the nineteenth to the twenty-first centuries, and find answers to the question of what can be discovered if we are prepared to look below the surface.

David Eden
Meinhard Saremba

PART I

Background

1 Savoy opera and its discontents: the theatrical background to a quarrel

DAVID EDEN

The West End theatre as we know it is a Victorian inheritance. Many theatre buildings still stand from this period, but more importantly the methods of production and patterns of audience behaviour which we take for granted were established then. Those who work in the contemporary theatre often take exception to this state of affairs. They look on theatre-land as hideously bourgeois and seek, albeit in vain, to reclaim it for the working class. The Victorians experienced the same problem in reverse. For them the challenge was to overcome the disrepute of working-class association and establish the theatre as a domain of the respectable bourgeoisie. The Savoy operas have their full share of this ambition; but they are end products rather than prime movers. Their roots lie deep in the eighteenth century, or earlier, and we regard them as 'entirely original' only because we have ceased to be aware of those roots. Above all it should be understood that their ancestry does not lie in 'opera' as the term is generally used, but in the popular London alternatives to it.

Theatre regulation

Following the Puritan interregnum, which banned all forms of public entertainment, King Charles II in 1662 granted letters patent to Thomas Killigrew and William Davenant for the performance of 'tragedies, comedies, plays, operas, music, scenes and all other entertainments of the stage'.[1] One patent became established at the Theatre Royal, Drury Lane, while the other eventually devolved upon the Theatre Royal, Covent Garden. In 1766 George III granted a summer patent to Samuel Foote at the Little Theatre in the Haymarket, which duly became the third Theatre Royal. Theatres operating outside the patents were technically illegal, and ran under constant threat of interference by the authorities.

A situation already sufficiently complicated was made more so by censorship, instituted by the Licensing Act of 1737. The purpose of the Act was partly to protect the patents, partly to suppress political attacks on the government – notably those of Henry Fielding, whose *Pasquin* (1736) was seen as a satire on the corrupt Walpole administration. By the terms of the Act all new plays had to be read and licensed by the Lord Chamberlain's office, and the non-patent theatres were abolished. In practice the unlicensed theatres continued to be tolerated provided they eschewed politics, particularly personal attacks on identifiable politicians. Social satire, exposing the follies of the age, was less objectionable to the censor, but the puritanical objection to *all* theatre remained as a significant social and religious force throughout the century and beyond.[2]

Avoiding regulation

As might be expected, the proprietors of the three patent theatres jealously guarded their rights. Anyone who wished to run a non-patent or 'minor' theatre had to find ways of producing works to which the terms of the patents did not apply. The result was a lengthy, sometimes rambunctious, battle between 'legitimate' and 'illegitimate' drama, only ended by the Theatres Act of 1843, which brought the minor theatres into a licensing system. At the same time the rapid expansion of Westminster in all directions created new audiences, eager for entertainment of any kind. So far from being the grey-haired middle-class minority with whom we are familiar, these audiences really did include the great unwashed. They were vociferous in their likes and dislikes, and not above a riot when sufficiently roused, as for example in September 1809 when audiences created uproar for days on end after the Covent Garden management tried to raise ticket prices.[3]

Much of the strife between the patent and minor theatres arose because the terms of the patents seemed to embrace almost anything that could be put on the stage. Broadly speaking the patent theatres saw themselves as the guardians of Shakespearean drama and tragedy, spoken comedy, and opera, normally Italian opera. The minor theatres turned to mime and circus – because they contained no spoken language – and imported an Italian mongrel form, generically known as burletta, which 'proved a very elastic term, comprehending opera, serious and comic, farce, pantomime, melodrama, burlesque, in fine, anything except tragedy and comedy; the one hard and fast rule being that a certain number of songs should be introduced, and the notes of a piano occasionally struck throughout the performance'.[4]

As an almost infinitely flexible form the burletta became a staple of all theatres, patent and non-patent alike. It embraced ballad opera like *The Beggar's Opera* (1728) but differed from comic opera such as Arne's *Thomas and Sally* (1760) in that it required no composer because the songs were adapted from existing popular sources. The dialogue might be in prose or verse, including blank verse, and the story might be a straightforward comic tale, or a burlesque of a familiar subject. Lampe's *Dragon of Wantley* (1737) is a burlesque in both words and music. A further distinction lay in the performers: 'Ballad opera was designed for the player who could sing, comic opera for the singer who could make some attempt at acting'.[5] And the form persisted. The popular *Midas* (1766) is formally indistinguishable from the burlesque of a century later – the dialogue is in rhymed couplets, the songs are popular tunes fitted with new words, and the characters are the gods of Olympus brought down to earth.

Nineteenth-century development

At the beginning of the nineteenth century the theatre remained more or less where Walpole had left it, with the difference that the population of London had grown substantially in the meantime, and more 'illegitimate' theatres such as the Surrey (1782) had grown up to meet the demand for entertainment. The sentimental comedy of the eighteenth century had begun to give way to romantic melodrama, but burlesque and burletta continued as a popular staple, often in the form of an afterpiece.

Later in the century a new force began to enter the equation in the shape of the access provided by omnibus and railway services. These opened up the possibility of theatre attendance by the rapidly expanding suburban middle class, and facilitated the long runs which became an increasingly familiar feature from the 1850s onwards.[6] Henry Morley estimated that 15,000 people per night were attending theatres in the 1860s.[7]

From the point of view of a theatre manager the middle class provided an obvious source of income, the difficulty being that they often chose to protect their new-found status by religion and snobbery. In spite of their potential as audience such people would not go to the theatre for fear of what they might encounter on and off the stage. Clearly reform was required if they were to be attracted into the theatre, and if theatre itself were to lose the stigma of illegitimacy. According to all contemporary testimony the process of change was begun by Elizabeth Vestris (1797–1856) during her tenure of the Olympic Theatre from 1831. Together with her second husband Charles Mathews (1803–1878) she

> introduced for the first time in England that reform in all theatrical matters which has since been adopted at every theatre in the kingdom.
> Drawing-rooms were fitted up like drawing-rooms, and fitted with care and taste. Two chairs no longer indicated that two persons were to be seated.
> A claret-coloured coat, salmon-coloured trousers, with a broad black stripe, a sky-blue neckcloth with a large paste brooch, and a cut-steel eye-glass with

a pink ribbon, no longer marked the light-comedy gentleman, and the public at once recognized and appreciated the changes.[8]

Madame [Vestris] was an admirable manager, and Charles [Mathews] an amiable assistant. The arrangements behind the scenes were admirable. The dressing rooms were perfect, the attendants well chosen; 'the wings' kept clear of all intruders – no strangers or crutch and toothpick loafers allowed behind to flirt with the ballet-girls; only a very few private friends were allowed the privilege of visiting the green room, which was as handsomely furnished as any nobleman's drawing room, and those friends always appeared in evening dress . . . There was great propriety and decorum observed in every part of the establishment, great harmony, general content prevailed in every department of the theatre, and universal regret was felt when the admirable managers were compelled to resign the government.[9]

In tandem with her managerial reforms Madame Vestris secured the services of J. R. Planché (1796–1880) as playwright. The two worked together over a period of more than twenty years, developing a new, magnificently lavish, production style and an approach to costume based on historical accuracy. Planché's first work for the Vestris management, *Olympic Revels* (3 January 1831), followed a recent appearance by Vestris in *Midas*. Like *Midas*, *Olympic Revels* is a burletta, 'replete with word-play and puns, topical allusions to English life, and a prevailing mood of comic bathos that arises from the incongruity of such utterances in the mouths of classical gods and demi-gods'.[10] Its success paved the way for a series of works in similar style which Planché called extravaganzas. Extravaganza, pantomime and burlesque are virtually indistinguishable on the page.

In writing his extravaganzas Planché made frequent use of the magic world of eighteenth-century French *féerie*. He also introduced the dead-pan acting style which we associate with W. S. Gilbert: 'Planché's major innovation as stage manger was to insist that the characters of his extravaganzas be played "straight". Whatever the nonsense they spoke, however absurdly or grotesquely they were called on to behave, their manner should be intent and matter-of-fact.'[11]

The new burlesque

Unfortunately Planché's innovations were not wholly positive. 'Lowness (figuratively speaking) is the Sublimity of Burlesque', said Henry Carey, the librettist of *The Dragon of Wantley*.[12] In Planché's works the satirical sharpness of Fielding and Foote, and the 'sublime lowness' of burlesque, give way to something he would have called artistic refinement, and we can only call genial pap. 'This is not a burlesque', said Thackeray, 'it is an idyll'.[13] Others said that he 'wrote in white kid gloves' or that he 'lived on honey and nectar'.[14] Theatrical reformers welcomed his achievement, but audiences had by no means abandoned their taste for something more invigorating.

This left room for a further development of burlesque by a group of writers of whom H. J. Byron (1834–84) and F. C. Burnand (1836–1917) are the best remembered. The new burlesque, beginning in 1850,[15] took advantage of Planché's reforms, but rejected his good manners. It was irreverent, vigorously danced and acted, and above all characterised by far-fetched puns. The practice of writing words to existing popular music was retained, as were cross-dressing and the use of rhymed couplets in the dialogue. Its modern expression is the Christmas pantomime. The high-minded case against it was put by Henry Morley in some comments on Burnand's *Ixion, or The Man at the Wheel* (1863):[16]

> The whole success of the piece was made by dressing up good looking girls as immortals lavish in display of leg and setting them to sing and dance, or rather kick burlesque capers, for the recreation of fast blockheads. If Miss Pelham only knew how she looks in the eyes of the better half of any audience when she comes forward with sandy beard and moustaches disfiguring her face, and with long pink legs wriggling her body into the ungainly gestures of burlesque toeing and heeling, the woman in her would rise in rebellion against the miserable vulgarity of the display. As for the Hon. Lewis Wingfield, who dressed his thin figure in petticoats and spoke falsetto as Minerva – every man to his taste! His great success was an idiotic dance in petticoats that might stand for something in competitive examination for admission into the Earlswood Asylum, but as a gentleman's first bid for the honours of the English stage was a distressing sight to see.[17]

It was at this point in the history of burlesque that W. S. Gilbert made his entrance. Gilbert's ambition was always to succeed Planché – he sub-scribed to the testimonial edition of Planché's extravaganzas – but he began his career with a series of operatic burlesques, expertly carried out in the punning manner of Byron, who no less than Planché contributed substan-tially to the ethos we call Gilbertian.[18] Finally, in his first collaboration with Sullivan, Gilbert produced a classical burlesque in the time-honoured manner: *Thespis or The Gods Grown Old* (Gaiety Theatre, 23 December 1871).

In describing the theatrical ancestry of Gilbert's work we are also drawing attention to what was really new in his collaboration with Sullivan, namely the provision of original music by a gifted composer. Most of the music of *Thespis* is lost, but one of the choruses, 'Climbing over rocky mountain', was redeployed in *The Pirates of Penzance*. Here, in place of the traditional reach-me-down material, is music of beauty and dramatic presence such as the English stage had not heard since the death of Purcell. Sullivan's arrival transformed burlesque into opera.

Burlesque and satire

Because his best-known works were written in the 1880s it is easy to forget that Gilbert's earliest and most intense theatrical experiences were of pantomime in the 1840s. He wrote about pantomime,[19] and once said modestly that burlesque 'in its highest development calls for high intellectual power on the part of its professors'.[20] It is in this context that the various reforms attributed to Gilbert must be understood. Seeing greater potential in burlesque than his contemporaries, and determined to return it to its Planchéan state, he moderated the objectionable features of Byronian practice as described by Henry Morley, creating in the process an allotropic form peculiar to himself – 'burlesque in long clothes' as John Hollingshead called it. Above all the desire for respectability which had motivated the Vestris management returned with Cromwellian vigour in the mind of Gilbert – the 'Immaculate Schwenck'[21] – who boasted to William Archer of his ambitions in that direction:

> It is a mistake to suppose that I ever complained of the influence of the 'young girl in the dress-circle'. It is to her that I attribute the fact that most of the plays produced in the 'sixties and 'seventies were sweet and clean. I have always held that 'maxima reverentia' is due to that young lady. I am so old-fashioned as to believe that the test whether a story is fit to be presented to an audience in which there are many young ladies, is whether the details of that story can be decently told at (say) a dinner-party at which a number of ladies and gentlemen are present . . . I have always kept this test well before me in writing plays, and I have never found myself inconveniently hampered by it.[22]

Gilbert never explained why he thought these principles were desirable, and yet in adopting them he denied himself a very wide field of expression. His mind was too sharp for mere Planchéan good nature, but his determination not to bring the blush of embarrassment to the cheek of innocence made it impossible for him to perform the task of the satirist, which is to bring the blister of shame to the cheek of guilt. Like all writers of burlesque he made political jokes, but the official sensitivity that led the Walpole administration to suppress Fielding led in his case only to a letter of congratulation from the Prime Minister himself, Mr Gladstone, on the 'good taste' of *Iolanthe*.[23] A proper understanding of the nature of burlesque, and of the difference between burlesque and satire, is essential to any discussion of Savoy opera:

> He [Gilbert] has been honoured with the name of satirist. He was not a
> satirist. His wit was strongly ironical, but it was a burlesque wit. He has
> been widely considered as the originator of an entirely new style of writing.
> He was not that either. At the beginning of his career he wrote so-called
> burlesques on popular successes, and, like all the other humorists, he wrote
> in rhymed couplets garnished with puns. He was an extravaganza writer,
> deriving, as they all did, directly from Planché. But whereas Henry J. Byron,
> the Broughs, and the à Becketts were illegitimate descendants, denounced
> and denied by their parent, Gilbert was the acknowledged heir.[24]

It is their root in extravaganza–burlesque–pantomime that makes the Savoy
operas so apparently difficult to classify. Just as Mozart's *Die Zauberflöte* is
derived from opera seria, opera buffa, and the lost Viennese suburban theatrical entertainments, so they are an outgrowth of the forgotten repertoire
of the London theatre. Once the hinterland is excavated they become altogether more comprehensible. Katisha and Widow Twankey are sisters under
the skin.[25]

English comic opera

The story of the founding of the partnership between Gilbert and Sullivan is
well known. Richard D'Oyly Carte, then the assistant manager and musical
director of the Royalty Theatre, was in need of a short companion piece for
Offenbach's *La Périchole* – he had already, in 1870, suggested 'the starting
of English comic opera' to Sullivan.[26] Now he approached both Sullivan
and Gilbert, and was given *Trial by Jury* (25 March 1875). The success
of *Trial by Jury* and the ambition of Carte combined to make the further
collaboration of Gilbert and Sullivan a matter of deliberate policy. It is
important to recognise that without the initiative of Carte, and without
the binding contractual obligations incurred by Sullivan (especially) and
Gilbert towards him, the famous partnership might never have come into
being, and would certainly have ended earlier than it did.

In agreeing to compose for the burlesque stage Sullivan was well aware
that the dyer's hand must be subdued to what it works in. His father
had been a clarinet player in the orchestra at the Surrey Theatre, and his
approach to music was entirely professional and pragmatic – one has only
to look at his bohemian life-style to realise that he was not born to follow
Beethoven up the winding stair. On the other hand he had been educated
in the European tradition, and his creative capacity was altogether broader
and deeper than anything required by burlesque. His extraordinary ability
to invest a textual skeleton with living musical flesh made him the ideal
partner for any librettist, but his ultimate purpose was to create English

opera in the proper sense by giving expression to human emotion through musical drama.

Gilbert for his part realised that he must accommodate the values of Sullivan, but he stood apart from them because his horizons did not really extend beyond the execution of his own reforms. He was additionally fearful that his contribution would be devalued in full-blown opera. As a result he made concessions to music without any fundamental departure from his base camp in burlesque. His marked egocentricity made him a difficult collaborator, and in the end an impossible one.

The outline of all future problems can be clearly discerned in *The Sorcerer* (17 November 1877), the first of the deliberately planned works by Gilbert and Sullivan. The demands of the composer meant that the musical element of the new opera could not consist simply of a few comic songs – more was required. The effect is seen in concerted numbers, in a lengthy concerted finale to the first act, and in the way in which the chorus functions as a character in the action. All of these became standard features of later works. In deference to Sullivan *The Sorcerer* is also an English work, set in an English village, performed by English artists. A manifesto by D'Oyly Carte published in *The Era* sets out the stall in unmistakable terms:

> It is many years since the manager of any theatre in London devoted to musical performance has relied for his opening programme entirely on the products of an English author and composer. But the taste of English audiences is turning in this direction, and it is a matter of fact that of all the light operas native and foreign that have been given of late years the most remarkably successful has been the little piece *Trial By Jury*, the joint work of our English dramatist Mr W. S. Gilbert, and our English composer Mr Arthur Sullivan. In arranging, as I am happily able to announce that I have done, for a new opera of more important dimensions by the popular author and composer above named, I believe that I have secured an attraction which will at any rate – whatever be its ultimate result – command the attention of all who are interested in a legitimate lyric performance, a performance which will depend for its success simply on its merits and not on any meretricious displays of costume – or rather absence of costume – or by any objectionable suggestiveness of motive or dialogue. To such a performance I believe many will come who have stayed away from fear of having to sit through hours of dull and unwholesome frivolity . . . Author, composer, singers and actors are all English. I appeal to the public to come forward and support the undertaking.[27]

Thus far the composer is satisfied; but in the matter of the performers the old tension between singers who could not act and actors who could not sing was never resolved, leaving a permanent effect on the music as Sullivan adapted it to the limitations of the cast. It was Gilbert's fixed opinion that acting can be taught by repetitive drill, like soldiering, and he managed the production of his works accordingly.[28] A group of obedient novices was recruited for *The Sorcerer* and its successors because no established artist would have submitted to such parade-ground methods. Insofar as they put an end to the old approach to production which allowed the principals to wander the stage at will,[29] these methods made for reformation. Unfortunately they also made for mediocrity and ossification as Gilbert and his heirs refused to allow 'any deviation whatever' from the dialogue and stage business once they had been determined by him.[30]

The lozenge plot

A marked tendency to perseveration and rigidity informs the Gilbertian imagination at large. Sullivan experienced it most acutely through what he famously called the lozenge plot, of which *The Sorcerer* is the first example. Reduced to essentials, the lozenge is a charm of some kind which has the effect of creating magic but mechanical transformations in the characters; the 'plot' is the sequential process by which the charm first takes hold, then has its effects reversed. In the case of *The Sorcerer* the lozenge becomes a potion which causes the villagers of Ploverleigh to fall in love with each other *à tort et à travers*, as Sullivan put it; the spell is broken by the self-sacrificial death of John Wellington Wells.

With or without magic the very nature of burlesque is inimical to the expression of emotion. It is, in the words of Goethe's Mephistopheles, the spirit that denies. *The Sorcerer* is more inclined to the musician than some of the later operas, but even here the dominant force is the automatic effect of the love potion. The emotional lyrics are inserted into burlesque situations, and are sung by characters who emerge in their prose dialogue as the merest of logic choppers. This uncomfortable mismatch between the characters as they appear in prose and their emotional qualities as expressed in music is one of the defining features of Gilbert and Sullivan opera. Moreover Alexis, the tenor hero, shows the first signs of the sadistic streak in Gilbert that was later to drive Arthur Quiller-Couch 'almost out of the theatre' in nausea.[31]

At first the difficulties did not seem to matter. The extraordinary success of *HMS Pinafore* (1878), *The Pirates of Penzance* (1879) and *Patience* (1881) brought wealth to both collaborators and established a formula which the public have been determined to accept ever since. Before the writing of the next opera, *Iolanthe* (1882), Gilbert proposed the lozenge in the form of a coin as the subject of the plot; Sullivan rejected it as unreal and artificial.[32]

Princess Ida (1884), the successor to *Iolanthe*, is treated as an aberration by modern audiences because the dialogue is in blank verse. In Gilbert's own terms, however, it represents the final attainment of the Planchéan ideal. The spoken text was originally heard at the Olympic Theatre in 1870 as *The Princess*, a burlesque of Tennyson's *The Princess* (1847) with interpolated music by Offenbach, Auber and Rossini. In adapting the play for Sullivan, Gilbert added extra lyrics, including something 'emotional' for the Princess herself, but did nothing to transcend the burlesque formula. From Sullivan's point of view the libretto is regressive, notwithstanding the quality of the music he wrote for it. Matters came to a head in March 1884 when Gilbert again proposed the lozenge as the subject for the next opera. After some preliminary shadow-boxing, Sullivan came to the point (1 April 1884):

> I will be quite frank. With *Princess Ida* I have come to the end of my tether – the end of my capability in that class of piece. My tunes are in danger of becoming mere repetitions of my former pieces, my concerted movements are getting to possess a strong family likeness, and I have rung all the changes possible in the way of variety of rhythm. It has hitherto been word-setting, I might almost say syllable-setting, for I have looked upon the words as of such importance that I have been continually keeping down the music in order that not one should be lost.
>
> And this very suppression is most difficult, most fatiguing, and I may say most disheartening, for the music is never allowed to rise and speak for itself. I want a chance for the music to act in its own proper sphere – to intensify the emotional element not only of the actual words but of the situation.
>   I should like to set a story of human interest and probability, where the humorous words would come in a humorous (not serious) situation, and where, if the situation were a tender or dramatic one, the words would be of a similar character. There would then be a feeling of reality about it which would give fresh interest in writing, and fresh vitality to our joint work . . . I hope with all my heart that they [our views] may coincide so that there may be no break in our chain of joint workmanship.[33]

In reply Gilbert declared himself 'galled' and 'wounded' by Sullivan's proposals and put forward the following defence:

> When you tell me that your desire is that I shall write a libretto in which the humorous words will come in a humorous situation, and in which a tender or dramatic situation will be treated tenderly or dramatically, you teach me the ABC of my profession. It is inconceivable that any sane author should ever write otherwise than as you propose I should write in future.[34]

As his comments make clear, Sullivan was not attempting to steer Gilbert away from comedy but from inhumanity and mechanicality. After a meeting on 10 April which altered nothing, Gilbert offered to stand aside for 'one turn', thereby allowing Sullivan to work with a different collaborator. He explained himself as follows:

> I suggest this because I am absolutely at a loss to know what you want from
> me. You will understand how faintly I grasp your meaning when I tell you
> that your objections to my libretto really seem arbitrary and capricious.
> That they are nothing of the kind I am well persuaded – but, for all that, I
> can't fathom them.[35]

Gilbert's reason for withdrawal is surreal. Having attributed insanity to
his own methods a few days earlier, he now professed himself unable to
comprehend Sullivan's demands for humanity, describing them as arbitrary
and capricious. The argument continued without alteration in terms until
8 May 1884 when Gilbert was visited with the change of mind that gave us
The Mikado. Sullivan stated:

> Your letter of today is an inexpressible relief to me, as it clearly shows me
> that you, equally with myself, are loth to discontinue the collaboration
> which has been such a pleasure and advantage to us.
>   If, as I understand you to propose, you will construct a plot without the
> supernatural and impromptu elements, and on the lines which you describe,
> I gladly undertake to set it without further discussing the matter, or asking
> what the subject is to be.[36]

With these words the first great quarrel between Sullivan and Gilbert was
resolved. Sullivan had evidently spoken to friends about his argument with
Gilbert, and had given the impression that the new opera would be a fresh
departure. Not so, as William Beatty Kingston remarked in *The Theatre*:

> It came to be understood in musical and dramatic circles, that . . . a wider
> scope was to be allotted to Sullivan's genius, theretofore circumscribed by
> the tortuous limits of the unnatural; he was to be allowed to deal musically
> with the passions and adventures of possible human beings, instead of the
> weird whims of comical monsters, the creations of Mr Gilbert's eccentric
> imagination . . . The première of 14th ult. [14 March 1885] promptly
> dispelled this illusion, and with it the hope, entertained by many of those
> present on that occasion, that they were about to witness the musical and
> dramatic results of an entirely new departure on the part of Messrs Gilbert &
> Sullivan.[37]

The success of *The Mikado* gave Sullivan an extended period of leisure,
during which he visited his brother's widow and her family in California.
Reaching New York on 29 June 1885, he received a suggestion from Gilbert
for another work:

> I think something might be done with a story founded on Frankenstein and
> the monster. Grossmith (as Frankenstein) constructing a monster
> (Barrington) which he (Grossmith) has to serve, and with every possible
> inconvenience upon him, might make a good plot. What do you think?[38]

Sullivan must have rejected this idea before setting out across America. Having arrived at San Francisco in July, he gave an interview to the *San Francisco Daily Chronicle* in which he set out his ambition to write an opera with 'characters of flesh and blood, with human emotions and human passions'.[39]

Gilbert, who had remained in England during these events, despatched a draft libretto at the beginning of October. It seems he had tried once more to gain acceptance for the lozenge, but had now settled for the melodramatic burlesque we know as *Ruddigore* (22 January 1887).

In *Ruddigore* the fundamental incompatibility between himself and Sullivan is exposed for all to see as Gilbert weakens the burlesque potential of his ideas by the insertion of parlour sentiments which deny Sullivan the dramatic and emotional scope he desired even while seeming to provide it. The lovers behave like characters from musical comedy,[40] and the introductory dementia of Mad Margaret collapses into a flaccid ballad, 'Only Roses', which was not even written for the purpose, having first appeared in the *Illustrated Sporting & Dramatic News* (10 December 1881).[41] When Dame Hannah is improbably united with her ghostly lover, Sir Roderic, they too sink into the flowery language of the drawing room. The second act is dominated and distorted by the musically substantial ghost scene in which at last Sullivan broke free. Gilbert for his part had preconceptions about how it should sound:

> My own impression is that the first act led everyone to believe that the piece
> was going to be bright and cheery throughout, and that the audience were
> not prepared for the solemnity of the ghost music. That music seems to my
> uninstructed ear to be very fine indeed, but out of place in a comic opera. It
> is as though one inserted fifty lines of *Paradise Lost* into a farcical comedy. I
> had hoped that the scene would be treated more humorously, but I fancy he
> thought his professional position demanded something grander and more
> impressive than the words suggested.[42]

Hearing Sullivan's superbly imagined setting of 'The ghosts' high noon' we think Gilbert must at least have wanted some sort of solemnity for his walking pictures, but apparently he expected the composer to treat them as a joke.[43] Many contemporaries agreed. 'This charnel-house business, references to funeral shrouds, churchyard bells and grey tombstones has no humorous side', said the *Saturday Review*; 'powerful it is, but not within the limits of any sort of comic opera'.[44]

To Victorian audiences *Ruddigore* was not an established classic to be forgiven its faults, but an entertainment like any other to be rejected if it failed to please. It soon became apparent that a successor would be required, and on 9 May 1887 Sullivan met with Gilbert and Carte to discuss the

situation. Gilbert again proposed the lozenge, as we learn from Sullivan's
diary:

> Gilbert and Carte came. Former again urged his old plot to be considered,
> the one we almost split upon before. He read it to us and proposed various
> modifications of an important character. A sort of provisional compromise
> was arrived at, that if, after he had written part of it, it did not turn out in
> a manner that appealed to me, or that it was not satisfactory for musical
> requirements, no more should be said about it.[45]

The impasse of 1884 was now repeated as the lozenge stuck in Gilbert's
throat while *Ruddigore* declined at the box office. Lacking a newly written
replacement, a decision had been taken to revive *HMS Pinafore*. Sullivan
went to a rehearsal on 31 October 1887 where he met Gilbert, who had
unexpectedly changed his mind:

> Gilbert told me that he had given up the subject over which there had been
> so much difficulty and dispute (charm and clockwork) and had found
> another about the Tower of London, an entirely new departure. Much
> relieved.[46]

New directions

Gilbert's 'new departure' is known to us as *The Yeomen of the Guard*.
However, the minds of both Sullivan and Carte were beginning to turn
away from the Savoy Theatre altogether. On 13 February 1888 Carte wrote
to the composer saying the time had come to begin afresh with a new
company in a new theatre. Precisely what they intended is not clear, but
they evidently wished to take leave of burlesque and occupy a musically
more substantial field. Probably they did not intend a grand opera house;
more likely is a desire to create something resembling the Paris Opéra-
Comique or the German Spieloper – a theatre where spoken dialogue was
retained in the place of recitative, but where the music was substantive
nevertheless.

Gilbert expressed himself unable to understand 'the reasons that urge
you to abandon a theatre and a company that have worked so well for us,
and for whom we have worked so well'.[47] Nevertheless Carte persisted with
his plans, buying a plot of land in Shaftesbury Avenue. His formidable wife
Helen laid the foundation stone of what was to become the Royal English
Opera House on 15 December 1888, *The Yeomen of the Guard* having been
produced after acrimonious rehearsals on 3 October. According to his own
statement Gilbert originally conceived *The Yeomen of the Guard* in terms of
the lozenge plot:

1 The Tower Furnishing Company's advertisement. *Kensington and Hammersmith Reporter*, January 1888.

Bored by waiting for a train at an Underground station [Uxbridge] I found myself gazing at the poster for a furnishing company [Tower Furnishing Company] with a 'Beefeater' as the central figure. I thought a Beefeater would make a good central figure for another Savoy opera, and my first intention was to give it a modern setting with the characteristics and development of burlesque – to make it another *Sorcerer*, but I decided to make it a romantic and dramatic piece, and to put it back into Elizabethan times, and as written it became my favourite.[48]

In its present form as an historical-romantic drama the *Yeomen of the Guard* represents a massive concession to Sullivan's values, and as such a victory for the composer. But Sullivan was unappeased. On 9 January 1889 he telephoned Gilbert and told him of his intentions:

Called, Carte, then Gilbert. Explained to latter my views as to the future, viz, that I wanted to do some dramatic work on a larger musical scale, and that of course I should like to do it with him if he would, but that the music must occupy a more important position than in our other pieces – that I wished to get rid of the strongly marked rhythm, and rhymed couplets, and have words that would give a chance of developing musical effects. Also that I wanted a voice in the musical constructions of the libretto. He seemed quite to assent to this.[49]

Gilbert responded with a reasonable letter detailing the practical difficulties in the way of Sullivan's proposal, and pointing out the unsuitability of his own personal style for the purposes of grand opera. He may have imagined Sullivan's ambitions as grander than they were (20 February 1889):

> There is no doubt about it, the more reckless and irresponsible the libretto has been, the better the piece has succeeded – the pieces that have succeeded the least have been those in which a consistent story has been more or less consistently followed out. Personally, I prefer a consistent subject – such a subject as the 'Yeomen' is far more congenial to my taste than the burlesque of 'Iolanthe' or 'The Mikado' – but I think we should be risking everything in writing more seriously still. We have a name, jointly, for humorous work, tempered with occasional glimpses of earnest drama. I think we should do unwisely if we left, altogether, the path which we have trodden together so long and so successfully.[50]

In his reply Sullivan repeated what he said after *Princess Ida*, namely that he had 'lost the necessary nerve' for comic opera, and again stressed the extent to which he had already accommodated Gilbert:

> But now we must decide, not argue. You say that in a serious opera, *you* must more or less sacrifice yourself. I say that this is just what I have been doing in all our joint pieces, and, what is more, must continue to do in Comic Opera to make it successful. Business and syllabic setting assume an importance which, however much they fetter me, cannot be overlooked. I am bound, in the interests of the piece, to give way. Hence the reason of my wishing to do a work where the music is to be the first consideration – where words are to suggest music, not govern it, and where music will intensify and emphasize the emotional effect of the words.[51]

Gilbert immediately abandoned all pretence of sympathy with Sullivan's position (19 March 1889):

> If you are really under the astounding impression that you have been effacing yourself during the last twelve years – and if you are in earnest when you say that you wish to write an opera in which 'the music shall be the first consideration' (by which I understand an opera in which the libretto, and consequently the librettist, must occupy a subordinate place) there is most certainly no 'modus vivendi' to be found that shall be satisfactory to both of us.
>
>   You are an adept in your profession, and I am an adept in mine. If we meet, it must be as master and master – not as master and servant.[52]

The situation was saved by D'Oyly Carte, who had relinquished his hope of persuading Gilbert to co-operate in the enhanced opera scheme. Instead he proposed to use the new building as a home for English opera in general,

2 Rebecca defies the Templar in Sullivan's *Ivanhoe*.

thereby affording Sullivan the chance to realise his wider ambition. In return
Sullivan agreed to co-operate again with Gilbert (24 April 1889):

> I am enabled to do this all the more willingly since I have now settled to
> write an opera on a large scale (Grand Opera is an offensive term) to be
> produced next Spring. I have my subject of my own choice, [*Ivanhoe*] and
> my collaborator [Julian Sturgis]; also an agreement with Carte to keep the
> new theatre for me for this purpose, and not to let it to anyone else before
> then. In this manner I can realize the great desire of my life, and at the same
> time continue a collaboration which I regard with a stronger sentiment than
> pecuniary advance.[53]

What this letter means is that Sullivan and Carte had decided to detach
themselves from Gilbert as far as the production of musically substantial

opera was concerned. The Savoy was to remain as the house for Gilbert and Sullivan – the new theatre was to have a different function. On 8 May 1889 Sullivan suggested the opera we know as *The Gondoliers*:

> Carte tells me that you again proposed the subject of a theatrical company. I hope you will not press it, as it has already been the means of nearly breaking up our collaboration . . . I understood from Carte some time ago that you had some subject connected with Venice and Venetian life, and this seemed to me to hold out great chances of bright colour and taking music.[54]

The Gondoliers was created in an atmosphere of seeming goodwill and produced amid mutual congratulations on 7 December 1889. On the face of it the partnership was in good working order; and yet it was about to undergo the seismic disturbance known as the Carpet Quarrel, which provided the public with a new form of entertainment and effectively destroyed the working relationship between Sullivan and Gilbert.

Finale

Superficially the Carpet Quarrel is inexplicable. It began in April 1890 as a dispute over the bill for front-of-house carpets and ended in open court in September as Gilbert tried unsuccessfully to have the Savoy Theatre taken into receivership, claiming that he, not Carte, was the real manager of the theatre.[55] Gilbert was a serial litigant, but only one sufficient *casus belli* is before us – Carte's new opera house and Sullivan's *Ivanhoe*. Gilbert had refused the chance to participate in both, but he must have perceived them as a rejection of himself, which is precisely what they were. The Carpet Quarrel is a loud, public cry of anger which would have delivered the Savoy into Gilbert's hands if his application for receivership had been successful. The application failed because the finances of the theatre were secure. As it was, the bad blood generated by the lawsuit made the parting of ways inevitable. In the case of Sullivan the sense of relief was palpable: 'How have I stood him so long!! I can't understand.'[56]

After a lengthy period of gestation *Ivanhoe* saw production at Carte's Royal English Opera House on 31 January 1891. A fully sung work, masterfully written for orchestra, it was intended both as the final fulfilment of the ambition with which Sullivan and Carte had set out in 1877 and as the foundation stone for a national English opera. Conventional wisdom, much aided by a facetious review from Bernard Shaw, regards it as a failure. The truth is altogether more complex. *Ivanhoe* is, as Sullivan intended, a mixed work, some parts of which – for example the tournament scene – have been deliberately written to retain the attention of a popular audience. In other places the composer wrote music which any sensible listener will recognise as emotionally adult and dramatic in a way that has no real precedent in English opera. The difficulty lay in the fact that London, for all its suburban population and ease of communication, did not contain a large enough minority to sustain the massive cost of the opera house. Opera is the most expensive noise in the world. For the first three months of its life *Ivanhoe* actually took more money than *The Mikado*;[57] but this was not enough. Unable to sustain his running expenses, Carte abandoned the scheme early in 1892 after the box-office collapse of Messager's *La Basoche.* The British composers who were supposedly clamouring to establish a national opera simply failed to deliver the goods.

Meanwhile Gilbert made his point with *The Mountebanks* (4 January 1892). In this work the lozenge becomes a bottle of medicine which 'has the effect of making every one who drinks it exactly what he pretends to be'.[58] For sufficient reasons Nita and Bartolo, two members of a troupe of mountebanks, have been pretending to be waxwork models of Hamlet and Ophelia. Transformed by the medicine, they become real dummies: 'They walk down the stage mechanically, as though controlled by clockwork. Their keys are fitted with keyholes in the small of their backs. Each wears a placard inscribed "Put a penny in the slot".'[59] A similar process is undergone by the other characters in turn until the label on the bottle is burned and everything returns to normal.

The bifurcation between Sullivan's outlook and that of Gilbert is complete. *Ivanhoe* is humane and dramatic in the natural sense – a sophisticated variant of the European operatic tradition at large. *The Mountebanks* is a puppet play which turns Hamlet and Ophelia into burlesque automata. Despite the popular impression of seamless unity the collaborative works written according to these mutually exclusive principles show many signs of strain. In his bleaker moments Sullivan wondered whether it had all been worthwhile: 'The theatre is not the place for the musician. When the curtain is up the music interrupts the actor, and when it is down the music interrupts the audience'.[60]

3 Mechanised characters in Gilbert's *Mountebanks*: Hamlet and Ophelia as clockwork dummies.

2 Identity crisis and the search for English opera: the Savoy Theatre in the 1890s

WILLIAM PARRY

Relations between Gilbert and Sullivan were seldom harmonious, but the Carpet Quarrel of 1890 was so traumatic for all concerned that nothing would be the same afterwards. Indeed this seems to have been Gilbert's express wish. Beginning in April, ostensibly about the preliminary production expenses for *The Gondoliers*, the dispute reached its very public nadir in the law courts in September. One immediate result of the breakdown in relations was that there was no new Gilbert and Sullivan opera to follow *The Gondoliers* when it closed on 20 June 1891 after 554 performances. The problem for Richard D'Oyly Carte, the Savoy Theatre's thus far extraordinarily successful impresario, was how to fill the void. Carte responded to the challenge in many different ways, and the sheer variety of the productions which he mounted at the Savoy make this final decade the most interesting in the theatre's history; indeed it goes to the heart of what people have subsequently come to understand by the term 'Savoy opera'.

Experiments

The Nautch Girl (30 June 1891) was to be the test case, the first opera at the Savoy to which neither Sullivan nor Gilbert contributed. Carte's decision in this instance was to commission an opera that would be as much like its 1880s predecessors as possible, and to this end he sought out Edward Solomon (1855–95), an experienced composer, trusted (and doubtless recommended) by Sullivan himself. Solomon was well known as one of the foremost in the circle of composers capable of producing a comic opera that could hold the London stage. His *Billee Taylor* (1880) had been a substantial success on both sides of the Atlantic, and Carte had already been involved with him professionally. Lyrics were provided by Frank Desprez (1853–1916) and George Dance (1857–1932).

Desprez had been Carte's secretary, as well as the librettist of a handful of the curtain-raisers employed both at the Opéra-Comique and later at the Savoy.[1] He represented continuity, therefore, and was to be pivotal in maintaining some element of 'house style' in the new piece. A relative newcomer, George Dance contributed dialogue as well as lyrics; he was to be one of the most remarkable, if by no means the last, of Carte's professional discoveries in the 1890s. *The Nautch Girl* launched his London career, which went from triumph to triumph thereafter.

The Nautch Girl as it emerged was something of an 'Indian *Mikado*' – an experiment in taking the Savoy form beyond its initiators while remaining in the established vein. The *Times* critic commented 'both Mr George Dance and Mr Edward Solomon have, with perfectly laudable intentions, subordinated their own individualities to the traditions of the theatre, and have produced a work which, if brought out anonymously, would be unhesitatingly classed, by superficial observers at all events, among the rest of the "Gilbert and Sullivan" operas'.[2]

The new opera was rewarded with a run of 200 performances, which kept the theatre open until January 1892 – a significant achievement. But the most important thing about *The Nautch Girl* was what it was not: its writers were not Sullivan and Gilbert. There could, it seemed, be a Savoy Theatre without them, even if their influence continued to be felt. So successful was the experiment that Carte decided to fill the gap before Sullivan's next work should be ready with *The Vicar of Bray* (1882) – one of Solomon's previous efforts, heavily restructured and rescored from its earlier incarnation. Produced on 28 January 1892, *The Vicar of Bray* ran into the summer of 1892 (143 performances) and broke the mould to the extent that it was the first main-stage work not to have been written originally for the Savoy. It conformed sufficiently to the established pattern to 'work' in the theatre. Not every experiment was to enjoy the same success.

Advancing English opera

The librettist of *The Vicar of Bray* was one of London's leading playwrights, Sydney Grundy (1848–1914); and it was to Grundy that Carte turned to provide Sullivan with his next libretto: *Haddon Hall* (24 September 1892). This opera is important as the Savoy work which comes nearest to Sullivan's ideal of what his kind of opera should be, as characterised by his interview with the *San Francisco Daily Chronicle* in 1885.[3] In Sydney Grundy, Sullivan found a collaborator who was happy to accommodate his wishes, and it is fair to assume that the composer had more involvement in the process of libretto construction for *Haddon Hall* than had previously been the case. Uniquely, Sullivan asked Grundy to provide him with two versions of every lyric. Grundy said that Sullivan invariably chose the one he himself would have rejected. 'What's the matter with the others?' asked Grundy. 'Nothing', replied Sullivan, 'but I've been setting them for fifteen years'.[4]

The plot has its basis in a popular story, according to which Dorothy Vernon of Haddon Hall eloped with her lover, John Manners, around the year 1563. Grundy, however, set the piece during the English Civil War, one hundred years later than the historic events. This yielded the benefit of a contrast (both comic and serious) between Parliamentary Puritan and Cavalier Royalist. From the beginning, new territory is explored. Sullivan eschews the usual overture in favour of a short introduction which incorporates an off-stage chorus.[5] Its theme is the English home as a symbol of continuity, and as the backdrop to family life. The timbre of the piece is frequently darker than that in Sullivan's preceding operas for the Savoy (the composition of *Ivanhoe* had changed him), though *Haddon Hall* contains music as fresh and lively as any of them. The composer particularly enjoyed characterising the ridiculous Puritan Scotsman, the McCrankie, providing him with a perfect orchestral imitation of the bagpipes.

Much has been made of the span of uninterrupted music from the elopement scene in the middle of Act II, through storm music over a scene change, into the climactic moment when the lovers' flight is revealed to the whole household. The consistent quality of invention here is telling; as a search party is sent off in pursuit of the lovers, Sullivan writes some of his most sombre music on the mutability of fate – 'Time, the Avenger'. Coming at the end of the Act II finale this is a passage of extraordinary introspection: for a moment the world-turning nature of the Civil War and the upheaval it brought to so many English homes is at the forefront, as the music fades out in grim resignation.

Haddon Hall, then, pushes back the boundaries of what Savoy opera could deal with, and does so while remaining comic in the broader, non-Gilbertian, sense. Indeed the delicate balance between the comic, the dramatic and the romantic is its prime success. Together with *The Yeomen of the Guard* (1888) and *Ivanhoe* (1891) it makes up a triptych of works which come closest to the composer's conception of English 'national' opera. It is not too much to say that in these works Sullivan was at the zenith of his career. He had demonstrated that there could be a Sullivan without a Gilbert, and that a Savoy opera could be challenging and profound and still succeed.

In spite of much wrangling, mostly about the contractual terms on which the librettist should be readmitted to the Savoy, the period since the Carpet Quarrel had witnessed a gradual reconciliation between Sullivan and Gilbert. By the time *Haddon Hall* closed on 15 April 1893 they had already begun the negotiations that were to result in *Utopia Limited* (7 October 1893). Even so there was a hiatus while the new opera was readied for the stage. This led to the first – but not the last – of the failures in Carte's attempt to fill the void at the theatre. Credit is due to the impresario for the fact that he generally sought out not just new writers and composers,

4 Two great men fail to convince: *Jane Annie* by J. M. Barrie and Arthur Conan Doyle.

but men of genuine talent. Unfortunately the amassing of talent did not always translate into the production of a masterpiece.

Jane Annie (13 May 1893) was initially intended by Carte to be the work of J. M. Barrie (1860–1937), who was later to write *Peter Pan*. Thinking lightly of the task at first, Barrie suffered a nervous breakdown and called in the assistance of Arthur Conan Doyle (1859–1930), already famous as the creator of the Sherlock Holmes stories.[6] The resulting farrago, set in an intrigue-riddled girls' school, was roundly loathed by the critics, and rejected by the Savoy audience – its run of only fifty performances was the first real failure the theatre had suffered in its history.[7] Sullivan, who had declined to set the libretto himself, went to the first night and commented: 'dialogue dull – music *very* pretty'.[8] The score, provided by Ernest Ford, a protégé and former pupil of Sullivan, could not redeem an essentially unsalvageable book. The fact that it was the least like the earlier Savoy operas would not have gone unnoticed.

Dubious reconciliation

Much had happened since the closure of *The Gondoliers*, and *Utopia Limited*, when it finally came, was to find both collaborators altered men, their new work quite significantly less carefree than its Venetian predecessor. Here, Gilbert is in satiric mood – more pointedly so than in any opera since

Iolanthe. Utopia is an imagined South Sea island whose ruler, King Paramount, has sent his daughter, Princess Zara, to Girton College, Cambridge, for an English education. The part of Zara was played – unconvincingly, most agreed – by Nancy McIntosh (1874–1954) for whom Gilbert had formed a deep personal affection.

The Princess returns from Girton bringing with her the eponymous 'Flowers of Progress', who represent Britain in its different forms. The 'Anglicisation' which follows creates unsettling perfection, and the malign coterie around Paramount plot their revenge. The title of the opera has two meanings: the Anglicised Utopia is itself limited and imperfect; but more than this, the entire nation of Utopia becomes a limited company under the benevolent institution of the 'Joint Stock Companies Act of 1862' (a phrase which Sullivan managed to set to music at the conclusion of Act I). Thus a plot scheme which formed an amusing aside in *The Gondoliers* (in which the Duke of Plaza Toro incorporates himself the better to profit from his new-found royal connections) becomes central to *Utopia Limited.* Gilbert was, as is borne out by his own life, obsessed with the trappings of business and the law; *Utopia Limited* was the first serious intimation that such concerns could unbalance his work with Sullivan.

Indeed, the plot of *Utopia* is, taken as a whole, a disappointment. The large cast never quite coheres; the love stories (notably between King Paramount and the English tutor Lady Sophy, and between Princess Zara and the English Captain Fitzbattleaxe) always feel constrained by the satirical and legal elements – something that could scarcely be said for the genuinely emotive *Iolanthe.* In short, there is considerably less heart than in many of the preceding Savoy operas. Sullivan's response is coloured by this, and by the fact that he never seems to find the musical locus of Utopia, a 'nowhere' in the South Seas (though the arrival of the English party towards the end of Act I, with characteristic bravura, is notable for the change that it yields).

It is often recounted that Gilbert thought the Act I finale to be the best that Sullivan had ever written. This is revealing – the construction of the finale is not in the least musical or dramatic, providing little more than a series of prosaic solos from each of the British representatives punctuated by comments from Princess Zara and the chorus. The reappearance (with his trademark 'hardly ever' – 'give three cheers and three cheers more') of the now knighted Captain Corcoran from *HMS Pinafore* was popular on the first night, but the reference really only served to remind the audience of past glories, and of what *Utopia Limited* was not.

The opera ran for a respectable 245 performances. This was to be the benchmark of the runs of the 1890s, but it could not compare with the huge successes of the preceding decade. And it coincided with the emerging triumph of musical comedy at the rival London theatres. It was clear that the Savoy would have to maintain its audience in the face of new competition.

At this critical point Sullivan and Gilbert had a fundamental disagreement as to the direction that their work should take. Disagreement centred in part on Nancy McIntosh, who, Gilbert insisted, must be included in any new opera. When Sullivan refused, Gilbert, who was already withholding rights to his existing works, withdrew his consent for a proposed revival of *The Mikado*. On 13 March 1894 Sullivan sent Gilbert a letter in which he put an end to their collaboration – apparently, this time, for ever.[9]

Once again Carte was confronted by the problem of replacements, and there then followed the strange episode of two operas that were really four. *Mirette* (3 July 1894) was composed by André Messager (1853–1929), whose *La Basoche* had been largely responsible for the failure of the Royal English Opera House in 1891–2 (hardly an auspicious precedent). The libretto, originally written in French by Michel Carré (1865–1945), was translated and further developed by Harry Greenbank (1865–1899) and F. E. Weatherly (1848–1929). It was roundly criticised – 'the new international opera which is not comic' – and, being something like an opéra comique, was not at all what the Savoy audience had come to expect.[10] Its initial run of forty-one performances was the worst ever for a new production at the Savoy. Carte hired Adrian Ross (1859–1933), an established musical comedy librettist, to rework the piece.

The result of this salvage job, produced on 6 October 1894, was an almost new opera, much more in the musical comedy style, to which Messager also made significant amendments. The reward – sixty-one performances – was perhaps a scant one for what had become, to critical acclaim, a genuinely attractive piece; a piece, moreover, which had diverged further from the generally recognised Savoy model than anything previously seen at the theatre.

Its successor was *The Chieftain* (12 December 1894), which was a different sort of compromise, taking as its starting point *The Contrabandista*, on which Sullivan had collaborated with his old friend Frank Burnand, editor of *Punch*, as far back as 1867. Despite – or because of – new dialogue, a much revised first act and an entirely new second one, the piece did not catch on and closed after ninety-seven performances (the bitter weather of the winter of 1894–5 may not have helped). There was to be no new production at the Savoy for a year – Carte even leased the theatre to the Carl Rosa Opera Company. In the wake of *Utopia Limited*, it seemed, nothing would really work. Perhaps the answer lay with Sullivan and Gilbert after all.

Relations between the collaborators had not, in truth, completely broken down; and with the tacit understanding that Nancy McIntosh would not be included, the way was cleared for them to reunite. As negotiations continued through 1895, something even more significant took place. For, in addition to agreeing terms for *The Grand Duke* (7 March 1896), which was to be the next – and last – collaboration with Sullivan, Gilbert agreed to let Carte produce revivals of earlier works (impossible while Nancy McIntosh's professional involvement was still Gilbert's proviso for giving Carte his permission). From then on, gaps in the schedule at the Savoy could be filled by the most popular Gilbert and Sullivan operas of the past. An important business solution for Carte, this was the first indication that the operas were to be more than one-off pieces – they were to be timeless. *The Mikado*, the first revival, was as triumphant on its reappearance as it had been in 1885; in runs either side of *The Grand Duke* it totalled no fewer than 353 performances, which took it comfortably over 1,000 in its West End lifetime.

The proximity of *The Mikado* did not help *The Grand Duke*, a work which feels a generation rather than just eleven years later than its Japanese predecessor. The unfortunate truth is that the libretto was structurally flawed (even Gilbert, who was not prone to bouts of self-criticism, described his book as an 'ugly misshapen little brat').[11] Once again, initial plot strands appear only to disappear for good (the secret sign of the sausage roll does not – mercifully – appear much after mid-way through Act I). Perhaps the most critical weakness is the absence of the title character, Rudolph, between the beginning of the Act I finale and the final part of Act II; instead the opera is dominated by the bass-baritone Ludwig, a member of the troupe of actors which organises the coup against Rudolph. Ludwig is seldom off the stage, resulting in a profound sense of imbalance. When Rudolph finally reappears it is hard to remember who he is.

The opera's sub-title – *The Statutory Duel* – points to a further weakness. The conceit of this legal institution is that one person may legally 'kill' another in a game of cards and accordingly take over all the property, rights and responsibilities of the losing party. Here again Gilbert is at his most legalistic and contrived. There is little in the way of romance, and the opera proceeds on a formulaic basis to settle various scores via the statutory duel – couples unite and part not out of love but according to the turn of cards, their relationships defined not by genuine affection but by their respective roles in the acting company.

Sullivan, as with *Utopia Limited*, grappled not altogether successfully with the libretto of *The Grand Duke*, and he was obviously uninspired by a plot which had its roots in *Thespis*, his first collaboration with Gilbert, of some twenty-five years earlier.[12] One of his main problems was undoubtedly the *mise-en-scène* of the opera. Sensitive as ever to location and atmosphere, Sullivan managed to capture a small-minded and tin-pot German Grand Duchy as only he could; but it is hardly surprising if the resultant musical palette is less appealing than in *The Mikado* or *The Gondoliers*. That said, the opera is enlivened considerably mid-way through Act II by the arrival of the royal party from Monte Carlo, which has come to seal the putative marriage between Rudolph and the Prince of Monte Carlo's daughter. In Monte Carlo, at least, Sullivan was at home; and Gilbert even contributes a song about roulette – which is undoubtedly the highlight of the opera. It is not surprising to learn that when Gilbert, in Sullivan's absence, set to revising the opera, he cut this song and more of Sullivan's music (including the Baroness's charmingly drunken drinking song 'Come bumpers, aye ever so many'), but little of his own dialogue. None of this did anything to redeem the opera and, after 123 performances, it closed, to be replaced, once again, with *The Mikado*. Rutland Barrington (1853–1922) – a stalwart of the company in bass-baritone parts for many years – chose this moment to leave the Savoy and join the cast of the wildly successful musical comedy *The Geisha* at Daly's Theatre. *The Geisha* was eventually to run for 760 performances. The contrast between the two ventures could not have been greater.

Identity crisis

The indefatigable Carte refused to give up on new projects, however uninspiring recent experiments had been. But now he made a genuine error (perhaps out of sheer desperation) and turned again to the librettist of *The Chieftain*, Frank Burnand. The result was another of the great flops to grace the Savoy in the 1890s – *His Majesty* (20 February 1897). Sullivan was busy with his Diamond Jubilee ballet for the Alhambra Theatre, *Victoria and Merrie England* (one of the genuine triumphs of his last decade) so the way was clear for another composer. Carte engaged Sullivan's old friend, the Principal of the Royal Academy of Music, Sir Alexander Mackenzie (1847–1935). Mackenzie, though characterised by Bernard Shaw as a self-authenticating 'professor', along with Parry and Stanford,[13] emerges as one of the most engaging musical figures of his age, and was on consistently good terms with Sullivan.[14] Unfortunately Burnand's libretto was one of the wordiest and least inspiring of all Savoy pieces (which, given some of the disasters of the 1890s, was a significant achievement). Mackenzie's music was seldom anything but tuneful and well crafted, but did not work in context. That the composer felt he was going out of his way to compose in a Sullivanesque vein is apparent from an anecdote in his autobiography in which he mistakes, presumably some years later, military band excerpts from his own *His Majesty* for Sullivan.[15] A contemporary cartoon has Sullivan saying to his old friend: 'Not such child's play as you thought, is it, Mackenzie?'[16] Indeed it was not – *His Majesty* closed after sixty-one performances.

After the demise of *His Majesty*, *The Yeomen of the Guard* was produced with great success, running for 186 performances from May to November

5 *In Re His Majesty*: Sir Arthur to Sir Alexander – 'Not such child's play as you thought, is it, Mackenzie?' *The Entr'acte*, 6 March 1897.

1897, again demonstrating the power of the best works of the 1880s to attain new life. Carte, however, had even now not quite given up on the concept of a Savoy without Gilbert and Sullivan. A revival in much revised and reorchestrated form of Offenbach's *The Grand Duchess of Gerolstein* (4 December 1897), with the addition of witty new lyrics by Adrian Ross, lasted for 104 performances, but did little to make Carte think that *opéra-bouffe* would work any better than the alternatives that he had already tried. 'I left before the curtain fell', Sullivan remarked in his diary. Nevertheless there was always Sullivan. Carte mounted a revival of *The Gondoliers* while the composer made his latest – and by no means least remarkable – attempt at a new direction.

New departures

The Beauty Stone (28 May 1898) is described not as a comic opera but as a 'romantic musical drama'. This soubriquet has echoes of German Romantic opera, but in fact Sullivan wanted the opera to be, as he said himself, 'an entirely new departure' – a more earnest piece not devoid of comic elements but not hidebound to the Savoy tradition.[17] The result was an opera that conformed less to the widely recognised style than any thus far seen. It is one of the most extraordinary works to emerge from the Savoy Theatre, and its brief run of fifty performances has ensured its status as the most misunderstood. Once again, Carte sought out a pair of established writers in a further attempt to bolster his creative team. J. Comyns Carr (1849–1916) was not only an experienced playwright but also someone with whom Sullivan had already collaborated successfully, with his 1895 incidental music to Carr's *King Arthur* (which Henry Irving had mounted, with some spectacle, at the Lyceum). Arthur Wing Pinero (1855–1934) was and remains one of Britain's more successful writers for the stage from this period, and by 1898 was already well known for *The Second Mrs Tanqueray*. The combination of these two literary talents could have been expected to produce a libretto of genuine depth and quality. It did not.

The book for *The Beauty Stone* turned into a verbose mess. Like much Victorian literature set in the Middle Ages, it is suffused with a fusty air of arch medievalism. Sullivan described Carr and Pinero as 'gifted and brilliant men, with *no* experience in writing for music'.[18] He tried to persuade them that certain passages would be better treated musically rather than as dialogue; many of the lyrics that were agreed upon were set in odd metres and were of unwieldy length. The result was a work on the scale of opera seria (the longest, indeed, ever to appear at the theatre); this in itself may not have been a problem except for preponderance of dialogue over music. That said, there was much for Sullivan to tackle musically, and Carr and Pinero achieved two very important things. First of all they created six or seven long concerted pieces (Sullivan's description) allowing the composer to develop musical ideas across uninterrupted spans for longer than he had since *Ivanhoe*. Secondly, they forged strong characters amply suited to musical treatment. Foremost among these are the two dominating and contrasting females: the crippled Laine, whose life is changed by the intervention of the magic stone of the title, and whose prayer to the Virgin becomes one of the prominent motifs interwoven into the score; and the Eastern temptress Saida, who in her cunning and sensuous beauty is everything that Laine is not.

With *The Beauty Stone*, too, we have music of quite a different nature from anything yet seen at the Savoy. A quotation from one of Sullivan's newspaper interviews makes clear the extent of his preparation. It may surprise those who assume that he never thought intellectually about music:

> *The Beauty Stone* is written in an oriental vein. I have tried to give it an unconventional colour. The conventional oriental colour in music is gained by the use of certain intervals, such as the augmented second and the

diminished fifth; but I have rather tried to give it an oriental colour by
means of the languor of the music and by adopting a scale of my own after
the Greek modes . . . It is quite my own invention, that scale: but if you like,
you can mention that it is a compromise between the Phrygian mode and
the Hypomixolydian mode.[19]

Saida's *scena* in Act II ('Though she should dance till dawn of day'), in which
this modal invention appears, is one of the most memorable in the whole
of Sullivan's output; and it is very far from being alone. Hamstrung by its
libretto, however, this was not enough to satisfy audiences who had come
to the theatre 'expecting a comic opera with all the quips, cranks and jokes
pertaining thereto'.[20] *The Beauty Stone* closed after fifty performances, and
Carte reverted to *The Gondoliers*.

This almost cruelly swift closure must have represented a psychological
blow to Sullivan and Carte, calling into question the likelihood that anything
outside the vein of musical comedy could hold a London stage. *The Beauty
Stone* demonstrated most powerfully the fact that the Savoy audience could
not be expected to support every venture presented on the Theatre's stage,
even when Sullivan was the composer. Indeed the opera proves that not
every work launched at the Savoy Theatre can fit comfortably into the
description 'Savoy opera'. Such consistently strong music deserved better
dialogue, and a different theatre.

Compromise

A failure to invite Gilbert to the opening of *The Beauty Stone* (whether by
error or design) was to be the cause of the next and, as it turned out, final
breach between Sullivan and Gilbert. On 17 November 1898, at a revival
of *The Sorcerer* for its twenty-first anniversary, Gilbert refused to speak to
Sullivan as they took their call. They were never to meet again, except in the
street, when Gilbert cut Sullivan dead.[21]

There was little to be done in this situation but to turn, if not to musical
comedy, then to comic opera in the Savoy tradition which could be relied
upon to pack out the house. *The Rose of Persia* (29 November 1899) was
that opera. It followed in a long tradition of successful comic operas and
musical comedies on exotic themes; indeed the Savoy had filled most of
the first half of 1899 with *The Lucky Star* (7 January 1899), an almost
complete remodelling of Emmanuel Chabrier's *L'Etoile* (1877) set in an
idealised Hindustan. *The Lucky Star* was perhaps the most consistent nod
in the direction of musical comedy yet made by the Savoy. 'How are the
mighty fallen!', Sullivan stated in his diary on that day. 'Good story – plot.
Dialogue without wit or point – some of the lyrics very good but the book

doesn't *read* like Gilbert's do – very weak. Music disappointing – not in the least "catching".' Nevertheless, Carte's choice was rewarded with a run of 143 performances – nothing compared to past successes, but more than the total accumulated by every single one of the new works since *Utopia Limited*. All of this boded well for the latest opera in an oriental vein. The other thing that boded well was Carte's choice of Captain Basil Hood (1864–1917) as the librettist.

Basil Hood was an experienced musical comedy writer who came as close to the Gilbertian model as anyone, and who was to be the Savoy's most successful writer after Gilbert.[22] Although, as in *The Nautch Girl*, the influence of *The Mikado* is evident (exotic theme, court intrigue, threatened beheadings, Eastern potentate, and a happy ending forged around a semantic nicety) Hood's book is based on *The Arabian Nights*; its combination of exotic location, genuine romantic feeling and broad humour was clearly invigorating for the composer. Passages of real operatic power intertwine with music in a much lighter, brisker vein; *The Rose of Persia* owes its preponderance of dance numbers to musical comedy, as it does its winning second act duet between Rose-in-Bloom and the Sultan ('Suppose, I say, suppose') – the baby-speak hereabouts could have been otiose, but it emerges triumphant when coupled with Sullivan's lush accompaniment. Two very different numbers were the big successes of the night: the tenor lead's drinking song 'I care not if the cup I hold' (one of the most popular numbers of the composer's final decade), and Rose-in-Bloom's 'Neath my lattice', which is of truly operatic proportions. Relief is palpable in Sullivan's diary entry: 'I conducted as usual. Hideously nervous as usual – great reception as usual – great house as usual – excellent performance as usual – everything as usual – except that the piece is really a great success, I think, which is unusual lately.'[23]

The Rose of Persia emerges as the best compromise between comic opera and musical comedy that the Savoy was to achieve. Its 213 performances were, for a Savoy opera at this stage in the theatre's life, a tremendous success. As Kurt Gänzl says, a decade previously it would probably have run two or three times as long.[24] But this was Sullivan's final complete score for the Savoy – he was to begin another, but did not live to finish it. By the time *The Rose of Persia* closed in June 1900, both Carte and Sullivan were ailing, and would be dead within the year.

Coda

After the rift with Gilbert, the fortunes of the Savoy lay more often than not in the hands of Carte and Sullivan; this was a testament not just to their professional and contractual relationship, but also to the genuine (though complex and delicate) friendship that they enjoyed. The legacy of these years is unquestionably more than a footnote to the achievements of the 1880s. In *Haddon Hall* and *The Beauty Stone*, Sullivan composed two of the most important operas of his career, both of which contribute immensely to our understanding of his lyrical gifts. Carte for his part never ceased to seek a solution to the problem of replacing Gilbert and Sullivan in the context of the rise of musical comedy – a solution that would not be a wholesale sell-out to the new and more populist form. Like any other brave theatrical manager he made severe errors of judgement along the way.

In the event no consistent operatic style was to emerge in the 1890s. Carte experimented with old style comic opera, with imitations of Gilbert and Sullivan, with Sullivan and Gilbert themselves, with opéra comique and opéra-bouffe, with romantic opera and with musical comedy. Only at the end of the decade did Sullivan's collaboration with Hood in *The Rose of Persia* show what the answer might have been: a style of broader English comic opera that incorporated some of the brighter, fresher elements of musical comedy. In the complex (but never dull) process of reaching this point, Carte might justifiably have hoped for more successful outcomes than were achieved, given the artists whom he commissioned.

In truth, the term 'Savoy opera' had become indelibly associated with its originators, Sullivan and Gilbert, as early as 1890. By 1900 it was already apparent that their collaborations of the 1870s and 1880s had staying power. But tastes had changed, and the task of filling the Savoy with new comic opera was quickly becoming impossible. *The Emerald Isle* (27 April 1901) stood at the end of the era. Sullivan strove to complete the work through his final illness in autumn 1900, but his health finally collapsed on St Cecilia's Day, 22 November 1900. Edward German (1862–1936) – the last but not the least Carte 'find' – did an outstanding job of composing the numbers left unset by Sullivan (approximately half of the total) and orchestrating all but the first two. Hood's libretto is witty and sharp, and its Irish setting must have been a wonderful inspiration for Sullivan, whose ancestral roots lay there. The composer responded, despite his appalling physical condition, in an extraordinary manner, and it is hard to imagine how music so fresh could have been written on what turned out to be his deathbed. The final pages of Act I (which must be some of the last music that he wrote) contain the loveliest tune of his career, as haunting and enchanting an Irish melody as could be imagined, as the soldiers are called to their fate in the fairy-haunted caves. The sheer ease with which it captures the situation – like so much of Sullivan's music for the stage – makes it almost impossible to believe that it is not folk music.

> 'Come away', sighs the Fairy Voice,
> 'Come to the caves of Carrig-Cleena!
> For there I make all aching hearts rejoice,
> Come, come away!'

3 Resituating Gilbert and Sullivan: the musical and aesthetic context

BENEDICT TAYLOR

Arthur Sullivan's operas based on W. S. Gilbert's librettos occupy a strange and to some extent bewildering place in nineteenth-century music. As both an outgrowth of a (so-called) 'serious' tradition of operatic culture (as is made witness not only by Sullivan's rigorous training and fluent proficiency in the mainstream tradition of German music but in the numerous allusions to and parodies of this august operatic lineage contained within these works) and at the same time seemingly the predecessors to a less well-regarded line of operettas, musicals and shows, the Savoy operas dwell in a strange no man's land between the serious (respectable) and popular (frivolous). This ambivalence is seen as borne out by that strange and still-present formulation, the double-barrelled, bicephalic entity referred to by all as 'G & S', even in contexts when only the music is being expressly referred to. At the same time, and not unrelatedly, these works have been afforded a remarkably polarised reception between enormous popular affection and critical opprobrium. To understand how this reception history has come about and where these works might most profitably be situated it is necessary to investigate more deeply the relationship of these pieces to their musical and aesthetic background, the sources, models and inspiration from which this unique series of operas grew, and to explore the impact such aesthetics might have had for their divided critical reception.

Musical background and influences

The position and reception of the Gilbert and Sullivan operas must be understood within the context of the cultural-sociological state of music in Britain prior to 1870. The considerable artistic culture Britain had was decidedly a literary one, based on common-sense virtues and rational thinking. A distrust of music was deeply rooted in the cultural mentality. Since the eighteenth century, the arts had been perceived by many as dangerously seductive and effeminate, a mischievous foreign influence that would lead to the emasculation of the British traits of reason and common-sense empiricism.[1]

Music was of course the most insubstantial and dangerous of all, in its insidious capacity for infiltration of the emotions and wayward freedom from rational explanation. 'Music is certainly a very agreeable Entertainment', wrote Joseph Addison in 1711, 'but if it would make us incapable of hearing sense, if it would exclude arts that have a much greater tendency to the refinement of human nature; I must confess that I would allow it no better quarter than Plato has done, who banishes it out of his commonwealth'.[2]

Years later Sullivan himself left the recollection that 'At any great meeting on the subject of music, archbishops, judges, politicians, financiers – each one . . . will depreciate any knowledge of music with a smug satisfaction, like a man disowning poor relations'.[3] Yet obviously there was a love of music among many. The upshot was that music was imported – a profession for foreigners to dabble in, who were of course allowed (even perhaps expected) to be wayward, morally suspect and over-emotional. Hence the extraordinary list of distinguished foreign musicians who were to visit Britain: Handel, J. C. Bach, Haydn, Clementi, Weber and Mendelssohn, to name just a few. As a result, those native talents that aspired to musical eminence found the going tough. Sullivan, like Thomas Beecham almost a century later, would complain of the hardships and obstacles facing the British musician confronted by such foreign competition. There was little institutional provision for 'serious' instrumental music, and opera (invariably given in Italian) was there to be chatted over. Britain was not *das Land ohne Musik*, but the native talent it possessed received scant encouragement from the existing state of society, and the path of musicians such as William Sterndale Bennett or George Macfarren was normally one of slow, sad decline from promising beginnings and overseas recognition, when exposed to accumulated years of public apathy. Music was simply not built into the society and cultural institutions of the country.[4]

It is against this social and cultural backdrop that the rise of Sullivan's career to the 1870s and the initiation of his partnership with W. S. Gilbert should be charted. The details of Sullivan's early career are well known: on winning the first Mendelssohn scholarship in 1856 and gaining a thorough training in that bastion of Germanic music, the Leipzig Conservatory, a performance in 1862 of his graduation piece, music to Shakespeare's *The Tempest*, established him overnight as the great hope of English music. Thereafter Sullivan turned his attention to ballet (*L'Île Enchantée*), opera (*The Sapphire Necklace*, 1864, now mostly lost), symphony (1866), a cello concerto, overtures, songs (including the five notable Shakespeare settings and the first English song cycle, *The Window*, to words by Tennyson), numerous hymn settings and a small number of slight, though charming instrumental pieces.

The achievement in these works is often considerable; the symphony, for instance, is one of the brightest to emerge from the decades between Schumann and Brahms, and would remain unsurpassed in English music until Elgar four decades later. Stylistically, the influences of Mendelssohn, Schumann and Schubert in particular are felt in the more substantial orchestral works, but from the beginning in *The Tempest* there is the peculiar, intangible stamp of Sullivan emerging confidently from this familiar background. At the same time, such serious productions would not in themselves keep Sullivan's body attached to the vertiginous flights of his soul, and in order to make a living he turned increasingly to the lucrative market for songs and ballads, a need which would eventually be satisfied by the financial independence provided by the extraordinary operatic success with Gilbert.

The operatic backdrop to the emergence of Gilbert and Sullivan's form of musical theatre in the 1870s is multifaceted. Standing behind any English operatic work of the time is the earlier tradition of ballad opera, a genre not directly relatable to the Savoy operas but present as a general precedent. More recently, the nineteenth century saw the growth of a genre, English Romantic opera, that survived into the twentieth century, even if this tradition is now little known; significant works include John Barnett's *The Mountain Sylph* (1834), Michael Balfe's *The Bohemian Girl* (1843), W. V. Wallace's *Maritana* (1845) and Julius Benedict's *The Lily of Killarney* (1862). This heritage provided an immediate context for a more serious (if hardly heavy) English opera, and indeed what we have of Sullivan's early *Sapphire Necklace* clearly lies in this tradition. Two influential models can be found for Gilbert and Sullivan's earliest work: French *opéra-bouffe* and the English theatrical burlesque. Offenbach's *opéra-bouffe* – itself in part an outshoot of Auber's opéra comique – was the initial impetus for Sullivan's first comic operatic outing with his friend F. C. Burnand as librettist, *Cox and Box*, and both *The Zoo* (to a text by B. C. Stephenson) and *Trial by Jury* (Gilbert) of 1875 were run as starters to Offenbach works, though they quickly became the main attraction of the evening. Gilbert's work grew out of the world of burlesque, and his first collaboration with Sullivan, the long-lost *Thespis* (1871), comes from this more humble stable.

In conjunction, Sullivan brought his training in the wider European tradition to bear in his comic operas. He had been exposed to a wide range of operatic music in Leipzig and later at Covent Garden under Costa, besides having prepared vocal scores of numerous repertoire operas.[5] Perhaps the most decisive influence and role model for his turn to comic opera was the figure of Rossini, whom Sullivan later claimed was probably the first person who 'inspired me with a love for the stage and things operatic'.[6] Sullivan had met the Italian composer in Paris in 1862 and by all accounts got on splendidly with the ageing master. Beyond this influence, the line of comic operas in German (Lortzing, Nicolai, Cornelius) and French opéra comique (epitomised by Auber) must have provided notable precedent for his endeavours. Sullivan's early comic works therefore relate to and stand at the confluence of several traditions. While Offenbach was the immediate catalyst, Sullivan would draw on a wider and deeper reserve for his comic operas.

Musical characteristics

The qualities indelibly associated with Sullivan scarcely need extensive exposition. Alexander Mackenzie, in an early account that remains one of the most perceptive and understanding to this day, identifies Sullivan's characteristic 'gifts of melody, graceful clearness of instrumentation, as well as a dramatic sense (which obtains results by obviously simple means)'.[7] To these qualities one could add a deft sense of piquant harmonic colour, and not least a remarkable gift for imaginative and metrically apt word-setting. This latter quality is the one aspect of Sullivan's compositional technique that has received adequate scholarly attention, and it is worth remembering that if Gilbert's texts are commonly held up to be a more significant aspect of the combined work than in many other operas, much of the credit must go to Sullivan for enabling the words, in all their wit, to be perceived so clearly in the first place. Indeed, the two creators are the bequeathers of a near-perfect fusion of word and music rarely equalled in the history of musical drama.

A further important feature of Sullivan's music is of course his keen sense of musical humour as a correlate to Gilbert's own comic gifts. This is seen especially in the use of parody that accompanied Sullivan throughout his career. The delight in parody and humorous pastiche obviously was fairly innate: Clara Barnett, a colleague at Leipzig, left an account of the composer during his student years taking 'a wicked delight in sitting at the piano and parodying a Rossini cavatina'.[8] As has often been noticed, though, Sullivan's attitude to parody changed gradually across his operas. We see a general progression away from the obviously satirical *Cox and Box* and *Trial by Jury* with their often hilarious parodies of operatic tradition, through the sometimes ballad-opera feel of *The Sorcerer* and *HMS Pinafore* to the more complex, nuanced relationship of the mature Savoy style to earlier operatic tradition. Increasingly there is the infiltration of characteristic 'English' elements – *Pinafore*'s glees, *Ruddigore*'s hornpipes, gavottes and older dances (*Sorcerer*, *Gondoliers*, *Haddon Hall*), madrigals (*Mikado*, *Ruddigore*, *Yeomen*), ballads (*Patience*, *Iolanthe*). By the time of the move to the new, purpose-built Savoy theatre in 1881, Sullivan's comic operas were indisputably an art form in their own right, forming a new and distinctive tradition, *sui generis.*

A closer investigation of the celebrated 'ghost scene' from *Ruddigore* (Act II) reveals several of the deeper musical qualities Sullivan could bring to his comic operas. This scene is notable as an instance of where the composer did not rein in his creative talent (causing no little irritation with Gilbert), and is consequently valuable for understanding the range of his musical capabilities in these works.

The opening chorus ('Painted emblems of a race') immediately sets the solemn tone of the scene, a sombre D minor, the male chorus accompanied by low strings and punctuated by *piano* brass. In tone and idiom this passage immediately suggests the influence of mid-century Italian opera, most particularly the 'Miserere' chorus from Act IV of Verdi's *Il trovatore*, which was doubtless in the back of Sullivan's mind. This in itself is probably more a case of Sullivan calling on an allusion for straight expressive effect than of intended parody of this style.[9] We are moving comfortably along familiar lines then, until Sullivan slips in a surprise at the approach to the cadence; the dominant moves down to a (major) subdominant chord and suddenly the Dorian mode opens up before us. From a fairly conventional, if effective, Verdian pastiche, a whole new realm is disclosed, an unmistakably English, crumbling Gothic atmosphere, stepping out from the past 'into the world once more', that forms one side of *Ruddigore*'s distinctive sound-world.

Modality thus constitutes one of the integral elements of this scene, most notably the startling Phrygian passage of 'Set upon thy course of evil'. The other feature is a pronounced chromaticism that seems to spill out of the prologue from Sullivan's *The Golden Legend* of the previous year. The music is suffused with diminished-seventh complexes – a standard technique for musical horror, but treated with a systematic urge that recalls Liszt. Where these two elements intersect is in the emphasis on the flattened-second scale-degree contained within the Phrygian scale and the concomitant tritone made with degree $\hat{5}$. For the former, one should note the prominence given at the start of the scene to the Neapolitan harmony, E-flat – the home tonality of Sullivan's opera. The latter interval is contained within the diminished-seventh complex and makes numerous appearances throughout the scene.

It is seen in the eerie parallel-tritone part-writing of 'Last of our accursed line' and with the frightening continuation of the Phrygian passage, ascending via an octatonic scale from C to a climactic impasse on F-sharp. The emphasis on the tritone is then taken up at a larger scale in the ensuing number: 'When the night wind howls' – in Gervase Hughes's words, 'unquestionably the finest piece of descriptive music that Sullivan ever wrote', in which 'we may find . . . an apotheosis of his matured harmonic resource'.[10]

This song contains several characteristic Sullivan harmonic traits, most pertinently here the quasi-modal modulation to the flattened leading degree (D–C) followed by a common-tone switch from C to A-flat, characteristic of many nineteenth-century composers with an ear for harmonic colour but perhaps most familiar to Sullivan from Gounod. The upshot of these two typical progressions is, however, the quite atypical polarity created between the D minor outward frame of the piece and the tritonally dissonant A-flat passage at its centre. Truly these ghosts are *diaboli in musica*.

The orchestration throughout is a model of imagination harnessed to clarity, and when the limited resources of the pit orchestra he had at his disposal is taken into consideration, Sullivan's achievement becomes even more impressive. The influence of Berlioz is often read into this song, though in truth there is no exact model for Sullivan by now. Thus, as this example shows, Sullivan would bring to a lighter more popular genre the skill and resources of a prodigiously gifted musician trained in the 'serious' Germanic tradition of Leipzig, and in time transform it into something unique and unparalleled. Just as Gilbert and Carte had a large part in turning the morally and socially suspect theatrical world of the burlesque into something eminently respectable, so would Sullivan transform the musical potential of light opera/*opéra-bouffe* into a genre comparable to that of Rossini, Auber or Lortzing.

Aesthetic qualities and critical problems

Sullivan was not prone to extensive philosophical reflection on the purposes and aesthetics of music. In common with many professional composers of an earlier age, writing music was his job, and he did it without feeling the need to construct elaborate systems or specious polemic to justify his ways. Yet on several occasions he left evidence of his general views on his music that can be enlightening for the modern reader trying to understand his aims. As he more than once complained to Gilbert, music should 'act in its own proper sphere', arising out of and intensifying the emotional elements of the situation. The stories set should be of 'human interest and probability', with a balance of dramatic, humorous and romantic aspects.[11] An interview given to the *San Francisco Daily Chronicle* in 1885 presents a good picture of the composer's aesthetic aims.

> The opera of the future is a compromise . . . Not the French school, with gaudy and tinsel tunes, its lambent light and shades, its theatrical effects and clap-trap, not the Wagnerian school, with its sombreness and heavy ear-splitting airs, with its mysticism and unreal sentiment; not the Italian school, with its fantastic airs and *fioriture* and far-fetched effects. It is a

> compromise between these three – a sort of eclectic school, a selection of
> the merits of each one. I do not believe in operas based on gods and myths.
> That is the fault of the German school. It is metaphysical music – it is
> philosophy. What we want are plots which give rise to characters of flesh and
> blood, with human emotions and human passions. Music should speak to
> the heart, and not to the head.[12]

What is evident from this account is that Sullivan valued such qualities as
emotional directness of communication, empathy and human relevance,
and a stylistic pluralism that is not afraid to draw on a variety of national
and historical styles. Attributes often prized in the Romantic era – such
as the fixation on the artist's own subjectivity and extreme emotional
states, the individual genius, misunderstood in his lifetime, writing 'for
posterity', and a radical, progressive musical language – are clearly not pri-
orities for Sullivan. Such personal characteristics are notable as many of
them potentially give rise to problems in relation to prevalent nineteenth-
and twentieth-century aesthetic ideologies, which may in part explain the
sometimes negative reception his work has been afforded.

A consequence of his polystylism is that the charge of 'eclecticism' has
often been levelled at Sullivan. This term is commonly understood nowadays
as an insult of some (indefinable) form, though Sullivan himself was quite
open in expressing this feature – 'I am very eclectic in my tastes'[13] – 'a sort
of eclectic school' – which, to the contrary, he seems to view as a positive
attribute. A consequence of this relation to earlier music is that Sullivan's
music is also often marked by a certain conservatism of style and models.
The criticisms here seem to be based on the assumption that (a) Sullivan's
music is 'derivative' and insufficiently original, and (b) that these attributes
are defensible criteria for aesthetic judgement. Both propositions are in fact
open to question.

Towards the end of the eighteenth century new aesthetic ideologies in
England and Germany began to see artistic truth and value as residing
in the individual creator-genius, endowed with a unique subjective identity and originality, whose art works thus stand outside society and prior
precedents. Beauty, earlier in the eighteenth century the central category
of aesthetic judgement, becomes replaced by truth, understood either as
metaphysical truth (related to the incomprehensible sublime or profound),
emotional truth (often equated with the emotionally extreme and unstable) or historical truth (i.e., the modern and progressive). This explains
the latent criticism directed at Sullivan through the 'eclectic' label, as the
wealth of allusions, parodies and echoes of other music might seem to mil-
itate against any chance of artistic originality and personal 'authenticity'.
Yet this assumption is fundamentally undermined by the simple fact that

his music is so unmistakable; there are in fact few more characteristic composers. 'Eclectic', as a criticism levelled against Sullivan, is thus an empty
charge, as no one has ever doubted that his music possesses in abundance
an unmistakable individual quality, despite the separate elements that have
gone to make it up. In a word, Sullivan sounds inimitably like Sullivan, and
always has. One might better read 'eclectic' as 'synthetic', as the music of a
pre-Romantic composer such as Mozart clearly was. Essentially, Sullivan's
taste coincides with a more eighteenth-century Enlightenment outlook
on art.

More substantial is the claim of conservatism. Despite some exceptions,
it would be hard to deny that Sullivan's music is not the most radical in existence. However, one must critically examine the grounds upon which this
feature, if taken as a criterion for judgement, is based, since the unquestioned
adherence to the ideology of modernity that lies behind this assumption
became increasingly untenable in the last decades of the twentieth century.
Accounts that actually seek to understand Sullivan's music rather than auto-
matically deciding its artistic value on an external scale of progressiveness
must therefore move beyond the discredited clichés of unthinking criticism. Recent scholars have found more enlightening ways of understanding
Sullivan's historical approach by relating it to a richer, more subtle understanding of historical time than the simplistic linear model progressivism
admits.[14]

Bound up with this stylistic conservatism is a desire for directness of
communication, witnessed by Sullivan's insistence on music that 'speaks
to the heart'. Mackenzie notes Sullivan's distrust of over-complex/elaborate
means, speaking of 'his maxim of respecting the "fitness of things"; with
the result that the "human touch" went very straight to its mark, and he
took care that that touch should not be weakened, or obscured, by either
unnecessary complications or diffuseness'.[15]

Directness of communication means working within publicly understood linguistic/expressive conventions, which explains the important function of Sullivan's conservatism of language. An obvious result of this is his
music's accessibility and, as a consequence, popularity.

This is one reason – its apparent straightforwardness – why his music
may be reviled or patronised by those wanting more complex commu-
nicative techniques. It is only too easy to be able to dismiss something
open and straightforward; because Sullivan does not condescend to us,
we condescend to him.[16] Clearly Sullivan cannot possibly be held to be a
'bad' composer in terms of technical proficiency or competence – indeed,
he was one of the most gifted composers of the nineteenth century and
had received a rigorous technical grounding.[17] His fault, as much as it is
one, is merely that his music is largely 'conventional', and seeks to convey

emotional states in an uncomplicated, direct manner accessible to many, not the few. Yet there is no definitive way of judging the emotional 'truth' of artistic expression (if there were, it is unlikely that academics and critics would have privileged access to it), and the numerous generations that have been captivated by his music might well bear out Percy Young's contention that 'Sullivan's simplicities frequently carried their own kind of profundity'.[18]

One place where the issue does become more clouded is concerning the issue of Sullivan's parodies. Opera – that most unrealistic of art forms – has so many expressive conventions and dramatic stocks-in-trade that it is amusing for a really talented composer and author to send it up. This gives a nice twist of irony to the issue above: Sullivan is doing it just as well or better than the model, showing how easy it is to copy or send up a style. As Thomas Dunhill contended with 'Poor wand'ring one' (*Pirates of Penzance*), Sullivan's music is 'fully equal to any of the songs it sets out to satirise'.[19] Hence, appropriately, the last laugh is *on* operatic snobs, not *by* them. The resistance to Gilbert and Sullivan encountered in some surely relates to this parody of sacred operatic cows, which shows all too uncomfortably how baseless the snobbish fetishisation of certain names at the expense of others is (what else would explain the anger, the seemingly personal resentment detractors hold against these works? It has no musical basis). And, typical of Sullivan's humane qualities, he does this affectionately, unmaliciously; hence it is easier to be scornful about this and ignore the satire, as it is too subtle for some detractors' minds.

Cultural issues

These Romantic aesthetics that prized originality, sincerity and profundity had a further consequence in imbuing music with a moral imperative. Art has a serious ethical function; *eo ipso* all music must be serious music. By far the longest-lasting and most damaging effect on Sullivan's reputation has been a cultural snobbery against popular music instigated during his lifetime and perpetuated long afterwards: the idea that true art must be serious, highbrow and ethically exemplary – what has been called the 'gospel of earnestness'.[20] As early as 1883, *The Musical Review*, following the announcement of Sullivan's knighthood, wrote that 'Some things that Mr Arthur Sullivan may do, Sir Arthur ought not to do ... it will look rather more than odd to see announced in the papers that a new comic opera is in preparation, the book by Mr W. S. Gilbert and the music by Sir Arthur Sullivan. A musical knight ... must not dare to soil his hands with anything less than an anthem or a madrigal; oratorio ... and symphony, must now be his line.'[21] A view that was becoming increasingly widespread was that comic opera was at best a negligible activity for a composer of Sullivan's talents, and at worst a prostitution of his ethical duty, a betrayal of 'gifts greater, perhaps, than fell to any English musician since the time of Purcell'.[22]

This divide between serious and popular became increasingly evident during the nineteenth century and relates to a general 'Teutonicising' of English music and culture. Certain composers, recalled Charles Maclean, 'almost exclusively German', were regarded in the Victorian era 'as "classical"; while the music of everyone else was treated as something out of the pale'.[23] Though Sullivan had been trained in Germany and was a forceful advocate of Schumann and Schubert at a time when these composers were little appreciated in England, his aesthetics stopped short of the more extreme manifestations of a view which in a morally charged Victorian culture held art and entertainment to be mutually exclusive. These aesthetic and ethical values were spread through the value-system of a new group of critics and composers occupying leading institutional positions in Britain. In their groundbreaking and provocative study of the 'English Musical Renaissance', Robert Stradling and Meirion Hughes detail how a small group of musicians and critics emanating from a narrow range of institutions (Oxford, Cambridge, the Royal Academy and Royal College of Music) propagated their own ethical and aesthetic agenda and as a consequence wrote their own values into the 'official' history of English music heard ever since. The effects of this ideology can be still seen in standard accounts of the development of English music over a century later.[24]

To be sure, one might justly see Sullivan himself as affected by this dichotomy in his constant desire to write a grand opera or something more worthy of his talents and his recurring dissatisfaction with the Savoy as a medium for his talent. But, though this aspect is undoubtedly present to an extent, this does not really point to Sullivan's distaste for comic opera *tout court*; documentary evidence suggests it was more the inadequate provision for 'human emotions and situations' in Gilbert's librettos and the feeling that the forms of these works restricted his creative potential that dissatisfied Sullivan. And when he did write a grand opera, *Ivanhoe*, the music has since been criticised for stepping out of the Savoy in places. The assumption that this was a subconscious reversion from a composer used to a lighter style is hardly a satisfactory explanation;[25] one might better view this as demonstrating how good tunes, humour and popularity were not categorically distinct from serious music for Sullivan, unlike for many critics of his time and since. The two occupy differing stages on a continuum between weightiness and levity, as demonstrated by the intermediary style of the near contemporaneous *Yeomen of the Guard* or *The Beauty Stone*. This snobbery against Sullivan's lighter music, conditioned by the underlying imperative

6 Sullivan the musician: conducting the Leeds Festival. *Illustrated London News* (23 October 1886), p. 421.

of moral earnestness and perpetuated by successive generations of critics whose desire for critical judgement no doubt outweighed their sensitivity to art (and finally, it must be said, their knowledge of Sullivan's music), ultimately has fed into a wider snobbery against the Savoy operas. Little of this has significant musical basis; rather, it is primarily directed against a social class and culture associated with these works. This is due above all to the phenomenon of amateur performances and their association with middle-class Middle England. (The clear distasteful social snobbery here shows that this quality is still very much alive – and hence that Gilbert's satire still has targets, ironically actually perpetuating these works' relevance.) As David Cannadine has demonstrated, these operas, with the satire they poke at national institutions and the middle classes, eventually became institutionalised themselves and associated with these same conservative values.[26] And the standards of amateur operatic performances are, obviously, not always the highest. (This is not to disparage amateur performances but merely to suggest that if most people's exposure to a repertoire comes from this source they are unlikely to hold it as highly in esteem as one featuring glittering star soloists in international opera houses.)

The dominance of the amateur operatic society was caused by the deleterious effect of the D'Oyly Carte's monopoly on performances. Until 1961 the copyright on the Gilbert and Sullivan operas was owned by the company created in their lifetime for their performance, who jealously guarded the rights and materials to these works, only allowing amateur groups to perform them (i.e., those who were unlikely to prove much threat to the D'Oyly Carte's hegemony). Even Sullivan's orchestral scores were not readily available for study (the well-known vocal scores give little indication of the full range of Sullivan's instrumentation). This is one of the major reasons why the Savoy operas still largely occupy a position outside the mainstream repertoire of major opera houses such as Covent Garden. Throughout the first half of the twentieth century, when opera companies in England were looking to establish a national repertoire, Sullivan's works – by far the most popular survivors from the previous century – could not be considered. In place, earlier works by Balfe, Wallace and Benedict were revived. By the 1960s, it was too late: English opera had found a new mythical founder in the figure of Britten. If all this had not been the case, the story of the growth of English opera may well have been substantially different from the present historical narrative.

It must also be admitted that the D'Oyly Carte Company themselves were not always the most musically accomplished of bodies. It may be a historical fact that the original performance conditions in Gilbert and Sullivan's lifetime were musically limited, but such works are always capable of a new lease of life. Sullivan's music should be allowed to shine in more fitting conditions; like all works of art, his operas are greater than their original production capabilities. 'It is only when we treat Sullivan with the same artistic respect that we show to Mozart and Schubert' wrote one commentator in 1938, 'that his peculiar genius can shine untarnished'.[27]

Conclusions: musical position and significance

To understand and appreciate Sullivan's music one has to stand above the ingrained aesthetic norms passed down from one particular, rather narrow, strand of Romantic thought and reinstate the values of beauty, human sympathy, popular comprehension and accessibility valued in an earlier age. Like Rossini, Sullivan was not fully in sympathy with Romanticism in its more extreme, individualistic aspects. His music indeed has more affinities with that of Mozart or Rossini than with contemporaries such as

Brahms or Wagner. (In this light, it is notable that a distinguished opera scholar such as E. J. Dent would hold that 'a course of Mozart in English might be the best step towards educating our on-coming public to a really intelligent appreciation of Sullivan.'[28])

The reasons why Sullivan's operatic reputation has not followed that of Mozart or Rossini are bound up with this cultural situation of music within nineteenth-century Britain. In Vaughan Williams's opinion, Sullivan was 'a jewel in the wrong setting',[29] while for James Day, similarly, 'Sullivan narrowly missed becoming an English Mozart . . . simply because Victorian art had to be serious and "chivalrous" for it to be taken seriously'.[30] In his sense of harmonic and timbral colour, and the matchless gift for melody, Sullivan often calls to mind his near-contemporary Bizet, with whom he shares many affinities. The parallel between the two might indeed be instructive for understanding Sullivan's cultural position and what he might have achieved had there been a stronger operatic tradition in England. Both composers, precociously talented, tended towards a post-Mendelssohnian/Schubertian idiom and were at their happiest in the smaller set-piece forms typifying the opéra comique that gave free reign to their unmistakable talents. (Sullivan's affinities with French music and culture have often been noted – probably more so indeed than with any other national style.) The major advantage Bizet had over Sullivan was in being born in a country with a strong operatic culture, which enabled him to work within established traditions and institutional frameworks even if ultimately he would transform them (and, perhaps, in dying at just the right time to become mythologised). Without such a serious operatic heritage behind him Sullivan would fall foul of aesthetic avatars that sought to distance his music from what was considered serious culture.

Yet perhaps Sullivan's achievement was in fact commensurate with his potential. Within the aesthetic context of the time, Sullivan's inclination for eclectic, synthetic music was in retrospect best suited to such comic operas. In these his comic gifts, his skill at parody of other music and flair for melody, rhythm and word-setting, would find its best vehicle. One should be wary of suggesting, because of this, that these works are the exclusive repository of his genius; Sullivan's musical qualities were diffused throughout all his output and many of his greatest 'serious' works could not have been written within the confines of Gilbert's texts and the style imposed by the conditions of the Savoy. Yet such was the nature of Sullivan's talents and the cultural-aesthetic circumstances in which he lived and followed, that the comic operas with Gilbert provide perhaps the most consistently perfect expression of his inimitable qualities and without doubt the most enduring. Sullivan's music – in its stylistic pluralism, accessibility, its good-natured blend of wit and sentiment, comprehensibility and erudition, moving happily between high and low styles, and its own particular beauty – would have fitted perfectly within an eighteenth-century aesthetic, but suffered in an age and culture that in hindsight can only be described as well intentioned but misguided. In Ian Parrott's words, 'He was essentially the most broad-minded musician in perhaps the most narrow and unoriginal school of thought in musical history'.[31] Only now, with the passing of time (but constancy of Sullivan's presence in the repertoire and English culture), we may perhaps outgrow the narrow prejudices of a less understanding age, and recognise the unique talent that Sullivan possessed. Works that are still going strongly a century after their creation suggest that the 'ephemeral', insignificant 'triviality' of such creations – and the aesthetic under which they have been judged – has been mistaken.

4 'We sing as one individual'? Popular misconceptions of 'Gilbert and Sullivan'

MEINHARD SAREMBA

As head of the Vienna Hofoper, Gustav Mahler developed his credo that in each performance an opera has to be created anew. This led to his conviction: 'What people of the theatre call tradition is nothing more than their laziness and their slipshod work'.[1] This notion is especially relevant for branches of musical theatre where the shadows of 'tradition' are especially long and hauntingly darkening, as in the so-called Gilbert and Sullivan, or Savoy operas.

W. S. Gilbert suggested in an 1891 interview that 'the burlesque stage was in a very unclean state' and that he and Sullivan had made up their minds 'to do all in our power to wipe out the grosser element'.[2] Arthur Sullivan said in 1885 that in comic opera he 'adhered to the principles of art which I had learned in the production of more solid works, and no musician who analyses the score of those light operas will fail to find the evidence of seriousness and solidity pointed out'.[3] Gilbert believed that some of Sullivan's music was out of place in comic opera, and this is not surprising, considering that he seems to have been more concerned about burlesque and moral standards – 'never to let an offending word escape our characters'[4] – whereas his collaborator reveals a wider range of artistic ambition. From the mid-1880s onwards there are repeated statements by Gilbert to the effect that the text 'must be played exactly as I wrote it'.[5] There is good reason to assume that this was not only due to issues of copyright but also because Gilbert, the librettist, feared losing control of the works. Usually the performers had to be true to the melodies but not necessarily the words, so he tried to take possession of the operas again as a producer. His detailed prompt-books helped to cement a performing style that may have been innovative for the late nineteenth century but had become antiquated by the early twentieth century, ignoring developments during Gilbert's lifetime such as the innovative stimulus propounded by Adolph Appia or Edward Gordon Craig concerning stage settings and theatre as a creative form of art.[6]

Even at the beginning of the twenty-first century, the works by Sullivan and Gilbert are often treated as though they belong in a parallel universe. Today Charles Mackay's 1841 book on *Extraordinary Popular Delusions* could be extended with a chapter on 'Gilbert and Sullivan' or 'Savoy opera', because this term itself is a misnomer – the first Sullivan operas at the Savoy Theatre were not premièred until *Iolanthe* (1882) and they did not come to an end with *The Grand Duke* (1896). There are a number of myths – in the sense of fictitious and unproven beliefs – which are still lurking in the minds of admirers and enemies alike: that the text is authoritative; that the works are operettas, in which the music is peripheral; that 'Gilbert and Sullivan' are inseparable, and cannot be transplanted elsewhere.

In order to gain full appreciation and a wider perception of these comic operas it seems necessary to bid farewell to at least these most common misconceptions of fans and the so-called Gilbert and Sullivan scholarship which is more knowledgeable about words than music. The crucial question is: are these works merely a sociological phenomenon that deserves nothing more than a marginal note in music histories, or are they substantial operas that can claim their place in the history of European music theatre?

Music makes the (opera-) world go round

The first myth is that these works are the librettist's operas. This notion devalues them for musicological research and the professional repertoire. There are numerous books and essays that spread the fallacy that Sullivan had provided nothing more than a musical complement for Gilbert's literary brilliance and in consequence they have been too often treated as 'plays with music' instead of comic operas.[7]

All his life Sullivan was searching for the ideal librettist. He was unwilling to write his own texts – as did Lortzing, Wagner or Tippett – but he made substantial demands and contributions to the story outline and its musico-dramatic realisation. A detailed analysis of Gilbert's librettos for *Princess Toto* (music by Frederic Clay) and *The Sorcerer* – both premièred in 1877 – would reveal a strikingly different approach resulting from Sullivan's insistence on 'humanity'. The idea that Sullivan simply did what Gilbert told him is misleading. In his music Sullivan reveals how the individual is lost in a chaotic environment bigger than him- or herself. The complex finales (for example, *Iolanthe, Ruddigore, Yeomen of the Guard*) depict the disillusionment of life with sometimes abrupt tempo changes and a focus on individual characters or groupings. During the first-act finale of *Iolanthe* (at about twenty-five minutes of music the longest of all), the bright and swinging fairy music gradually charms and overpowers the 'manly' march-like tunes and pompous Verdian allusions of the peers' music. The march tune that concludes the finale functions as an antithesis to the earlier *maestoso* march of the peers. As the *allegro marziale* indicates, the music reveals the fairies' perspective on the invaders – the conflict reaches the culmination of the crisis. In the operas by Sullivan and Gilbert the protagonists constantly ask themselves: *Am I doing the right thing? Who can I trust? Who and how shall I love?* It is the music that enhances the emotional uncertainty (which is hardly ever brought out to full effect in recordings or on stage): how can we change the course of life – does a book with rules of conduct give advice? In *Ruddigore,* Rose's emotional turmoil is illustrated with a strong contrast to the *tempo di valse* of her aria; when she refers to her book the violins have large interval leaps at Fig. A in the critical edition of the full score (where a *piano* flute line tries to placate her agitation at 'But here it says'), or are played staccato with the woodwind *tacet* altogether in Fig. C (at 'Where can it be?'). In all the operas we get interim solutions – a closer look reveals that, in the end, people are often not really helped or 'redeemed'. In *Ruddigore* we observe that prophecies can easily become self-fulfilling and dangerous – hence the *grave e maestoso* style of the ghosts' music and the often driven and nervous *allegro con brio* excitement of the human protagonists. Can Ko-Ko and Katisha really live happily after the end of *The Mikado*? (Trills in the violins and woodwind and a dynamic range from *piano* to *fortissimo* can be interpreted as emotional instability and doubt.) What about Sergeant Meryll and Dame Carruthers after the curtain falls in *The Yeomen of the Guard*? (In contrast to the duet for Hannah and Roderic in *Ruddigore*, there is hardly a trace of true affection in the Allegro vivace e con brio of 'Rapture, rapture', which rattles off like a musical clock or toy and reveals an ambiguity similar to some Mozart finales.) Is the premise true, as presented in *Utopia Limited*, that we cannot live in perfection but have to accommodate ourselves to the 'attendant blessings' of mass societies? (The music seems to indicate a feeling of insecurity with its hammering rhythm in the finale after the preceding turmoil of the chorus 'Upon our sea-girt land'.) In Sullivan's approach, abrupt changes of gear suggest an ambiguity within Gilbert's apparently easily intelligible moments.

Although Sullivan hardly ever reflected upon his art in essays and manifestos, he had a natural ability to detect mannerisms and artificial 'one-big-happy-family' posturing. What did he mean concerning 'seriousness' in his comic operas? Sullivan had encountered sufficient social and artistic rejection – for example the Scott Russell love affair in the 1860s[8] and criticism of his inclination to the stage[9] – in order to grow as a creative personality. His 'If-you-cannot-beat-them-join-them' attitude related him to Elgar – Sullivan worked his way up from even lower social origins – and led to an ambiguous, sometimes disillusioning, outlook in most of his comic operas. Accepting this disillusioning bias is, for example, to perceive that the words in the Major-General's song in *The Pirates of Penzance* are fired by a military man like bullets from a machine gun and that there is more in this scene than just a jolly 'Anything-you-can-sing-I-can-sing-faster'. One may dismiss these features as standard operatic devices, but in works by composers who surpass many of their contemporaries there are more things between the notes and staves than are dreamt of in our philosophy. An epoch-making, influential book like Ernst Lert's *Mozart auf dem Theater*[10] has yet to be written about Sullivan.

What are the conclusions? If stage productions are based on musical and dramatic analysis instead of anecdotes and gossip[11] concerning stage tradition, directors, producers and performers might see things from another perspective and come closer to the core of the works. Jonathan Miller's idea that 'the more you get the Japanese trimmings right, the more you get the opera wrong'[12] had already been noted decades earlier. As early as 1926, designs by Charles Ricketts for a new D'Oyly Carte production of *The Mikado* were regarded as questionable. 'If *The Mikado* makes a mockery of Japan, how does it help matters to render the costumes more realistic?' wrote the reviewer in *Punch*: 'I doubt if there is a single joke in the whole play that fits the Japanese'.[13] Both approaches looked to the future, but generally the production history of Sullivan's operas developed like the well-known jumping procession in the Luxembourgian town of Echternach – three steps forward and two steps back! The operas are not 'frozen' in the Victorian age, but there are elements that are still relevant to modern times – for example, the Mikado's order to carry out executions resembles 'operation Phoenix' of the Vietnam War in the 1960s during which the village elders were obliged to fulfil monthly rates of killing.[14]

Even the seemingly harmless March of the Peers in *Iolanthe* has more to offer. Presenting it as an oratorio-like parade misses the point of the subtle crescendo in the score where the music becomes increasingly intensified to a point where it is too aggressive for the situation. This menacing crescendo should be mirrored in the staging because Sullivan's treatment is much more than a cheerful ceremonial march tune.[15] For him this march seems to be the musical equivalent of a famous cartoon by James Gillray, 'The March to the Bank'.[16] Gillray's etching of 1787 is a vicious attack on an institution: it shows the march of the guards who protected the Bank of England, but instead of protecting they arrive with sabres rattling and trample down the people. After publication, the troops were forbidden to march in this provocative way. Similarly, the March of the Peers in *Iolanthe* is not a carnival parade but (from the fairies' point of view) a procession of unwelcome intruders. Consequently, the musical presentation should have an aggressive bite and find an analogous staging.

As a producer Gilbert was the major-general who gave orders to his army of performers on stage and perpetuated his strategy in prompt-books – he rehearsed and staged the librettos regardless of Sullivan's music, which he considered as merely the icing on his own cake. However, the mechanised magic of the first productions cannot be revived by means of prompt-books,

7 James Gillray: *The March on the Bank* 1787.

which would only lead to the 'puppet-shows' that Sullivan had become fed
up with. For today's productions, stagings have technical facilities at their
disposal that Gilbert could never have dreamt of, with film projections,
lighting, etc., so modern stage capabilities should be used carefully – in
accordance with Sullivan's scores – to follow in the footsteps of Craig and
others.

Comic operas instead of 'satirical operettas'

The second myth was created when the works became regarded as 'operettas'
that are full of satire. The condescending attitude of the academic musical
establishment not only had a detrimental effect on the acknowledgement
of the works in the English-speaking world (outside the 'various circles
of "G & S"-addicts')[17] but also on a wider perception of them in the
world of opera.[18] Some observers realised early on what was happening.
In 1928, the composer Thomas Dunhill summarised the developments in
his book *Sullivan's Comic Operas*: 'Macfarren . . . dubbed his colleague "The
English Offenbach" . . . Unfortunately the remark was given permanence by

its inclusion in Macfarren's article on Music in the *Encyclopaedia Britannica*. It was never intended as a compliment, nor was it taken as such.'[19] Alexander Mackenzie called it an inappropriate comparison, as the methods of the two composers as well as the quality of the librettos for their operas had been totally different.[20] Assessments like that of E. J. Dent in 1925 have been forgotten:

> Sullivan was called the English Auber by people who wanted to flatter him, and the English Offenbach by people who wanted to snub him. Neither was a very happy nickname. He might more justly have been called the English Lortzing, since he undoubtedly learnt more than a little from the composer of *Czar und Zimmermann* whose comic operas he heard during his student days at Leipzig. But Sullivan owed very little to anyone. His genius was thoroughly his own.[21]

Sullivan and Gilbert never used the term 'operettas' – all of their stage works have individual descriptions. Calling these comic operas 'operettas' implies a degradation which much too often results in routine and second-rate musical standards.[22] Owing to unreflective negligence even Mozart's *Le nozze di Figaro* was announced as 'operetta' on theatre playbills in the late eighteenth century. Today this would be unthinkable, since it has been agreed to stick to the original description as *comedia per musica* (in the first edition) or *opera buffa* (in Mozart's own list of works). This is not merely a semantic detail, but of primary importance for the approach and casting: do we want a soubrette or lyrical voice for Susanna; a singing actor or a proper baritone for Figaro?

Ignoring or even denying musical qualities shifts the focus and upgrades other aspects which lead to the misconception that all the works by Sullivan and Gilbert contain nothing but satire that seemingly unmasked Victorian life and society. Critics, especially on the European continent, demanded from productions that the 'satire' be sharper, the staging more absurd, etc. In fact, Gilbert was not a satirist in the true sense but was mainly influenced by burlesque. The operas were never banned. Queen Victoria herself invited the cast of *The Gondoliers* to Windsor and *The Mikado* to Balmoral. She enjoyed the shows, and Prime Minister Gladstone wrote to congratulate Sullivan on the good taste of *Iolanthe* – a supposedly political satire! Only in 1907 were productions – even amateur productions – of *The Mikado* tactfully withdrawn due to a state visit by the Japanese Prince Fushimi to Britain. Gilbert never questioned the values of society, which is one of the secrets of his popularity. As a writer he never really threatened middle-class convictions because his basic beliefs upheld bourgeois values. (*Princess Ida* in these days of women's liberation seems to be hopelessly old-fashioned, even if Sullivan wrote some of his best music for it.)

8 A contemporary take on *Ruddygore* – The Prime Minister, Mr Gladstone, says to George Grossmith, who played Robin: "A crime a day, George! Why, I can play that part as well as you." *What should Robin in today's productions look like? Moonshine*, 12 February 1887.

At best the librettos brought political cartoons and caricatures on stage – so they can be as amusing, savage or even trenchant as they were and still are. A problem with all nineteenth-century librettos is that topical allusions are soon forgotten, like a newspaper the day after it is published. Fortunately there are far richer and more varied qualities in the works. They may not be a vicious attack on Victorian life or a means of changing the world, but as operas they focus on emotional states. In operetta, emotion is always make-believe or even fake. In comic opera, the characters are granted moments of honesty and truth.[23] Although Sullivan was a loyal subject to Her Majesty the Queen, he was not overly reverent – Bernard Shaw commented that he was responsible for ten or a dozen godless mockeries of everything sacred to Goss and Bennett[24] – but brought great flexibility and variety to his operas. As soon as we accept that Gilbert's concept remained static, whereas Sullivan accepted and rejected ideas according to the situation, new perspectives on production will emerge. The music reflects the situations of those who live in a commercialised society, a world-power which influences a major part of the planet. The consequences of the Industrial Revolution were disorientation and wide social gaps (similarities to our own time are obvious). This is why audiences are still comfortable with the emotional problems of the characters and why they can accept the hilarious absurdity and sensitive emotion. In his operas Sullivan takes these emotions seriously.

Human comedy and range of expression

A third myth is established when commentators take Sullivan for granted while talking about Gilbert and Sullivan. The composer himself was proud of the achievements in his stage works: the interaction between concert hall and stage provided a positive stimulus to his creative imagination. In his comic operas, above all, Sullivan wanted to distinguish a national opera, sung in English, from the tradition of ballad opera (which was not capable of development) and cheap music hall entertainment, vaudeville, extravaganza and the influence of Italian opera on the repertoire. While Gilbert was concerned with refining burlesque, Carte's and Sullivan's concept was larger when they began to establish a national (comic) opera for the purpose of competing with French stage works. In order to overcome a strong foreign competitor one cannot beat a rival at his own game easily – consequently they had to fall back on other sources. Whereas at the beginning of Sullivan's career, French opéra comique (for *The Contrabandista*) or Offenbach's one-act plays (for *Cox and Box*) and Greek travesties (for *Thespis*) may have been models, Sullivan later relied on other sources of inspiration. 'If *The Sorcerer* is a great success it is another nail in the coffin of *Opéra Bouffe* from the French', he wrote.[25] As a 'hammer' for his 'nails' he gained inspiration from two major sources: Rossini and the German tradition of the Singspiel.

After their first encounter in December 1862, Sullivan met Gioacchino Rossini whenever he went to Paris. As Rossini's output encompasses almost as many dramatic as comic works, he inspired Sullivan's compositions for music theatre in the widest sense. From April to July 1863 Sullivan learned more about the stage when he worked at Covent Garden, which had, among other pieces, Rossini's *Guillaume Tell* in the repertoire. Comic opera *and* dramatic works *plus* opera on a grand scale based on national topics – even at a time when his reputation was limited[26] – Rossini's output remained the model for Sullivan's career and music, as evidenced in several rhythmic patterns and constructions of long finales.

In the context of his ambition to work on convincing human plots and characters, Sullivan's admiration for Wagner's *Die Meistersinger von Nürnberg* is revealing. 'You see, I am taking a lesson', Sullivan said to the critic Herman Klein, who met him in Covent Garden. 'Well, why not? This is not only Wagner's masterpiece, but the greatest comic opera ever written.'[27] Little wonder that the overture to Sullivan's own favourite work, *The Yeomen of the Guard*, is modelled on the *Meistersinger* prelude, which he had conducted.[28]

When Wagner's opera was premièred in 1868 (five months before Rossini's death), it represented the peak of a development which culminated in the consolidation of a national opera in Germany. One of its forerunners had been Lortzing's opera *Hans Sachs* (first performed in Leipzig in 1840), which Wagner knew. Another important contribution to German opera was made by Peter Cornelius, a devotee of Wagner. Sullivan was acquainted with his work because while in Leipzig, Liszt had invited him to the Weimar première of a modern, through-composed German comic opera: *Der Barbier von Bagdad* by Cornelius (1858; later, in the early 1890s, Sullivan encouraged the English première of Cornelius's work by students of the Royal College of Music at the Savoy Theatre). In his first opera with Gilbert under the auspices of Carte, Sullivan tried his hand at a through-composed comic opera, too, for which *Trial by Jury* offered a good opportunity. As Gilbert was not capable of providing, or willing to develop, librettos for through-composed works (the adaption of H. H. Milman's *Martyr of Antioch* being an exception), Sullivan's later comic operas came closer to the achievements of Mozart and Lortzing (although he was capable of mastering bigger structures, as evidenced by *The Martyr of Antioch*, *The Golden Legend* and *Ivanhoe*). The developments in Germany were of special importance because France and Italy, with their comparatively unified evolution of music theatre, had been the leading operatic nations for hundreds of years, whereas the situation of English opera bore a resemblance to that in Germany in the early nineteenth century. When Sullivan went to Germany for the first time, he experienced an operatic culture that was yearning to break free from other influences. Mozart set a model with his two large-scale operas in the native language. E. T. A. Hoffmann continued the tradition by composing operas and writing essays on music aesthetics.[29] In the 1820s, Heinrich Marschner championed a concept of a series of comic operas for the general music lover, but unlike Sullivan he could only toy with this idea because he lacked financial backing such as the Englishman had through Carte's management. Nevertheless, with Weber (a friend of Sullivan's teacher George Smart), Spohr, Marschner, Nicolai, Lortzing, Flotow, Cornelius and Wagner, the Germans had already achieved what the English only half-heartedly attempted: a national comic and romantic opera.

In Leipzig during the 1850s and 1860s it was almost impossible not to learn about Albert Lortzing, whose most important operas were premièred there. A friend recalled

> sitting with him [Sullivan] at a concert once where somebody had sung *Einst spielt' ich mit Zepter und Krone* from Lortzing's *Zar und Zimmermann*. He assured me that although not particularly well rendered, that ditty had

almost moved him to tears with its sweet pathos, adding 'How wonderful is the power of music that with a few simple notes rightly put together, it can stir our tenderest heart strings and melt a time worn old buffer like me.'[30]

The German Singspiel, or light opera (mainly with a music/dialogue structure similar to French opéra comique, *à la* Auber),[31] was by no means unknown on stages in Britain and the USA.[32] Sullivan realised that his commitment on a broad scale – responsibility for the Leeds Festival for eighteen years, writing orchestral works and dramatic cantatas (inspired by Liszt and Berlioz) and composing operas from one-act pieces to those on a grand scale – was vital to create the basis of a high-quality English music repertoire. (See Appendix 4, Sullivan's archetypes of English opera.) As his lecture 'About Music' (1888) reveals, Sullivan committed himself to the improvement of musical taste, fighting against ignorance among politicians and audiences. 'We must be educated to appreciate, and appreciation must come before production', he said. 'Give us intelligent and educated listeners, and we shall produce composers and performers of corresponding worth.'[33]

How could these achievements – comparable to those of Smetana for the Czechs – have been neglected? It was due to cultural politics and the myopic management of the D'Oyly Carte Opera Company that Sullivan's operatic output – which provided England with the 'foundation stones' for a wide range of operatic styles – was disparaged. Both contributed to the exclusion of these important works from the repertoire of the newly founded national English opera ensembles of the early twentieth century and their followers. An old-fashioned performing style and an omnipresent amateur movement – a special phenomenon which is relevant for musical education but should not preclude a professional approach – have led people to the erroneous conclusion that Sullivan is simple, easy-going and harmless. As his sources of inspiration reveal, Sullivan's music encompassed a wide spectrum of expressiveness which made his comic operas more advanced than those of any of his contemporaries.

The decisive factor of his collaboration with Gilbert was the tension between author and composer. Sullivan's music often reveals a subversive structure. When Gilbert has light entertainment in mind, he gets a serious approach; when he wants to make fun of people, Sullivan treats them with empathy and respect. This tension is present from the beginning, for example Alexis's first aria in *The Sorcerer* or the duet for Frederic and Ruth, 'You told me you were fair as gold', in *The Pirates of Penzance*. Sullivan does not always mock the melodramatic devices of Italian opera – he often uses them in order to express emotion. There is a huge difference between real feelings and parody. A comic situation arises close to the end of *Trial by Jury* where all the participants in court get stuck in a chaotic situation that cannot be solved – a nice dilemma for everybody. The music of the ensuing ensemble number overtly refers to a scene in Bellini's *La sonnambula* in which villagers ask themselves whether the heroine is faithful or not. Here Sullivan's pathetic, serious approach functions as counterpoint to the legal complications – and with this allusion he perhaps subtly questions the faithfulness of the plaintiff. His music can be described as parody only in situations where the 'high style' (of so-called 'serious' music) is inadequate for the situation. Another example of dramatic operatic expression at an inappropriate moment could be the 'farmyard effects', as Sullivan called them,[34] of the coloratura in Mabel's 'Poor wandering one' in *The Pirates of Penzance*.

The dramatic style has to be taken seriously where Sullivan trusts the emotions, for example when lovers who belong to different social classes express their feelings, as in the duet for Ralph and Josephine, 'Refrain audacious tar', in *HMS Pinafore*. Here Sullivan uses the dramatic style of Italian opera because it matches the emotional circumstances. There is no reason for parody as this would make fun of the characters who discuss serious problems of their relationship. These aspects connect Sullivan to Mozart and Lortzing. As in Rossini's operas, rhythm, melody and cumulative layouts of solos, ensemble numbers and especially Act I finales (compared to Offenbach's static 'departure finales' in *Orphée aux enfers* or *La belle Hélène*) are of vital importance for Sullivan. Sometimes he even goes further than Rossini; where the Italian composer breaks up words or sentences regardless of their context, Sullivan always takes into consideration the character and the dramatic situation. When he flavours the rhythm of 'Were I thy bride' in *Yeomen of the Guard* with subtle instrumentation, he creates a seduction scene with restless, sultry, even sexy music. (Oh yes, the Victorians were less prudish than they are supposed to be . . .) On the surface the works may appear attractive and charming – but there are elements that do not quite match, and they reveal an ambiguity which makes it vital to rethink Sullivan's approach.

For Sullivan, the individual sound-world of each work is decisive. This is reminiscent of what Verdi called 'la tinta musicale' – the individual musical colour which he wanted to give to a piece. Sullivan's *tinta musicale* encompasses an aerial fairy-like tone in *Iolanthe*; more dramatic, darker colours in *Ruddigore*; a lyrical, rural eighteenth-century atmosphere in *The Sorcerer*; swift Mediterranean lightness in *The Gondoliers*; the nautical air of *HMS Pinafore*; the ethereal tone of the aesthetes in *Patience*; and the respectful sound depiction of the Tower in *Yeomen of the Guard* (whereas Sullivan's treatment of Torquilstone in *Ivanhoe* is altogether bleaker). As in Verdi's works such as *Rigoletto*, *Simon Boccanegra* or *Don Carlos*, there can be complementary or contrasting colours to the *Grundton* ('priming paint') – an idea already championed by Weber. The contrapuntal complexity of *Princess Ida* is challenged by the rough-and-ready sounds of disagreeable men like King Gama and the hulking brothers; the somewhat self-absorbed exotic tunes of *The Mikado* are flavoured with the full range of European opera.

In an interview Sullivan admitted that writing comic opera was a much more demanding task than composing orchestral or choral works.[35] In his dramatic works (*The Martyr of Antioch*, *The Golden Legend*, *Ivanhoe*, etc.) he adopts a more homogeneous style. In comic operas he makes use of the method Mozart adopted for *Die Zauberflöte*: while the mesmerising chords of the overture set the 'high' tone, the palette ranges from *up* one minute to *down* the next, from jolly songs to two attempts at committing suicide. There is a different 'cloth' for each piece of music – in March 1889 Sullivan himself even used the term that his characters are 'clothed with music'.[36] Sullivan's style may be described as 'classical pluralism': 'classical' in the transparent handling of the orchestra (even with large forces),[37] 'pluralistic' in the way he adopts any style that he thinks appropriate for the characterisation of atmosphere, scene or person. Dance elements are not as important as in French or Austrian comic works. Certainly there was a 'formula' behind the making of the Savoy operas, with features such as a patter song in most of the pieces, the tenor hero, the comic role for the baritone, an unmarried elderly lady, etc. (the entertainer Anna Russell made fun of this 'formula' when creating her musical sketch *How to Write Your Own Gilbert and Sullivan Opera*).[38]

All works were written for a fixed ensemble, the Savoy Company, which limited artistic licence to a certain extent. Nevertheless within this framework Sullivan was able to develop and integrate a wide variety of stylistic elements: even the inevitable patter songs are far from monotonous. In fact, they are extremely individual and range from the snobbish tone of Sir Joseph Porter in *HMS Pinafore* to the dream-like 'nightmare song' in *Iolanthe* which staggers from one alarming situation to another. The importance Sullivan attached to orchestration is evident from a letter to an American friend in 1879: 'Orchestral colouring plays so large a part in my works that to deprive them of this is to take away half the attractions'.[39] Adaptations from Sullivan's opera scores were not only a problem in the USA. In January 1887 Sullivan sought 'to take all necessary steps to stop the sale of these piratical copies in any part of Germany, and if necessary to take legal proceedings'.[40] According to his diary,[41] the composer hated disrespectful treatment of his works ('cuts, additions, changes etc. – I was furious') but he was delighted by a serious musical approach ('very good on the whole. – The principals are all opera artists.'). Nevertheless, some arrangements and perversions of Sullivan's orchestration that are performed today come close to the worst abuses of the past. It is because of Sullivan's artistic ambitions that the style of his music is among the most refined in all comic opera of the late nineteenth century.

Gilbertandsullivan the Obscure: separating the twins

For the 150th anniversary of Arthur Sullivan's birth, in 1992 the Royal Mail issued a set of stamps not with a portrait of the composer but with motifs from five Gilbert and Sullivan operas. Although this gesture should be appreciated, it is ridiculous that an artist with major individual achievements is presented in the context of only part of his output. One of the die-hard myths is that the works are described as 'made by G & S' because the names cannot be separated. The odd consequence was that two important artists merged into a super-human-box-office-careerist as *Gilbertandsullivan*, so that today many people find it difficult to distinguish between them. It was, however, common in Victorian theatrical practice to link the names of author and composer on the playbill (for example as with Gilbert and Clay or Hood and Sullivan, a practice that survived in some, but not all, twentieth-century musicals). In the strange case of Gilbert and Sullivan it also became a marketing strategy. It remained part of the policy of the D'Oyly Carte Company to sell their products with this logo because they wanted to make money from amateur societies and touring companies all over the world. So 'G & S' developed into a trademark for fans and potential customers.

In order to justify Gilbertandsullivan as Siamese twins it is often said that the text suggests the music and vice versa. This is tenuous, if not flawed, because the lines do not suggest the music easily. For the aria 'Were I thy bride' alone (in *Yeomen of the Guard*) Sullivan had tried eight different versions before he arrived at the definitive one.[42] Today people already know the music to the text and sometimes even lines of long-known Mozart-, Verdi- or Puccini-translations bring the music to mind. That the music suggests the lines is a simply a phenomenon of familiarity which is also true for other composers – even Mozart's *Die Zauberflöte* in which the libretto is regarded as inferior.

The twin-like 'G & S' combination emphasises the industry of comic opera production. It was a huge commercial success: by 1880 Sullivan was earning roughly £10,000 a year (about £7,000 from comic opera). This was an important factor in Sullivan's decision to turn his attention to stage works. His earnings from comic opera between 1879 and 1890 amounted to £90,000. Gilbert was similarly well off – by today's standard they would both have been millionaires.[43]

That the letters 'G & S' worked like a company logo led to unfortunate consequences decades later. From the beginning of the twentieth century, linking the two names helped the musical establishment to deprive Sullivan of all individuality and exclude him from England's music history as one of the leading and most inspiring musicians.[44] Gilbert has suffered, too, because his extensive output has rarely been a topic for a literary study. At least Sullivan's wider achievements are increasingly acknowledged today. As it is not common in opera to label *Falstaff* 'by Boito *and* Verdi' or *Don Giovanni* 'by da Ponte *and* Mozart', Sullivan and Gilbert, too, should be acknowledged in their own right – Gilbert in the field of literature and the relatively new subject of libretto research[45] and Sullivan in musicology.

Despite the importance of the librettist's contributions, good operas survive because of the music. Some decades ago a leading English magazine wrote: 'It is Sullivan's music rather than Gilbert's plots and words that have maintained the popularity of these works for so many years'.[46] Sullivan tried to impart human credibility not only to the later works – *The Yeomen of the Guard* may be an exception for Gilbert, not for Sullivan – but added it whenever he could. One of the main differences between Sullivan and Gilbert is that Gilbert shows a hostile attitude towards the world, while Sullivan is full of empathy. Gilbert was rarely able to put any deep-felt emotion and characterisation into the roles of the plays and operas. In the poem *My Dream* of 1870 he described what he was especially good at – 'to dwell in Topsy-Turvydom – Where vice is virtue – virtue, vice: Where nice is nasty – nasty, nice.'[47]

Although, for a short while, Sullivan and Gilbert were members of the same Masonic Lodge Sullivan's outlook on life was different. Influenced by the humanity of Freemasonry and his friendship with Dickens and Trollope, Sullivan translated the anfractuosities of Gilbert's literary world – bleak, sparkling or grotesque – to the musical stage.[48] He sees the good side even in evil characters and his music transcends mechanical topsy-turvydom. Like Dickens and Trollope, Sullivan treats characters with sympathy and, by doing so, he becomes the moving spirit behind the artistic aspiration of the operas. Sullivan's *comédie humaine* is based on nineteenth-century optimism, his attitude closer to that of Dickens and Trollope than to Hardy's pessimism or Gilbert's misanthropy.

If his writings are to be believed, Gilbert never trusted love; Sullivan, on the other hand, did. He did not trust institutional arrangements (Fanny Ronalds's married status was valuable because she could never ask him to marry her) so the music in *Trial by Jury* reveals sympathy with free love and the defendant, whose entrance recitative is not a corruption of Italian opera but an expression of fear. The plaintiff intends to decoy him with the help of a code of law – but observe the subtle change from her demure entrance music to the lustful 'I love him' where the mask falls. In the Jurymen's chorus Sullivan does not mock Handel but characterises the 'honourable' gentlemen with an old-fashioned style of music that highlights their antiquated attitudes (just as Alfredo's father in Verdi's *La traviata* sings in a style reminiscent of his youth). When Gilbert repeatedly makes fun of middle-aged spinsters, Sullivan counterbalances with touching moments, as in *Patience* with Lady Jane's aria or in *The Mikado* with Katisha's second-act aria. This aria – after the curtailing of the second verse before the première – was sometimes cut in performance,[49] which reveals the attitude towards Sullivan's contribution. The pieces were regarded as Gilbert's creations, to be dealt with on his terms, ignoring the fact that the composer gives more depth to them than intended by the librettist. Sullivan's working methods reveal how carefully he examined the emotional situations of the librettos. The first version of the tenor aria 'Is life a boon' in *The Yeomen of the Guard* is rather conventional; not until Sullivan has arrived at the definitive version does he achieve a convincing reflection of a person who is about to be executed.[50]

Those English writers who demanded, almost half a century ago, that 'Sullivan's name – not Gilbert's – must lead the partnership'[51] remained lonely voices crying in the wilderness. The question may be asked: did Sullivan and Gilbert really 'sing as one individual'? Even if some reviews of the period suggest that music and text resulted from the same brain – invariably assumed to be that of Gilbert – it is revealing how Sullivan set the duet 'Replying we sing as one individual' from *The Gondoliers*. Sullivan and Gilbert are not twins, and as a result the subdued setting sounds as though Sullivan is deliberately mocking the exhausted cooperation which – at that time – he supposed to be the last. For both it should rather be: 'we sing as *two* individuals'.

Separating the 'Siamese twins' would be an operation that led not to the death of one of them but to the release of both from the 'prison' of the label. The company called 'Gilbert and Sullivan' is limited because it is mainly something for economics but hardly anything for studies of literature or musicology. If we unscrew the firm's nameplate and replace it, for example, with 'Sullivan: *Patience*, libretto by W. S. Gilbert', it would be much easier to free worn-out conventionalities from their shackles. As 'G & S' they were business partners – as Sullivan and Gilbert they were masters in their own spheres who can be treated independently of each other.

He is an Englishman – and a part of European music history

The fifth myth is the popular delusion that Sullivan's comic operas are not suited to the stage beyond the English-speaking world. To assume that wider international acknowledgement of the works is irrelevant, because they are already performed throughout the English-speaking world, reveals an ignorance of the background: as the first step towards a national (comic) opera they were composed as a contribution to the operatic heritage. It is the music that provides the cosmopolitan substance and for which these operas deserve a place in the international repertoire. To assume that a continental audience would not accept 'English topics' is ridiculous. Even countries 'separated by a common language' – as George Bernard Shaw characterises England and the USA – enjoy these operas, though one might ask why Americans fancy stories about peers, fairies or the British Navy. Not only is British comedy popular abroad on screen, today's repertoire of comic operas in German-speaking countries, for example, is entirely multi-cultural, with works by Rossini, Smetana, etc. In addition, some of the major German Spielopern in the repertoire are set in England – Nicolai's *Lustige Weiber von Windsor* and Flotow's *Martha*.

In the second half of the nineteenth century there are no comic operas – apart from Verdi's *Falstaff* – that can compete with Sullivan's stage works (mainly – but not entirely – those with librettos by Gilbert). The English-speaking world should be proud of this and encourage wider dissemination, rather than insisting that they belong on English soil and cannot be translated. Performances of comic operas (with dialogue) in countries other than that in which they originated, often demand translations; this would exclude 'Gilbert' from 'G and S'. That the works are not translatable seems to have become an immutable fact. However, if the world did not stop turning as a result of the many translations of Shakespeare, it will also not do so because Gilbert's words are translated. As early as 1953 Audrey Williamson stated in her influential *Gilbert and Sullivan Opera: A New Assessment*:

> If *The Mikado* has transplanted successfully there is no real reason why
> others of his operas should not do so, for it is by no means true that in all of
> them the satire is too specifically English to be understood. *The Mikado* may
> have the widest humorous appeal . . . a Navy is still a Navy anywhere, and
> the *Pirates of Penzance* have their counterparts . . . The setting and tale of
> *The Yeomen of the Guard* might well seem more picturesque to a foreign
> audience than a British one: the opera was in fact performed in Germany,
> under the title *Der Königsgardist*, at Kroll's Theatre, Berlin, in 1890, and
> the reason for its early withdrawal had nothing to do with its appeal and
> quality . . . The difficulties of translation, presented by Gilbert's intricate
> rhymes and metres, are admittedly enormous; but they have been overcome
> in the case of *The Mikado* in many countries, at least to the satisfaction of
> the local inhabitants. The music has a universal appeal and it is a pity
> Sullivan's talents have had no chance of international recognition.[52]

Experience has proved that being English is not a necessary qualification for a careful reading or an appropriate *mise-en-scène* of Sullivan's stage works.

An entirely comic approach puts up a barrier whereas involving the audience emotionally is imperative. There is a dramatic, comedic and human quality in Sullivan's music that can only be fully explored when Gilbert's advice, 'It is often useful to shake off conventionalities',[53] is realised. Not until we put on stage what is beneath the surface of the music can we come to a complete appreciation of the works. Sullivan's comic operas on Gilbert's librettos form an important part of music history. They are operatic world literature and should be treated as such. Tradition does not mean adoring the ashes, but keeping the fire burning.

PART II

Focus

5 The operas in context: stylistic elements – the Savoy and beyond

RICHARD SILVERMAN

A study of the correlation between the so-called Savoy operas and Sullivan's other major works seems at first glance a non-controversial subject of musicological inquiry. Sullivan was by no means unique in writing works that succeeded on the popular stage and in the concert hall. Elgar and Copland are highly respected composers who wrote popular marches or ballets in addition to symphonies and concertos. Leonard Bernstein is famous – aside from his great conducting career – as the composer of *West Side Story*, but *Age of Anxiety*, *Jeremiah* or *Chichester Psalms* are not proscribed because of his Broadway popularity. George Gershwin wrote popular songs and Broadway musicals. He also wrote concert works and the great American opera. His reputation in both fields is exemplary.

Sullivan's comic operas and serious works were frequently performed during his lifetime. After his death in 1900, the comic operas retained enormous popularity, while the concert works gradually sank into oblivion. Very early acoustic recordings were made of *The Yeomen of the Guard* and *HMS Pinafore* in addition to extensive excerpts from *The Golden Legend* and *Ivanhoe*. World War I precipitated the collapse of the Victorian–Edwardian world order – the society of which he was a distinguished member – thus terminating Sullivan's reputation as a great composer. Only in those works that stood aside from – indeed parodied – that now discredited sociopolitical system did Sullivan's music live on as a vital force.

For much of the twentieth century, when not linked with that of Gilbert, Sullivan's name was associated with hymns or quasi-religious songs like 'Onward Christian Soldiers' and 'The Lost Chord': works that were embarrassingly out of fashion in a century dominated by two world wars, totalitarianism, mass murder and thermonuclear bombs. Not only did Sullivan's major choral works disappear from the concert hall, they were ignored by the recording industry during the eras of the 78 and the LP. Generations of classical music listeners were given no opportunity to judge the quality of music widely enjoyed by their nineteenth-century forebears. In the latter decades of the twentieth century there was a gradual exploration of Sullivan's orchestral music. Eventually, the Irish Symphony and all of the extant concert overtures were recorded.

Within the first 100 years of the composer's death, the plight of his major choral works remained dire. Any study comparing them with the comic operas would have been, of necessity, a very limited enterprise. Only a small number of musicologists with access to long out-of-print editions or to the autograph scores themselves were in a position to discuss – for example – the influence of *The Golden Legend* upon *Ruddigore*, or the latter's anticipations of the *Macbeth* music. In the first decade of the twenty-first century, the animus towards Sullivan has finally abated sufficiently to allow several of his major choral works to appear in professional recordings. While several significant gaps still remain, the interested reader will now have access to enough of Sullivan's *serious* music to retain an aural reference to the music being discussed below.

Instrumentation

In comparing the comic operas and the concert works, one must first acknowledge that they were written for different audiences and for performing forces of different size and ability. The pit orchestra available to Sullivan was quite small. In *Cox and Box*, the woodwind section contained only one flute (alternating piccolo), oboe and bassoon, plus two clarinets. The brass contained pairs of horns, cornets and trombones. One percussionist and a small string section completed the orchestra. The orchestra for *Trial by Jury* is of the same size. In *HMS Pinafore*, we find a second flute added. Only near the end of the collaboration with Gilbert – *Yeomen of the Guard*, *Gondoliers*, *Utopia Limited* and *Grand Duke* – was Sullivan able to increase the orchestra's power with the addition of a second bassoon and a third (bass) trombone.

Consistent with the small pit orchestra, the voices available for Savoy comic opera were not expected to reach the last row of Covent Garden. Hanslick noted approvingly in his 1886 review: 'The vocal parts in *The Mikado* are so easily encompassed, and restricted to such a modest range, that big lungs and technical virtuosity are no more prerequisites for their performance than they were for the musical comedies of Adam, [J. A.] Hiller, Monsigny, and Gretry'.[1]

Sullivan's early concert works use an orchestra consistent with his Leipzig Conservatory training: woodwinds in pairs, four horns, three trombones, timpani and strings. However, Sullivan was clearly aware of Berlioz's music as well. The latter scored for a much larger orchestra than his German contemporaries and included exotic instruments such as the cor anglais, the cornet, the ophicleide and the harp. Sullivan made use of the exotic Chinese Pavilion in *On Shore And Sea* and he called for a cor anglais in the

Example 5.1 Contrasting scorings in the *Overture di Ballo*

Example 5.2 From the Overture to *HMS Pinafore*

early ballet *The Enchanted Isle* and, many years later, in *The Golden Legend* and *Ivanhoe.* He never used it at the Savoy, nor did he require a powerful bass instrument like the tuba or its forerunner, the ophicleide, in the comic opera orchestra. The ophicleide is a brass/wooden hybrid that first appeared in Paris in 1817. It was largely out of use by 1860, but Sullivan retained a preference for this French 'original' instrument of Berlioz's youth. In a letter to the Philharmonic Society, he wrote that his new overture – *Marmion* – would require only one additional instrument: an awful ophicleide which he transformed by a play on words into 'awfiklide'.[2] Even more antiquarian is the instrumentation of the *Overture di Ballo* which called, not for the two tubas as the modern edition lists, but for an ophicleide and a serpent![3]

While the Savoy orchestra would be overwhelmed by a tuba or the less powerful ophicleide, there is a similarity in scoring shared by the *Overture di Ballo* and the overture to *HMS Pinafore* (which Sullivan wrote himself). Sullivan appears to have had Berlioz in mind in the gallop of the *Overture di Ballo* where – at 'HH') he alternates contrasting groups:

A: full woodwinds plus horns, trumpets and trombones.
B: flutes, oboes, clarinets and strings (see Ex. 5.1).[4]

Earlier at bar 351:

A: woodwinds plus horns, trumpets, trombones (2) and ophicleide.
B: oboes, clarinets, bassoons plus bass trombone, serpent and strings.

Similar passages can also be found in *Marmion.*

In the *HMS Pinafore* Overture we also find similar instrumental groupings (six bars before Fig. 202 f.; Ex. 5.2):[5]

A: flute, oboe, clarinets, bassoon, full brass and cellos.
B: all of group A plus piccolo, cymbals, bass drum and full strings.

The *Overture di Ballo* marked the end of Sullivan's early period as a composer of orchestral music. The symphony, cello concerto, and all but one of the concert overtures belong to the period ending in 1870. Sullivan considered a return to orchestral music in 1887 when he suggested to the Leeds Committee that he might accept a commission for a symphony for the 1889 festival. In light of the huge success enjoyed by *The Golden Legend* in 1886, Sullivan probably expected a ready acceptance. Instead, the committee was evasive. In fact, Leeds was hoping to acquire a new work from Brahms. Only after the latter declined on the grounds of retirement, was an offer made to Sullivan. By then his interest had waned. No doubt his feelings were hurt, but a glance at some of his diary entries for this period reveals a depressing picture of a man who, only in his mid-forties, was undergoing a serious decline in health. He was suffering from pain, fatigue, haematuria, repeated infections with ulcerations, and oedema so severe that at times he was unable to walk. That he somehow found the strength to compose *Macbeth*, *The Yeomen of the Guard*, *Ivanhoe* and *The Gondoliers* during the next three years is a testament to his determination and courage.

In contrast to the theatre music Sullivan composed in the 1870s, *Macbeth* has an overture, the first major orchestral piece since *Di Ballo*. Coincidentally, Sullivan composed a symphonic overture for *The Yeomen of the Guard* in the same year. Thus, we are afforded a rare opportunity to examine the orchestration of two major scores, one from the Savoy and one from the concert stage, composed at the same point in Sullivan's career.

The *Macbeth* overture published in 1893 – and available in several recordings – differs from its original Lyceum Theatre version by being thirty-seven bars longer and of weightier orchestration. The theatre orchestra that Henry Irving made available was substantial: forty-six instruments including two harps. There were the standard woodwinds in pairs, two horns, the ubiquitous two cornets, three trombones, harps, timpani and strings. (The published 1893 version adds another pair of horns, a tuba, additional percussion, and replaces cornets with trumpets.) The numerically smaller Savoy orchestra for *The Yeomen of the Guard* was composed of woodwinds in pairs (except for the single oboe), the same brass complement as *Macbeth*, timpani, no harp, and strings.

When comparing the overtures, two obvious differences are immediately apparent. In form, *Yeomen* is 'old-fashioned'. It is in the sonata form of the 1860–70 works, while *Macbeth* has a programmatic structure. Secondly, the *Macbeth* overture demands a higher level of technical proficiency from its players, especially flutes, clarinets, violins and violas. The latter were given some prominence in the Irish Symphony, but subsequent scores relegated them to the background. In both overtures there are animated violin passages leading to powerful statements by the brass. The brass was enlarged in the *Yeomen* overture by the addition of a bass trombone. This allowed the composer to write full chords for the trombones. It also gave him the opportunity to reinforce the Savoy's weak bass line by doubling the second tenor trombone with the bass trombone and the new second bassoon. This occurs at the beginning of the work in the rising brass theme and at crucial points where a deep pedal point is sounded. In the *Macbeth* overture, where the orchestra had a more substantial string section, there is less need to double the second and third trombones, but Sullivan still uses this technique when a deep sustained bass note is required. We also find two horns doubling the bass trombone at the octave. This roughly anticipated Rimsky-Korsakov's later advice to double the tuba with two horns at the octave above. In earlier Savoy scores like *The Mikado*, we also find Sullivan achieving variety within the small brass complement by putting the second horn below the two trombones and then in the subsequent passage, reversing the arrangement.

In the *Yeomen* overture, the writing for woodwinds is of the highest order. After the introductory passages for full orchestra, one hears a virtual parade of beautiful woodwind solos for clarinet, bassoon, oboe and flute. In the development section we find further prominent woodwind solos especially for clarinet, alternating with flute and violin passages of soaring melody. In other Savoy operas we encounter equally felicitous examples of Sullivan's wonderful writing for woodwinds. *Princess Ida*, Act II, contains an especially rich vein:

- The trio 'Gently' has solos for clarinet and bassoon.
- The trio 'I am a maiden' has an animated bassoon part that may remind one of the active double bassoon passages in 'A certain man had two sons' in *The Prodigal Son*.
- The ensemble 'The world is but a broken toy' has beautiful solos for clarinet and flute.

Of particular interest too is the virtuoso flute writing in Sir Roderic's ghosts' high-noon aria from *Ruddigore*. The fluttering bats and night birds eventually wend their way from the Savoy Theatre to the Lyceum where they reappear as depictions of the Chorus of Spirits of the Air in *Macbeth*.

Another prototypical Savoy passage occurs in Pooh-Bah's aria 'Young Man Despair'. The phrases in this bass aria are punctuated by fanfare-like flourishes in the cornets. Moving from Titipu to the road to Salerno in *The Golden Legend*, scene 3, we find Lucifer disguised as a friar mocking the Pilgrims. He is also accompanied by brass fanfares, but much weightier in scoring, and far more complex in harmony than their *Mikado* counterparts.

While the employment of the woodwinds in *The Yeomen of the Guard* is of the same high level found in the early concert overtures, their use in *Macbeth*

Example 5.3 String writing in *Macbeth*

is different. In this overture there are two solo passages for oboe and one for clarinet. Otherwise, there is more use of the woodwinds as a section – as in Berlioz – and doubling of the strings. Some established, standard Sullivan devices are still present: the frequent deployment of clarinets in octaves and the doubling of horns by clarinets and bassoons. Rimsky-Korsakov later discouraged the use of the same woodwind instrument in octaves.[6] Sullivan clearly found it an effective technique and pleasing sound since he used it often. The string writing in *Macbeth*, like the woodwinds, is also more block-like. We find a major theme spread out in two octaves for the violins, violas and cellos (Ex. 5.3).[7]

In earlier orchestral pieces this level of doubling was reserved for fast scale-like passages, not for broad melodies. The latter, when doubled, were violins I and II or violins and violas (the Irish Symphony), or violins and cellos (*Marmion*). In *Macbeth* more combinations of instruments play more of the time than in the early orchestral works. This thicker style of string writing is encountered in scores by Saint-Saëns such as *Samson and Delilah* and the Organ Symphony. Sullivan was especially familiar with the latter since it had its première at a Philharmonic concert on 19 May 1886 during his tenure as director. Saint-Saëns conducted his new symphony, but also appeared as soloist in Beethoven's Fourth Piano Concerto. That work and the rest of the programme were conducted by Sullivan.[8] Sullivan's familiarity with Saint-Saëns's music is also evident in *The Rose of Persia*. The dance sections seem clearly influenced by *Samson and Delilah* and the *Algerian Suite*.

Orchestra and voice

In the matter of vocal support by the orchestra, one finds some similarities in Savoy and concert works in the use of the woodwinds. In the comic operas, the woodwinds' role in supporting the voices is more obvious. For example, the tenor aria 'When first my old, old love' in *Trial by Jury* commences with the singer's line. For the second phrase the vocal line is doubled by the flute. This is a common Sullivan practice, whether the instrument be flute, clarinet or oboe. In the concert works, Sullivan was writing for larger more confident voices, so the need for exact doubling support in the orchestra was less requisite. In 'Love not the world' from *The Prodigal Son*, the contralto begins her melody with a simple string accompaniment. For the second phrase, she is doubled by a flute, but for only four bars. For much of the aria, the singer is not doubled, except for two bars in the clarinets, until the flutes and clarinets join her in the final section of the aria. In the tenor aria, 'Come ye children', the singer is doubled by the violins from the onset. At the second phrase, the tenor is joined by an oboe. In another tenor aria, 'Father, give me the portion' the singer is on his own for the opening phrases until eventually being doubled by a clarinet. At the onset of the aria, the violins move in a peripatetic manner sometimes coinciding with the singer's melody, but just as often wandering away. In fact, at one repetition of 'portion of goods' (bar 20) the first violins freely imitate the tenor's melody at the distance of one and two beats, resulting in two blatant dissonances: minor seconds. The singer (Sims Reeves) was expected to stay on pitch without any woodwind support.

In the Savoy works, important harmonic clashes between voice and orchestra are also encountered, but several interesting examples involve multiple voices, underlining the old adage about strength in numbers. In Act III of *Princess Ida*, King Gama's three sons, Arac, Guron and Scynthius – who appear as dim-witted as the three trolls, Burt, Tom and William that Bilbo Baggins encounters in the Hobbit – prepare to fight Hilarion, Cyril and Florian by removing all of their armour to the strains of Arac's aria in the manner of Handel. The ensuing battle is fought against a chorus peppered with seconds.

In the previous act, Gama's sons had clumsily tried to convince Ida to yield in order to save their lives. In the trio 'We may remark' Sullivan illustrates their awkwardness by placing minor seconds in each phrase. The three brothers cannot even sing in tune!

In *Ruddigore*, the final chorus of the ghost scene presents music of a much darker – and to Gilbert's thinking, inappropriate – mood. Having successfully tormented Robin, the ghosts transform from spectres into paint and canvas images by way of an eerie, descending chromatic sequence. It begins with a minor second: G ♯ in the chorus against A ♮ in the orchestra. Moving from Ruddigore Castle to Strasburg Cathedral, another chorus of male voices (monks?) also commences with a minor second in the first bar 'Nocte surgentes' of the magnificent conclusion to the Prologue of *The Golden Legend*. *Ruddigore* was composed only months after *The Golden Legend*. That there are many echoes of Sullivan's masterful cantata in it is hardly surprising. An obvious influence is the chromaticism in Sir Roderic's second-act aria, but there are smaller subtle connections too. In 'Cheerily

carols the lark' Mad Margaret cries out her name in a theme that rises from
Db to Fb and then falls back down to Db, but an octave lower. In scene 4 of
The Golden Legend, Elsie cries 'Alas ! Prince Henry!' Her theme rises a third
from A to C and after a diversion to G♯, back to C, thus encompassing a
phrase that rises and falls by a minor third. In the Act I finale to *Ruddigore*,
Hannah sings 'Winter is the time to sleep'. In the second refrain her contralto
melody descends A–F♯–D. In *The Golden Legend*, scene 2, Ursula's contralto
melody at 'paint the dusky windows red' also descends by thirds: G–E–C.

Harmony

The major choral works and comic operas of the 1870s use the harmonic
language characteristic of Sullivan's Leipzig training. There are diminished-
seventh chords, modulations to far-off keys by means of secondary dominants, some use of modes (as in the *Festival Te Deum*), but the chord
progressions follow expected paths and usually resolve quickly enough to
retain the sense of key. According to Goldman,

> chords that are employed as extensions or interpolations are, in the 18th and
> early 19th centuries, generally resolved, or led to a resolution, within a short
> time span. In all cases, they are directed towards a point that is not distant,
> and to which a relation is seldom hard to perceive. With the development of
> later 19th century style, these chords are often extended in time, or several of
> them may occur in succession, with the result that basic tonal processes are
> temporarily in abeyance.[9]

The young Sullivan's loyalty to the harmonic style of Weber,
Mendelssohn and Schumann is not surprising. His education was conservative and the country to which he returned was very conservative in
its musical ideas. Schumann was little known, and the assertion of Franz
Liszt that any chord could resolve to any other chord was heresy in the
musical circle of Potter, Goss or Sterndale Bennett. Unlike Gade and Bruch,
Sullivan did eventually embrace more 'modern' harmonic devices. In 1880,
he returned to the oratorio idiom with *The Martyr of Antioch*. In this 'sacred
music drama' Sullivan added a harp to the instrumentation and added a
new quality to the tonality: harmonic ambiguity. In the *Martyr* we find chromaticism, the use of the half-diminished-seventh chord and the extended
appoggiatura floating leisurely over a seventh chord. In the music for the
pagans the harmony is no longer sharply focused on traditional progressions, but is able to move more slowly and in an ambiguous fashion. The
music for the Christians is more conventional and foursquare. In contrast
the pagans' unrestrained music seems almost sensual. In succeeding works

Example 5.4 From *Patience*, Act I finale

of the 1880s like the *Imperial Ode* and *The Golden Legend*, Sullivan adopts more of these 'modern' harmonic practices. In the *Imperial Ode* there are progressions like half-diminished sevenths moving to diminished sevenths to ninth chords. There are abrupt modulations to distant keys. In the Prologue to *The Golden Legend* there is no home key at all, but a constantly shifting chromatic flux.

The first Savoy work following *Martyr of Antioch* was *Patience*. In contrast to its predecessors, *Patience* relies less on broad parody of grand opera, but adopts a delicate lyrical style that becomes even more refined in *Iolanthe* and *Princess Ida*. The influence of the *Martyr* is much stronger in those two works than in *Patience*. In the latter, the device of using an important theme in the orchestra against which a new melody is heard in the voices is likewise encountered in the *Martyr*: 'The love-sick damsel' and the Act I finale of *Patience* (Ex. 5.4[10] and Ex. 5.5[11]). In terms of mood, the pagan damsels and the twenty love-sick maidens seem languorously alike. From the vantage point of harmony, *Patience* breaks little new ground with the notable exception of the scene in which Bunthorne is discovered by the love-sick maidens: 'I am a broken hearted troubadour . . .'. The sudden introduction of chromaticism following a beautiful oboe solo is startling and gives this passage a magical character. The spell is then broken by diminished-seventh chords as the finale races to a breathless mock Italian opera conclusion.

In *Iolanthe* and *Princess Ida*, Sullivan's experiences with the expanded harmonic palette of the *Martyr* are far more evident. Following the splendid overture, *Iolanthe*'s opening chorus has an orchestral introduction which uses augmented chords and hints at whole-tone harmony. The fairy queen's summoning of Iolanthe is rich in chromaticism. Even seemingly simple passages contain harmonic surprises. When Phyllis sings 'For riches and rank . . .' the harmony is straightforwardly diatonic in B-flat. When she reaches 'untrue' it shifts to the minor, but then slides chromatically through a whole-tone chord before sliding again as (her) 'heart that's breaking'. Chromaticism is also well represented in the Lord Chancellor's reference to 'Anderson's library'.

Example 5.5 From *The Martyr of Antioch*, 'The love-sick damsel'

In 'O Goddess wise' Princess Ida seems very much akin to Margarita (*Martyr of Antioch*) in her self-righteous ecstasy. In this aria we find one of the many instances in which Sullivan employs the French augmented-sixth chord. He often places it in second inversion and almost always resolves it directly to the dominant, rather than first stopping at the second inversion of the tonic. In the trio 'Gently, gently' French sixths are repeated, but the resolution delayed until the dominant (G) begins sounding like the tonic. Only when Sullivan flattens the note F does the pull back to the tonic (C) become irresistible. The beginning of the Act I finale of *Ruddigore* is likewise ambiguous. Starting in F minor, it seems to move towards C major by the sixth bar with a pre-dominant chord (German sixth). However, the harmonic progression does not resolve convincingly for fourteen bars until an F♮ makes clear that C, and not G, is actually the tonic.

The score of *Princess Ida* is an excellent primer on Sullivan's ability to underline the stage action with harmonic colouration. In the trio 'The world is but a broken toy' an exotic sequence of IV–I progressions subtly emphasises 'unreal its loveliest hue'. In the finale to Act II, 'Defiance' is undermined by the instability of the home key (E-flat) which is shaken within only one bar by a strong pull towards D-flat. As Act III unfolds with Ida's school under siege, the uncertainty of its defenders is illustrated by the restlessness of the harmony. C minor moves to D-flat major to D major to G major. In the C major section 'Please you do not hurt us' secondary dominants shift the harmonic focus to F and then E minor until another augmented sixth – this time the German variety (rare in *Princess Ida*) – returns us to the original home key. In Ida's aria 'I built upon a rock' her 'fire has died away' via a diminished-seventh to half-diminished-seventh progression. A similar sequence in the Act I finale of *The Yeomen of the Guard* at '1,000 marks alive or dead' then moves towards the tonic by means of a secondary dominant sequence, but the arrival at the tonic is far from the customary V–I conclusion. A subdominant with added sixth moves to an ambiguous chord that serves as a reluctant dominant. It can be described as a half-diminished seventh of VII or a ninth chord of V, but lacking the root. This ambiguous 'dominant' to tonic conclusion underscores Elsie's bewildered state of mind as the curtain falls. In Act II, Sullivan surprises us at 'The river must be dragged' by not employing the diminished-seventh chord (so overworked in *Ivanhoe*). Instead the Lieutenant gives his orders via a dominant seventh. *The Yeomen of the Guard* is illustrative of Sullivan's continuing harmonic growth by way of *The Golden Legend* as well as his ability to invoke an earlier era by adding elements of Baroque practice and modality. The 'cock and bull' duet in Act II employs typical Baroque chord progressions – like Grieg in his *Holberg Suite* – while the entrance of Jack Point and Elsie Maynard is set to music in the Lydian mode. The latter, combined with the quintuple rhythm, produces a sound world not unlike that of Bartók's *Mikrokosmos*. In *Ivanhoe*, Tuck, that very warlike friar who is fond of wine and drinking song, is also revealed in his sacred persona by passages of simple hymnal diatonicism mixed with hints of modality.

Counterpoint

This subject falls into two categories: imitation and synthesis. The former refers to the traditional practices of canon and fugue. Post-Mendelssohnian sacred works would be expected to contain sections of imitative counterpoint and Sullivan duly conformed in *The Prodigal Son*, *The Festival Te Deum* and *The Light of the World*. Fortunately he was a skilful contrapuntist. The canons and fugues in these works are dramatic and compelling. *The Martyr of Antioch* has no fugues, but Sullivan returned to the form in the Epilogue of *The Golden Legend*. Complex in harmony and vivid in its scoring, that fugue is Sullivan's finest essay in the form. On the operatic stage, the fugue is treated as a comical device. The Mikado's reference to it as a form of punishment is well known. In a more subtle vein, the Lord Chancellor has a fugal leitmotif, the complexities of imitative counterpoint being appropriate to the intricate workings of the legal mind. In *Ivanhoe*, the scene in Act II in which King Richard, in disguise as the black knight, is the guest of Friar Tuck is the only lighthearted section of the opera. In this scene, king and friar compete in singing ability and physical prowess. As they await a rustic dinner of 'ven'son pie and rosy wine', the orchestra accompanies its preparations with a fugue.

The combining of themes or synthesis is a hallmark device in most Gilbert and Sullivan comic operas. Sullivan was not the first composer to use this device. Berlioz employed it in *The Damnation of Faust*. However, Sullivan combined themes with far more exactitude than Berlioz and made this device a conspicuous characteristic of his style. Often, two sections of chorus were involved, thus the term 'double chorus'. A typical example is 'Welcome gentry' in *Ruddigore*. Sullivan also used this device beyond the Savoy, in serious works of a dramatic nature such as *The Martyr of Antioch* – 'Now glory to the God' – and *Ivanhoe* – 'Fair and lovely is the may'.

Sullivan also synthesised themes with combinations of chorus and individual voices. *The Pirates of Penzance* provides good examples in the police 'When the foeman bars his steel' versus Mabel and Edith's 'Go ye heroes' or the Chattering Chorus with the general's wards singing 'How beautifully blue the sky' against Mabel and Frederic's 'Did ever [maiden wake], [pirate loathed]'. In the 'big, black, block' trio of *The Mikado*, we find three separate male voices combined. Sullivan also employed this type of mixed ensemble in *The Golden Legend*. In the Prologue, there is a three-part juxtaposition of Lucifer, the Powers of the Air (female chorus) and the Bells (male chorus singing in Latin). This example highlights the contrasting moods of the protagonists. Similarly, as Act II of *The Yeomen of the Guard* opens, an ensemble compares the frustration of the Warders in their impotent search for Fairfax and the scorn heaped upon them by Dame Carruthers. *The Yeomen of the Guard* is the only opera by Sullivan and Gilbert that may be accurately labelled a romantic rather than a comic opera. In this it is related to *Haddon Hall*. Both operas have secondary comic elements, but the overall mood is of real people involved in serious matters. *Haddon Hall* and the later *The Beauty Stone* have happy endings, while *Yeomen* ends tragically.

Drama

Much of the comic operas by Sullivan and Gilbert is parody of grand opera. Scenes of real human drama are conspicuous by their rarity, *The Yeomen of the Guard* being the most obvious example. In *The Sorcerer* the brewing of the love potion is a spoof of the casting of the magic bullets in *Der Freischütz*. *The Sorcerer* also contains scenes that are not parody. Constance is a young woman suffering from unrequited love. She is neither mad nor a desperate, overstuffed middle-aged spinster. Her aria 'When he is here' is a lovely heartfelt song that candidly reflects her feelings. The object of her affection is Dr Daly. He is neither pompous like Sir Marmaduke, arrogant like Alexis, nor faintly sinister like J. W. Wells. His loneliness is genuine. His Act I ballad and Act II song are fine examples of the pastoral style Sullivan used so effectively in the opening section of *The Light of the World*. A Victorian audience, well read in Trollope's popular novels, would find nothing incongruous or grotesque in a clergyman seeking domestic tranquillity in a good marriage.

The Sorcerer is also unusual in containing a death scene. Mr Wells's decision to 'yield up his life to Ahrimanes' is a mere trapdoor stunt. His disappearance evokes no more concern than a job transfer. Death seems more of an ominous reality near the conclusion of *Iolanthe*. Until then, the Fairy Queen appears no more sinister than Lady Jane (*Patience*) with a horned helmet. Her words and music assume real menace as she dooms a traitorous subject. Iolanthe's previous plea to the Lord Chancellor and the warning cries of the Fairy Chorus were poignant. Even the smug Lord Chancellor was deeply affected by the sudden reappearance of his long 'dead' wife. But *Iolanthe* is no tragedy. Gilbert resolves all difficulties in the ensuing dialogue; and the opera ends happily.

Sullivan's major attempt at music drama was *Ivanhoe*, which premièred little more than two years after *The Yeomen of the Guard*. Both works are set in Britain's historical past; and each contains a famous poignant soprano aria. In addition, a major character dies in each opera: one from a heart attack, and the other from a broken heart. While the final scene of *Yeomen* progresses naturally and inexorably to Point's tragic end, the demise of the Templar is rushed. A member of the audience whose attention briefly wandered could easily miss this crucial event. The Templar's rage at Ivanhoe's arrival is not sufficiently exploited musically to make his sudden cardiac arrest dramatically convincing. If Elsie had simply looked up at Fairfax and recognised Meryll before singing 'Leonard my loved one' the situation would be analogous.

Ivanhoe exerted little overt influence upon the two remaining collaborations by Sullivan and Gilbert. Grundy's *Haddon Hall* libretto is a mixture of drama and comedy, so it is not surprising to find Sullivan drawing upon his grand opera experience in setting it. For example, Sir George Vernon's 'In days of old' is mined from the same vein of hearty, nostalgic, Olde England style as Cedric's rousing drinking song in *Ivanhoe* Act I. The next to last completed opera by Sullivan, the little known, but musically impressive medieval romance, *The Beauty Stone*, is rich in genuine drama. The beneficial influence of *Ivanhoe* is especially strong in Act II, scene 1 with its echoes of 'Happy with winged feet', King Richard's 'I ask not wealth', and the *Les Huguenots* inspired Heralds' music from the Act I tournament scene.

The two final operas with librettos by Hood are largely a return to Gilbert's topsy-turvy style. *The Rose of Persia* is an Iranian variation of *The Mikado*. In the unfinished (by Sullivan) *Emerald Isle*, the reluctance of the troops to assault the caves of Carrig-Cleena is strikingly similar to the cowardice of the police in *The Pirates of Penzance* Act II, 'Go ye heroes go to glory'. However, the Act I finale of *The Emerald Isle* undergoes a radical transformation when it concludes with a reprise of the hauntingly beautiful 'Come away sighs the Fairy's voice'. Sullivan's ethereal final thoughts remind one of the music of a very young composer; the magical trio of the third movement of the Irish Symphony.

Great expectations

An audience leaving *The Mikado* was expected to have a smile on its face and a cache of infectious tunes in its memory. Listeners to *The Golden Legend* would have departed feeling uplifted, having experienced a variety of sensations from exhilaration, to sadness, to catharsis. Sullivan's range was sufficiently broad to encompass a diversity of situations and emotions. In consequence, he used many of the same devices in both his comic and serious works, but they were applied with different emphasis and complexity consistent with the requirements of the composition. Sullivan's music for the Savoy, his concert works and his choral compositions are different facets of the same jewel. In *The Tempest* his formidable talent undermined the complacency of a nation that honoured Wren, Turner and Dickens, but kept music at arm's length as an exotic plant cultivated by foreigners. He cleared the path that was subsequently trod by Elgar, Delius, Vaughan Williams, Walton, Britten, Tippett and others.

Appendix: The orchestration of Sullivan's major works

Title	Year	Woodwind								Brass				Percussion		Special
		Flute	Oboe	Clarinet	Bassoon	Piccolo	Cor anglais	Bass clarinet	Double bassoon	Horn	Trumpet	Trombone	Tuba/ophicleide	Drum	Other	
The Tempest	1862	2	2	2	2	1				2	2	3		2	4	
L'île enchantée	1864	2	2	2	2	1	1			4	2	3	1	1	3	Harp
Kenilworth	1864	2	2	2	2	1				4	2	3	1	1	4	2 cornets, bass trombone, ophicleide, harp
Symphony in E	1866	2	2	2	2					4	2	3		2		
In Memoriam	1866	2	2	2	2	1				4	2	3	1	2	4	Organ, ophicleide
Marmion (concert overture)	1867	2	2	2	2					4	2	3	1	1		Ophicleide, alto tuba
The Contrabandista	1867	2	1	2	1	1				2	2	2		2	1	Sax horn in F, 2 cornets
The Prodigal Son	1869	2	2	2	2	1			1	4	2	3	1	2		'Organ, ophicleide'
Overture di Ballo	1870	2	2	2	2	1				4	2	3	2	2	4	Ophicleide alt. to tuba or double bassoon instead of serpent
On Shore and Sea	1871	2	2	2	2	1				4	2	3	1	2	4	Chinese crescent, cornet, ophicleide alt. to tuba
Festival Te Deum	1872	2	2	2	2	1		1	1	4	2	3	1	3		'Organ, ophicleide, military band'
The Light of the World	1873	2	2	2	2	1			1	4	2	3	1	3 ?	2	Organ, harp, ophicleide
The Zoo	1875	1	1	2	1					2	2	2		2	Var.	2 cornets
Trial by Jury	1875	1	1	2	1					2	2	2		2	3	2 cornets
Henry VIII	1877	2	2	2	2	1				4	2	3	1		4	
The Sorcerer	1877	2	1	2	1	1				2		2		2	4	2 cornets
HMS Pinafore	1878	2	1	2	1	1				2		2		2	4	2 cornets
The Pirates of Penzance	1879	2	1	2	1	1				2		2		2	4	2 cornets
The Martyr of Antioch	1880	2	2	2	2	1			1	4	2	3	1	1	1	Harp, 2 cornets, ophicleide, organ
Patience	1881	2	1	2	1	1				2		2		2	4	2 cornets
Iolanthe	1882	2	1	2	1	1				2		2		2	4	2 cornets
Princess Ida	1884	2	1	2	1	1				2		2		2	4	2 cornets

(cont.)

Appendix: (cont.)

Title	Year	Woodwind								Brass				Percussion		Special
		Flute	Oboe	Clarinet	Bassoon	Piccolo	Cor anglais	Bass clarinet	Double bassoon	Horn	Trumpet	Trombone	Tuba/ophicleide	Drum	Other	
The Mikado	1885	2	1	2	1	1				2		2		2	4	2 cornets
The Golden Legend	1886	2	2	2	2	1	1	1	1	4	2	3		2	Var.	Organ, harp
Ruddigore	1887	2	1	2	1	1	1		1	2		2	1	2	4	2 cornets
The Yeomen of the Guard	1888	2	1	2	2	1				2		3		2	4	2 cornets
Macbeth Overture (concert version)	1888	2	2	2	2	1	1			4	2	3	1	2		Harp
The Gondoliers	1889	2	1	2	2	1				2		3		2	4	2 cornets
Ivanhoe	1891	2	2	2	2	1	1	1		4	2	3	1	2	var.	Harp, bass trumpets on stage, treble flute in G
Haddon Hall	1892	2	1	2	2	1				2	2	3		2	4	2 cornets
The Foresters	1892	2	1	2	2	1				2		1			1	2 cornets
Imperial March	1893	2	2	2	2	1		1		4	4	3		1	3	Harp
Utopia Limited	1893	2	1	2	2	1				2		3		2	4	2 cornets
The Chieftain	1894	2	1	2	2	1				2	2	3		2	2	
The Grand Duke	1896	2	1	2	2	1				2		3		2	4	2 cornets
The Beauty Stone	1898	2	1	2	2	1				2		3		2	4	2 cornets
The Rose of Persia	1899	2	1	2	2	1				2		3		2	4	2 cornets
Te Deum laudamus	1902	2	2	2	2	1			1	4	4	4		1	var.	Organ, fluegelhorn, 2 euphoniums

6 The librettos in context: Gilbert's 'fables in song'

HORST DÖLVERS

The nineteenth century abounded in parables, *contes*, emblematic tales, reveries, etc., and fables of the Aesopian type had their fair share of this blossoming. It can be shown that in the course of the century the latter tended to evolve from vessels of instruction, often at schools, into rather brittle repositories of humour, if not plain nonsense. In a light-hearted vein, the most common narrative structures of the fable – a problem or confrontation, their complication by an idiosyncratic action, and a pointed ending – often suffered parody. In a different context, that of shop ballads, they underwent humorous erotic re-encoding. A popular book of the time representative of both tendencies is *Fables in Song*,[1] a collection that Edward Robert Bulwer, First Earl of Lytton, the son of the novelist, brought out in 1874, seven years before Gilbert's and Sullivan's *Patience*. In their verbal wit and their sheer exuberance of linguistic play, abounding in allusion and pastiche, Bulwer's two volumes specifically invite comparison with Gilbertian fable persiflage.

Fables in abundance

The best-known milkmaid in English musical drama lends her name to a spoof on the aesthetic craze of the 1890s. One of its main targets, poor poetic Grosvenor, deprived of Patience (as, no less, of patience), despairs of getting away from the love-lorn maidens who pursue him: 'Oh, Patience . . . Alas, they will die of hopeless love for me, as I shall die of hopeless love for thee!' In this quandary, the Poet, as a last resort, attempts to read to them two of his poems (not exactly mind-stunning achievements), which, fable-wise, have heavy morals attached to them. Here are the endings of tales of Gentle Jane ('who was good as gold') and Teasing Tom ('a very bad boy'):

> . . . And when she grew up (Jane) was given in marriage
> To a first-class earl who keeps his carriage!
> . . . The consequence was (Tom) was lost totálly
> And married a girl in the *corps de bally*!

Great fun this: a multiple play on sound, accent and rhyme. More fun lies in the slippage of the signifiers (ostensibly two rather unlikely life stories as a blueprint of poetical justice) into the abyss of centuries of allusion. For the polarity of goodwill and bad ways had been worked out emphatically in apprentice guides and similar educational tracts from the eighteenth century onwards, books that contrasted honest work with sloth and vice, from Hogarth's *Industry and Idleness* (1747) to Hannah More's 'The Two Shoemakers' in her *Cheap Repository Tracts* (1795–8). The Savoy audience would have known these works or others like them. From the beginning of the nineteenth century this contrast – a staple topic in fables for the young – was projected even into the animal and insect world, as in fables for the nursery that taught bee-lore to infants: 'Velvet, though she was pretty, she was not good ... Busy, who was only a plain brown bee, was at work from morning till night'.[2] The least that can be said is that Gilbert, tongue in cheek, pokes fun at the infantile, though (we may be sure) ballet-girls-loving Grosvenor. Surely, he is conversant with literature at its simplest.

The Idyllic Poet's efforts are to no avail. The young ladies keep on gushing. Now, might a more explicit fable do the job? 'Remember the fable of the Magnet and the Churn ... I will sing it to you.'

> A magnet hung in a hardware shop,
> And all around was a loving crop
> Of scissors and needles, nails and knives,
> Offering love for all their lives:
> But for iron the magnet felt no whim,
> Though he charmed iron, it charmed not him;
> From needles and nails and knives he'd turn,
> For he'd set his love on a silver Churn!
>   His most aesthetic,
>   Very magnetic
> Fancy took this turn –
>   'If I can wheedle
>   A knife or a needle,
> Why not a Silver Churn?'
>
> And Iron and Steel expressed surprise,
> And needles opened their well-drilled eyes,
> The penknives felt 'shut up', no doubt,
> The scissors declared themselves 'cut out',
> The kettles they boiled with rage, 'tis said,
> While every nail went off its head,
> And hither and thither began to roam,

Till a hammer came up – and drove them home.
  While this magnetic
  Peripatetic
Lover he lived to learn,
  By no endeavour
  Can a magnet ever
Attract a Silver Churn!

The sad tail of the poet's tale (to lift this from Lewis Carroll) is utter discouragement, 'the girls straggle away'.

The fable is skilfully integrated into the main text.[3] The 'clever lyric' is, of course, an allegory for the futile love of the ladies (as the magnet) for Grosvenor (as the churn). This, at least, is what Grosvenor may think he can 'drive home' poetically. At the same time, Grosvenor's fable is sadly allegorical of his own love for Patience, the milkmaid. In the larger context of the Savoy operas the tools enact topsy-turvydom caused by misplaced passion, like that imposed by Princess Ida on her girl graduates: 'Let Chaos come again'.[4] Recognising a recurrent sado-masochistic motif in *Patience*, one critic has regarded the assortment of needles, penknives, scissors and boiling kettles 'offering love' as anything but accidental.[5]

More significantly, as an allegory the tale of the Magnet and the Churn integrates into a specific, and venerable, set of intertexts. It can certainly be read as a parody of biblical parables,[6] but Grosvenor, in calling it a *fable*, actually proves himself well versed in the field of literary terms. A fable, originally one of the 'primary forms' as defined by André Jolles in 1930,[7] aims at conveying truths (often unpalatable ones) about invariants of human behaviour. It is a fictitious tale about an event in the past told for the sake of a point that is moral.[8] 'The Magnet and the Churn' illustrates magnificently the Aesopian type of fable sometimes called *apologue*.

Apologues are mostly told about a small number of animals, plants or objects. They are short, and told in what may be called a sceptical, pessimistic, if not cynical vein. They focus either on behaviour that, though ruthless, is pursued by their protagonists as pragmatically profitable. Or they may, no less worldly-wise, teach resignation in view of calamities that frustrate even modest expectations. Thus, their world is conceived as inhabited by agents who are either selfish and cunning, or Fortune's fools. La Fontaine's swallow comes to mind, whose insolent pillage and destruction of the spider's web demonstrate that those who are strong and ruthless are favoured by Jupiter.[9] The second perspective is well known from the turtle whose dream of flying comes true but who is dropped from the eagle's beak. Or think of the sensitive ass that finds a lyre but is unable to touch its strings with its hoof. Or of the fox who swims for a cheese that is only the reflection of the moon in the water, or of the mouse that wants first the wind, then a tower for a strong husband but has to make do with the strongest of all, one of her kind – since mice gnaw even palace walls to pieces.[10] 'The Magnet and the Churn' fits in with this latter model: sober reflection may well show that passionate lovers are foolishly blind to reality, and that more often than not this is hammered home to them and their entourage in unpleasant ways.

A plea for playfulness

Parody was rife in the fable genre; one thinks of Lewis Carroll's 'The Mock Turtle's Song' that begins "'Will you walk a little faster?", said a whiting to a snail'.[11] Playful erotic innuendo pervaded much album verse, as in Joseph Skipsey's 'The Bee and the Rose', which ends, passionately, with "'Come back, thou villain!" cries the Rose / "Come once more kiss me, if thou darest!"'[12] When Lord Lytton published his *Fables in Song* in 1874,[13] Robert Louis Stevenson frowned upon playfulness of that kind in a review of Lytton's collection in the *Fortnightly Review*.

John Morley, publisher of the *Review*, had praised Lytton's fables as 'full of fancy . . . the verse and form most brilliant . . . swift, sustained, light-winged, penetrating'.[14] Stevenson, though politely chiming in with Morley's enthusiasm, puts forward a remarkable hypothesis about recent changes in the fable genre. He points out a tendency of fables to incorporate, in a 'real-istic way', 'unanswerable problems of life'. His argument, itself Darwinian, takes account of a spirit of the times deeply affected by the more provocative theses of Charles Darwin, whose *Descent of Man* had been published only three years before. In 1874, the fable, in Stevenson's view, could no longer be what it had originally been, 'fantastic . . . a bit trivial, somewhat playful, old stories of wise animals or foolish men . . . the point of the thing (being) a sort of humorous inappropriateness'. Rather, after 'the theory of evolution', it had to lose its pleasantry:

> a comical story of an ape touches us quite differently after the proposition of Mr Darwin's theory . . . a man is no longer the dupe of his own artifice, and cannot deal playfully with truths that are a matter of bitter concern to him in his life.[15]

Against this verdict, Gilbert, in 1884 (like Lytton before him), would appear to put in his veto. Although he was not averse to picking up bitter concerns (for example, suicide, or the death penalty) the obligation to leave playfulness and humorous inappropriateness in order to make the fable, in Stevenson's words, 'quite a serious, if quite a miniature, division of creative literature' did not concern him overmuch. Or so it seems. For this is his response to the new importance of being earnest, in *Princess Ida* (1884):

A Lady fair, of lineage high,
Was loved by an Ape, in the days gone by,
The Maid was radiant as the sun,
The Ape was a most unsightly one –
   So it would not do . . .
With a view to rise in the social scale,
He shaved his bristles, and he docked his tail,
He grew mustachios, and he took his tub,
And he paid a guinea to a toilet club –
   But it would not do . . .
He bought white ties, and he bought dress suits,
He crammed his feet into bright tight boots –
And to start in life on a brand-new plan,
He christened himself Darwinian Man!
   But it would not do,
   The scheme fell through –
For the maiden fair, whom the monkey craved,
   Was a radiant Being,
   With a brain far-seeing –
While a Darwinian Man, though well-behaved,
At best is only a monkey shaved!

Of course, this text elaborates as familiar a motif as did the tales of Gentle Jane and Bad Tom, since for centuries vanity and mimicry had been conceived and caricatured as apes or monkeys gulling their victims. In Gilbert's own time topical satire was virtually invaded by monkeys – Robert Buchanan, for instance, evoked Darwin in his abusive rhyme directed at Swinburne 'The Monkey and the Microscope' (1872).[16]

Fable codes creating plausibility

Over and above any intertextual and topical paraphernalia, however, fables partake of age-old plausibility codes. For the stories that fables tell are certainly improbable and a-mimetic – if apes may (do we know?) fall in love with humans, they certainly do not strive 'to rise in the social scale'. If fables, in spite of their non-realism, woo the reader into a mixed attitude of amusement, reflection and assent this is because they depend on an adequate reading (or decoding) competence.

It is this competence which makes the reader recognise the fables' agents within culture-specific correlations. First, they are tied to a fairly stable set of characteristics and values, and it is this which constitutes their verisimilitude: 'The wolf is cruel and cowardly, the fox wily, the bees infinitely busy'[17] – although pointed deviations from these assumptions (as with Velvet the bee, pretty, but not good) make sense as well. This verisimilitude works largely in unison with linguistic stereotypes – apes tend to 'ape' other beings. In addition, codes that are historically variable relate groups of characters and their attributes to specific social positions – ladies of 'lineage high' were supposed in Gilbert's days to be 'radiant as the sun', 'fair' and 'with a brain far-seeing', while underlings appeared 'most unsightly'. Finally, pre-coded plots arise out of deep, possibly culture-independent, experience. These plots create what comparative studies have posited as fable types, which overlap with folk tale types.[18] In addition to the excessive-desire-and-frustration type (cf. Mouse and Wind), the Ape fable blends into at least one other type of experience – seen as it were from outside. An intruder may try to assimilate himself, in outlook and behaviour, to the prevailing norms of a group – but he still remains a (potentially dangerous) outsider. The wolf in sheep's clothes is unmasked, as is the magpie among doves.[19]

Thus, the 'Ape in love' song may have appealed to its hearers as 'true' in a sense beyond topical issues. This decoding is what makes people understand fables at a basic level and accept them as common sense, on a largely subconscious plane.

Plausibility and oscillation of meaning

The specific charm of fables, of course, lies in semantic and pragmatic inter-pretations of their decoding. They may fit into contexts that add meaning to mere sense. In texts of some subtlety such contexts tend to oscillate, and readers may be seduced into wavering between alternatives that need to be negotiated. Thus in Gilbert's fable the implications of the Darwinian link and its playful handling are by no means clear. True, the experiment of Princess Ida's Academy for Women is meant to be ridiculous and to be played for smiles – but this does not quite hold for Ida's words introducing the project as devoted to 'nobility of brain' while social distinctions are disregarded and 'beauty counts for naught'. Even less so since earnestness of mind is here joined by moral impetus: 'If we succeed / We'll treat (Man) better than he treated us'. It is this reforming spirit that for the ladies entails an exclusion of 'Sensual Man' – and one may well feel that in this context the Ape fable (in Stevenson's words) 'loses its pleasantry'.

But then, Lady Psyche's reading of the fable bases the project on a non sequitur: 'We are all taught, and, *being taught, believe* / That Man, sprung from an Ape, is Ape at heart'. Or do we? The repetition of 'taught', fumbling, uneasy, gives her words away as traces of an interior dialogue, which is rudely made audible in Cyril's response, 'That's rather strong'. After all, the doctrine is based on mistaken semantics: 'man' = 'male', and Cyril acts as a close reader. Apparently the plot's suggestion of unpleasantness may be easily defused into muddled thinking and an indictment of the English language. Thus, in a volte-face, the ending turns out to be conventional: Ida, finally, sighs: 'I love thee – come!' Still, the statements (and overstatements, in the Ape fable) of the Academy's tenets claim an authority which, by the textual frames, is by turns affirmed and undermined. The fable's intertextual and textual affinities work together to destabilise the plot.

New players in old plots

As has been indicated, writers of original fables may replace Aesopian agents by non-Aesopian variants, retaining the fable type and its roles. One of the best-known Aesopica is that of the fox who disdains the coveted grapes as too sour because they are beyond his reach.[20] Similarly, Richard Dauntless, 'a Man-o'-war's-man' in Gilbert's *Ruddigore*, tells a yarn of a thwarted attempt to loot what initially looked like a French merchant ship – but turned out to be anything but an easy prey: 'She proved to be a Frigate – and she up with her ports / And fires with a thirty-two!'

> Then our Captain, he up and he says, says he,
>   'That chap we need not fear, –
>   We can take her, if we like,
>   She is sartin for to strike,[21]
>   For she's only a darned Mounseer . . .
> But to fight a French fal-la – it's like hittin' of a gal –
>   It's a lubberly thing for to do . . . '
> So we up with our helm, and we scuds before the breeze
>   As we gives a compassionating cheer:
>   Froggie answers with a shout
>   As he sees us go about,
>   Which was grateful of the poor Mounseer . . .
> And I'll wager in their joy they kissed each other's cheek
>   (Which is what them furriners do),
>   And they blessed their lucky stars
>   We were hardy British tars
>   Who had pity on a poor Parley-voo . . .

The pattern of experience honoured by this fable is that of turning defeat into a smug pretence of satisfaction. As with the Ape fable, this text may have sparked off conflicting interpretations in Gilbert's days. Certainly Richard, a braggart who is able to laugh at himself ('I may say, without exaggeration, that the marciful little *Tom Tit* has spared more French frigates than any craft afloat!'), was to be played for laughs. But at least some listeners may have realised that what appeared to be a foxy way of keeping up one's self-respect (thus hilarious) was no less an indictment of the delusions arising out of chauvinism, a celebration and, at the same time, a debunking of the British tar.

Erotic innuendo: new plots for old players

At first sight, nothing more than another substitution of agents appears in Hannah's fable of the flower and the oak tree, also in *Ruddigore*:

> There grew a little flower
>   'Neath a great oak tree:
> When the tempest 'gan to lower
>   Little heeded she:
> No need had she to cower,
> For she dreaded not its power –
> She was happy in the bower
>   Of her great oak tree!
>   Sing hey,
>   Lackaday!
>   Let the tears fall free
> For the pretty little flower and the great oak tree.

True to stereotype, the oak tree proves mortal while the flower survives. But the moral implied is emphatically different:

> Said she, 'He loved me never,
>   Did that great oak tree,
> But I'm neither rich nor clever,
>   And so why should he?
> But though fate our fortunes sever,
> To be constant I'll endeavor,
> Aye, for ever and for ever
>   To my great oak tree !'
>   Sing hey . . .

Since antiquity, the oak had occurred in several variants of an Aesopian fable that contrasted the tree, strong but doomed to die, with some weak and pliable reed or weed, a vine or a willow. As G. Wren points out, Gilbert had used this image in a song in *Princess Ida*: 'I leant upon an oak, / but in the hour of need, / alackaday, / my trusted stay / was but a bruised reed'.[22] To replace, in this constellation, the pliant plants of natural growth by 'a pretty

9 *The Oak and the Reed*: illustration by Thomas Bewick to Aesop's *Fables*, 1818.

little flower' and invest the oak with a bower, traditionally an emblem of courtly love and intimacy, gives Hannah's song a tone that is totally different from the apologue proper. This chimes in with the substitution of litheness triumphant by the pathos of a constant lover. The age-old moral is provocatively replaced, even parodied, by a sentimental appeal: 'Let the tears fall free . . . ' The refrain suggests a merger of the fable form with traditional ballads. All this indicates that here the textually implied reactions of the reader/listener are different from those that have been discussed so far. As a matter of fact, fable material had for quite some time already been adopted by a literature of polite entertainment.[23]

From the beginning of the century onwards, a number of Aesopian motifs and structural features – shortness, anthropomorphism, collusion or conflict, the whole told for the sake of a point that is moral or at least useful – had been converted into playful allegories of stereotypical erotic situations. In ballad-related verse of the *Heidenröslein* type, a small repertoire of animals and plants and their relationships were re-encoded as erotic ciphers. Goethe's poem itself, in its setting by Schubert, may have served as a powerful model, since in the course of the century it was given several further musical settings by English composers, settings which enjoyed considerable popularity in Victorian drawing rooms. The deluge of album verses of this kind is now almost completely forgotten. On and off, Moore's *Irish Melodies* (1801–34) are still sung in Ireland ('The Last Rose of

Summer'), and Gabriel Fauré saved Victor Hugo's 'Le papillon et la fleur' from oblivion.

These offspring of Aesopian apologues went along with two powerful conventions of the Victorian drawing room – that of evading embarrassing subjects by playful innuendo, and a consensus that matters of love and sex could be illustrated for the young, as it were in passing, through a set of idyllic nature miniatures. Not only the botanical subset of the fables' agents (one thinks of fir and bramble, thistle and ear of wheat, lily and rose, *Amaranthus et Rosa*), but also butterflies and bees slipped into *vers de société*.[24] Lord Lytton, for instance, in his *Fables in Song*, coyly developed erotic innuendo into a warning against premature sexual experience when in his idylls 'green grass-blades [are] aquiver / With joy...', while young flowers, 'in haste to be cherished', are nipped in their buds.[25] Philip Bourke Marston's 'The Rose and the Wind' was a cautionary tale with its moral preserved, though now adequately sentimentalised:

> *The Beech.* – 'Broken she lies and pale, who loved thee so?'
> *The Wind.* – 'Roses must live and love, and winds must blow.'[26]

Even before the commencement of the Savoy project Gilbert had tampered with erotic innuendo in fable form by providing Sullivan with one of these unfair discriminations against the wind – 'The Distant Shore' (1874). In *The Pirates of Penzance* (1880) the hybrid genre is fully developed:

The Fickle Breeze

> Sighing softly to the river
>   Comes the loving breeze,
> Setting nature all a-quiver,
>   Rustling through the trees!
> And the brook in rippling measure
>   Laughs for very love,
> While the poplars, in their pleasure,
>   Wave their arms above!
>   River, river, little river,
>   May thy loving prosper ever.
>   Heaven speed thee, poplar tree,
>   May thy wooing happy be!
> Yet, the breeze is but a rover,
>   When he wings away,
> Brook and poplar mourn a lover!
>   Sighing well-a-day!
> Ah, the doing and undoing
>   That the rogue could tell!

When the breeze is out a-wooing,
   Who can woo so well?
      Pretty brook, thy dream is over
      For thy love is but a rover!
Sad the lot of poplar trees,
   Courted by the fickle breeze.

This lyric may well have been written in hope of success in Victorian drawing rooms, be it spoken or sung to the piano. Indeed Gilbert and Sullivan were by no means unwilling to contribute to the remunerative genre of so-called shop ballads. Besides 'The Distant Shore' they produced 'The Love that Loves Me Not' (1875) and 'Sweethearts' (1875). Out of their (pre-Savoy) operas the ballad 'Little maid of Arcadee', from *Thespis* (1871), was printed immediately for the drawing room (Cramer, 1872), as was 'Silvered is the raven hair' (with alternative words) from *Patience*.[27] In those years there existed a tremendous demand for this genre, so that many of Gilbert's later Savoy lyrics, certainly 'amorous in effect' like 'The Fickle Breeze', reveal an intent to rival the songs from, say, operas by M. W. Balfe, composer of *The Bohemian Girl* (1843), that were printed and sold by the thousands.[28] Shaw famously showed himself little amused by 'the string of hackneyed and trivial shop ballad stuff'.[29]

Hannah's fable quoted above of the rose and 'the sheltering oak that all too soon proves unworthy'[30] is of the shop ballad type, too. No less than the texts discussed earlier, this fable is well integrated into the plot of the play. In its bittersweet, even forgiving, mood it is only one of two distinctive reactions by female characters in *Ruddigore* to male betrayal of love. The other is Mad Margaret's well-known 'To a Garden Full of Flowers', where the vision of roses is one of prostitutes (Wren) while the protagonist, a violet – traditionally their opponent – has to experience the gardener's injustice.

Mock-serious allegorical fabulation

Among Gilbert's writings there are a number of longer, non-Aesopian allegorical tales in verse. These fables spread leisurely and without the formal and material constraints of apologues into narratives whose allegorical import often combines with the creation of a humorous narrative voice. 'A hive of bees, as I've heard say, / Said to their Queen one sultry day, / "Please your Majesty's high position . . . / We rather think, with a due submission, / The time has come when we ought to swarm".' Her Majesty sulks, a bee named Peter takes the matter into his own hands ('Surely a bee can swarm

alone?'), is convicted of being drunk ('Peter has been at the old brown
sherry. Old brown sherry is much too strong –') and is sent to Coventry:
'In dismal dumps he lived to own / The folly of trying to swarm alone!'[31]

Linguistically, this plot is developed out of a semantic collision within
a hypothetical phrasal verb (*swarm alone*) when one of its components is
taken literally.[32] The moral is obviously that a bad English phrase entails a
life sentence: 'All came of trying to swarm alone'. Again, Lord Lytton's more
philosophical *Fables in Song* come to mind with their plot developed out
of idioms taken literally. There a thistle that is cut by the sweep of a scythe
consoles himself, 'One may lose his head'. The denizens of the sea are proud
of their president, 'gracing our President's Chair to see / Such a pearl of an
oyster!' A pantheistically inclined windmill who believes in being moved
by the Spirit of Nature has to realise that 'philosophy often ends only in
wind'.[33]

The Bab Ballads (1869), a collection of nonsense with deeper meaning
on a level with Edward Lear's *Book of Nonsense* (1845), contain many more
examples of mock-serious allegorical fabulation. There is, for instance, a
street ballad about the horrific ending of an 'extremely bulky' Discontented
Sugar Broker, who had 'everything a man of taste / Could ever want, except
a waist, / And discontent / His size anent'.[34] His physical exercises, however,
have an unexpected result, and the ending is close to that of Wilhelm Busch's
gruesome cautionary tale of 'Max and Moritz':

> I hardly like to tell you how
> This dreadful story ended . . .
> I hate to preach – I hate to prate –
> I'm no fanatic croaker,
> But learn contentment from the fate
> Of this West India broker . . .

Conversely, a happy ending is affixed to Sparkeion's ballad parody, in
Thespis, about the 'Little maid of Arcadee', who, after having been jilted,
'grew so thin and pale – until / Cousin Richard came to woo! / Then
again the roses grew!' Ko-ko in *The Mikado* sings a song about a little bird
that parodies an exemplum, a tale to induce immediate moral action, in
order to rouse Katisha's love: 'And if you remain callous and obdurate, I /
Shall perish as he did . . . ' A parable in the form of an extended logical
argument ('rule of three') occurs in Princess Ida's blank verse sermon to her
students:

> Attend, while I unfold a parable.
> The elephant is mightier than Man,
> Yet Man subdues him. Why? The elephant
> Is elephantine everywhere but here (*tapping her forehead*),

And Man, whose brain is to the elephant's
As Woman's brain to Man's – (*that's rule of three*) –
Conquers the foolish giant of the woods,
As Woman, in her turn, shall conquer Man . . . [35]

Give the term 'fable' a less restricted meaning than 'Aesopian' and all these Gilbertian texts and many more can be read (and sung) as *Fables in Song*.

7 'This particularly rapid, unintelligible patter': patter songs and the word–music relationship

LAURA KASSON FISS

The analysis of comedy in Gilbert and Sullivan comic operas regularly centres on Gilbert's librettos, as if they were the sole source of humour. Indeed, Sullivan seems to have shared this view, although Gilbert did not. Gilbert once said of Sullivan, 'He used to maintain, oddly enough, that there was no such thing as humour in music, but in my humble judgment he was, himself, a musical humorist of the very highest order'.[1] To be sure, words and music each have humour, but there is a third kind of humour at work in Gilbert and Sullivan, as is most vividly shown in their patter songs.[2] This humour stems from the formal relationship between words and music. In patter songs, consonants and vowels tumble over each other in sheer sonic joy, careering at the absolute edge of intelligibility. The question of intelligibility that these songs raise forces a re-evaluation of the boundaries between words and music. It then seems necessary to ask how this effect is produced and why the patter song's status on the border of intelligibility is funny.

Despite the frequent use of the term 'patter song' in Gilbert and Sullivan criticism and reviews, the form is not clearly defined. Its properties are usually left to be inferred from examples like 'I am the very model of a modern Major-General'. Even the gold standard of music dictionaries, *The New Grove Dictionary of Music*, does not give a richly formal definition: 'A comic song in which the humour derives from having the greatest number of words uttered in the shortest possible time'.[3] A patter song is not defined by its structure at the level of bars or sections (like a blues or a symphony), but by a much smaller unit of measure: the relationship between words and time. The first definition of the patter song, from the 1880 edition of Grove's *Dictionary of Music and Musicians*, written by J. A. Fuller Maitland, is almost identical to that in the current edition of *New Grove*, but the slight difference is instructive. A patter song, Maitland writes, is 'a kind of song, the humour of which consists in getting the greatest number of words to fit the smallest number of notes'.[4] Understanding the words of the patter song not in relation to the shortness of time but the number of notes stresses that the humour of the song derives from the relationship between music and text.

History of patter and the patter song

By 1880 the association between the patter song and Gilbert and Sullivan was sufficiently strong to feature in Maitland's definition. It had been less than a decade since Gilbert and Sullivan's initial collaboration, *Thespis*, and they had only really hit their stride with *The Sorcerer* in 1877. Of the patter song, Maitland says, 'Its latest development is in the operettas of Messrs. Burnand, Gilbert, and Sullivan, in all of which patter-songs fill an important place. Excellent instances are "My aged Employer" in "Cox and Box," and "My name is John Wellington Wells" in Gilbert's "The Sorcerer".'[5] By the 1907 edition of the *Grove Dictionary*, the entry for 'Patter-Song' indicates that 'My name is John Wellington Wells' was 'the first of a whole series'.[6] Gilbert and Sullivan had taken their place as integral to the definition of the patter song as a form.

But Gilbert and Sullivan did not invent or even inspire the term 'patter song'. It seems to have originated around the 1830s with reference to popular entertainment, but the word was quickly applied to opera as well. The patter song probably gained its name from the usage of 'patter' to describe a form of speech: Maitland's entry begins by defining 'patter' as 'the technical – or rather slang – name for the kind of gabbling speech with which a cheap-jack extols his wares, or a conjuror distracts the attention of the audience while performing his tricks'.[7] He then describes its use in music with the implication that a patter song has characteristics of this 'gabbling speech'. Spoken patter also appeared in the music hall to introduce songs or between verses.[8] Its rhythmic, sonorous nature creates an overall effect more important than any individual word. Thus a patter song is a song that resembles speech that resembles music.

Maitland indicates that the term 'patter song' came from the illegitimate stage: 'This form of song has for long been popular with "entertainers" from Albert Smith to Corney Grain, and probably owes its name to a song sung by Charles Mathews in "Patter versus Clatter".'[9] The play *Patter Versus Clatter*, a burletta produced by Madame Vestris at the Olympic Theatre, opened on 21 May 1838, and its first song has the following opening:

> When a man travels he mustn't look queer
> If he gets a few rubs that he doesn't get here
> And if from Calais to Paris he stray
> I'll tell him the things that he'll meet on his way.
>   Dover heights
>   Men like mites
>   Skippery-cliffery-Shakespeare
>   Can't touch prog
>   Sick as a dog
>   Packenem-rackenem makes pier.[10]

10 Charles Mathews as Mephistopheles in F. C. Burnand's *Faust and Marguerite*.[11] Caricature by W. S. Gilbert. *Fun*, 23 July 1864.

This song has four long verses of rapid-fire rhymes, bracketed on either end by the refrain 'When a man travels . . .'. The libretto resembles a number of Gilbert and Sullivan patter songs in the rapid rhymes and verse–chorus organisation. But Mathews's libretto contains nonsense words like 'packenem-rackenem', while Gilbert's does not. Perhaps the content here matters less.

When Maitland says the patter song 'has for long been popular', he seems to mean since the mid-nineteenth century: Albert Smith became known in the 1850s for lectures punctuated by comic songs and Corney Grain performed at the German Reed Gallery of Illustration, starting in 1870.[12] But almost as soon as the term 'patter song' was invented it was retroactively applied to a long-established operatic tradition. Music critics in *The Times* used the term 'patter song' in the 1850s with reference to works by Rossini, Mozart and Auber, as in 'a veritable "patter-song" in the *buffo* style'.[13] Current opera studies use the term 'patter song' to apply to a tradition beginning with eighteenth-century intermezzo and opera buffa, from Pergolesi, through Mozart and Haydn to Rossini and beyond.[14] Of course, the patter song has also continued in musical theatre, producing such wonderful specimens as Stephen Sondheim's 'Getting Married Today' from *Company*

(1970). Maitland cites a number of examples of patter song from classical music, from 'Haydn's "Durch Italien, Frankreich, Preussen" from *Der Ritter Roland*'[15] to 'Dulcamara's song in Donizetti's *L'elisir d'amore*'.[16] These songs differ somewhat from Gilbert and Sullivan's patter songs in style, and in some the 'patter' is a section in a larger aria that may also contain slow sections.

Gilbert and Sullivan's patter songs bridge the operatic and the popular. Sullivan was doubtless familiar with the intermezzo–buffa tradition, and the man who originally sang most of the patter songs, George Grossmith, was rooted in the popular tradition. Gilbert and Sullivan cast Grossmith in the title role of *The Sorcerer* in 1877 largely on the basis of his ability to sing patter songs: he was asked to sing the newly written patter song 'My name is John Wellington Wells' at his audition.[17] Grossmith (1847–1912) went on to play a lead baritone role in every Gilbert and Sullivan comic opera from *The Sorcerer* in 1877 to *The Yeomen of the Guard* in 1888 (nine out of a total of fourteen,[18] not including revivals), and he sang at least one patter song in each. Grossmith was more closely tied to the style of the music hall than that of opera. Before 1877, he was a self-described 'amateur' singer, performing comic sketches and songs, generally of his own composing, at various venues in London and in the provinces.[19] This material was in the style of the popular patter song: Corney Grain, the aforementioned popular patter singer, shared Grossmith's music publisher, and advertisements for each appear on the other's music. Even after he became a stage success, Grossmith continued to perform at private London parties, earning as much there as at the Savoy.[20] These performances probably resembled his stage performances. Certainly Grossmith's Savoy performances did not rely principally on an operatic vocal timbre; he did not have that sort of singing voice. In an autobiography, speaking of his childhood, he says, 'There is a period when the voice breaks, but I do not think I ever had a voice to break'.[21] One review of *Ruddigore* called him 'neither an actor nor a singer, but simply the most amusing little man ever seen'.[22] Apparently, Grossmith's performances were not about music; perhaps they were not even about words. Nonetheless, without being 'an actor', who might place greater emphasis on words, 'nor a singer', who might place greater emphasis on music, Grossmith is 'most amusing'. The patter song in its original delivery seems to emphasise neither words nor music; the humour comes from a different or combined source.

Grossmith's compositions blur the line between speech and song. He performed this personal repertoire at private parties while a member of the Savoy, on tour in America and in the provinces after he left the Savoy in 1889, and at a command performance in 1890.[23] Parts of this repertoire also made their way into print, and a number of Grossmith's songs and musical sketches survive. The sketches in particular combine spoken and sung text with a variety of degrees in between. 'A Juvenile Party', for instance, includes text spoken with no accompaniment, spoken over chords (with chords changing on a particular word), and set to particular notes – sometimes in a manner reminiscent of an operatic recitative, other times with much more variation of pitch. This sketch also incorporates familiar tunes like 'Here we go round the mulberry bush' and 'My grandfather's clock'.[24] These sketches have a spontaneous character in which speech flows into song. Grossmith reports in his first autobiography, *A Society Clown*, 'With regard to the "patter" portion of the sketch, that is the last part I write, and I alter it from time to time during its delivery – cutting out portions that do *not* "go," and extemporising observations and retaining them if they *do* "go"'. He probably uses 'patter' here in the music hall sense, referring to the spoken sections. This patter is improvisational and mutable in a way that Gilbert and Sullivan's works are not. Although there is a current tradition of changing the words to the patter songs and there seems to have been a certain amount of extemporising by the original cast in spoken dialogue, Gilbert and Sullivan generally insisted that the words and notes of the songs be sung as written.[25]

While the phrase 'patter song' is a nineteenth-century coinage, the word 'patter' is much older. From the beginning of its use, this word signified a convergence between speech, sound and noise. It derives from the prayer 'Pater-Noster' or 'Our Father', and the oldest meaning recorded in the *Oxford English Dictionary* is from the fifteenth century, used as a verb: 'To repeat the Paternoster or other prayer, esp. in a rapid, mechanical, or indistinct fashion; to mumble or mutter one's prayers'.[26] Since prayers were often chanted or sung, 'patter' seems to have referred to rapidly delivered songs from the outset. In this original meaning, patter is song sped up to a state at which words and song degenerate into noise; it can hardly be a complimentary term. The implication seems also to be that the content of the song is denigrated: if the words are indistinct, the supplicant can hardly mean them. Speed here approaches sacrilege, and the unintelligible is insincere.

Other definitions of 'patter' indicate an alternative language, as in 'The cant or secret language of thieves or beggars, "pedlars' French"; the peculiar lingo of any profession or class; any language not generally understood'.[27] Unintelligibility here is prized and partial. This secret language is not insincere, but encoded. What is not 'generally understood' (or 'generally heard') can be understood by the initiate. The general public hears only noise or meaningless sound. Patter of this sort thus divides its audience. One man's patter (secret language or even song) is another man's patter (meaningless noise).

Patter can also mean meaningless sound, even of a kind not produced by a human voice, as in 'the pitter-patter of tiny feet'. Gilbert and Sullivan use this sense of 'patter' in 'Dance a Cachuca' from *The Gondoliers*:

> To the pretty pitter-pitter-patter
> And the clitter-clitter-clitter-clatter –
> Clitter – clitter – clatter,
> Pitter – pitter – patter,
> Patter, patter, patter, patter, we'll dance.

This is one of only two instances of the word 'patter' in Gilbert and Sullivan's comic operas. In this case it simply means noise, but of course the word would have conjured an association with the patter song. Here, 'patter' indicates the sound of music: it's something to dance to. The patter song draws attention to the sound of words: the words make a pattering sound as they go by. 'Patter' indicates the sound of music and the sound of words and, by its double meaning, collapses them.

Does intelligibility matter? (matter, matter, matter, matter)

The other use of the word 'patter' in Gilbert and Sullivan refers to a patter song, in 'My eyes are fully open to my awful situation' from *Ruddigore*, nicknamed 'The Matter Patter': 'This particularly rapid, unintelligible patter / Isn't generally heard, and if it is it doesn't matter!' Paradoxically, this joke requires its own words to be close to unintelligible: this joke would not be nearly as funny in a slow, sedate song. At the same time, the joke raises questions, fundamental to the patter song, about the relationship between intelligibility and hearing and about how much any of it matters.

One apparent reading of this couplet is that this patter song is sung so quickly that its words are not individually discernible; they cannot be properly 'heard'. But these words could be intelligible even if they were not heard. Librettos were sold in the Savoy Theatre's lobby for *Ruddigore*, as for other operas, and a significant number of audience members read along with the production. Contemporary reviews of *Ruddigore* mention the sound of simultaneous page-turning in the audience, indicating that many audience members were following along during the performance: 'everyone seemed to have a book of the words, so that when it came to the bottom of a page there was a flutter as of Somerset House pigeons at feeding time, or as if you had suddenly pulled the wrong cord of a Venetian blind'.[28] These readers had an edge in patter-song comprehension, and if they did not hear all the words, it mattered less. Of course, not everyone could purchase these librettos; presumably lower-middle- or working-class

Example 7.1 Opening of 'The Matter Patter'

My eyes are ful-ly o-pen to my aw-ful sit-u-a-tion; I shall go at once to Ro-de-ric and

patrons in the pit or gallery would be unlikely to spend the money. For them the caviar of the patter songs might not be 'generally heard'.

But hearing is also a talent. The patter song resembles its cousin the secret language. It is a test of its audience's ear: catching the complex phrases may be as much of a skill as enunciating them. The singer and the audience together push the boundaries of intelligibility. Also, the patter song takes on a different valence after its first performance. In modern productions, a large subset of the audience will be expected to be familiar with the opera already. Where there is not a libretto or supertitles, the audience still contains seasoned Savoyards whose foreknowledge of the words makes understanding them easier. But many modern productions write new verses or replace lines in the well-known patter songs. To be sure, this freshens the allusions, but it also replicates the original listening experience: it makes the words more of a challenge to the hearer.

But perhaps the joke is that the patter song fundamentally is not about the words; the words here don't 'matter'– they are merely excuses to make funny noises. This particular couplet comes at the very end of 'The Matter Patter', the rest of which does matter to the plot of *Ruddigore*. This last couplet can then appear as a sort of joke, as if to say, 'I can fill up these last lines with whatever I like because it's not going to be understood anyway'. One might read this as a protest on Gilbert's part against the writing of patter songs that Sullivan goes on to set in a manner that makes them 'unintelligible'. But since Sullivan wrote the music after Gilbert wrote the words, by writing this couplet, Gilbert practically required a setting that would make the words nearly 'unintelligible'. But, again, if the words completely fail to get across, the joke is not funny. This joke requires and exploits the status of the patter song at the very limit of intelligibility where words and notes balance uncertainly between comprehensible sounds and 'unintelligible' noise.

The above is predicated on the assumption that 'unintelligible' refers to the words. But does music have an intelligibility of its own that may be lost? The notes of the 'Matter Patter' are quite intricate, each one moving to a different pitch, creating an ornamentation around a basic melodic structure (see Ex. 7.1).[29]

At high speeds, this ornamentation may not be heard and the notes may register as being at or around the same pitch as each other. It is not just music infringing on the intelligibility of words: the music also loses intelligibility, and music and text together represent the problems of intelligibility.

Text-setting

The general impression a patter song gives is an ironic mixture of control and lack of control. This is partly due to the speed, but it also has something to do with the text-setting. In patter songs, text is set syllabically, which means each syllable gets its own note. The vocal lines tend to be somewhat simple, with largely congruent or arpeggio motion (moving along scales or chords). Although there are few large leaps, a large vocal range is usually covered, sometimes as much as an octave in a few bars. Patter song melodies are quite distinctive; it would be very difficult to mistake 'I've got a little list' for 'I am the very model of a modern Major-General'.

Although the melody lines are not particularly difficult, patter songs are virtuosic in their enunciation. The lack of melismas (the carrying over of one syllable to another note) means that each syllable must be articulated quickly on a single note. It is a truism of vocal technique that music is carried on the vowels and words on the consonants. To make the words more intelligible the singer gives more time to the consonants, and to make the music more intelligible the singer gives more time to the vowels. This is why the pitch is ordinarily sustained on a vowel sound. It is possible to sustain a pitch on a voiced consonant like 'd' or 'v', but the sound is considered less pleasing, and unvoiced consonants like 't' and 'f' cannot hold a pitch at all. Time is borrowed from the sustaining of the note to insert the appropriate consonant. If more time is given to the consonants, the words are emphasised more. When there is one brief note to be divided up between a vowel and four consonants, allocating the appropriate time to make both intelligible is both a technical and an interpretive challenge. One could describe this phenomenon as a battle for intelligibility between words and music. But to see words and music as in competition in a song is the same as seeing vowels and consonants as in competition within a word: both are necessary; one is unintelligible without the other.

But unintelligibility is precisely what patter songs flirt with. The text-setting characteristic of patter songs, words with many consonants set to a rapid, steady pulse, ratchets up the consonant–vowel tension. Consider this line from 'The Nightmare Song' ('When you're lying awake with a dismal headache' from *Iolanthe*): 'In your shirt and your socks (the black silk with gold clocks), crossing Salisbury Plain on a bicycle'. These are all fairly common words. Only a couple exceed two syllables and there is only one proper noun, 'Salisbury Plain', a location familiar to an English

Example 7.2 From 'The Nightmare Song'

In your shirt and your socks (the black silk with gold clocks) cross-ing Sal's-bu - ry Plain on a   bi - cy - cle.

audience. But try reading the sentence aloud at a high speed, or at least at a constant speed, which is how it is notated in Sullivan's score (see Ex. 7.2).[30]

It is surprisingly difficult to say. This difficulty is due to the large ratio of consonants to vowels, especially in the transitions between the words 'gold' and 'clocks' and 'clocks' and 'crossing'. Each has four consonant sounds in a row: /ldkl/ and /kskr/. Since the notes are so short, the usual practice of borrowing time from the vowel (and the pitch) is complicated. The singer must adjudicate time carefully between vowel and consonant. And this phrase is quite simple compared to the proper names and technical terms that many patter songs contain.

Patter songs tend to fall into two categories: the narrative and the list. The narrative patter song is fairly straightforward: it is one in which a story is told. 'The Nightmare Song' is one example; others include 'When I went to the Bar as a very young man' from *Iolanthe* and 'For thirty-five years I've been sober and wary' from the original version of *Ruddigore*.[31] The list patter song is more common and more classic. Its most famous examples are 'I am the very model of a modern Major-General' from *The Pirates of Penzance* and 'As someday it may happen that a victim must be found' from *The Mikado*, which is often referred to by its refrain, 'I've got a little list'. These songs generally establish a category and enumerate its components. In the case of 'I am the very model', the list is of 'information' Major-General Stanley knows, and in 'I've got a little list', it is of people Ko-Ko would execute if called upon to act in his ceremonial position as Lord High Executioner. The narrative songs have higher stakes of intelligibility: since there is a continuous narrative, the audience is probably more interested in hearing each word. An item in a list can be more easily relinquished than a link in a narrative chain.

List songs pose a challenge to intelligibility in that their items are incongruous and therefore cannot be predicted. The nature of the list also permits the introduction of terms and proper names that are difficult to pronounce and understand. Some lists are more rapid-fire than others. Some, like 'If you want a receipt for that popular mystery' from *Patience*, rattle off incongruous terms at a rapid pace without much rationale or principle of selection: 'Beadle of Burlington – Richardson's show / Mr Micawber and Madame Tussaud!' The humour in this particular song is the incongruity of the items in the list, which are supposed to be the 'elements' that make up a heavy dragoon. Incongruity is a factor in the more expanded lists as well. For instance, in 'I am the very model', 'I can tell undoubted Raphaels from Gerard Dows and Zoffanies' rhymes with 'I know the croaking chorus from the *Frogs* of Aristophanes'. The rhyme is pleasurable because the eighteenth-century German–English painter and the ancient Greek playwright have little in common except for the Anglicised sound of their names. The association works best when heard: the words are not as pleasingly correspondent on the page because the 'f' sound in 'Aristophanes' is spelled with a 'ph'; moreover his name would originally have been written in a different alphabet. The rhyme is intensified because of its quantity: it stretches over three syllables, a triple rhyme. It is a triumph of sound over sense.

Conclusion: words, notes, song

The pleasure of the patter song is a rediscovery of the pleasure of language. The speed and text-setting push the words to the very edge of intelligibility, but they still remain words: they still carry content. Perhaps it is the relief that linguistic chaos has not entirely descended, or the recognition that funny sounds underlie all language, that elicits laughter. Consider which characters usually sing the patter songs: the Lord Chancellor, a major-general, a king and other figures of official authority. It is humorously incongruous for these dignified characters to utter what comes close to nonsense, yet it implies that their ordinary mode of speech is already nonsense, or close to it.

Patter song is an exaggeration of properties inherent to language, music and song. Therefore, some of these observations are true for song in general, not just the patter song. As a side effect, it can be difficult to determine the line between patter song and song in general. For instance, within Gilbert and Sullivan there are many border-line cases. Bunthorne's song 'If you're anxious for to shine in the high æsthetic line as a man of culture rare' from *Patience* was originally sung by George Grossmith and has some of the sensibility of a patter song, but it is relatively slow and contains ornamentation and melismas. It could be considered a variation on the patter song form: in keeping with the opera's parody of the Aesthetic movement, this is a patter song aestheticised. Also, the term 'patter song' is usually applied to solo songs, but there are several ensemble pieces in Gilbert and Sullivan that have very similar constructions. The 'Matter Patter' is clearly labelled 'Patter-trio' in the libretto and refers to itself as a 'patter'. Several other ensemble pieces have characteristics of the patter song, including the 'to sit in solemn silence' section of 'I am so proud' from *The Mikado* and the 'Chattering Chorus' ('How beautifully blue the sky') from *The Pirates of Penzance*. Perhaps the patter song, like the folk song, provides Gilbert and Sullivan with a form on which to offer variations.

The existence of a third type of meaning besides the meaning of the words and the meaning of the music is not unique to the patter song. This meaning is often used for comedic effect in a variety of song genres: since humour thrives on incongruity, an exaggerated discrepancy between words and music can be funny. In all songs, but especially in a form like the patter song, it makes little sense to talk about the effect produced by the words as separate from the effect of the music. Words and music both make sound and, in the patter song, they also make noise.

8 Standing still and moving forward: *The Mikado, Haddon Hall* and concepts of time in the Savoy operas

MICHAEL BECKERMAN

In 1892 Arthur Sullivan without Gilbert, and *with* Sydney Grundy, offered the English public an 'Original Light English Opera', entitled *Haddon Hall*. Although its eventual run of 214 performances at the Savoy Theatre was far less spectacular than that of *HMS Pinafore, Patience* or *The Mikado*, the work must be counted a popular and critical success which was attested by more than twenty reviews of the production.[1] Notwithstanding such critical acclaim, however, *Haddon Hall* has failed to recapture the stage in spite of several revivals. Most simply blame Grundy's libretto. Jane Stedman has criticised Grundy's style in comparison with Gilbert's and has claimed that, although some of Sullivan's librettists were 'markedly successful in writing non-musical plays, none gave Sullivan what Gilbert's librettos gave him'.[2] From the very beginning *The Daily Telegraph*, which had praised Sullivan's music highly, took Grundy to task: 'The great weakness of the libretto . . . is the dramatic insignificance of the main characters' (26 September 1892), while the *Pall Mall Budget* on 29 September insisted that the work had 'a want of balance in the idea – a structural deficiency which it is very hard to forgive'. Bernard Shaw made his *Haddon Hall* review a vehicle to derogate the absent Gilbert, 'whose great fault was that he began and ended with himself';[3] however, though he attributed the work's success to 'the critical insight of Mr Grundy', even he found segments of the libretto quite clumsy. Perhaps Nigel Burton reflects the prevailing modern view when he says that *Haddon Hall* 'is saddled with an impossible libretto by Sydney Grundy, but merits a full recording on account of its considerable quantity of good music'.[4]

Though much of the attack on Grundy is based on an actual or implied comparison with Gilbert, critics universally seem to be unaware that, questions of quality aside, the two are utterly dissimilar dramatists working in radically different dramatic modes. *Haddon Hall*'s success is a direct result of the fact that Sydney Grundy, certain flaws in his libretto notwithstanding, gave Arthur Sullivan precisely what he wanted.

The iconic and dialectic mode

We often use the term 'drama' as if it were synonymous with conflict. Thus what we may identify as the dialectic mode of dramatic presentation is so commonplace that we might mistakenly assume it to be the central ingredient of all types of theatrical performance.[5] In its purest state the dialectic mode presents eternal conflicts of the human condition covered by the skin of conventional plot and design. *Hamlet* is a useful example of this mode since it stages not only the rivalry between the guilt-ridden schemer and the tormented prince – evenly matched rivals – but Hamlet's internal struggle as well. In this dialectic mode, the future is uncertain: the audience thus becomes conscious of movement towards a goal, of passage through time.

Yet not all types of presentation utilise the dialectic. In the USA, July 4 parades, pageants and all manner of pastorals offer the spectator scenes free from conflict, an image of perfected time. These may be considered examples of the iconic mode. 'In a world where iconic time holds sway', states Bernard Beckerman, 'change can only produce corruption, for where there is perfection, the ideal, whatever its nature, can only endure; it can never improve'. Thus, working in iconic time, a dramatist 'tends to create an image of an idea rather than an image of time passing',[6] and iconic presentation 'in its purest form endeavours to create an illusion of stasis'.[7] It is important to note the two modes of presentation which have been identified above are rarely present as theoretical absolutes, but most often overlap and coalesce in the course of a play, musical or opera.

Applying these theories of modes to the study of *Haddon Hall* and *The Mikado* does not suggest that they provide the only way to approach the works. Yet exploring them through this lens reveals how powerful is the role played by stasis in regulating the flow of what are, on the surface, entirely different kinds of theatre.

Sydney Grundy's libretto for *Haddon Hall* is based on the true story of Dorothy Vernon's elopement from Haddon Hall with her secret lover John Manners in the sixteenth century. The libretto is divided into three parts: Act I – The Lovers; Act II – The Elopement; Act III – The Return. This seems to correspond to traditional notions of conflict and resolution. Yet there is no real struggle; the conflict is purposely minimised, for Dorothy's father, Sir George Vernon, the genial host of Haddon Hall, is hardly a villain, while the resolution is also never in doubt. Instead of becoming aware of a passage towards something, we have the illusion of standing still. *Haddon Hall* tends to resemble a collection of *tableaux vivants* and in that sense may be considered an example of the iconic mode.

11 Stately home opera: *Haddon Hall. Illustrated Sporting and Dramatic News*, 8 October 1892.

The iconic mode in its purest form is not merely characterised by stasis but also embraces a 'steady state of being, an undifferentiated timelessness that demonstrates an abiding truth'.[8] This 'abiding truth' is evident in the very first lines of the libretto, a chorus in praise of English country houses:

> Ye stately homes of England,
> So simple yet so grand;
> Long may ye stand and flourish,
> Types of our English land.

The world of the text is timeless and is symbolic of the assumed English virtues of grandeur and simplicity. There is no Gilbertian irony in this text. The ensuing series of *tableaux* that comprise the initial section of *Haddon Hall* amplify this sensibility. A pastoral dance with choral accompaniment, 'Today it is a festal time', is briefly interrupted by Dorothy's companion Dorcas, whose ''Twas a dear little dormouse' metaphorically describes the young woman's reluctance to marry her father's choice, the strident hypocrite Rupert. The pastoral tone then resumes with yet another song for chorus, 'Nor violet, lily, nor bluebell we bring', and the first section of the opera concludes with the climactic madrigal, 'When the budding bloom of May', for chorus and soloists.

From the beginning of *Haddon Hall*, then, a sense of stability and sta-sis is evoked. The twin forces which eventually disturb the pastoral bliss – Dorothy's love of and elopement with John Manners against her father's wishes, and the caricature chorus of Puritans led by Rupert and the ultimate stage Scotsman The McCrankie – are so overstated and, in the case of the Puritans, so 'consciously ridiculous'[9] that they cannot be considered to be forces of opposition; they exist merely to enhance the overall sense of stabil-ity. Thus, although one may speak of dialectic moments which occasionally dot the libretto of *Haddon Hall*, particularly during the elopement itself, the entire thrust is strongly iconic.

The kind of stasis described above can be problematic in the theatre since 'the dramatist who creates action in iconic time fights his medium . . .' He 'challenges the very nature of his discipline, and, if successful, triumphs through the challenge'.[10] It may seem somewhat premature to speak of *Haddon Hall* as an artistic triumph – in any case, that is always a subjective matter. Nevertheless, before one can argue for the work's unity and specific quality of its iconic time, we must see how Sullivan responded to Grundy's text, and we need to compare it with his response to Gilbert.

Madrigals

One of the most characteristic bits *of Haddon Hall* is the madrigal text 'When the budding bloom of May', which crowns the series of quasi-pastoral revels which comprise the opening of the work. The text glorifies love and nature, and in no way conflicts with the preceding material, but rather complements and reinforces it. The language is slightly archaic, simple, yet elevated; the prevailing sentiment seems to be summarised by the final lines: 'All creation seems to say, / "Earth was made for man's delight!" ' Although there is a fleeting reference to darker images in the second stanza – 'When the leaves of autumn sigh, / "Nearer death and further birth" ' – it seems merely a reminder to partake of life's joys and is in no way foreboding; time stands still in a delightful universe.

Gilbert's well-known madrigal from *The Mikado*, 'Brightly dawns our wedding day', though similar in certain superficial ways, occurs in a dia-metrically opposite dramatic situation. Peep-Bo and Pitti-Sing have been reminding Yum-Yum that her husband to be, Nanki-Poo, will be beheaded in a month. Attention is thus focused on the personalities involved and their fate – qualities completely lacking in *Haddon Hall*. We become aware of the passage of time. Yum-Yum's tears, oddly enough, are only allayed by Nanki-Poo's reference to a more iconic mode: 'These divisions of time are purely arbitrary . . . We'll call each second a minute – each minute an

Example 8.1 *The Mikado*, 'Brightly dawns our wedding day', opening

hour – each hour a day – and each day a year.' The principals then vow to be 'perfectly happy' and begin to 'Sing a merry madrigal'. Yet these words are in marked contrast to the stage directions which read, at the beginning, 'All break into a forced and melancholy laugh' and, at the conclusion, 'ending in tears'. Much of the pungency of this scene derives from admitting an iconic moment into the course of a dialectic situation.

At first glance Sullivan's two musical settings may appear to be quite similar. Both are strophic, with identical music for both stanzas, something uncharacteristic of madrigals in general and the Victorian madrigal in particular.[11] The similarities in external form are likewise clear: both have a main statement in the tonic key, a move to the dominant, a return to the original material, and a fa-la coda. Yet within these parameters, there are differences of tone, rhythmic structure and harmonic quality which correspond to the specific dramatic situation in which each occurs.

This is evident from the opening bars of the two pieces. The *Mikado* madrigal, with its sprightly Allegro con spirito, begins with a fanfare-like leap from the tonic to the dominant note and, in the first two phrases, swiftly outlines the basic harmony with block chords (see Ex. 8.1). The *Haddon Hall* piece, on the other hand, is much more restrained. The tempo is Allegretto moderato, the motion is primarily stepwise, and the chords are filled with non-harmonic tones (see Ex. 8.2). In addition, the initial cadences are conspicuously blurred: the first, half cadence, by a tonic inflection (on 'red and white') and the second, full cadence, by an added tone in the melody line.

Example 8.2 *Haddon Hall*, 'When the budding bloom of May' opening

These elements would not have great impact were it not for differences of rhythmic design in the two pieces. 'When the budding bloom' is not only stepwise in terms of melodic motion, but also its rhythmic phrasing is unfailingly regular. It breaks down, except for the very final section, into clear four-bar phrases, with the real accent on every second bar – a form which is almost antithetical to 'Brightly dawns our wedding day', where phrase structure is irregular from the start (2 + 4 or 4 + 2), and becomes even more so, particularly during the coda, where it is completely dissolved. (In this case it may be noted that the coda is simply an extension of the introduction.) The *Mikado* madrigal actually begins on the second half of the bar, and part of the musical interest derives from the way the actual downbeat oscillates from one half of the bar to the other. For example, on the words 'What though mortal joys be hollow', the accent is on the second half of the bar (Ex. 8.3a), while on 'Though the tocsin sound ere long' it moves to the first half. The bell imitation which follows blurs the distinction entirely (Ex. 8.3b). Perhaps the two madrigals differ most in their harmonisations, particularly the tension between tonic and dominant. While the *Haddon Hall* piece, with its added tones, is much richer in short-range harmonic colour, it is remarkably static in terms of its long-range design. The first section begins and ends in the tonic; almost every real accent is on the tonic note. The second section, of equal length, begins and ends in the dominant, and the first half of this is a simple dominant pedal. There is thus

Example 8.3a *The Mikado*, 'Brightly dawns our wedding day'

Example 8.3b *The Mikado*, 'Brightly dawns our wedding day'

no real tension of the kind produced by prolonging resolution, and this lack, taken with the rhythmic regularity, weakens any long-range harmonic sense.

In the *Mikado* madrigal, by contrast, harmonic changes are approached through transitional passages. For example, on the words 'Fickle moment prithee stay' (Ex. 8.4) there is a modulation to the dominant. A series of sequences beginning on 'What though mortal joys be hollow' seems to lead back to the tonic, but there is a long, unexpected subdominant extension which prolongs the tension and heightens expectation – and finally a move to the dominant on 'Yet until the shadows fall', preparing for the return of the main theme. This piece is replete with unexpected turns; in fact, the *Mikado* madrigal spends more time away from the tonic than in it. It may also be noted that while the *Mikado* madrigal refers stylistically to things outside itself in its word-painting and madrigalian imitations, the *Haddon Hall* piece, with its stately tempo and non-imitative texture, seems more in the spirit of a generic Victorian part song than a true madrigal.[12]

Example 8.4 *The Mikado*, 'Brightly dawns our wedding day'

This is not to suggest that the *Mikado* is a perfect example of the dialectic mode. Indeed, compared with, let us say, Pamina's despairing 'Ach, ich fühl's, es ist verschwunden' from Act II of *Die Zauberflöte*, it would appear quite iconic. So, the forward drive, comparative uncertainty and formal design of 'Brightly dawns our wedding day' plays on our expectations in a more dialectic manner and makes us aware of movement towards something, while the predictable rhythms, plodding gait and simple harmonies of the *Haddon Hall* madrigal are more iconic, tending to create the illusion of stasis.

Musical personality

The harmonic stasis of *Haddon Hall* is not confined solely to the madrigal but is rather a fundamental characteristic of the work's musical personality. The prelude begins with a quotation of Dorothy Vernon's song, a piece which plays a critical role in the opera since it returns to conclude both the first act and the work as a whole. The tune never articulates a real harmonic contrast and, like the madrigal, frequently refers to notes and chords a third distant from the tonic, giving it a rounder, less pressing shape which, taken together with its tempo and rhythm, tends towards stasis (Ex. 8.5). To reinforce further the harmonic profile of the opening bars, the chord pattern is duplicated almost exactly in the following choral dance, 'Today it is a festal time'.

The dialectic and iconic modes of presentation affect the spectator's perception of passing time. It is surely no accident that the question of time

Example 8.5 *Haddon Hall*, Dorothy Vernon's song, 'When yester-eve I knelt to pray'

plays an important and actual role in *Haddon Hall* – a role of which Grundy and Sullivan must have been aware. In a telling moment, at the conclusion of Act II, it becomes clear to Sir George Vernon, the master of Haddon, that his daughter has eloped. Much confusion and commotion ensue; there are cries of 'horse, to horse, the fugitives pursue'; chaos reigns. Suddenly the atmosphere changes, and the act ends with the following lines:

> Time the Avenger,
> Time the Controller,
> Time that unravels the tangle of life
> Guard thee from danger,
> Prove thy consoler,
> And make thee a happy mother and wife.
> Brief is all life;
> Its storm and strife
> Time stills.
> And thro' this dream
> The nameless scheme fulfils;
> Until one day
> Thro' space is hurled
> A vacant world,
> Silent and grey.

This is an extremely strange passage; though supposedly a scene of great conflict, it contains its own resolution. 'Time', or rather 'timelessness', is being praised as that which solves the dilemma since it 'unravels the tangle of life' and stills its 'storm and strife'. We even have the specific reference that 'time' – i.e., what we have called 'iconic time' – will enable or perhaps even force Dorothy Vernon to become a conventional 'happy mother and wife'. *Haddon Hall* had seemed for a moment to swirl into the churning sea of dialectic time; now 'Time the Avenger' prevails, returning the proceedings to the iconic. This order of things will continue forever, until the planet is without life, 'a vacant world, silent and grey'.

Example 8.6 *Haddon Hall*, 'Time, the Avenger'

Sullivan's musical setting here is masterful. The passage which precedes it is derived directly from grand opera and is a kind of continuous recitative for the entire on-stage cast. The harmonic fabric is extremely unstable with unpredictable rhythms. As the scene continues there is a gradual deceleration, a shift to a lilting 9/8 Andante con moto and a modulation to C major. The initial part of the above text is then sung by the chorus in unison (Ex. 8.6). The conclusion of Act II, then, produces the illusion of time stopping, of total stasis, at precisely the moment where an artist working in the dialectic mode would desire the most unrest and uncertainty. It is thus not surprising to find that Grundy himself acknowledged the fact that *Haddon Hall* inhabits a universe where time is skewed. On the score of the work itself we find the disclaimer that 'the clock of time has been put forward a century, and other liberties have been taken with history'. Shaw remarked upon this phenomenon in his review:

> It only remains to warn the matter-of-fact theatre goer that from the hour when, at the beginning of the piece, Sir George Vernon points to the sixteenth-century façade of Haddon Hall, and remarks that it 'smiled before the conquest', to the final happy moment when Charles I, having beheaded Cromwell in 1690, or thereabouts, restores the property to the evicted parent of the heroine, *Haddon Hall*, in history, costume, logic, and everything else of the kind, is perfectly impossible.[13]

This topsy-turvy world is hardly the free-standing fantasy of Gilbert with its constantly implied social critique, but rather it is the timelessness of stasis where years and centuries hardly matter – in other words, a timelessness which is but a part of the endless perfection of England and English life.[14]

Drama inclines naturally towards the dialectic, and indeed the dramatic possibilities and psychological nuance revealed in the plot of *The Mikado*, for example, are much richer than in *Haddon Hall*. Yet an examination of the score reveals that musically much of *Haddon Hall* equals or exceeds Sullivan's work for Gilbert. Since it seems absurd to argue that Sullivan wrote fine music for *Haddon Hall* because he was able to perceive the dialectic implications in a basically iconic situation, we might suggest that Sullivan had a natural tendency to respond to that notion of 'perfected time' which we have termed iconic.

A survey of Sullivan's life and activity reveals that, in contrast to Shaw, he was a man very much in harmony with his time. Yet Sullivan, who certainly agreed with Shaw in many ways regarding the general quality of English musical life, believed in the genre of the oratorio and maintained a lifelong interest in religious songs and hymns. Indeed, he was clearly dependent on traditional notions equating seriousness and virtue. Thus we may not be surprised to find that Grundy's extremely conventional libretto found favour with Sullivan, who was socially and artistically committed to the status quo.[15]

Indeed, what may appear to us to be an almost absurdly iconic libretto, an actual 'dramatic pageant', elicited a depth and sincerity from Sullivan which is only rarely present in his works with Gilbert; and of those, perhaps only *The Yeomen of the Guard* features a similar level of involvement and invention.[16] Although from the vantage point of conventional dramatic criticism *Haddon Hall* lacks a fundamental dialectic thrust, the composer seems to have been predisposed to its subject matter and approach.

Perhaps it is important to remember that a composer's predisposition towards one mode or the other may be a determining factor in the final quality of the composition. For example, the libretto of *Die Zauberflöte* has some astonishingly iconic touches: the final battle between the forces of dark and light seems a ridiculous anticlimax, and the so-called 'trials' of Tamino and Pamina are so light that generations of directors have bent themselves into contortions trying to make the sad little flute march sound terrifying. Indeed, the libretto is so replete with pat moralising that Ingmar Bergman, in his charming film, had the appropriate texts ornately printed on placards. Yet in addition to setting such texts convincingly, Mozart added an entire dialectic component where the strophic folk-song style epitomises the more iconic world of Papageno while the sonata arias of Tamino and Pamina inhabit the arena of conflict, struggle and trial. Thus, in this case, the composer's inner sense drove him far beyond the limitations of the libretto.

The iconic mode, as indicated above, implies stasis; yet not all kinds of stasis are identical. Indeed, the iconic mode need not even be 'the truth of virtue as long as it is a perfected state of being, even of evil'.[17] There is an overriding sensibility which illuminates what can be called the perfected time of *Haddon Hall*. The opera is distinguished not only by images of pastoral bliss but also by an almost constant reference to darker forces: the

Example 8.7 *Haddon Hall*, Act I instrumental coda

sighing of the autumn leaves in the madrigal, the 'tangle of life' from the Act II conclusion. These contrasting images, however, are never a threat to the placid and stolid characters of the drama, yet these reminders of the universe of conflict, struggle and even death serve to tinge *Haddon Hall* with melancholy and sentimentality. Earth is made for man's delight, yet one aspect of that delight is a dollop of sorrow. This is the sensibility upon which Grundy drew for *Haddon Hall*, and it is this quality which radiates from Sullivan's score.

This mixture of devotion to convention, pastoral artlessness and vicarious sentimentality is not merely a quality associated with *Haddon Hall*, but rather is one of the primary tendencies of Victorian drama and perhaps even of Victorian consciousness. *Haddon Hall* is nothing more or less than a paean to Victorian stability and virtues. From the outset of the work the pastoral is linked with the everlasting presence of England's stately homes. Sullivan further ties these images together by quoting the main theme of 'Ye stately homes of England' in a short instrumental coda following the conclusion of the madrigal in Act I. In the final act, Sir George Vernon leads the assembled multitudes in a high-spirited, yet perfectly serious bit of reaction, praising the time when 'mirth was mirth and worth was worth / In the grand old days of yore'. This piece, which further creates the illusion of timeless virtues preserved, is so strongly reminiscent of 'Rule Britannia' that Sullivan must have relied on the great song for his example of patriotic fervour (Ex. 8.7). In most of Gilbert's writing such conventional moralising and chauvinism become the butt of jokes and snipes. In Sullivan and Grundy's *Haddon Hall*, however, the unrealistic and unappealing Puritans are straw men who provide a foil for the glorification of contemporary values such as sentimentality, chastity, simplicity and manifest destiny embodied in the heroine and her father. Indeed, the main protagonists are so devoid of life that one may assert that the real hero of the piece, in the 'title role' as it were, is *Haddon Hall* itself. This stately English country house, this motionless structure, becomes the ultimate icon representing sturdy virtue – a perfect reflection of contemporary ethos.

Haddon Hall concludes with a return of Dorothy Vernon's song from the Act I finale: a virtual *leitmotif* which had begun the overture to the work as well (see Ex. 8.5). The final lines once again emphasise references to struggle and conflict:

Though storms uprise and cloud the skies,
And thorns where roses grew,
Come sun come snow, come weal come woe,
To thine own heart be true.

The naive little tune itself gives away the lie: there is no struggle – it is all implied, seen from a safe place far away; it never really happens.

In discussing the relationship between Shakespeare's *The Taming of the Shrew* and the earlier *The Taming of a Shrew*, Bernard Beckerman asserts that Kate's final speech of conciliation is, in the latter version, 'cosmic and moral rather than contractual and biological. Its argument is eternal, unchanging. It assumes the pervasiveness of iconic time.'[18] Though Dorothy Vernon is no Kate, her final lines are also cosmic commandments. They seem to challenge the status quo, yet are intent on the glorification of sentimentality. 'To thine own heart be true', far from being an invocation to lawlessness and freedom, is an invitation to obedience, conventional morality and timelessness. The realisation of these attitudes in dramatic form, frozen in iconic time, is the weakness but also the strength of *Haddon Hall*'s libretto. For, considering the transcendent sincerity of the music, we cannot doubt that Grundy's work had the ring of truth for its composer.[19]

Haddon Hall is an extreme example of the iconic – an example that could almost function as a prototype against which other works could be measured. This is of course why it was chosen. However, we might note that, seen in relation to the more famous examples of nineteenth-century musical theatre, all works by Sullivan and Gilbert would be considered as veering towards the iconic spectrum. In fact, even *The Mikado* seeks to reinforce Victorian sensibilities, albeit in a more subtle manner than *Haddon Hall*.[20]

Apart from any usefulness the concepts applied here might have in terms of approaching music and theatre in Victorian England, the notions of iconic and dialectic may permit more nuanced evaluations of musical compositions and practices. Since our entire approach to great art stresses the dialectic, indeed elevates it to a prime position, one may discover that many of the least-respected genres and composers are not guilty of the crime of 'bad music' but merely may be identified as iconic. Thus when we praise Mendelssohn's symphonies and ignore his oratorios, when we dismiss the great bulk of nineteenth-century choral music, or when we sneer with Bernard Shaw at Sullivan's *Ivanhoe* – or even when we scratch our heads in puzzlement upon encountering Mozart's *Maurerische Trauermusik*, we might first ask what mode the composer was working in, and then we need to ask if he worked completely and well within it.

9 Musical contexts I: motives and methods in Sullivan's allusions

JAMES BROOKS KUYKENDALL

The influence of one piece (or style) of music on another is a perplexing issue. The continuum of musical references ranges from the subtlest detail (for example, a similarity in orchestration or a motivic resemblance) to whole-scale appropriation, and examples have been decried or defended as coincidence, plagiarism, incompetence, creative economy, tribute, poetic resonance and brilliant satire. 'Borrowings' have long attracted musicological interest;[1] recent studies have turned to more subtle allusions and the meanings behind them. Christopher Reynolds's sophisticated analysis of motivic allusions in nineteenth-century art music explores a complex (and intentional) interrelationship between four parties:

> An allusion requires four elements: a composer (author), the new composition, the old composition, and the audience. A composer creates a new work that refers to an existing work (or works) in order to imbue the new work with a meaning that someone will recognize and interpret.[2]

The situation of musical allusions in the comic operas of Gilbert and Sullivan is somewhat more complicated. It is by no means clear that Sullivan's references were always intended to be recognised as such, nor indeed if he was always conscious of the allusions latent in his music. To be sure, there are clear examples of actual quotations which he expected to be recognised and appreciated: the fugue subject from Bach's G minor organ Fantasia (BWV 542) given to clarinet and bassoon as the Mikado sings 'By Bach, interwoven with Spohr and Beethoven' is only the most famous such case ('A more humane Mikado', *The Mikado*, Act II).

The allusion to and near-quotation of the music of other composers is a running theme in Gervase Hughes's *The Music of Arthur Sullivan* (1960), still the only monograph on Sullivan's music. The breadth of Hughes's references makes his study an entertaining read. His useful chart of 'Sullivan's Contemporaries' (ranging chronologically from Spontini to Milhaud) perhaps illuminates his approach to his subject: Sullivan's music naturally springs from a context.[3] Hughes disappoints because of a tendency to treat the musical references he observes as curiosities happened upon on the way, without exploring their larger significance in the music.

The conclusion that Sullivan's style is essentially cosmopolitan is presented apologetically:

> Attention has several times been focused … on the diverse influences to which Sullivan was subject; indeed it has been impossible to exculpate him altogether from the charge of eclecticism. No doubt some readers have wondered where this was leading; they may have heard a piece referred to as being 'typical Sullivan', which now begins to look like a contradiction in terms.[4]

Probing deeper where Hughes and others have stopped, a more nuanced understanding of Sullivan's allusions reveals a complex web of references which act on different levels – some accessible at the most superficial level, some much more opaque. The stylistic pluralism that characterises 'typical Sullivan' is not mere curiosity. On the contrary, Sullivan's wide-ranging musical interests, partially manifested through a series of works that had a great popular following, had lasting consequences on the trajectories of English music.

Type 1: local colour and characterisation

When the libretto afforded the opportunity, Sullivan sometimes adopted a musical language descriptive of the characters or setting. This is standard procedure in opera, where librettists have often favoured distant locales and remote history – either for crowd-pleasing exoticism or, as often in Italian opera, to get sensitive political issues past the censors. In musical terms, this sort of local allusion generally involves only the most superficial level, but its effects are accessible to audiences. Operatic composers have generally taken advantage of the widened musical scope encouraged by exotic settings – for example, the use of non-Western scales or non-standard instruments. Sometimes this included musicians on the stage, which Sullivan exploited in some of the original productions: a military band to accompany the entry of the peers in *Iolanthe*, Lady Jane's cello in *Patience*, a bagpipe played by McCrankie in *Haddon Hall* and – judging from photographs – the banjos and violins played by the 'Flowers of Progress' in the minstrel song 'Society has quite forsaken all her wicked courses' in the second act of *Utopia Limited*.[5]

In the operas by Sullivan and Gilbert, the richest vein of music used as local colour is *The Mikado*, with 'Japanese' inflections in the score, not only by the quotation and reworking of Japanese melodies ('Miya sama' in Act II), but – as Michael Beckerman has argued – in the recurring pentatonicism of Sullivan's melodic figures (for example, 'If you want to know who we are', 'The sun whose rays', 'See how the fates', 'There is beauty in the bellow of the blast').[6] Sullivan did not pursue this at every possible opportunity: Nanki-Poo's 'A wand'ring minstrel I' (with the string accompaniment that only barely suggests the 'native guitar' Gilbert instructs him to carry) is Victorian through and through, with evocations of the drawing room ballad, military march and sea shanty.

Elsewhere Sullivan's nautical music is equally marked, reminiscent of the ballads of Charles Dibdin and the old folk tradition of sea-songs to some critics.[7] The chorus of welcome for Richard Dauntless in the first act of *Ruddigore* is so constructed that the music would not fit any other situation. Even in the introduction, the reworking of the Bridesmaids' initial 'Fair is Rose as bright May day' motif, now set over a jaunty rhythmic accompaniment with the single bass note sounded throughout, becomes a near quotation of the choral 'Yeo-ho, heave-ho, Hurrah for the home-ward bound' (from 'A wand'ring minstrel I'). The rapid, *à la* hornpipe violin obbligato was fashioned from the same fabric that Sullivan had used in 'A British tar is a soaring soul' in *HMS Pinafore*. Out of this figuration, on short notice, Sullivan crafted the hornpipe that follows Richard's song, borrowing a rhythmic cliché familiar from the traditional tune 'Jack's the lad', perhaps the most universally familiar hornpipe. Of the authentic flavour of Richard's 'I shipped, d'ye see', a comparison with Stanford's later 'The Old Superb' (the last of the *Songs of the Sea*, 1904) reveals that they drew from the same well.

Type 2: humour in incongruity

One comic device frequently encountered in the Gilbert and Sullivan operas is the calculated mismatch between a character and his expression. Ralph Rackstraw's hyper-inflated language ('a living ganglion of irreconcilable antagonisms') is a verbal example, but Sullivan also uses a similar technique in his music. In the earlier works – particularly the less formal, one-act works *Cox and Box* (1866, libretto by F. C. Burnand), *Trial by Jury* (1875) and *The Zoo* (1875, libretto by B. C. Stephenson) – the music sometimes tends towards an exaggeratedly melodramatic lampoon of Italian opera. A good example is the trio 'Who are you, sir?' in *Cox and Box*, as the music presents one stock operatic gesture after another: the reiterated hammerstroke chords at the beginning (so characteristic of Rossini); the short phrases in which the orchestra echoes the questions posed by the characters; the duet-cadenza 'Yes, 'tis the hatter/printer' which concludes the slower first section; the artificial repetition of the text delaying any new developments (note the second time through 'Printer, printer, take a hin*ter*'); a lively parlando ('Your room! If on that you're bent'), where the orchestra carries on the musical substance under the interjections of the soloists; and the overly extended cabaletta – the faster concluding section – made to seem all the more absurd by its text, which consists of the single repeated word 'Rataplan'. The 'Rataplan' marching-song idea is itself an operatic allusion, with examples in Donizetti's *La Fille du régiment* (1840) and Verdi's *La forza del destino* (1862). Sullivan employs each of these techniques in the works with Gilbert, but nowhere in such concentrated conjunction as here. Significantly, Sullivan seems to have tired of carrying on burlesque for its own sake, coming to prefer instead more subtle jabs, or (as discussed below as Type 3) drawing on operatic techniques for musical assistance rather than comic effect.

Cox and Box also presents early manifestations of two similar recurring musical comic incongruities: Handelian mock-heroics and sincere (even tender) settings of absurd texts. In each case, the composer sympathetically matches the music to the character's attitude, and not to meaning revealed in the words. For Bouncer's fond reminiscences of his military service ('I mounted a horse / In Her Majesty's force'), in which 'somehow the enemy didn't come', Sullivan writes a quasi-Handelian aria, complete with the characteristic echoes from the orchestra at cadences as the singer prepares for the next phrase. The music suggests military glory which Bouncer revels in but does not deserve.

'Thank heaven, he breathes again!' from *The Zoo* and 'All hail, great judge' in *Trial by Jury* are similar cases, treating the relatively mundane with a pseudo-grandeur; as Donald Burrows has written, this sort of irony,

> was effective because the Handelian style was at that time associated with serious English oratorio choruses, and also with music for national or ceremonial occasions. It was an aspect of the satire that the Judge [in *Trial by Jury*] was a less worthy character than those to whom Handel's own choruses were usually addressed with this type of music, such as victorious Old Testament leaders.[8]

Perhaps the most famous example of this is 'This helmet, I suppose' in Act III of *Princess Ida*, where the three warriors prepare for battle by ponderously rationalising and removing their armour – the precise opposite of 'Arm, arm ye brave!' from Handel's *Judas Maccabaeus*. Sullivan's setting – with overly repeated text ('as many a guardsman knows' appearing four times in the first verse), walking bass line, and extended melisma at the word 'off' – captures the most easily parodied aspects of Handel's heroic style (for example, the bass duet 'The Lord is a man of war' in *Israel in Egypt*).

A Handelian reference, however, need not be a joke as such. Gervase Hughes hears in 'Hereupon we're both agreed' (in *The Yeomen of the Guard*,

Act II) a Handelianism that is 'surely spontaneous and not a parody'.[9] The significant change as Sullivan matures is not that he becomes more facile at parodying various musical styles, but that his motivation for employing this skill changes. If Sullivan was aware of a Handelian sound to this duet (perhaps most evident in the refrain), it was perhaps an appreciative tribute – borrowing from Handel a mood that fits the merriment of the characters.

Regarding the tender music Sullivan gives to absurd situations, the earliest example is perhaps also the *ne plus ultra*: Box's lullaby to the frying bacon, set with an arresting delicacy. Here the idea for the lullaby was clearly Burnand's; Sullivan's deadpan approach heightens the effect, as it clearly matches the sentiment of the character. Similarly, Frederic's plea 'Oh, is there not one maiden breast' (*The Pirates of Penzance*, Act I) is entirely sincere, and Sullivan's music is too. It is as impressive a tenor solo as Sullivan ever wrote, particularly at its climax on the top B♭, even though the composer knows his audience will chuckle at Frederic's inept references to a 'homely face and bad complexion'. The Fairy Queen's impassioned 'O Foolish Fay' (*Iolanthe*, Act II), and the mock nobility of Richard Dauntless's 'Within this breast there beats a heart' (*Ruddigore*, Act I) are comparable examples.

Type 3: structural models

Perhaps Sullivan felt that his burlesques of Italian opera in *Cox and Box* and the other early works were overly transparent and not sufficiently creative for a composer of his abilities. He moved beyond generic, surface-level references (although in some cases these remain) to concentrate instead on how to make large-scale dramatic structures cohere by means he could learn from continental models. There are many different situations in which we can find a correspondence between the musical structure of a scene in the standard operatic repertoire and in Sullivan's comic operas, and it may not have mattered to the composer whether the audience was aware of any allusion.

The remark, commonly found in the literature on the Savoy operas, that the ensemble 'A nice dilemma we have here' from *Trial by Jury* was modelled upon 'D'un pensiero e d'un accento' from Bellini's *La sonnambula* (1831), misses the essence of Sullivan's dramatic achievement in this number.[10] There is nothing in the libretto to suggest the scope of the piece that Sullivan composed. There are four couplets, each allotted to a single character, followed by 'ALL. A nice dilemma, etc.'. Sullivan recognised that this was the great static moment of the drama, at which the court is faced with the insoluble legal problem of 'burglaree'. His solution was a grand *largo concertato*: precisely what an Italian librettist would prepare for – and the composer would do – in similar circumstances.

The *largo concertato* was characteristic of an interior finale (that is, the finale of an act other than the last), where a dramatic revelation prompted a period of reaction by the characters, one by one, in a slow but showy ensemble. Often the chorus participated in a 'groundswell' effect, building to the climax. The action would then resume with faster sections leading to the fall of the curtain. In *La sonnambula*, Amina awakes from her sleep-walk to find herself accused of infidelity (cue *largo concertato*), and the wedding is called off. Compare this to similar shocking moments in other familiar operas: in Rossini's *Il barbiere di Siviglia*, the Count avoids arrest for being drunk and disorderly by revealing his true identity to the officer (cue), and the characters are left puzzled by the situation; in Donizetti's *Lucia di Lammermoor*, the wedding party is interrupted by the sudden return of Edgardo (cue), and it is clear that no one in the love triangle will come to a happy end.

Sullivan's setting of 'A nice dilemma' is not merely burlesque: it has a crucial effect on the structure of the whole work, which otherwise trips along at an ever-increasing pace. Although Sullivan does not use this technique again in the same way, there is still a trace of it in the Act I finale of *The Yeomen of the Guard*, where the tolling bell interrupts the family reunion (cue *largo concertato*, 'The prisoner comes to meet his doom', which is ended abruptly by the news that the condemned man has escaped). In both *Trial by Jury* and *Yeomen*, the most important aspect of the *largo concertato* allusion is the structural importance for the larger work, not merely a superficial stylistic resemblance.

It is doubtful that Sullivan ever encountered Abramo Basevi's 1859 *Studio sulle opere di Verdi*, but anyone familiar with the mid-century Italian opera repertoire would be aware of the multi-section structures that Basevi described. In several of the early collaborations with Gilbert, there are multi-section duets which suggest an emulation of the concept labelled by Basevi as *solita forma*. In essence, *solita forma* is a duet pattern evident already in the libretto which results in a four-section musical structure beginning at the switch from recitative into rhymed verse:

Tempo d'attacco:	rhymed verse, with lyrical and primarily parlando vocal writing, dramatically kinetic.
Adagio:	rhymed verse, lyrical melody, dramatically static.
Tempo di mezzo:	rhymed or unrhymed verse, parlando or even recitative vocal writing, dramatically kinetic.
Cabaletta:	rhymed verse, faster tempo, often with the vocal parts joining (whether in unison, thirds or sixths), dramatically static.

While this reduction of the *solita forma* model may seem fairly straight-forward, Basevi sought to describe a complex tradition in the simplest terms. The multiplicitous varieties that are found in the music have led to a vast literature on manifestations of (and departures from) the *solita forma* convention.[11]

The complexities of the subject notwithstanding, even the simplified *solita forma* model above can reveal correspondences within the Gilbert and Sullivan canon. The clearest *solita forma* duet is that of Frederic and Mabel in Act II of *The Pirates of Penzance*:

[*Tempo d'attacco*:] Allegro agitato:	'Stay, Frederic, stay!' Two rhymed verses, one for each character; lyrical vocal writing over an extremely active (quasi-parlando) accompaniment, with increasing exchanges between the singers, and with one brief passage singing together; the argument about Frederic's duty is dramatically kinetic.
[*Adagio*:] Andante:	'Ah, leave me not to pine' Two rhymed verses, one for each character, with concluding 'fa-la-la-la' together; static.
[*Tempo di mezzo*:] Recitative:	'In 1940 I of age shall be' The text is metrical (10.11.4.10.4.11) and rhymed to match (*abcacb*), but set as recitative; kinetic, presenting the solution to their problem, namely to outwait Frederic's indentures.
[*Cabaletta*:] Allegro vivace:	'Oh, here is love, and here is truth' One rhymed quatrain, sung mainly together in harmony (with requisite parallel thirds and sixths of love duets) to fastest tempo; static.

There are not many multi-sectional duets in Sullivan's works, and so few other places where any *solita forma* influence can be detected. The duet earlier in the same work – Frederic's duet with Ruth – is in three sections, but in a modified da capo form (very rare for Sullivan): 'Oh, false one, you have deceived me!' – 'My love without reflecting' – 'Faithless woman to deceive me'. Lady Sangazure and John Wellington Wells have a four-section duet in Act II of *The Sorcerer* that comes closer to *solita forma*, mapping perfectly onto the dramatic scheme:

[*Tempo d'attacco*:] Andante non troppo lento:	'Oh, I have wrought much evil in my spells' (kinetic).
[*Adagio*:] Andante:	'Hate me! I drop my H's' (static).
[*Tempo di mezzo*:] Allegro:	'At what I'm going to say', together with Andante: arioso 'To a maiden fair' (kinetic).
[*Cabaletta*:] Allegro agitato:	'O agony, rage, despair!' (static).

Basevi's description of aria form is more complicated, but Josephine's *scena* (Gilbert's label) in Act II of *HMS Pinafore* seems at least to nod in the direction of the Italian models:

Andante:	'The hours creep on apace' (static).
Chant:	'On the one hand, papa's luxurious home' (kinetic).
Allegro con spirito:	'A simple sailor, lowly born' (static?).

In this instance, however, there is less evidence in the lyrics: Sullivan has imposed the shift at 'On the one hand' and this creates a three-part structure. In any case, whether Gilbert conceived of any of these songs and duets as Italianate multi-section pieces is impossible to tell; his own knowledge of Italian opera suggests that it is possible.[12]

The Italian solo or duet pattern disappears after *The Pirates of Penzance*, and this is probably related to a shift in Sullivan's conception of the comic opera genre. In continental opera and operetta, the public display of the voice was a *sine qua non*; in the genre that Gilbert and Sullivan were forging together, the trained soloist as such was not the focus. Although there are striking solo songs, they are comparatively few, and given to the lead soprano (for example, 'Oh, goddess wise' in *Princess Ida*, ''Tis done! I am a bride' in *The Yeomen of the Guard*), while there is a marked increase in small ensemble pieces. Sullivan excelled at these, whether of the madrigal type (for example, 'When the buds are blossoming' in *Ruddigore*, its close cousin 'When the budding bloom of May' in Sydney Grundy's *Haddon Hall*, and in 'Strange the views some people hold' in *The Grand Duke*) or the verse-ensemble (for example, 'I am so proud' in *The Mikado*, 'How say you, maiden' and 'When a wooer goes a wooing' in *The Yeomen of the Guard*, and 'Then one of us will be a queen' in *The Gondoliers*). Vocal bravura virtually disappears. After *The Pirates of Penzance* little can compare to Mabel's 'Poor wand'ring one' and the cadenza that introduces it; the most demanding soprano role after Mabel, dramatically and vocally, is Julia Jellicoe in *The Grand Duke*. In both cases, the demands are stylistic necessities, as Mabel's alludes to the French opera waltz tradition, and Julia is given a true melodrama ('I have a rival! Frenzy-thrilled, I find you both together') in addition to two lengthy solos and extensive ensemble writing. The other shining moment of virtuosity is Rose-in-Bloom in *The Rose of Persia* (1899, with a libretto by Basil Hood), a part written to display the unique voice of Ellen Beach Yaw (1869–1947); when in the original production she was replaced, some of the music had to be changed to accommodate a more typical range and ability.

Type 4: speaking the same musical language

When even in the new Savoy opera genre, however, the libretto afforded Sullivan a serious 'operatic' situation, the composer generally responded with correspondingly 'operatic' music. Thus the conclusion – one might say cabaletta – of the Act II finale of *Princess Ida* ('To yield at once to

12 Rosemary Joshua, Anne Collins and Anne-Marie Owens in the ENO production of *Princess Ida* (1992).

such a foe') seems straight out of Verdi with its galloping rhythm and Ida's
acrobatic melody soaring over the chorus. 'Di quella pira l'orrendo foco',
the polonaise call-to-arms which concludes Act III of *Il trovatore* (1853),
could be regarded as a prototype for Sullivan's treatment. The allusion –
if there is one – is no more than the subtlest bow to the earlier composer,
but by borrowing the *tenore di forza* call-to-arms topos for the defiant Ida
Sullivan characterises her as every bit the equal of her foe Hildebrand and
his troops. Significantly, the effect is weakened when the chorus takes over
material that rightfully belongs only to the hero(ine) (at 'Tho' she is but a
girl').

This example is contentious, but it represents a method that recurs in
Sullivan's music: a situation elicits from him a familiar reaction 'along
certain well-established lines', as Ian Parrott has written.[13] Supernatural
moments, for example, have been seen to bear a certain family resemblance. Arthur Jacobs makes a nice distinction in his description of the
incantation in Act I of *The Sorcerer* which 'evokes (rather than mocks) the
casting of the devil's bullets in Weber's *Der Freischütz*. As in that model, the
spells are called by number, an off-stage chorus sings in 6/8 time; "spooky"
diminished seventh chords are heard, with shrieks from the woodwind.'[14]
Of course Weber had no monopoly on diminished-seventh chords

(especially in such contexts); the specific allusion to *Der Freischütz* is just as much in Gilbert's libretto as it is in the score, but Sullivan's response to the stimulus is clear. This is not the sort of allusion labelled Type 3 above, because it acts only on the superficial level; the scene is only a brief vignette, and lacks the weight that Weber gives it as the culmination of an act. Sullivan's treatment is altogether lighter, particularly because of the stylistic volte-face for the ensuing return of the villagers, to which he gives a Beethovenian luminescence.

The ghost scene in Act II of *Ruddigore* has some of the same traits exhibited in the incantation, but it includes other references as well. In particular, Sullivan's brass writing harkens back to well-established operatic traditions of brass – specifically trombones – in supernatural scenes. Act II of Mozart's *Don Giovanni* – one of the operas Sullivan had edited for Boosey & Hawkes – has splendid examples of unworldly trombones at the appearance of the dead Commendatore; a closer connection may be Act III of Mozart's *Idomeneo*, a work Sullivan had studied with a view to a performance at the 1886 Leeds Festival, a few months before setting to work on *Ruddigore*.[15] In Roderic's song 'When the night wind howls', the sinuous chromatic descent of the ghosts' chorus ('Ha! Ha! high-noon ... then is the ghosts' high-noon!') is accompanied by the introduction of just such 'supernatural' brass sonorities. The sustained brass chords as the ghosts return to their frames (the second 'Painted emblems of a race') are analogous. These artful allusions only increase the grim nature of the scene, and would have contributed to the dissatisfaction that prompted Gilbert's complaint that the music gave the effect of 'insert[ing] fifty lines of *Paradise Lost* into a farcical comedy'.[16] (It should be noted that there are instances where Gilbert seems to suggest a musical reference which Sullivan decides, for whatever reason, not to follow: the 'Tea-cup Brindisi' in *The Sorcerer* is a brindisi in situation only – a communal drinking song – and not in musical style. For *Iolanthe*, Gilbert costumed the Fairy Queen to resemble Wagner's Brünnhilde, but there is no hint of Wagner in her music. The costume may have been Gilbert's own stylistic 'humour in incongruity'.)

That Sullivan was influenced by the music of Felix Mendelssohn is unremarkable. Mendelssohn's music pervaded the London concert scene and regional choral festivals for decades after his death in 1847: what Victorian composer escaped his influence?[17] In his concert works, Sullivan's emulation of Mendelssohn is clear. His Symphony (1866), written soon after his return from Leipzig, seeks to rival the older composer's model even in its conception. Two of Mendelssohn's symphonies (the *Scottish*, No. 3, and *Italian*, No. 4) were direct responses to his youthful travels abroad. Sullivan's letter to his mother from an Irish holiday in 1863 is so worded as to suggest that he recognised a responsibility to fulfil his studies at Mendelssohn's own

Leipzig Conservatory by taking up the dead composer's mantle as the great (and no longer adopted) Victorian composer:

> I feel my ideas assuming a newer and fresher colour, and I shall be able to work like a horse on my return. Why, the other night as I was jolting home from Holestone (15 miles from here) through wind and rain on an open jaunting-car, the whole first movement of a symphony came into my head with a real Irish flavour about it – besides scraps of the other movements.[18]

The flavour was more Mendelssohnian than Irish: the two ascending scalar passages in the slow introduction must allude to the reiterated 'Dresden Amen' that frames the introduction to Mendelssohn's Symphony No. 5, the *Reformation*; the first theme in the first movement is a close cousin to the first theme in Mendelssohn's Violin Concerto (with which it shares the same key of E minor), and Sullivan's stormy development of it evokes Mendelssohn's turbulent overture *The Hebrides* (another work inspired by his Scottish sojourn); the other movements follow Mendelssohnian models – especially the folk-like scherzo.

After these, the Mendelssohn orchestral music best known to Victorian audiences was his overture *A Midsummer Night's Dream*, op. 21 (1826), and its subsequent incidental music, op. 61 (1843). Allusions to these works – and even near-quotations – turn up frequently in Sullivan's music, especially in his incidental music *The Tempest* (1861) and the ballet *L'île enchantée* (1864). In the comic operas, the strongest associations with *A Midsummer Night's Dream* are found in *Iolanthe* and *The Yeomen of the Guard*; in both of these cases the allusions are subtle, and reflect a common musical response to a given dramatic setting.

Act II of *Yeomen* opens by moonlight to the chorus 'Night has spread her pall once more'. Sullivan's opening gesture – a single chord sustained through a swelling and fading crescendo–decrescendo – is prototypical Mendelssohn, whose scores are filled with opening and closing 'hairpins' in close succession: < >. Sullivan's setting is in a broad triple metre, with the long melody presented first by unison strings (with cellos in their intense upper register). The accompaniment is very subdued – chords sustained in the winds, over a sustained tonic bass. As the melody concludes, the accompaniment drops away to leave only the trilled leading tone in the melody. After the cadence, the brass has a brief solemn fanfare, and the women's chorus enters over a string accompaniment of chords repeated in quavers (9/8 time). Dame Carruthers has a verse in the parallel minor, punctuated by a cornet tattoo. The men's chorus, when it enters, maintains the slow triple metre, but with the beat subdivided in two rather than three (thus 3/4 time: the main beat stays the same). The concluding section returns to the home tonic B-flat major, with the women on the original 'Night has spread her pall once more' and the men echoing 'Warders are we, whom do we ward?' as if a horn-call.

Many, though not all, of these characteristics are found in the Con moto tranquillo 'nocturne' of Mendelssohn's *Midsummer Night's Dream* music, which accompanies the enchanted sleep of the lovers that ends Act III. There are no fanfares here: Sullivan has supplemented the night music with martial passages to fit his own dramatic needs. Nonetheless, the musical similarities are remarkable: the emotive opening melody is given to a solo horn, though the strings (with high cellos) have melodic moments later; the reiterated 9/8 string chords are there soon enough; the shifting between 3/4 and 9/8 is present throughout, but is somewhat more fluid in Mendelssohn's version (so as not to awaken the lovers); the horn melody is stated again over a fuller texture, in an ABA' form; and in the coda the long leading-tone trill is isolated before its final resolution. Sullivan's *Yeomen* chorus is not a direct reworking of Mendelssohn's nocturne, but the correspondences between the two pieces suggest that Sullivan wanted to evoke a similar mood: night, perhaps even an enchanted or quasi-Shakespearean night. From there he went his own way, but not without borrowing (consciously or not) a battery of musical gestures.

The fairy music of *A Midsummer Night's Dream* was a natural model for Sullivan in *Iolanthe*, and although this has been mentioned by other writers, it has not been examined in detail.[19] Mendelssohn depicts the fairies through several distinct orchestral textures: high, rapid, transparent string writing (as at the beginning of his overture); high, rapid chordal figuration (as in the Scherzo); repeated staccato winds with pizzicato string figuration (as in the song 'You spotted snakes' at the words 'Philomel with melody'). Of course Mendelssohn did not reserve such textures exclusively for *A Midsummer Night's Dream*, and indeed his affinity with Shakespeare's play may have been the result of a stylistic predisposition for such transparent writing; in any case, they are employed so consistently in *A Midsummer Night's Dream* as to signify an intentional 'fairy' effect – and in fact Mendelssohn's usage may betray the influences of other fairy-tale works like Weber's *Oberon* (1826).

The overture to *Iolanthe* turns to Mendelssohn twice in the gossamer scherzo-like figuration beneath which Sullivan quotes the Fairy Queen's 'O, Captain Shaw' melody (albeit now transformed to 2/4 time). The chorus 'Tripping hither, tripping thither' seems to be modelled on Mendelssohn's finale 'Through this house give glim'ring light'. In both, the staccato (detached) writing is taken to an extreme ('we are dain-ty lit-tle fai-ries'), but with some legato passages: compare 'When you know us, you'll discover that we almost live on lover' with Mendelssohn's 'First rehearse the song by rote'. (Note also the 'scherzo' texture of the overture at 'Arm ourselves with lover's darts'.) The introduction to 'Strephon's a Member of Parliament', the fairy entrance in Act II, begins with a masterful reworking of Mendelssohn's 'Philomel with melody' scoring (with pizzicato strings) before turning to the 'scherzo' wind writing; when the voices enter the accompaniment becomes much more mundane. Sullivan's fairy masterpiece, however, is 'In vain to us you plead', in which the 'Philomel' scoring is maintained nearly through-out: the *moto perpetuo* pizzicato violin line above the repeated woodwind chords results in an astonishing likeness to 'You spotted snakes'.

An intriguing case of Sullivan's intertextual references is the quasi-patriotic 'He is an Englishman' in Act II of *HMS Pinafore*. Gilbert's lyrics are satirical, but Sullivan fits the Boatswain's sincere expression to a tune which seems always to have sounded somehow familiar. As I have argued elsewhere, Sullivan's melody synthesises characteristics of four musical styles perceived by Victorians to be prototypically 'English' (the Handelian Baroque, national airs in the Dibdin tradition, Victorian hymn tunes, and military marches); moreover, descriptions of the tune generally cite one of these styles as being the model.[20] The larger significance as a fountain-head in what might be termed the 'Pomp and Circumstance' style is due to Sullivan's reuse of the tune in his 'Grand National Ballet' *Victoria & Merrie England* (1897), composed to celebrate Queen Victoria's Diamond Jubilee. The work is an historical pageant, including scenes of 'Ancient Britain' and 'Christmas Revels'; the culmination, '1897 – Britain's Glory', clearly defines that glory in military terms. The dancers are attired in various military cos-tumes, and enter the stage regiment by regiment with appropriate musical accompaniment. At the entry of the Volunteers, the orchestra plays 'He is an Englishman'. Sullivan's reuse of the melody comes at a significant moment for British nationalist expression in art: 1897 was arguably the climax of the British Empire under Victoria. Sullivan's synthesis of hymn, folk and Handelian elements in the trio of a patriotic march composed for an explic-itly imperialist and royal celebration could hardly be more momentous: with this tune he prepared a place in the ears of his audience for the 'Pomp and Circumstance' style that was forming at that very moment. (Elgar's first *Pomp & Circumstance* March was premièred in 1901 to astounding popular success.)

Lasting significance

Herein is the great significance in Sullivan's cosmopolitan musical style, and his larger musical career: he helped his audience to hear music in a differ-ent way. Even in the aesthetically unprepossessing genre of comic opera, Sullivan stretched the ears of his audiences so that indigenous music could be recognised not only as having its own voice but also as an outgrowth of a larger international tradition. Sullivan's musical allusions provide precisely that grounding.

In his time Sullivan was not regarded merely as a composer, but as a public musician (in the way we might speak today of a 'public intellectual'). Even now it is difficult to situate him among his British colleagues: he does not fit naturally among the symphonists Parry, Stanford and Mackenzie, nor the church musicians Goss, Parratt and Stainer, nor his comic opera successors Cellier and German. He has American counterparts in Victor Herbert *and* John Phillip Sousa *and* Horatio Parker. Perhaps a closer comparison is Leonard Bernstein. To be sure, Sullivan was not a great educator through words (with no activity analogous to Bernstein's 'Young Peoples' Concerts'), but he was an innovative concert programmer – championing Schumann and rediscovering Schubert – in ways not unlike Bernstein's efforts for Haydn and Mahler. Notably, for both Sullivan and Bernstein – and for that matter the versatile Wynton Marsalis – their compositions have been the *most* criticised of their many musical activities. The phenomenal success of the comic operas played a part in the construction of a national musical sensibility: an audience that sat through a first-act finale at the Savoy one evening was better prepared on the next to hear an Evensong featuring the quasi-'symphonic' treatments of the Canticles in the new settings of Stainer and Stanford; Sullivan's word-setting demonstrated that English texts could effectively be set to music even outside of the walls of the church. Most importantly, his facility within a wide variety of current and historical musical styles in both his compositions and his concert programming familiarised his audience with the cosmopolitan musical scene more than any other individual before Henry Wood.

When Sullivan arrived in Leipzig to finish his studies, he looked back in astonishment at the provincialism of the accessible musical life in his homeland. He wrote to his mother on 31 October 1860 that 'it is my opinion that music as an art in England will go to the devil very soon if some few enthusiastic, practical, and capable young educated musicians do not take it in hand'.[21] When he died forty years later, he had done much to improve the situation.

10 Musical contexts II: characterisation and emotion in the Savoy operas

MARTIN T. YATES

A proper understanding of Sullivan's creative stance is central to any discussion of the musical contribution to the Savoy operas. During the course of an interview given to the *San Francisco Daily Chronicle* in 1885 he made what amounts to a 'mission statement' regarding his approach to composition for the stage. 'I adhere', he said, 'to the principles of art which I had learned in the production of more solid works, and no musician who analyses the score of those light operas will fail to find the evidence of seriousness and solidity pointed out'.[1]

The use of the word 'serious' does not mean that Sullivan wished his music to be sombre and sad, but that it should be responsive to any stimulus, whether comic or serious – he certainly did not see emotional seriousness as the antithesis of comedy. In addition a central part of his stated seriousness of purpose emerges as a belief in real emotion, which for him was intuitively linked to a sense of humanity. Expressing scepticism towards Italian, French and Wagnerian opera, he rejected the maxim that opera is of life, but larger than it. Rather he was inclined to make emotion not 'unreal and artificial' as he put it, but as real as possible – a natural reaction to credible experience. Time after time he ensures that his musical settings remain sympathetic to the characters themselves, giving them a degree of dignity even while embracing their sometimes unpleasant Gilbertian features.

The music of humanity

The fundamental values of Sullivan's art emerge from the beginning. In 1869 the young composer was attracted to the parable of the Prodigal Son. Using the Preface to the published score he gave deliberate expression to his viewpoint:

> the Prodigal himself has been conceived, not as of a naturally brutish and depraved disposition – a view taken by many commentators with apparently little knowledge of human nature, and no recollection of their own youthful impulses; but rather as a buoyant, restless youth, tired of the monotony of home, and anxious to see what lay beyond the narrow confines of his father's farm.

As if to bear out these remarks the dramatic sections of *The Prodigal Son* are altogether more successful musically than the theological choruses. A similar effect can be seen in *The Light of the World* (1873), which rejects 'the spiritual idea of the Saviour' in order to portray 'the Human aspect of the Life of Our Lord on earth'.[2] Indeed it is consideration for the earthly aspects of the story that distances Sullivan's works from the general trend of Victorian oratorio.

By the same token it was his concern with the feelings and dignity of the protagonists that eventually brought Sullivan into conflict with the increasingly 'topsy-turvy' creations of Gilbert. In the altercations that followed the production of *Princess Ida* in 1884 he forcibly expressed his need for believable characters in realistic situations, whether comic or serious. This is hardly an unreasonable stance for an operatic composer, even though it has sometimes been misunderstood. In any case the position taken was an essential part of Sullivan's artistic outlook as works outside the Gilbertian canon, like *Ivanhoe* and *Haddon Hall*, bear witness.

Local colour and characterisation

Establishing an overall characterisation is just as important as creating the characterisation of groups and individuals. A composer sets the prevailing tone, in which mood and atmosphere persuade the listener that the music belongs to one specific work and no other. 'Local colour', in this sense, was very much part of Sullivan's ethos. The preface to Victor Hugo's play *Cromwell* (1827) describes the purpose of local colour:

> It is not on the surface of the drama that local colour must lie, but at its basis in the very heart of the work, and from there it should spread to the surface of its own accord naturally, evenly, and one might say to every corner of the drama, like sap rising from the roots to the last leaf on a tree.[3]

While speaking specifically of the art of the playwright, this statement also describes the tendency of composers like Meyerbeer (in *Les Huguenots*) and, later, Verdi (in *Aida*) to use the unifying power of local colour as a basic ingredient of their work, not merely something added for effect. Sullivan was attracted to the story of the Prodigal Son in part because of the opportunities it offered for local (oriental) colour, and was to prove himself adept at creating a 'prevailing tone' which spreads 'to every corner of the drama'. *The Mikado* – with its pentatonic flavouring derived from the musical setting of 'Miya Sama' – and the historically themed *Yeomen of the Guard* are both outstanding examples of this skill. In *HMS Pinafore* the tang of the sea is evident throughout, and every bit as potent as the atmosphere evoked by Britten over seventy years later in his nautical opera *Billy Budd.*

Iolanthe is another work which benefits from local colour, albeit of a different kind. As the first notes of the overture rise from the depths of the strings, and are answered by the woodwind, seemingly whispering the name of Iolanthe, the composer evocatively conjures a world of fancy. This 'fairy' mood is maintained throughout a score in which the composer consistently reaches a high level of attainment.

Utopia Limited brings out an interesting if not always successful response from the composer. Even though set on a South Sea island, the libretto proved less of a stimulus to Sullivan than might have been imagined. There is some local colour, mainly in the opening chorus and 'Quaff the nectar', but with the arrival of the visitors from Victorian England the inhabitants of Utopia are gradually Anglicised or 'Victorianised', so Sullivan's musical dramaturgy changes in consequence.

If *Utopia Limited* offered little real stimulus in terms of local colour, *The Grand Duke* did evoke a more characteristic score from the composer, despite the fact that the libretto is totally lacking in those genuinely human feelings which he craved. Gilbert's dowdy Germanic tone is conjured in the first moments of the overture, and the opera is full of imaginative touches like the waltz song 'Pretty Lisa', the mock-Greek chorus which opens Act II, and the sunny music associated with the Prince of Monte Carlo – especially his wonderfully characterised 'Roulette' song, with its French café-style music. Ignoring the cynicism of the words, Sullivan creates a moment of real tenderness in Lisa's song 'Take care of him'.

As part of the musical 'backcloth' of each work, Sullivan's characters – however one-dimensional or 'cardboard' they might be in origin – are 'clothed in music' (Sullivan's phrase) that humanises them and makes them more substantial than the words alone would suggest. In particular Sullivan was responsible for the 'toning down' of Gilbert's more heartless effusions, especially his mockery of older women. By the same token the composer treats the lumbering British Bobby in *The Pirates of Penzance* with obvious affection and warmth. Villains are never given ugly or brutish music. The treatment of Dick Deadeye in *HMS Pinafore* suggests ugliness without being ugly in itself, and even the miserable Rudolph of *The Grand Duke* is treated with a modicum of sympathy.

In *Princess Ida*, the work which followed *Iolanthe*, the positively 'academic' feel of their music is achieved by frequent use of a moving bass line and the sequential development of phrases. The two elements coalesce in 'I am a maiden' in which Sullivan deftly shows how Hilarion, Cyril and Florian, having broken into the ladies' academic world, are now imbued with the same musical colour. Arac is afforded something more in the princely setting of 'This helmet I suppose', while even the waspish Gama is given music which reflects his character without resorting to musical ugliness.

Wilfred Shadbolt, the brutish jailor of *The Yeomen of the Guard*, was originally provided with a song, 'When jealous torments', which expresses his anger and frustration without resorting to brutish sounds. This important piece of characterisation became the victim of a cast alteration when Rutland Barrington left the Savoy and was replaced by the newcomer W. H. Denny for whom this solo may have been regarded as a little too demanding. It was not restored until a recording by the New D'Oyly Carte Company in 1993.

Melodic metamorphosis

Sullivan achieved unity in his scores by binding together the musical tone of the work through the use of local colour and the music given to the characters. At times this involved employing motifs – the Lord Chancellor's introductory fugato is an obvious example – but a more subtle technique involved the metamorphosis of themes which is evident even in a relatively early work like *HMS Pinafore*. Here Sullivan uses the traditional hornpipe as his local colour, and several of the vocal lines are influenced by its melody (Ex. 10.1). The melodic fragment (*a*) appears in the Captain's first song, while (*c*) is Sullivan's variation on (*b*)(Ex. 10.2). The melody is then extended and used for the refrain in Sir Joseph Porter's song (Ex. 10.3). This melody

Example 10.1 Traditional hornpipe

Example 10.2 *HMS Pinafore*, No. 4 Captain Corcoran's song and Chorus

Example 10.3 *HMS Pinafore*, No. 9 Sir Joseph Porter's song and Chorus

Example 10.4 *HMS Pinafore*, No. 10 Trio and Chorus

And his fist be e-ver rea-dy For a knock-down blow.

Example 10.5 *HMS Pinafore*, No. 10 Trio and Chorus

And his fist be e-ver rea-dy For a knock-down blow.

Example 10.6 *HMS Pinafore*, Act I, finale

And this should be his cus-to-ma-ry at - ti-tude,

reappears in the trio for Ralph, the Boatswain and the Carpenter, and is quoted exactly by Ralph (Ex. 10.4). However when the chorus join in the refrain the same words are fitted to a melody that has been slightly changed (Ex. 10.5). Finally this melody is repeated exactly, but to different words, in the finale to Act I (Ex. 10.6). Throughout the opera there are evocations of the hornpipe, such as the dance which follows 'Never mind the why and wherefore' and between the verses of the duet 'Kind Captain'.

Sullivan used these compositional techniques successfully in other operas with Gilbert, and with even greater impact in later works like *Ivanhoe* and *The Beauty Stone*.[4]

Characterisation through word-setting

Sullivan made sung English sound natural and inevitable, with stresses and climaxes perfectly timed to bring out the essence of the words. Though basing himself on what he called 'word-setting' – a 'one-note-per-syllable' principle – he worked with considerable freedom inside these parameters, and frequently found ingenious ways to set Gilbert's text. Generally speaking he managed so well that the words and music seem indissoluble, as with the 'What never?' joke in *HMS Pinafore* and 'No possible doubt whatever' in *The Gondoliers*. Sometimes, however, possibly due to haste or some really uncongenial piece of Gilbertism, the setting hardly gives the words a chance at all – as in 'Oh sweet surprise, Oh dear delight' (*Utopia Limited*).

Fortunately such occasions are rare, and when an inspired setting does occur the effect is bewitching.

Such a setting is that of 'The sun whose rays' in the *Mikado* second act, where the music transcends Gilbert's cynical words to produce a most beautiful and heartfelt song in which the character of Yum-Yum comes fully alive. In his own analysis of this song,[5] Sullivan first examines the short lines of the lyric in detail, then explores their rhythmical variety and, in the refrain, writes two different settings of the *same* words. He then matches this rhythmic analysis with a marvellous melody, the combination making the song distinctive. Though mainly in a major key, there is a moment when a minor-key phrase is introduced. At the words 'He don't exclaim' the change from G major to D minor – the string chords supported by a long-held oboe note – is exquisite; and at the climax the effect of the rhythmical variety in the word-setting is enhanced by the interweaving of oboe and clarinet. Sullivan wrote this song while pacing from room to room during a sleepless night. One can almost hear the effect of the moonlight.[6]

As an example of skilful word-setting in the service of characterisation during a dramatic moment we may take an incident in the first-act finale of *Iolanthe*. The Fairy Queen tells the Lord Chancellor who she is – 'Oh Chancellor unwary' – and he responds with 'A plague on this vagary'. The setting is identical for twelve bars; then, in the last five, the changes begin. The Fairy Queen's notes are smooth and connected – she is confident; the Lord Chancellor's are detached and hesitant – with several chromatic notes – giving the ending a different 'feel' as he struggles with the realisation of her identity.

Detail of this kind comes not from the words but from how the composer sets them. Sullivan lifted the ideas and words of his librettist onto a higher plane, thus ensuring an extra dimension to the emotion and characterisation.

Character development

Often a character grows musically during the course of an opera as Sullivan makes increasing demands, developing and deepening the characterisation. In *HMS Pinafore* Josephine, very much the conventional 'lass that loves a sailor', suddenly achieves musical prominence with a remarkable *scena*, 'The hours creep on apace'. This piece steadily builds through recitative and reflective passages to a tremendously operatic climax. Similarly one can follow the musical change in Patience from the carefree milkmaid who 'cannot tell what this love may be' to the much more serious and reflective person of 'Love is a plaintive song'.

In *The Yeomen of the Guard* Elsie is first presented as a shy singer of street ballads, but from then onwards appears in most of the big musical moments, and is at the forefront both dramatically and musically of all the perilous situations in the opera.

The part of the Lord Chancellor in *Iolanthe* calls for an actor/singer of great dramatic ability if the demands of the role are to be negotiated successfully. These demands range from the comedy of his first songs – especially the light airiness of 'When I went to the bar' (achieved by setting the voice in 6/8 against a 2/4 accompaniment) through the difficult but wonderfully composed 'Nightmare' song, to the pathos of the scene with Iolanthe.

Thus too does Sullivan deepen the characterisation of groups. In the madrigal 'Brightly dawns our wedding day' (*The Mikado*) the word-setting and the contrapuntal interweaving of the four voices perfectly capture the mood of regret, even though the characters are trying to be cheerful. As with 'The sun whose rays' a minor phrase mirrors the words 'What though mortal joys be hollow?' and a sequence of 'fa-la-la'. At the end, as the final 'fa-la-la's fade away to *pianissimo*, it is the music which gives depth to the characters by reflecting the true feelings of each person.

Regret is the prevailing musical mood for a quartet in the Act I finale of *The Gondoliers*. Here the two men, Marco and Giuseppe, are bidding farewell to their loved ones, Gianetta and Tessa. The verses for the two girls are particularly well handled by Sullivan to show their contrasting personalities. Short lines are again set with rhythmical variety, and the emotional impact is deepened when the men's voices join them in 'O my darling, O my pet'. On this occasion Sullivan's perfection comes close to matching that of Mozart's trio 'Soave il vento' in *Così fan tutte* without attaining that trio's ambiguity. Mozart's sincere and touching music hides the fact that the situation is ridiculous, while persuading the audience into believing it is not.

Ambiguity

On other occasions Sullivan himself proved adept at the creation of ambiguity, for example in his handling of Ko-Ko's wooing of Katisha at the end of *The Mikado*. Once again the situation is farcical, and the audience have laughed heartily at Ko-Ko's attempts to win the heart of this terrifying maiden. Had he responded to Gilbert's sado-masochistic humour the setting of 'Tit Willow' might have been a very different affair, with all sorts of 'bird' effects in the woodwind or loud trombone 'splashes' as the unhappy bird plunges into the billowy wave. Instead, by choosing a simple approach, Sullivan creates a genuinely moving moment. He is responding to the humanity of Ko-Ko's efforts to control his feelings and behave convincingly while in a state of desperate emotional turmoil, and in doing so ensures that this part of the story succeeds dramatically. Unless the effect is shattered by stage antics, the audience is persuaded that the pathetic Ko-Ko *can* win the affection of Katisha.

In *Ruddigore* the Gilbertian concept of Richard's whirlwind romance of Rose, both in the dialogue and in how the scene develops, is cynical and absurd. It is left to Sullivan's music in the duet 'The battle's roar is over' to persuade the audience that the lovers are sincere in their emotions. Sullivan, in providing a rich and serene setting, is responding to the imagery of the sea, and the idea of a 'safe haven' in love. The potent melodic pattern of a rising fourth and a falling third suggests the movement of waves, as do the vocal lines when the voices join together: 'And thou and I love'. Here the lower strings play a different wave-like pattern while the harmony includes a beautiful enharmonic change (on a D ♭/C ♯) in which a D-flat-major chord on 'sigh' becomes an E-major chord on 'love'. The coda continues the first wave pattern in the orchestra, while the calmness of the voices suggests they have reached their safe haven.

An extended scene of musical ambiguity is found in the first-act finale of *Patience*. Once again the dramatic situation is ludicrous. The maidens have deserted the poet Bunthorne, and for a fleeting moment return to their old loves, the Dragoon Guards. They sing a sextet – 'I hear the soft note'. The maidens are not really sincere in their change of affection, but the music persuades us that they are. As the music continues to weave its spell so we continue to believe, until the entrance of another poet, Grosvenor, abruptly changes the mood.[7] The sextet has been questioned as a lapse into 'churchiness' and defended as a merely wicked parody. Such comments – like the complaint that it stops the action – are beside the point. Sullivan is vindicated because the music makes the audience believe in the maidens' change of heart, thus intensifying rather than delaying the appearance of Grosvenor.

Characterisation of the chorus

Throughout the operas the collaborators were careful in their delineation of group character. Occasionally Gilbert provided jingling rhymes – for example 'Here's a man of jollity' in *The Yeomen of the Guard* – but Sullivan did much to mitigate the effect. On the whole there were few lapses where banal words were fitted with banal music,[8] and Sullivan certainly never perpetrated such a gaffe as did Stanford in *The Travelling Companion*, in

13 The Fairies have the stage to themselves in *Iolanthe*. Carl Rosa Opera 2008.

which a chorus of ordinary peasants are provided with what can only
be described as the most ordinary music. Even in *The Grand Duke*, his
final opera with Gilbert, Sullivan was able to create some interest in the
characterisation of the chorus, and Rudolph's court functionaries fulfil
their ceremonial role with style, and a rather good tune ('The good Grand
Duke of Pfennig Halbpfennig').

In preparing for the reprise of the 'heighdy' duet during the second-
act finale of *The Yeomen of the Guard*, Sullivan shows his subtlety in the
characterisation of the chorus. Point sings 'I have a song to sing, O' and the
chorus reply with 'Sing me your song-O' – fully harmonised and marked
pp. However when Elsie sings her phrase, the choral 'What is your song-O?'
is marked *ff*, with each word stressed – a telling moment of differentiation.

In his pioneering study of Sullivan's music, Gervase Hughes cites 'Comes
a train of little ladies' (*The Mikado*) as a supreme example of Gilbert and
Sullivan's happy collaboration: 'in capturing an atmosphere of youthful
femininity trembling deliciously on the threshold of womanhood'. [9] It may
be noted that Sullivan adds an extra dimension to the characterisation by
a minor phrase in a major key setting to mirror some of the words, like
'Each a little bit afraid is' and 'Are its palaces and pleasures / Fantasies that
fade?' The dotted-note rhythm given to the strings also adds its distinctive
contribution to the characterisation of this piece.

In pompous contrast the March of the Peers (*Iolanthe*) stands as one of the most impressive and sustained pieces of group characterisation achieved by Sullivan in any opera; yet even in *Iolanthe* it is matched by the delicacy with which he portrays the fairies. The finale to Act I of *Iolanthe*, in which he maintains the characterisation of both chorus and individuals, is also one of Sullivan's most significant structural achievements. Including within itself changes of tempo and 'the ebb and flow of rhythmical tension', the finale is considered by James Day to be 'the finest piece of sustained musico-dramatic construction by any British composer before Britten'.[10]

Generally speaking the treatment of the chorus in Savoy opera stands out against the contemporary trend for a 'wallpaper' chorus, employed only to add atmosphere and drama when required. It was left to Britten, nearly fifty years later, to pick up the threads, and in *Peter Grimes* to make the chorus a true protagonist of the drama.

Emotional expression

Britten's remark, 'the more simple I try to make my music, the more difficult it is to perform'[11] seems particularly apt with regard to Sullivan, who often used the simplest of means to create an emotional effect. A typical case is the duet 'I have a song to sing, O!' in *The Yeomen of the Guard*. It is well known how much trouble the setting of this duet caused the composer, particularly because he was aware of the dramatic and musical significance of its place in the opera:

> I was awfully nervous, and continued so until the duet 'Heighdy' which settled the fate of the opera! Its success was tremendous; three times encored!![12]

Had the composer failed here, the end of the opera, where the duet reappears, would not have had the same emotional impact. Yet the simplicity of the setting – mainly two chords and a drone bass – is not only apposite for letting the melody expand to match the increasing complexity of the words, it also allows the composer to develop the melody and its rhythmical impulse during the coda which forms the climax to the opera, thus providing the work with its emotionally dramatic ending. The skill of Sullivan in finding the right music for the right situation has been recognised by Nigel Burton:

> The greatness of *The Yeomen of the Guard* lies in its profound humanity; Point was the finest of Gilbert's creations and Sullivan never wrote more touching music than that which depicts the terrible fatality of the Jester's dilemma.[13]

Burton is thinking especially of the quartet 'When a wooer goes a wooing' in which Sullivan's poignant melody, his expressive use of the D-flat major key, and subtle chromatics all emphasise the pathos of the situation. Both Point and Phoebe have been alienated by the romance of Elsie and Fairfax – Phoebe's distancing is achieved musically by the use of C-sharp minor for her verse – and the change of mood from the much lighter previous trio ('A man who would woo a fair maid') is skilfully achieved by Sullivan. The characters do not act in a frenzied or hysterical way, and the drama seems more powerful because of their restraint.

The character of Phoebe greatly appealed to the composer, and he gave her some of the most heartfelt music in *The Yeomen of the Guard*. Her opening song, 'When maiden loves', shows how carefully he delineates her feelings. Here is a young girl, more or less engaged to Shadbolt the jailor, but dreaming of being in love with the handsome Colonel Fairfax. The way Sullivan sets the words and builds an evocative orchestration of pizzicato chords and suggestive spinning phrases on the violas gives the song a wistful yearning quality rather than a positively 'in love' exultation. The most telling moments occur when the 'spinning' phrases cease, and words like ''Tis but a little word – heigh ho!' are set more freely (they are marked *meno mosso*) allowing the 'heigh ho!' to be stressed by the unaccompanied singer. Sullivan also makes use of the technique employed in 'The sun whose rays', in which certain phrases are repeated but in a slightly different setting. In this instance the words 'Lies hidden in a maid's "Ah me!"' are repeated to form the expressive coda.[14]

There are several layers of dramatic intention in Phoebe's second song, 'Were I thy bride'. The song is used to persuade another character, Shadbolt, that she is sincere in her feelings towards him – the beauty of the setting belies the fact that it is a sham, and Phoebe is not sincere at all. As Phoebe delivers the *coup de grâce* – 'I'm *not* thy bride' – it is very difficult not to feel a pang of sympathy for him, because the music has succeeded in wooing the audience as well as Shadbolt. The anti-climax is all the greater because with these final words this lovely song comes to an end.[15]

The funeral march in the first-act finale is finely felt and developed by the composer, though not with Wagnerian strength. Fairfax is no Siegfried – the requirement is to portray the impending doom of a prisoner, not the death of a hero. Sullivan sets the tone exactly, and the prayer for Elsie which follows the march expresses her sadness without becoming too forceful – she has never actually seen the condemned man, even though she is married to him!

The finale to Act II abounds in contrasting emotions. The serene opening chorus, 'Comes the pretty young bride', is followed by the thoughtful trio for Elsie, Phoebe and Dame Carruthers where, again, the use of D minor at the words 'Some lurking bitter we shall find' in an F major setting adds a slight sense of melancholy. This is soon justified as the calm is shattered by the disclosure that Elsie's husband still lives. Sullivan allows a frenzied outburst, 'Oh, day of terror', in which the communal shock of the announcement is mirrored in the music. Elsie's moving plea which follows is changed to joy as she discovers that the unwelcome 'husband' is in fact the man she loves.

A similar richness of emotional response is to be found in many episodes of *Iolanthe*, especially in the music for Iolanthe herself. From the moment she emerges from the stream – her words surrounded by a halo of muted strings – to her final impassioned plea to the Lord Chancellor, Sullivan shows a deep empathy for her character and the situation in which she finds herself. Sullivan excelled in his setting of her song 'He loves', and the second verse, where the voice is supported by tremolando strings alone, rises to an intense and passionate climax.

The plangency of this song is maintained throughout the following scene, and every heartfelt moment leads the listener more deeply into the drama. The Lord Chancellor's almost offhand rejection of Iolanthe's plea makes her self-sacrifice inevitable, while the fairies' cries of 'Forbear, forbear' add to the sense of desperation. Finally, as Iolanthe declares 'I am thy wife', the fairies break into a wailing cry in which their descending notes are matched by ascending phrases on the violins. Even the Wagnerian overtones of the Queen's pronouncements are skilfully woven into the musical fabric without incongruity. The whole scene shows a true operatic composer responding to the emotional situation with prodigious skill.

Wanton perfection

There are many occasions when, in the process of providing an extra dimension to the emotion, Sullivan's genius carried him beyond Gilbert's words into what may be termed, using Nietzsche's striking phrase, moments of 'wanton perfection'.[16] Four such moments may stand as *pars pro toto*.

Amidst the librettist's rather conventional layout lies the melodic purity of the duet between Mabel and Frederick, 'Ah! Leave me not to pine' in the second act of *The Pirates of Penzance*. Scored for voices and strings alone, the major-key melody is unexpected but utterly right for this poignant moment. One would have expected a minor key here, but as Gluck showed in 'Che farò', the major key can be just as effective. For a brief moment the characters spring into life, and we can believe the sincerity of their emotions as expressed through the music.

A second moment is the duet 'There was a time' for Casilda and Luiz in *The Gondoliers*. Having just engaged in a dialogue of Gilbertian silliness, the two characters are transformed by the beauty and inner warmth of the music. The key of F-sharp major is unusual for Sullivan. But it allows him to make an expressive modulation to D major during the singers' repetition of 'Ah woe is me!' At this moment the quavers of the first lines are extended into crotchets which give a rhythmic and melodic emphasis to such words as 'One heart, one life, one soul'. 'Oh bury bury', where the voices join, is intensified by the steady tread of the woodwind and the passionate tremolando of the strings. This leads towards the moving climax of a beautiful and heartfelt duet which emphasises the real emotion of the characters.

The finale to Act I of *The Gondoliers* provides two striking examples. At the beginning of the finale, 'Kind sir you cannot have the heart' stands out as a moment of real tenderness. The apposite word-setting, the beautiful melody and the orchestral support all fit together so exactly that it is hard to say which is the more effective. As a result the character of Gianetta gains a depth of feeling not previously in evidence. Sir Jack Westrup has described this song as 'one of the most perfect things of its kind in the literature of song'.[17]

In the concluding moments of this finale all the elements of Sullivan's genius come together in a spectacular way: his immaculate word-setting, his melodic richness, his use of local colour, his skilful construction and his unerring sense of theatrical effectiveness – all supported by masterly orchestration. As the four unaccompanied voices finish their sensitive phrases 'Do not forget you've married me' Sullivan changes the mood and tempo in preparation for the moment when the girls bid farewell to the men and send them on their way to the 'island fair'. In transforming Gilbert's words Sullivan floods the scene with music of utter beauty – tinged with a mixture of rejoicing and regret. As the curtain descends, the music, now marked *largamente*, continues in a richly scored and sensuously beautiful seascape, suffused with Mediterranean warmth.[18] It would be hard to find a comparable moment in the whole of English operatic literature.

New perspectives

While Sullivan may not have regarded the Savoy operas as his main *modus operandi*, he nevertheless gave the greatest care to their composition and endowed them with the same 'inner warmth' which permeates so much of his music. The writing of opera with spoken dialogue was more or less forced on him by a long British tradition, but he deserves to be afforded the same consideration shown to other operatic composers rather than be regarded as a purveyor of light and simplistic music. By the same token the works written with other librettists, and the cantatas (which contain much 'operatic' work), are well worth investigation because they show the very skills which Sullivan brought to the works with Gilbert, sometimes, as in *Ivanhoe*, on a much larger scale. Future musicological research needs to fully investigate these compositional techniques in order that Sullivan's significant accomplishment can be understood and valued.

Above all the appreciation of Sullivan's achievement requires that performances should be based on the complete uncut full scores, with 'lost' numbers reinstated. Musical values must be a priority, with attention shown to the detail of vocal lines and orchestration. The modern practice of introducing celebrity performers who cannot sing or even act[19] is damaging in this respect, as is the habit of relying on vocal scores which frequently bear no relation to the true sound-world created by the composer.

Sullivan the true man of the theatre was of course fortunate to find a collaborator of genuine talent, but it is Sullivan the artist who sets the tone of the operas and supplies the grounding for the expression of emotion and character. In doing so he provides everything that the composer *should* provide in the creation of stageworthy opera.

PART III

Reception

11 *Topsy-Turvy*: a personal journey

MIKE LEIGH

All modern art is ridiculous: what is the point of a painting if it doesn't look like anything? Picasso couldn't draw a straight line; how can you have poetry that doesn't rhyme? Proust is boring, Dickens verbose, Samuel Beckett pretentious. Schoenberg is an ugly cacophony; Brecht is all propaganda and no drama; Bergman relentless doom and gloom. Diane Arbus was nothing more than a voyeuristic pervert, Bob Dylan is an overgrown teenager with nothing to say, and the Marx Brothers aren't funny.

Philistinism has many causes. Ignorance, of course. Fear of the unknown. Fear of the over-familiar. Snobbery. Stunted antennae, absence of a sense of humour, spiritual blindness and deafness; notions of art and culture as fashionable gesture rather than reflection of life or expression of truth; inability to pay attention; the need to hide behind a safe position. And a lack of joy of the soul – of generosity.

Thus, Gilbert and Sullivan operas are a load of outdated camp nonsense – dead fossils of a remote Victorian age. Gilbert's plots are superficial and mechanical, his characters mere puppets – ciphers; his lyrics are doggerel, his rhymes contrived and excruciating, his characters sexless. And his world view is insular and prudish, and devoid of life.

As for Sullivan, he never wrote an original tune – everything was derivative pastiche. His music is either humdrum, repetitive rum-ti-tum or church music with bells on. In short, he has nothing to commend him, and is best left to the oblivion of the vast, barren English musical desert that lies between Purcell and Elgar.

All in all, the works of Gilbert and Sullivan are smug and twee, and pander to the simplistic philistinism of the mindless 'safe' English middle classes. And, in any case, they can't decide whether they are operas or musicals.

Yet we know that Sullivan was a highly original and inventive composer of great breadth, depth and skill, with a capacity to express life's joys and pain as great as that of Mendelssohn or Mahler. (And that conclusion could almost be reached on the evidence of the Savoy operas alone, although it shouldn't.)

We know, too, that Gilbert, apart from being the greatest lyricist in the English language, could scale unquestionable poetic heights. This he certainly achieved with a profundity of which those other two classic

Victorian comic writers, Edward Lear and Lewis Carroll, were quite incapable. Yet Carroll is even honoured in Poets' Corner in Westminster Abbey – a privilege consistently denied Gilbert on the grounds of his superficiality.

Gilbert and Sullivan were consummate craftsmen. Each understood his medium, and together they displayed an exemplary capacity to write specifically to the strengths of their company, both theatrically and musically. Sullivan's mastery of the orchestra, of individual instruments, of the needs of singers and of musical architecture, was matched by Gilbert's impeccable control of the theatrical unities. The panâche he displays as he spins his far-fetched yarns derives from his assured sense of structure. He is, in short, a great story-teller, with a capacity to bring elegance and simplicity to material that, in lesser hands, might have been vulgar, cluttered and clumsy.

Yet objections to their work persist, always ignoring its enduring popularity over 130 years. Highbrow snobbery accounts for much of it, but there is also a very specific form of philistinism at work here. Your standard vehement loather of Savoy opera will inevitably be the victim of stale, unimaginative and inept productions, both professional and amateur, or of pompous elderly relations and schoolmates, who sang badly and incessantly; or of hideous memories of the ignominy of playing members of the opposite sex in school productions of dubious motivation.

Humour and lightness of touch do not preclude gravity, as this writer can testify. Our philistine detractors would of course tell us that they would not disagree with this in principle; they would merely insist that the particular problem with Gilbert and Sullivan is an endemic facetiousness.

Obviously, this complaint is primarily aimed at Gilbert. How can one take seriously a puppet-show in which characters instantly metamorphose into somebody else, or exchange their identity merely by the arbitrary intervention of external forces, be they potions or lozenges, or spontaneously altered rules and laws? Of course Sullivan himself was apparently afflicted by this reservation about Gilbert's work, but, if he really did think this, he failed to see the wood for the trees, as do the detractors.

W. S. Gilbert took life extremely seriously. As I say in my introduction to *The Complete Gilbert and Sullivan* (Penguin Classics 2006):

> Gilbert saw the world as a chaotic place, in which our lives are brutal accidents of birth, fate and human blunder, a jungle of confusion and delusion, where we all aspire to be other than what we are, and where nobody is really who or what they seem to be.
>
> Power. Status. Rank. Duty. Hypocrisy and affectation. Youth and old age. Gilbert's obsessions inform all these operas, his greatest being the arbitrary nature of society's rules and regulations. He was a failed barrister in his

youth and a lay magistrate in his old age. He loved the English legal world, not least for its theatricality, and he himself was compulsively litigious. But, for all his appearance of the very model of conservative respectability, his merciless lampooning of the heartless constraints of laws and etiquette reveal him, underneath it all, to have been a genuine free spirit and a true anarchist. Doubtless he would have denied these descriptions, but his subversive tendencies are beyond dispute, and he could hardly have been called a conformist.

The two principal elements of all Savoy Operas are law and identity. Actual magic crops up in only three of them, but material change, caused by supernatural intervention, is only a variation on the manipulation of laws and rules.

If a key to understanding the operas is to see Gilbert as an anarchist, it may also be useful to approach them as the work of a proto-surrealist. With great fluidity and freedom, he continually challenges our natural expectations. He makes bizarre things happen, and turns the world on its head. Thus, the Learned Judge marries the Plaintiff, the soldiers metamorphose into aesthetes, and so on, and nearly every opera is resolved by a deft moving of the goalposts.

Sullivan's mortal sin is often identified as frivolity rather than facetiousness. Other complaints revolve around his uninventive repetitiveness, and in his inability to furnish Gilbert's words with anything more than fancy wrapping. All of which is, again, the precise opposite of the truth. In fact, he displays an endless capacity for challenging and subverting Gilbert's material, taking us on quite unpredictable journeys.

With every piece of art or culture, the public is divided into three camps: those who love, those who hate, and those who neither know nor care. In the case of Gilbert and Sullivan today there has grown up an unusual extremity in all these positions. So one of my many intentions in making *Topsy-Turvy* was to confront the expectations of each faction.

For a proportion of the uninitiated general public, both in and beyond the UK, the discovery of Gilbert and Sullivan through seeing the film came as a minor revelation and a pleasant surprise, and I would like to think that to some extent general interest in the operas grew as a result. These things are hard to measure, but, for example, the range and quality, not to mention the very presence, of new and classical Gilbert and Sullivan CDs grew noticeably after the film's success, not least at the Oscars.

Ten years on, apart from a wide range of stage productions, there is a remarkable amount of Gilbert and Sullivan and related material to be found on the internet in general, on which, at the time of writing, there are nearly 150 dedicated sites. On YouTube in particular, there are nearly 300 items. These range from numerous extracts from all fourteen operas, including *Thespis*, to nine renderings of Sullivan's part song 'The Long Day Closes' (including one by a Spanish choir), and a four-year-old boy singing Tom Lehrer's 'The Elements' to the tune of 'A Modern Major-General'.

One of *Topsy-Turvy*'s central tasks is to make us look at Gilbert and Sullivan's work within the context of their personal and professional lives, stripping it of its accumulated baggage of coy whimsy, instead revealing its true spirit – bold, clear and robust.

This seems to have had something of a positive effect on many detractors, although inevitably the diehards remain entrenched. But it has been heartening to hear of many yielding concessions in the vein of 'I normally hate Gilbert and Sullivan, but I found myself warming to it, in spite of . . .'. However, my intentions, such as they are, regarding the Gilbert and Sullivan fans, are best considered within an analysis of all *Topsy-Turvy*'s motives and objectives.

Of all the various subversions at work in the film, the first was the act of making it at all, confronting all expectations of a film by me – gritty, realistic film-maker tackles chocolate-box subject! – as well as expectations of a film about Gilbert and Sullivan – chocolate-box subject gets gritty, realistic treatment!

Another subversion was of the so-called bio-pic, although plainly *Topsy-Turvy* is no such thing, either conceptually or structurally. It drops anchor in 1884–5, and stays there, only dealing with the events of those fifteen months. Its ancestor, Launder and Gilliat's *Story of Gilbert and Sullivan* (1953) is very much a conventional bio-pic, covering forty years (1869–1907).

But *Topsy-Turvy* deliberately subverts inevitable bio-pic expectations; the audience de-codes the film as though it was a bio-pic, and it has frequently been referred to as one in the press.

Only twice in the film do I deploy sub-captions. The first, at the beginning, reads, 'London, January 5th 1884'; the second, exactly half-way through, announces, 'February 12th 1885. News reaches London of the killing of General Gordon by the Mahdi's troops at Khartoum.' Yet this device, sparingly used as it is, together with the inclusion of a few key actual events – two first nights, the sword falling off the wall, the Mikado's song conflict – serve to create the illusion of a bio-pic narrative. In other words, we borrow from the convention.

To some extent inspired by Gilbert himself, my preference usually is to contain the overall dramatic action within a limited time-frame, notwithstanding the inherently flexible nature of cinematic time. This liberates me to explore character, rather than committing me to having to deal with sprawling, diffuse narrative for its own sake.

However, the primary reason for choosing not to make *Topsy-Turvy* a bio-pic was simply that the events of 1884–5 make for a very good story. No doubt an action-packed epic could be made out of the subterfuge surrounding the two simultaneous first nights of *The Pirates of Penzance* in New York and Paignton, Devon; but, quite apart from the prohibitive cost of such a film, Gilbert, Sullivan and D'Oyly Carte's relationship in 1879 was still too harmonious to be dramatically interesting. Conversely, there was the legendary Carpet Quarrel a decade later, but by this time the relationship was positively dysfunctional, and in any case this is a dry tale of money and litigation, unrelated directly to artistic endeavour or theatrical presentation.

By contrast the *Mikado* story cried out to be a film, with the bonus that the opera itself is the most popular of the series. Major themes were there to be exploited – masks and reality, integrity and the struggle of the artist, relationships, work. From Sullivan's winter illness and his decision to quit, through the failure of *Princess Ida* and the heatwave, the revival of *The Sorcerer*, the collapse of the triumvirate and the arrival of the Japanese Village, culminating in the preparations for, and the success of *The Mikado* itself, the potential was rich, dramatically and cinematically, with great scope for a visual and musical feast.

This aim, to make a sumptuous, exotic period film on a low budget, con-stituted *Topsy-Turvy*'s one other subversive objective. I have already referred to the notion of viewing an apparently chocolate-box subject through the sharp lens of reality, but I was also concerned to subvert the English period costume drama itself. This arose from my severe distaste for the genre, not least its unintelligent, stilted acting style.

Which brings us to the final reason for avoiding the bio-pic. I hate the convention of actors on film ageing over decades. It quite prevents us from suspending our disbelief. By staying within one relatively short time-frame, the actors can settle into a total reality, and we are undistracted by the mechanics of their performances. And, by glorious coincidence, in 1998 both Jim Broadbent and Allan Corduner were respectively exactly the same ages as Gilbert and Sullivan in 1885.

Although the main through-line of *Topsy-Turvy*'s drama hangs on the fate of Gilbert and Sullivan's collaboration, much of the film works by cumulative rather than causal narrative – that is, character-driven action evoking spirit and atmosphere. The rehearsal scenes; Gilbert wishing Lucy goodnight; the costume fittings; actors in their dressing-rooms; Gilbert at the dentist; Sullivan visiting a Paris brothel.

A substantial proportion of this material is total invention, albeit sug-gested by and drawn from painstaking research. The commitment was to create an accurate, if subjective, picture of Gilbert and Sullivan's world. For it is subjective – unapologetically so. It is a highly personal, fact-based poetic piece, deriving initially from my own fascination with the Savoy operas and their authors, as well as my long professional life in the theatre. It is also my

14 Jim Broadbent and Allan Corduner as Gilbert and Sullivan in *Topsy-Turvy*.

response to the shadow still cast by the Victorian Age on the lives of all of us born in the middle of the twentieth century.

Manchester is a great Victorian city. To grow up there after World War II was still to live in an inescapably Victorian environment. The nineteenth century hung in the recent air. We were surrounded by Victorian architecture, from the dark, satanic mills that still blackened the skies and pumped multi-coloured toxic effluent into the River Irwell, to neo-Gothic exotica like Waterhouse's beautiful Town Hall of 1887.

Many of us lived in Victorian houses. In Salford, we walked Dickensian cobbled streets, played in Victorian parks with cast-iron bandstands (sometimes sporting bands grinding out Gilbert and Sullivan), and we went to school in Victorian buildings. There we were taught by Victorian people, with late Victorian and Edwardian memories and attitudes, like our grandparents.

We studied nineteenth-century history, we read Victorian literature, and nineteenth-century music accompanied our lives. Manchester has a great musical heritage. It was the birthplace of the Hallé Orchestra and the Northern School of Music, and Sullivan visited and was performed there in his early twenties. The city's musical activity was still vibrant in the 1950s. Sections of the Hallé visited our schools, the amateur operatic movement was strong, as were the brass bands, and the annual five-week visit of the D'Oyly Carte Opera Company to the Manchester Opera House was always an instant sell-out.

I was taken to see *The Mikado* there at the age of six in 1949. I was instantly hooked. By the time I left home to go to London at seventeen to throw myself into what turned out to be the crazy, creative, avant-garde Swinging Sixties, I knew the Savoy operas backwards. I could recite the *Bab Ballads*, and I'd read Gilbert's *Original Plays*. Leslie Baily's *Gilbert and Sullivan Book* was my bible, I'd sung *The Long Day Closes* in the school choir, I'd given my bridesmaid in *Trial by Jury* (on the same bill), as well as my Duke of Plaza-Toro in a competition at the Manchester Branch of the national Gilbert and Sullivan Society. And every February was dominated by as many D'Oyly Carte shows as I could wangle.

In short, like thousands of others, I had become your typical G & S fan. What a curious breed we are: healthily devoted to the operas, yet often secretive about our passion in many a social context. And what joy when one stumbles across a fellow conspirator! The sheer delight of a spontaneous sing-song, or the exchange of Gilbertianisms!

Occasionally one unearths pockets of lively communal Gilbert and Sullivan activity in surprising places. One night in the late 1960s I found myself, quite by chance, at the Manchester Press Club, after hours. This was an annual all-night booze-up, consisting of all the male members of the visiting D'Oyly Carte, together with their rehearsal pianist, leading the journalists, compositors and other print workers through most of the Savoy repertoire. Lubricated by much ale and thick cheese-and-onion sandwiches, Gilbert's lyrics were interpreted with gloriously disgusting innuendoes, and some naughtily rewritten versions that were obviously a secret D'Oyly Carte tradition. It was great fun. On several occasions I have heard 'Tit-Willow' rendered beautifully by folk-singers, and I have it on good authority that rousing Gilbert and Sullivan choruses have been heard in the working-class pubs of Republican West Belfast.

I myself sat on this private passion over the many years of writing and directing my plays and films. Enjoyment of the operas grew with the progression from disc to cassette to CD, which afforded an ever-widening range of recordings. Most importantly, one could now discover Sullivan's wider oeuvre. From time to time I would catch a post-D'Oyly Carte production, such as Tyrone Guthrie's *Pinafore* and *Pirates*, which were impressively natural and un-camp; Frank Hauser's *Iolanthe* at Sadlers Wells, which was neither, Joe Papp's glorious *Pirates*, Jonathan Miller's inspired ENO *Mikado*, and Ken Russell's excruciating and deeply irresponsible *Princess Ida*, also at ENO.

One exotic feature of Victorian Manchester that survived into the 1950s was Shudehill, an ancient, sloping street of second-hand bookshops and stalls, now long gone. By the time I was twelve I had acquired my life-time addiction. I had begun with 1880s copies of *Punch*, for a mere sixpence each, and progressed to books related to Victorian life and theatre in general, and Gilbert and Sullivan in particular – a library that has, of course, grown ever since.

The idea of a film about Gilbert and Sullivan inevitably gestated over the years. But as I found my own voice and style, with my natural commitment to character-driven, contemporary tragi-comic social observation, it never seemed an appropriate scheme to pursue. Apart from any artistic, thematic or political considerations, it remained to be seen whether I would really have anything to say through such a film, let alone whether anyone would back it. But by the early 1990s I had begun to realise its serious potential, and my producer Simon Channing Williams agreed that we should explore the possibility in earnest. However, the big question was, who could play Gilbert and Sullivan?

Then, one freezing day in January 1992, we were shooting a short film called *A Sense of History* for Channel 4. Jim Broadbent had written this as a monologue for himself, and I had agreed to direct it. Half-way through a take, as Jim strode through a snow-covered farmyard as the appalling 23rd Earl of Leete, I had a clairvoyant flash. Of course! Jim could and must play W. S. Gilbert! I shared the thought with him soon afterwards, and he was very excited. But it was to be five years before *Topsy-Turvy* would happen.

Since 1965 I had developed my organic method of creating contemporary original dramas without scripts, through extensive discussion, research and improvisation, working with my actors over long periods of preparation. Now I was going to be confronted not only by my first period piece but also, for the first time, by working from extant historical material.

Having made the very contemporary *Naked*, and knowing that the Gilbert and Sullivan film was a possibility, I decided to conduct an undercover experiment in the guise of a stage play I now created for the newly restored Victorian Theatre Royal, Stratford East, previously home to Joan Littlewood's Theatre Workshop.

This was *It's A Great Big Shame!* which took its title from the song made famous by the great music hall comedian Gus Elen (1862–1940), best remembered for *The 'Ouses In Between*. The first act dramatised the song, which concerns the huge drayman bullied by his diminutive shrewish wife. It was set in 1893, the second act taking place 100 years later, in the same house.

The experiment was successful. Clearly, it was possible, with time and patient research, for authentic Victorian language and behaviour to be achieved truthfully and organically by intelligent actors.

With regard to dramatising in this mode real historical figures and events, my assumption, later confirmed, was that the answer would lie in absorbing the facts into the bloodstream, so to speak. We would then create our characters and explore their situations as though they were fictitious, except that our narrative choices would be informed by the facts.

By 1997 Simon had raised the money, albeit with much difficulty. Whilst we were making two further films (*Secrets and Lies* and *Career Girls*), preparations for the Gilbert and Sullivan film continued seriously. We hired a researcher, and set about casting ninety actors, fifty of whom could really sing or play musical instruments. *Topsy-Turvy* contains no tricks: each actor is really doing it.

After considerable anxiety over who would play Sullivan, it became clear that Allan Corduner was the only first-class actor qualified for the job. Apart from looking reasonably like the composer, Allan is a consummate pianist, and I exploit every opportunity to show him actually tinkling the ivories.

The whole of 1998 was spent rehearsing and shooting *Topsy-Turvy*. Everybody on both sides of the camera immersed themselves enthusiastically not only into Gilbert and Sullivan and their world, but into every aspect of Victorian life – history, politics, morality, religion, education, economics, transport, literature, music, art, dance, newspapers, magazines, food, etiquette; and above all, theatre and language – formal and popular.

The film was mostly shot in a disused school and an old house near Watford. The Savoy scenes were shot at the Richmond Theatre in West London, the oyster scene at the Institute of Directors in Pall Mall, and the Japanese Village was built in a studio.

The film cost a meagre £10 m. This is remarkable, as it looks far more expensive, thanks to the extraordinary resourcefulness of my team, two of whom won Oscars. The world première was at the Venice Film Festival on 3 September 1999. Jim Broadbent won Best Actor. My Director's Statement in the Festival Notes read:

> *Topsy-Turvy* is a film about all of us who suffer and strain to make other people laugh.
>
> Gilbert and Sullivan dominated the musical theatre in the English-speaking world of a hundred years ago, and I have always been fascinated not only by their personalities but by the way in which they and their collaborators fought and struggled to produce such harmonious, delightful and profoundly trivial material.
>
> The film is an attempt to evoke their world, and to bring it to life. For me, it is also somehow a last chance to glance briefly over my shoulder at the quickly receding past, before embarking on the imminent journey into the new century.

The film is, first and foremost, a celebration of Gilbert and Sullivan. We savour Gilbert's language through his verse and dialogue, from his legendary repartee, and from sections of his and Sullivan's correspondence, which I have stitched into the dialogue of the film.

A sense of Gilbert's style also informs my live dialogue. Writing by collaboration through rehearsal with the actors, as I always do, I kept a wide range of Victorian reference constantly by my side; but the text I found most useful was *The Savoy Operas*.

Topsy-Turvy explodes with Sullivan. Our aim was to treat the audience to a wide range of his festive palette. Apart from the extracts from the three shows, Carl Davis in his score managed to includes themes from all but two of the operas (*Trial by Jury* and *Utopia Limited*), as well as *The Long Day Closes* and the incidental music to *The Merchant of Venice*.

Topsy-Turvy: The film

Notes, scene by scene

Page numbers in brackets refer to the published *Topsy-Turvy* screenplay.

Scene 1: Front credits

The girls sing 'So please you, sir, we much regret' (*The Mikado*, Act I). An *hors d'oeuvre* to whet the palate. Piano accompaniment rather than full orchestra immediately suggests the working environment. (Page 3)

Scene 2: The theatre

By 1884 the tradition had grown up for the 'Gods' at the Savoy to fill up an hour or so before first nights. Working-class fans would lustily sing favourite numbers from the previous operas. My original intention was for this to be the action of the title sequence. Accordingly, one bright, warm Saturday in August 1998 we filled the balcony of the Richmond Theatre with enthusiastic members of several amateur societies, appropriately dressed and made up as Victorian proletariat. They all knew their Gilbert and Sullivan, and could break out instantly into any number we asked for. We filmed a selection, but were particularly impressed with 'Hail Poetry' from the *Pirates*.

We were delighted. But when we looked at the rushes a couple of days later, we were horrified. The camera never tells lies. Through no fault of their own, our confident, ebullient middle-class amateur singers, all sporting glowing late twentieth-century holiday tans, were utterly unbelievable as working-class Londoners who had traipsed across town in open-topped omnibuses on a snowy night in 1884!!

I reluctantly cut this action, salvaging only the front part of the shot where the camera cranes up, now in silence, through the empty auditorium. Originally you could hear the singing as the camera moved up towards it. (Page 4)

Scene 3: Sullivan's apartment

Sullivan did leave his sick bed to conduct the first performance of *Princess Ida*. His kidney condition, alleviated here by a shot of morphine, was incurable in the nineteenth century, and eventually killed him. His man, Louis Jaeger, was German; Clotilde Raquet, his maid, was Belgian. (Page 4)
   *Music cue 1: *The Yeomen of the Guard* – the 'Private Buffoon' theme from the overture.

Scene 4: Street

In the brougham. Owing to impecuniosity there are only two exterior scenes in the film. At one stage, we planned lots, including Gilbert aboard his yacht, and Sullivan at the races. (Page 5)
   *Music cue 2: *The Yeomen of the Guard* – the 'Wooer goes a-wooing' theme from the overture.

Scene 5: Backstage

Helen: Helen Lenoir (Helen Cowper-Black, 1852–1913) was D'Oyly Carte's assistant. She married him on 12 April 1888 and ran the company before World War I.
   Frank: François Cellier (1849–1914). Sullivan's musical director and conductor. (Page 6)

Scene 6: Theatre

Sullivan conducts the overture to *Princess Ida*. Note the long shot of our healthy gallery folk. They will crop up from time to time, but not singing! Sullivan conducted sitting down, as was the custom in the nineteenth century. (Page 6)

Scene 7: Stage

In the wings. An armourer had been imported from Paris. (Page 7)

Scene 8: Corridor

Leading Victorian actors had their dressers sit outside their dressing rooms, on sentry-go. The call-boy at the Savoy was actually nicknamed 'Shrimp'. (Page 7)

Scene 9: Stage

'If you give me your attention', etc. Straight to the essence of Gilbert and Sullivan with one of the great patter songs. Stage designs and blockings are all as per the original productions of *Princess Ida*, *The Sorcerer* and *The Mikado*. (Page 8)

Scene 10: Green Room

Gilbert and the Armourer. Said to have really happened. Presumably somebody else was there, as the Armourer went straight back to Paris. Otherwise this leaves only Gilbert's word! (Page 9)

Scene 11: Backstage

Sullivan did collapse, and the Dr Lynch referred to was the Savoy Theatre doctor. We do not know if he attended the first night of *Princess Ida*. (Page 9)

Scene 12: Gilbert's house

The review read out by Gilbert was edited by me from several sources. Gilbert's portrait was based on photographs of him on his yacht. Lucy was in the habit of riding in Rotten Row on a fine morning. (Page 10)

Scene 13: Sullivan's bedroom

In making his avowal at this point to write grand opera, was Sullivan aware that in *Princess Ida* he had just composed his richest grand operatic score in the series so far? (Page 11)
   *Music cue 3: *The Long Day Closes*. Part song by Sullivan (1868).

Scene 14: Gilbert's bedroom

The Gilberts were childless. Regarding Gilbert himself, his sexual side is something of an enigma. Lucy Gilbert (*née* Turner, 1847–1936) was, however, a devoted wife, but there is little to indicate her personality, so for the most part, Lesley Manville and I made her up. But we did find the following anecdote quite useful. During World War I somebody asked her whether she found life difficult now that Sir William was dead. She replied that she didn't find it half so difficult as she had when he was alive.

Note the photograph of the real W. S. Gilbert on the table. The philosophical debate this provoked on the set about the nature of screen reality persuaded me to use it. (Page 13)

*Music cue 4: *The Yeomen of the Guard* – ''Tis said that joy in full perfection' from the finale, Act II.

Scene 15: Sullivan's drawing room

Weber's Piano Duet For Four Hands, op. 10, was very popular. Weber's inspiration to Sullivan is self-evident.

Mary Frances Ronalds (*née* Carter, 1839–1911) was a Bostonian. Married, but separated, she met Sullivan in Paris in 1867, and became his mistress from around 1870, by which time she had moved to London with her children. She became one of an élite of influential American women in London society. She refers here to another of these, Jennie Churchill (1854–1921), wife of Lord Randolph and mother of Winston. Lady Colin Campbell (1857–1911), whose article she quotes, would become notorious in the 1890s as the central player in a scandalous divorce case. Unbelievably, the judge instructed the jury to visit her house in Cadogan Place, S.W., to ascertain whether it was feasible for a male servant to have looked through the keyhole of a door, and seen her having sex on the floor. (Page 14)

Scene 16: Brothel

Sullivan is known to have visited high-class Parisian brothels. Our research unearthed the practice at these establishments of small obscene *tableaux* performed privately for select clients. Keen to include a little Offenbach somewhere in the film, I thought it would be fun to use here the Clockwork Doll song ('Les oiseaux dans la charmille') from *The Tales of Hoffman*. (Page 16)

Scene 17: Theatre

Gilbert seldom watched his performances. Lucy did so on his behalf, and reported back. The inaccurate absence of the chorus and other principals on stage is again due to our impecuniosity. We could not afford the necessary costumes. (Page 19)

Scene 18: Dressing room

Richard Temple (1847–1912) and Durward Lely (1852–1944) had both studied singing in Milan. By way of research Kevin McKidd unearthed Lely's unpublished autobiography in the local library of Lely's home town of Arbroath. This led to a surviving elderly lady, who gave Kevin a tiger's tooth talisman given in turn to her by Lely's son in the 1950s. Lely always wore it round his neck for luck on stage at the Savoy in the 1880s, and Kevin is actually wearing it in the film.

Similarly, the Royal College of Music lent us one of Sullivan's batons. However, Allan Corduner found it a little too heavy, so he conducts on screen with a lighter reproduction.

It is unlikely that Gilbert had Dick Deadeye speak with a Portsmouth accent in *HMS Pinafore*. Dramatic licence. (Page 20)

Scene 19: Gilbert's house

Note the collection of blue-and-white pottery on the shelves. A reference to *Patience*, Act I:

Such a judge of blue-and-white and other kinds of pottery –
From early Oriental down to modern terra-cotta-ry.

'O horror, horror, horror!'
(*Macbeth*, Act II, Scene 2). (Page 22)

Scene 20: Carte's office/Gilbert's house

'The everlasting bonfire' (*Macbeth*, Act II, scene 2).

Richard Barker, Carte's company manager, refers to John Hollingshead (1827–1904), the Victorian impresario, who built the Gaiety Theatre, where he presented *Thespis* in 1871. Now he was hosting Sarah Bernhardt (1844–1923), who was touring internationally as Lady Macbeth. Her performance was widely ridiculed in London.

Alexander Graham Bell (1847–1922) had invented the telephone only eight years before, in 1876. It is remarkable how quickly it had become a working tool. Gilbert's father, William Gilbert, was born in 1804, a child of the eighteenth century. This scene is about progress versus the old world. Note the old man's use of 'thank ye' and 'luncheon', as opposed to the modern (1884) 'lunch'. Research reveals that, unsurprisingly, the sound-quality of early telephones necessitated shouting. One of my many secondary agendas in this film is to show things you don't see in movies, such as 1880s telephones not being accorded the faculties of later technology. (Pages 23–4)

*Music cue 5: *The Grand Duke* – 'As o'er our penny roll we sing', from Act I. This piece is often know as the 'Habañera'.

Gilbert was significantly the product of a dysfunctional family: parents were estranged, and a little unhinged. (Page 27)

'Nobody respects the woman more than I do, and I can't stand the woman.' Gilbert actually said this about somebody else (a man). (Page 30)

Scene 21: Paris restaurant

*Music cue 6: *The Grand Duke* – The Dance from Act II followed by 'My Lord Grand Duke, farewell', from Act I.

The Savoy Theatre, built by Carte in 1881, was the first public building in the world to be lit by electricity. His generator was on an adjacent piece of wasteland. Much inspired by American hotels with their *en suite* bathrooms, he now set about building the Savoy Hotel. He incorporated the generator, which continued to supply the Charing Cross area until 1946. (Page 30)

Scene 22: Sullivan's apartment

Fanny Ronalds is singing her own composition, *Barcarole*, words by Edgar Barry. (Page 33)

Scene 23: Sullivan's apartment

The Lucerne lump sugar (p. 35) is a fiction: we made it up.

Much of the dialogue in this scene is distilled directly from Gilbert and Sullivan's correspondence.

The new libretto posed a problem, given the necessity for Gilbert to read it out. We used *The Mountebanks*, generally thought to be a later version of the disputed libretto in question, and which Gilbert staged in 1892, with music by Alfred Cellier (1844–1891), the brother of Frank, as in the film. (Page 37)

Scenes 24/25: Gilbert's house – Dentist

*Music cue 7: *The Grand Duke* – 'When you find you're a broken-down critter' from Act I. (Pages 37–8)

Scene 26: Mrs Ronalds' house

The young man is playing Fauré's Nocturne No. 4 in E-flat major, op. 36. Although Gabriel Fauré was only three years younger than Sullivan, his work at this time was regarded as avant garde, certainly from Sullivan's perspective. (Page 39)

Scene 27: Carte's office

'But answer came there none.' Gilbert is quoting *The Walrus And The Carpenter* (Lewis Carroll, *Through the Looking-Glass*, 1871). (Page 41)

> Shall we be trotting home again?
> But answer came there none.

Scenes 28/31: Theatre

A performance of *The Sorcerer*. The film commences with the slightest hint of *Princess Ida*, and so far that is all we have seen of Gilbert and Sullivan's work. But now, having got to know them, it is time to settle down to a substantial extract. *The Sorcerer* is, of course, one of the many lozenge plots to which Sullivan objected. Here it is the love philtre in the teapot. We see cause and effect – the casting of the spell, with its Incantation, and the local yokels waking up, each instantly falling in love with the first member of the opposite sex he or she sees.

I did not want this sequence to be merely an extract from the show. It is important that it is about work – the theatre as a factory. Thus we see the activity on stage, backstage, in the pit and in the auditorium. (Page 42)

Scenes 29/30: Dressing-room

Two principal ladies in their dressing-room with their dressers. Continuing the picture of workers in their habitat. Vulnerable actresses, coping with a tough life. Leonora Braham (1853–1931) had a son from a marriage to a man who committed suicide. She was alcoholic. Jessie Bond (1853–1942) did have a leg ailment, diagnosed for us by a consultant as a varicose condition, for which there was no cure in Victorian times. Her autobiography, *The Life & Reminiscences of Jessie Bond* (1930), helped us to formulate a picture of her personality, which was not wholly attractive, to say the least. On being introduced to Oscar Wilde, she writes:

> He deigned to stoop and shake hands with me; and I did not like the feel of his hand, nor did I like him, though I knew no harm of him then.

For their voice warm-up, the two actresses sing 'Long years ago, fourteen maybe', from *Patience*, Act I. (Page 46)

Scene 32: Sullivan's apartment

Like many composers, Sullivan did not write at the piano, which he said he would find limiting. (Page 50)

Scene 33: Carte's office

A proportion of the dialogue in this scene is taken from the protagonists' correspondence. The scene contains the film's only howler, of which I am deeply ashamed. Until 1924, Oslo was called Kristiana. (Page 50)

Scenes 34/35: Japanese village

About 100 Japanese men, women and children were smuggled out of Yokohama by a Dutchman called Tanaker. Few had the required exit visas, and many were on the run. It took fifty-three days to sail to Tilbury. Tanaker installed them in his curious Japanese Village Exhibition, in Humphreys Hall, which stood on the site now occupied by Imperial College. There they lived, slept and worked for over a year. At one stage there was a fire, and when Tanaker finally closed the exhibition, he shipped the community to Hamburg, where he remodelled the show, and sustained a further fire, and a rebellion.

Gilbert did, of course, visit the exhibition – frequently, in fact, taking photographs. But in reality he had already thought of *The Mikado* before it arrived.

At one stage, I had the notion of an Anglo-Japanese co-production, in which the whole Tanaker story, starting in Japan, would collide with the *Mikado* saga. Fortunately, this was too ambitious a scheme for anybody to take seriously, although JVC Japan were backers of the film.

When we consulted plans of the Japanese Village, we discovered that they included a theatre. Although there is no record of Gilbert visiting one at the Exhibition, it is obvious that he must have done so.

With the help of my two actors, Togo Igawa and Eiji Kushara, I distilled a famous confrontation scene from a well-known Kabuki play. The action obviously relates loosely to *The Mikado* Act II, when the Emperor is interrogating the three fibbers. (Page 58)

Scene 36: Gilbert's house

The notion that Gilbert bought the sword at the Exhibition is my invention. (Page 60)

Scene 37: Gilbert's mother's house

A further portrait of Gilbert's mad family. Anne Gilbert's exhortation to her daughter never to 'bear a humorous baby' evokes Gilbert's family nickname, 'Bab', the legend that he was captured by Neapolitan brigands at the age of two and ransomed for £25, and confusions surrounding various of his characters in their babyhood. (*HMS Pinafore, The Pirates of Penzance, Patience, Iolanthe, Princess Ida, The Gondoliers.*) (Page 61)

Scenes 38/39: Gilbert's house – Theatre

The sword falls off the wall. Probably apocryphal, but widely accepted. In the 1953 film, a gust of wind brings it down. Gilbert reported the incident in an interview given to the *New York Tribune* in August 1885 (reprinted in the *Pall Mall Gazette*, 24 August 1885). Some sources claim the weapon had been hanging there for years, but he had been in his new house for only a few months. I decided to go to the other extreme, making it a few hours.

*Music cues 8/9: *Ruddigore*: – opening bars of overture and 'I once was as meek as a new born lamb' from Act II.

At this point I break with two film conventions. Gilbert looks straight into the camera, i.e., he shares his inspiration with us; and we flash forward to the first extract from *The Mikado*. This is, of course, totally illogical, as he is imagining the finished piece, music and all. This flash-forward device afforded me licence to include far more of *The Mikado* than would have been possible had we only seen rehearsals and the first night. (Page 61)

Scene 40: Sullivan's apartment

Should we have actually seen Sullivan's progression from anxiety to laughter? Simpler story-telling as this might have been, it would not have been logical: he would not be listening to Gilbert had he not already been seduced. (Page 64)

Scene 41: Gilbert's house

*Music cue 10: *The Mikado* – 'Our great Mikado, virtuous man', from Act I. This is the tune of the song Gilbert is reading to Lucy, played very slowly. (Page 66)

Scene 42: Restaurant

Grossmith and Barrington really did eat bad oysters that day. This is a scene about actors, ordinary Victorian racism and Scottish nationalism. (Page 68)

*Music cue 11: *Patience* – 'The soldiers of our Queen', from Act I; 'So go to him and say to him', from Act II.

Scenes 43/44/45: Carte's office

George Grossmith (1847–1912), actor, comedian, popular solo performer, song-writer, dramatist and journalist. Wrote *The Diary of a Nobody* (1894) with his brother Weedon. His need to support both his family and his drug habit rendered him obsessed with money. He would invariably follow his evening stage performances with late-night solo performances at private parties, accompanying himself on the piano. He wrote songs, of which the most popular was 'See Me Dance the Polka' (1886). He would usually work during the day as the *Times* correspondent at Bow Street Magistrates' Court. (Page 70)

*Music cue 12 (under Barrington's scene, Page 71): *The Merchant of Venice* – 'Danse grotesque'.

Helen quotes *Macbeth* (Act II, scene 2 yet again) – 'A little water clears us of this deed'.

Scene 46: Dressing room

Temple refers to the Fenian bomb. The Fenian brotherhood waged a consistent Irish Republican campaign throughout the period, and into the twentieth century. (Page 74)

Scene 47: Sullivan's apartment

'A short sharp shock' (*The Mikado*, Act I). As this is Gilbert's most universally quoted line, I felt I had to give it pride of place. (Page 79)

Scene 48: Fitting room

*Music cue 13: *The Gondoliers* – 'Take a pair of sparkling eyes' from Act II.

Actresses behaving like actresses at a costume fitting. The corset controversy dominated preparations for *The Mikado*. At this period in the London theatre, actresses' costumes were usually arranged not by theatrical costume designers but by lady costumiers, such as Madame Leon, whose shop was in the Strand. Many of these ladies were either French or had French backgrounds. Madame Leon is clearly a Londoner, but she has a distinctly French style. (Page 80)

Scene 49: Fitting room

However, theatre designers did design the men's costumes as well as the sets. Wilhelm (William Pitcher, 1858–1925) was one of the most distinguished, and was still designing pantomimes during World War I. (Page 84)

'Unfortunately, your avocation as an actor compels you on occasion to endure the most ignominious indignities.' Gilbert really said this. (Page 85)

Scene 50: Stage

'A wandering minstrel' (*The Mikado*, Act I). The song is charming, subtle, succulent, delightful. But at the same time we are looking at grown men earning an honest crust by dressing up like dolls, with their wig-joins on display. (Page 86)

Scenes 51/52/53: Theatre

A core scene theatrically. What is real? Gilbert is obsessed by Japanese authenticity, yet *The Mikado* is as Japanese as fish and chips. He did bring people from the Japanese Village to advise his actors. I have invented the idea of his company's initial resistance. However, since the choreographer John D'Auban (1842–1922) had begun his career as a comic dancer on the music hall stage, the pantomimic preferences with which we have endowed him are not unlikely. (Page 87)

Scene 54: Gilbert's study

Gilbert planned his productions in advance, down to the last detail – every move, word, inflection, gesture. Anathema to most of us modern practitioners of his craft. But it must be remembered that he was one of the major pioneers of directing – or producing, as it was called until well after World War II. Prior to this period, there was no consideration of coherent *mise-en-scène* in the English theatre. The director was known as the stage manager, but his function was organisational rather than creative. The nearest thing to conceptual directing was the work of the various actor-managers, from Macready to Irving, whose priority was the organisation of the production round their own egocentric performances. (Page 95)

Scene 55: Rehearsal room

Gilbert's desire for authenticity applies to surface effect rather than to real-life character motivation. Grossmith's notion that Ko-Ko, a cheap tailor, might be played as a Cockney is, of course, perfectly logical. For Gilbert, having his words spoken beautifully, as by a gentleman, would have been of greater concern. (Page 96)

Scene 56: Theatre pit

This scene makes a pair with the previous one. Gilbert and Sullivan at work with their respective teams: compare and contrast. (Page 103)

Scenes 57/58/59: Auditorium

A theatre at work: dress rehearsal, notes, painful decisions, vulnerable actors, late-night fatigue, a benevolent management. Sullivan was more naturally gifted at rallying the troops than Gilbert.

Gilbert's decision to cut the Mikado's song is interesting. The opera contains two songs listing society offenders fit for punishment, the other being Ko-Ko's 'Little list' song in Act I. Surely the Mikado's song is far the more interesting of the two? (Page 108)

*Music cue 14: *The Yeomen of the Guard* – the 'Private Buffoon' theme (see music cue 1).

Scenes 60/61/62: Dressing rooms backstage

It is widely acknowledged that this scene (the reinstatement of Temple's song) really happened, although nobody knows how it took place, or who said what. For me, it is a key event in the film, dealing, as it does, with the political dynamics of the workplace. (Page 115)

Scene 62: Dressing room

And this scene lies at *Topsy-Turvy*'s emotional core – Temple's philosophical resignation to his fate; the warmth of his and Lely's comradeship; and his final heartfelt definition of theatre as life. (Page 114)

Scene 64: Gilbert's house

*Music cue 15: *The Grand Duke* – the Habañera again. (Page 116)

Scene 65: Auditorium

Anticipation, adrenaline. (Page 117)

Scene 66: Dressing room

Grossmith was unlikely to have been as unhinged as we make him. But he was pretty bad. Note some more photographs of a real protagonist, Grossmith, on the dressing-room table. (Page 117)

*Music cue 16: *The Yeomen of the Guard* – 'I have a song to sing, O!' from Act I and Act II. (Page 118)

Scene 67: Dressing room

How not to talk to actors about to face a first night! We researched Gilbert's respective attitudes to these two women. He kisses Jessie, but not Leonora. (Page 119)

15 *Topsy Turvy*: first night of *The Mikado*.

*Music cue 17: *The Yeomen of the Guard* – the 'Private Buffoon' theme (see music cues 1 and 14)

Scene 68: Dressing room

Showing Grossmith injecting himself is of course part of subverting expectations of the chocolate-box costume movie. (Page 121)

Scene 69: A dark, dank passage

A mad woman accosts Gilbert in a dark passage. My idea was that perhaps at this moment he gets the idea for *Ruddigore*, the next opera. I now think I should have had her shout one of Mad Margaret's utterances. (Page 124)
     *Music cue 18: This is really a piece of pure dramatic film music by Carl Davis. But if you listen carefully you will hear the 'More humane Mikado' theme, which Temple has just sung at the end of the preceding scene.

Scene 70: Theatre

Joyous extracts from the historic first performance of one of the most successful musical shows in theatrical history. A climactic happy end. Or is it? (Page 125)

Scenes 71/72/73: Gilbert's bedroom – Sullivan's bedroom – Leonora's dressing room

Gilbert, inspired and successful, constrained by his emotional impotence. Lucy, open and imaginative, constrained by her relationship. (Page 131) Sullivan, lighting up the world, constrained by his health. Fanny, loving and generous, constrained by society. (Page 133). Leonora, honest and drunk, constrained by life. (Page 134)

Scene 74: Theatre

Leonora is transformed by being on stage, and empowered by the magic of this beautiful, profound, ironic, reflective, haunting song.

It is Gilbert and Sullivan's gift to us. They have the last word, but we have the song. It is ours to keep and cherish.

The film is no longer about them. It is about us.

12 Amateur tenors and choruses in public: the amateur scene

IAN BRADLEY

For all Gilbert's disparagement of amateur tenors and those who sing choruses in public, amateur performances have been the bedrock of the enduring popularity of his work with Sullivan. The Savoy operas have been performed by amateurs virtually since their inception. The Harmonists Choral Society put on *HMS Pinafore* in the Drill Hall, Kingston upon Thames on 30 April 1879, less than a year after its professional opening. Since then, church halls and schoolrooms across the English-speaking world have resounded on winter evenings to the strains of would-be pirates, policemen, fairies and bridesmaids rehearsing for Spring productions.

Nowadays, Gilbert and Sullivan appeals to amateur performers partly because it is cheap to put on – being out of copyright there are no performing rights fees to pay as there are for most Broadway and West End musicals. It also tends to provide a more substantial role and challenging sing for the chorus than most musicals and requires less complex staging and fewer special effects. These latter factors were also important in its early appeal. As the official history of the amateur operatic movement in Britain notes:

> Relatively easy to stage with a good variety of parts, plenty of chorus work
> and box office appeal, they became instant favourites. *The Mikado, The
> Gondoliers, Iolanthe* and the rest of what are known collectively as the Savoy
> Operas provided the artistic springboards from which most amateur
> musical groups launched themselves, and indeed, many still do over a
> century later. No works have played a more important role in developing
> and sustaining the amateur movement and Gilbert and Sullivan remain the
> only artists to whose works numbers of societies are specifically designated.[1]

Origins and history of the amateur tradition

It is, indeed, not too much to claim that the Savoy operas gave birth to the whole amateur operatic movement on both sides of the Atlantic. Several of the earliest performing societies formed in the United Kingdom are still going strong, although most are no longer restricted to just Gilbert and Sullivan and have diversified into operetta and musicals. The Glasgow Orpheus Club put on its first show (*Trial by Jury*) in 1893 and has mounted

THE BREACH OF PROMISE "TRIAL BY JURY" AT THE ROYALTY.

16 *Choruses in Public*: an early illustration to *Trial by Jury. Funny Folks*, 24 April 1875.

annual productions without interruption ever since, remaining exclusively dedicated to Gilbert and Sullivan until 2000. Other societies still active more than a century after their foundation include Settle (first production *HMS Pinafore* in 1891), Sunderland (*HMS Pinafore*, 1894), Bristol (*The Sorcerer*, 1894), Stoke on Trent (*Patience*, 1896), Huddersfield (1897) and Hereford (*The Sorcerer*, 1898).

The British amateur operatic societies grew out of the great revival of choral singing that took place between 1840 and 1870. If Gilbert had his reservations about some of its manifestations, Sullivan enthusiastically supported the choral movement, conducting the annual Leeds Festival at which local choirs performed over four days. His great oratorios – *The Light of the World*, *The Golden Legend* and *The Prodigal Son* – were written for and enthusiastically performed by the choral societies sprouting up across the country, especially in its northern industrial heartlands. The growth of church choirs also gave a huge impetus to this choral movement and it is no coincidence that many of the dedicated Gilbert and Sullivan societies set up in the United Kingdom (and a significant proportion of those in the United States) had their origins in churches and chapels. The Savoy operas provided a suitably respectable and clean repertoire for their members to sing when they left the choir stalls and pews. Even now a significant number of performing societies retain a close church connection, with the Methodist link being the strongest.

The *petit bourgeois* respectability associated with chapel culture was for long an important element in the make-up of many British Gilbert and Sullivan performing groups. It is clearly evident in the circumstances surrounding the formation of one of the oldest which has remained dedicated to performing nothing but the Savoy operas, Plymouth Gilbert and Sullivan Fellowship. It was founded in 1923 by Horace Bickle, a local solicitor and Gilbert and Sullivan enthusiast who was concerned about the Americanisation of British culture and feared that 'if we were not careful the operas would be turned into musical comedy and all the lovely touches of humour would be lost and the whole thing brought down to the vulgar level of so-called American humour'.[2] He made clear that the chief object of his Fellowship, a term itself suggestive both of church gatherings and a tight community of like-minded devotees, was to preserve the 'Savoy Tradition', something that he felt could not really be left to the current management of the D'Oyly Carte 'judging by the awful mutilations of the last few productions I have seen'. This was by no means the only occasion that an amateur society would take upon itself the guardianship of the holy grail of Gilbert and Sullivan tradition when it felt that even the blessed D'Oyly Carte Company was treating it with insufficient reverence and respect. The Plymouth Gilbert and Sullivan Fellowship has staged at least one Savoy opera every year since it began, including a production of *Yeomen of the Guard* staged in the Citadel on Plymouth Hoe and *HMS Pinafore* performed on the warship HMS Antelope which later (1982) sank in the Falklands War.

Similar concerns led to the founding of the first major amateur performing group in the United States. The Savoy Company of Philadelphia, which proudly claims to be the oldest amateur theatre company in the world continuously dedicated solely to the production of the works of Gilbert and Sullivan, was set up in 1901 by Alfred Reginald Allen, a medical doctor concerned about the bizarre treatment that he felt the Savoy operas were receiving in the USA. His object was to 'gather together a group of like-minded friends to perform the works in their "original" English manner'. The Company treasures a letter sent by Gilbert to its president in 1904 in which he wrote: 'It is gratifying to know that the joint works of Sir Arthur Sullivan and myself are of sufficient interest to justify the promotion of an amateur company for the express purpose of interpreting them'.

The Savoy Company exemplifies many of the characteristics of the amateur Gilbert and Sullivan scene in the USA. It has a strong Anglophile streak, evidenced by the fact that its main rehearsal venue is the Germantown Cricket Club and that every public performance is preceded by two verses of 'God Save the Queen'. Until the 1960s, membership was confined to those listed in the Philadelphia Social Register and it is only relatively recently that the Company has shed its upper-class image.

The influence of the D'Oyly Carte Company

For most of the twentieth century, British amateur societies maintained a close relationship with the D'Oyly Carte Opera Company. Until the expiry of copyright in 1961, all amateur Gilbert and Sullivan performances had to be licensed by the company, which also exacted a performing rights fee and had a monopoly on hiring out band parts. The relationship continued until the company's demise in 1982. D'Oyly Carte performances remained the yardstick and model for amateur performers and its stars were eagerly sought after as honorary presidents and patrons of local societies. Retired company members supplemented their meagre pensions by such activities as making fans and copying out band parts for hire. Since the company's closure, several of its former members have found a second career acting as freelance directors for amateur companies on both sides of the Atlantic, so perpetuating the D'Oyly Carte style and influence well into the twenty-first century. One of the most prolific and sought after, Alistair Donkin, estimates that about 50 per cent of the blocking for the amateur shows that he directs is very similar, if not identical, to that for the D'Oyly Carte productions in which he himself took part as the old company's last patter man.

Amateur societies have long provided a route into professional performance. Perhaps the most distinguished Gilbert and Sullivan exponent to rise through the ranks this way was the conductor Sir Malcom Sargent, who began his life-long love affair with the Savoy operas at the age of eight when he became programme seller for the Stamford Operatic Society. At thirteen he was given a walk-on part in *The Mikado* as the Lord High Executioner's sword bearer. He enjoyed the experience so much that from then on he attended every one of the society's rehearsals and at fourteen he was acting as the rehearsal accompanist.

School productions have been a hugely important part of the amateur scene and equally, if not more, influential in kindling a life-long attachment to Gilbert and Sullivan. Until well into the 1960s, the Savoy operas were staple fare for both maintained (state) and independent (public) schools in

Britain and introduced many budding musicians and singers to the delights of performed music. Richard Suart, the leading contemporary exponent of the patter roles, first encountered Gilbert and Sullivan when he played the viola for a *Mikado* production as a first-year pupil at Sedbergh School. By his final year, he had graduated to playing the judge in *Trial by Jury* with the headmaster's wife leading the bridesmaids.

For much of the twentieth century there were essentially two distinct routes into amateur Gilbert and Sullivan performance in England. The first was located in the world of provincial, often northern, Nonconformity where those occupying Captain Corcoran's station in the lower middle class encountered the Savoy operas through chapel and grammar school. A prime example of someone nurtured in this tradition was Harold Wilson, Labour Prime Minister from 1964 to 1970 and 1974 to 1976, who, thanks to the enthusiasm of his Congregationalist parents, was word perfect in *The Pirates of Penzance* at six and first appeared on stage at ten as the midshipmite in a production of *HMS Pinafore* by the Milnsbridge Baptist Amateur Operatic Society near his home town of Huddersfield. The other way in, via prep and public school productions, involved generations of upper-middle-class boys and girls, predominantly from the Home Counties, cross-dressing in their single-sex establishments and graduating from playing sisters, cousins and aunts to peers, policemen and pirates as puberty kicked in.

The flavour of such productions was delightfully, if somewhat melodramatically, caught in one of the popular 'Mrs Bradley' Mysteries co-produced by the BBC and WGBH Boston in 2000. Entitled 'Death at the Opera' it centred around a murder committed back stage and provoked by a lesbian affair during an all-female production of *The Mikado* at Mrs Bradley's old finishing school. These productions lingered long in the minds of those involved in them. In 1980 a distinguished literary agent accosted a leading television newscaster in a London street with the words 'How would you like to be a fairy guardsman'. The two men had not clapped eyes on each other since appearing respectively as the Fairy Queen and Private Willis in their all boys' school production of *Iolanthe* twenty-five years earlier.

The D'Oyly Carte Company drew much of its fan base from these two groups. Its regular winter seasons at the Savoy Theatre, the scene of many a Home Counties family Christmas treat preceded by a meal in the Strand Palace Hotel, drew the aspiring performers from southern independent schools while its hugely popular appearances in Manchester, Bradford and Leeds attracted those who trod the boards in northern grammar school and chapel productions. Principals from amateur societies, which regularly block-booked tickets, would go again and again to study the way their role was performed by the D'Oyly Carte masters. There was always the chance that a particularly talented amateur might one day end up with the

Carte – right until the end of its life, this was a recognised and well-trodden route into the company.

The grounding that so many boys in particular received in the Savoy operas at school in the early decades of the twentieth century showed itself when they became one of the main entertainments mounted by British prisoners of war in the Second World War. Trevor Hills, who sang with the D'Oyly Carte in the 1950s, cut his Gilbert and Sullivan teeth performing *HMS Pinafore*, *The Mikado*, *The Gondoliers* and *The Yeomen of the Guard* in Stalag 383 in Bavaria between 1942 and 1945. The novelist J. G. Ballard has written movingly in his memoirs, *Miracles of Life: Shanghai to Shepperton* (2007), of the Gilbert and Sullivan productions that he witnessed as a boy in the internment camp set up by the Japanese in 1943 for British and other allied nationals living in Lunghua, a suburb of Shanghai.

The last forty years

Both school and amateur performances of Gilbert and Sullivan almost certainly reached their peak in the twenty years or so following the war. By the mid-1960s their popularity in British schools was beginning to wane, thanks partly to the Beatles and the rise of musicals, but much more because of the attitude of music and drama teachers that Gilbert and Sullivan was old fashioned and boring. Later, *Grease* and *Guys and Dolls* were to sweep all before them in secondary schools, while in prep and junior schools Gilbert and Sullivan gave way to the ubiquitous *Joseph and the Amazing Technicolor Dreamcoat*. Its librettist, Tim Rice, had himself been introduced to the Savoy operas at his Sussex prep school and often thought of them as he devised his quintessentially Gilbertian lyrics rhyming farmers and pyjamas. In the United States Gilbert and Sullivan held on for longer in schools, helped by the fact that many North American high schools maintained four-part singing and other traditional musical disciplines being abandoned by their British equivalents. An episode of the popular US teenage television series *Clarissa* which screened in the mid-1990s featured the eponymous heroine starring as Mabel in a high school production of *The Pirates of Penzance*. It is impossible to imagine such a story line in a comparable recent British television series set in a secondary school like *Grange Hill*.

It is not, in fact, clear whether there has been a decline in the number of amateur Gilbert and Sullivan performances since the 1960s, as is so often alleged by nostalgic Savoyards pining for the good old days of yore. Analysis of the yearbooks of the National Operatic and Dramatic Association (NODA), the umbrella body for amateur operatic societies in the UK, enables a statistical snapshot of the Gilbert and Sullivan 'market share' to be gained in any one year. Counting the number of amateur operatic productions in the first year of each of the last five decades produces the following figures:

Year	Total productions	G & S productions	% share
1961	996	167	16.7
1971	866	178	20.5
1981	803	123	15.3
1991	725	117	16.1
2001	942	173	19.1

These figures do not suggest that there has been any significant decline in amateur Gilbert and Sullivan performances either in actual numbers or as a proportion of all amateur operatic productions. Indeed, the figures for 2001 are higher in both respects than those for 1961. Research also shows that in all of these years at least one Savoy opera was among the top five most performed musical shows by amateur societies in Britain. In 1961 *The Mikado* (with thirty-two performances) was second in popularity only to *The Merry Widow*. In 1971 *The Gondoliers* and *The Mikado* (twenty-five) came fourth equal after *The Sound of Music*, *The Merry Widow* and *My Fair Lady*. In 1981 *The Mikado* and *The Gondoliers* (twenty-four) came third equal after *Fiddler on the Roof* and *The Merry Widow*. In 1991 *The Pirates of Penzance* (nineteen performances, including six of the Papp version) came fifth after *Carousel*, *South Pacific*, *Oklahoma!* and *Brigadoon* and in 2001 *The Mikado* (thirty-three performances, including five of the *Hot Mikado*) came third after *Oklahoma!* and *Fiddler on the Roof*.

As the figures indicate, there is no single out-and-out favourite among the Savoy operas in terms of amateur performance. This is confirmed by statistics compiled annually by the D'Oyly Carte with respect to the hire of band parts and scores, just about the only activity in which it has been engaged since the new company ceased production in 2003. *The Mikado*, *The Pirates of Penzance* and *The Gondoliers* are regularly the most requested, with *HMS Pinafore* and *Iolanthe* also consistently popular. In the United States the 'Piramikafore' trinity dominates the amateur as well as the professional scene with *The Gondoliers* being noticeably less popular. As Dan Rothermel, the long-serving musical director of the Savoy Company of Philadelphia observes, 'Brits like it because it isn't British, and that's exactly why Americans don't like it'.[3] Despite the growing popularity of the rescored and synthesiser-accompanied 'Papp' *Pirates* and 'Hot' *Mikado* among amateur companies, most amateur performances on both sides of the Atlantic continue to use traditional orchestral accompaniment closely based on Sullivan's own scoring, although with reduced parts. James Newby helped amateur societies hugely in the late 1990s by arranging the entire Gilbert and Sullivan repertoire for a fifteen-piece orchestra.

Altogether, there are around 150 amateur groups in Britain still dedicated to an exclusive diet of Gilbert and Sullivan and a good many of the 2,000 or so more general operatic societies still perform Gilbert and Sullivan from time to time. It is more difficult to estimate the extent of the amateur scene in the United States but on the basis of his extensive contacts and research Gayden Wren, entertainment editor of the *New York Times* Syndicate, has identified 196 amateur societies performing the Savoy operas on an annual basis, of which at least eighty-seven are exclusively dedicated to Gilbert and Sullivan.

Differences between the amateur tradition in the USA and the UK

There are marked differences in the social and age composition of performing societies on either side of the Atlantic. A rare academic study of the world of amateur Gilbert and Sullivan performance in Britain by Shani D'Cruz concludes that:

> Throughout the (twentieth) century, the social profile of amateur operatic societies has been predominantly white and lower middle class: principally traders, white-collar workers and professionals. Societies have acted as nodal points in over-lapping sets of people's social and leisure networks, particularly those of neighbourhood, friendship and family.[4]

D'Cruz is particularly struck by the appeal to women of performing in the Savoy operas. Despite the fact that Gilbert's 'positive representations of femininity are predominantly youthful' and his portrayals of older women more negative, with 'origins in the grotesque, cross-dressed dame of burlesque', she concludes on the basis of extensive interviews that 'older women in particular, aided by the possibilities of moving between performing and social identities that this leisure activity encourages, have made empowering and selective imaginative appropriations from these gender ideals'. She argues that the older women who predominate in amateur societies and enjoy playing fairies, young maidens and bridesmaids, however incongruous this may look, are simultaneously cocking a snook at ageism, Gilbert's fixation with elderly, ugly daughters and the modern obsession with youth and beauty:

> Operatic society identity has offered respectable, middle-class, sometimes conservative and often anti-feminist women the opportunity to play with and to satirise dominant constructions of femininity in ways which contained any risks to their reputations through the 'serious' leisure content.[5]

The overwhelming predominance of women in British amateur performing societies contrasts with the strong male bias among Gilbert and Sullivan fans, especially those of the more obsessive kind who constitute a kind of 'inner brotherhood' somewhat similar to that formed by steam-train enthusiasts and cricket addicts. There is, indeed, a strong overlap between these three groups, perhaps accounted for by a shared nostalgia for a vanished age or a fascination with lists and craving for a self-contained and orderly world which some psychologists have pointed to as indicative of mild autism.

US performing societies manage to achieve a more equal balance between the sexes and even to attract a good supply of amateur tenors, an increasingly rare commodity in the UK. Their age profile is also considerably lower, and among the bigger societies particularly principal roles are increasingly taken by young singers studying at, or recently graduated from, music academies who use performing with amateurs as a stepping stone in their professional singing careers. Amateur performers in the United States are more likely than their British counterparts to be drawn from the university-educated professional classes, with a high proportion of lawyers, scientists and engineers. This is in large part a reflection of the fact that Gilbert and Sullivan is looked on much more as high art and has a much greater intellectual appeal in the United States than in the United Kingdom. The US performing societies are disproportionately concentrated in areas with a preponderance of higher-education institutions and hi-tech industry on the Eastern and Western seaboards, with the Boston region having the biggest cluster. In contrast to the British amateur scene, which remains overwhelmingly white, they have broken away from being a White Anglo-Saxon Protestant preserve to encompass a much broader ethnic mix on stage. The 2003 Philadelphia Savoy Company's *Mikado*, for example, featured an Asian Indian Nanki-Poo, an African American Pish-Tush and a Jewish Mikado.

The significant following for Gilbert and Sullivan among the Jewish community in New York has spawned one of the most intriguing and successful 'spin-off' amateur performing societies catering for a niche market. The Gilbert and Sullivan Yiddish Light Opera Company of Long Island, founded in 1984 as an offshoot of the Gilbert and Sullivan Light Opera Company of Long Island, has performed *Der Yiddisher Mikado*, *Der Yiddisher Pinafore* and *Di Yam Gazlonim* (*Pirates* set on the coast of Israel) in synagogues, retirement homes and public halls not just in New York and down the Eastern seaboard but as far afield as Florida, Toronto and London. Highlights from these operas have also been recorded on CD with piano accompaniment. Not all the company members, who range professionally from dentists to cantors, are Jewish but they share a commitment to the survival of Yiddish and choose to perform the

Savoy operas rather than genuine Yiddish material partly out of a love for Gilbert and Sullivan but also because of a conviction that 'down-to-earth Yiddishkeit stands out all the more vividly against such a genteel, Victorian ever-so-English background'.[6]

It is not just in Britain and the USA that the amateur tradition thrives. There are at least twenty-three amateur groups regularly performing Gilbert and Sullivan in Australia and New Zealand and nearly forty in Canada. The main society in South Africa, set up in Cape Town in 1947 by a husband and wife team – he played the patter roles while she sewed the costumes – now performs a Savoy opera every other year, alternating with a musical. As one might expect, Gilbert and Sullivan tends to flourish in places where there is a sizeable British expatriate community. The Brussels Society began in 1975 when thirty-five people met on a wet February evening in the basement of the city's Anglican church. It has since extended its repertoire beyond Gilbert and Sullivan and changed its name to the Brussels Light Opera Company, but the Savoy operas are still a major feature of its programme. There have also been amateur performances further afield. A promising series of productions in the early 1980s by the British military team stationed in Kaduna in northern Nigeria, which featured a real-life colonel as the Major-General and an RAF Group Captain as the Sergeant of Police in *The Pirates of Penzance*, were brought to an end by a military coup. *HMS Pinafore* was performed for four nights in 1997 in the gardens of the British Embassy in Jeddah with the commercial secretary as the musical director. Jerusalem has a thriving performing society founded in 1984 by Robert Binder, who first encountered Gilbert and Sullivan in 1958 as a student in a US summer camp where a Hebrew version of *Pirates* was performed.

Summer camps have traditionally introduced many North Americans to Gilbert and Sullivan and several are continuing this function today. Camp Tecumseh in New Hampshire, which conforms to the British prep- and public-school tradition in being all-male, has done a Gilbert and Sullivan production every year since 1930 with around seventy boys rehearsing for six weeks for the end-of-camp show. The co-educational Interlochen Arts Camp in Michigan has an equally long tradition of putting on Gilbert and Sullivan shows, with anything up to 200 high-school students giving two performances in a 5,000-seat outside auditorium.

On the whole, amateur performers in the United States are more reverential of the D'Oyly Carte tradition and are more likely to stage conventional and period productions than those in Britain. This is in marked contrast to the professional scene where there have been some daring liberties taken recently – perhaps most successfully with the gay version of *HMS Pinafore* which opened in Los Angeles in 2001 and went on to Chicago and New York in 2003. The music was left intact but *Pinafore* became a ship in an alternative gay US Navy set up by a liberally inclined Democratic president and the entire cast is male apart from Bitter Butterball and gay apart from Dick Dockstrap. This first overtly gay reworking of Gilbert and Sullivan could be a sign of things to come. In Britain, aside from the wonderfully inventive and irreverent Opera della Luna with its saucy *Parson's Pirates* and *Rocky Horror Show*-inspired *Ghosts of Ruddigore*, it has tended to be amateur companies who have pushed the boundaries in terms of up-dated productions. Southampton, an unusually young society by British standards, set their 2003 *Princess Ida* in the 1960s with Hilarion, Florian and Cyril as teddy boys and Arac, Gurion and Scythion as bikers, serenading 'the brrrm, brrrm, brrrm of the Harley Davidson' in their song 'We are bikers three'. There have also been some effective contemporary stagings of the Savoy operas by schools, most notably by St Mary's Catholic High School in Astley, near Manchester, in a series of highly acclaimed productions through the 1990s which transferred the *Mikado* to a Nissan car plant in Sunderland, set *Yeomen* in Blackpool Tower and performed *Iolanthe* on roller skates.

The amateur scene today

Perhaps the most vibrant amateur Gilbert and Sullivan performances today are taking place in universities and colleges. There are over twenty university societies in the United Kingdom specialising entirely in the Savoy operas and a similar number in the United States, as well as others which regularly perform them as part of a wider repertoire. Several of the more dedicated and energetic student groups mount two or three full productions a year and they often enthusiastically tackle the less-popular operas which most other amateur societies shy away from, such as *The Sorcerer, Utopia Limited* and *The Grand Duke*. Student directors range from the ultra-traditional to the avant garde. A good number of student performers have no knowledge of Gilbert and Sullivan before coming to university. Of those who do, most were introduced by their parents or at school, although a growing minority first encountered it through watching Bart Simpson sing the score of *HMS Pinafore* to Sideshow Bob or the hero of *Family Guy* being serenaded by 'If you'll marry me' from *The Sorcerer* when he joins a football team.[7] Gilbert and Sullivan references remain ubiquitous in North American cartoons and television shows – *Frasier* and *West Wing* were peppered with them – in marked contrast to British TV soaps and sitcoms where they hardly ever feature.

A good overview of the vitality and originality of high school, college and university performances can be gained from a visit to the Edinburgh

17 *The Show Goes On*: flier for an amateur production of *HMS Pinafore*, October 2008.

Festival Fringe, where there are regularly half-a-dozen or more Gilbert and Sullivan productions a year, the majority coming from the United States. The 2005 Fringe programme, for example, included a *Hot Mikado*, a straight production of *The Pirates of Penzance* from a High School Festival in Texas, an up-dated *Gondoliers* about the efforts of George Bush to import democracy into the Middle East, a whistle-stop tour through every Gilbert

189 Amateur tenors and choruses in public

and Sullivan role by four performers in eighty minutes, a sing-along *Trial by Jury* with the principals' roles taken by students from four British university Gilbert and Sullivan societies and a *Starship Pinafore* performed by a Scottish university group.

If Edinburgh at festival time provides a snapshot of the variety and vitality of youth productions, the more staid surroundings of the pavilion gardens and Opera House at Buxton in the heart of the English Peak District showcase the best of more traditional and mature amateur performances from around the world. Begun in 1994, the Buxton International Gilbert and Sullivan Festival brings together up to 2,000 amateur performers and 20,000 fans every August for three weeks of virtually non-stop Gilbert and Sullivan activity. Its founder, Ian Smith, came to Gilbert and Sullivan through the classic northern Nonconformist route, having first performed with Methodist societies in West Yorkshire. Fanatical about the D'Oyly Carte tradition, he set up the festival partly to keep it alive. Former principals with the old company are brought to Buxton to run workshops and hand the sacred torch on to a new generation. The festival is not just backward-looking, however: there are youth and student productions and several initiatives to promote Gilbert and Sullivan among schools, including one which involved myself appearing on stage as the Sergeant of Police surrounded by primary-school pupils from Huddersfield. At the heart of the festival are the nightly adjudicated and competitive performances given by the cream of amateur societies from the UK, the USA, Canada and South Africa. The audiences who pack the Opera House to see them may be mature – a survey in 2007 revealed that more than 80 per cent of festival goers are over fifty – but the youth and exuberance of the performers points to the enduring vitality of the amateur tradition. The enthusiasm that the Buxton Gilbert and Sullivan Festival engenders is palpable and infectious – the spa gardens, pubs and streets surrounding the Opera House are filled with Savoyards singing choruses in public. What happens in Buxton every August suggests that the tradition of amateur tenors and others singing their hearts out in the Savoy operas is alive and well and likely to continue well on into if not through the twenty-first century.

13 Champions and aficionados: amateur and listener experiences of the Savoy operas in performance

STEPHANIE PITTS

'When you go home at night, it's still swimming around in your head. And when you wake up in the morning, the tunes are still there, you know. And I suppose there could be worse things in your head', says a member of the Edmund Rice Choral and Musical Society (ERCMS), interviewed in August 2001. 'I enjoy it when it's on, but I'm also glad when it stops and my life's my own again. I feel I can go and cut the grass, or do the mundane, ordinary things that just get left.'

The Savoy operas occupy a unique place in English performing history as a self-contained genre of light-hearted, accessible (though not always easy) tonal music with plenty of chorus involvement, solo parts of varying dimensions, and (in most cases) a guaranteed happy ending. For decades they have provided amateur performing groups with a reliable formula for fun in rehearsals and popularity with audiences. Out of copyright and with relatively straightforward costume and staging requirements, performing Gilbert and Sullivan is a reasonable aim for amateur groups, and one which musical societies from around the UK and further afield celebrate at the annual Gilbert and Sullivan Festival in Buxton, Derbyshire. An empirical study of audience and performer experience at the 2001 festival considers the impact of the Savoy operas on the individuals participating there and on amateur performing culture as a whole.

The Buxton Festival is a haven for devotees of the genre, who relish the language and wit of Gilbert's lyrics, the melodic power of Sullivan's music, and the opportunities that both provide for performers to develop and demonstrate their musical and acting skills. The three-week festival, held in the refurbished Edwardian opera house of this Derbyshire spa town, comprises performances by amateur groups, interspersed with professional productions and a large programme of 'fringe' activities, including interviews and masterclasses with past D'Oyly Carte performers, 'scratch' performances and a nightly cabaret.[1] The festival offers immersion in the Gilbert and Sullivan repertoire amongst like-minded enthusiasts, providing a sense of fellowship and community that is sustained between festivals by publications including the *Gilbert and Sullivan News* and websites such as Savoynet.

Audience members and performers at the 2001 festival had an expectedly high commitment to the music and the festival, but also demonstrated some differences in perspective, with the audience much more strongly committed to preserving the Savoy opera repertoire for future generations. Amongst the performers, a few dissenting voices were to be heard, noting the marginalisation of women in Gilbert's plots, and questioning whether the popularity of the canon could continue with younger audiences more accustomed to the glamour of West End musicals. The experiences of individual performers and listeners therefore help to shed light on broader debates associated with the Savoy operas, including the relationship between amateur and professional productions, and the responsibilities felt towards the repertoire and its continued performance in future decades.

Professional, amateur and audience relationships

The uniqueness of the Savoy operas within the musical repertoire is compounded by their unusual dual performing status: the operas have both a clear professional identity, established first by the D'Oyly Carte Opera Company, then by the English and the Welsh National Opera and the New D'Oyly Carte Company[2] and more recently by the revived Carl Rosa Opera, and a strong amateur base in the dedicated Gilbert and Sullivan societies that exist around the UK and, to a lesser extent, internationally. Whilst it is true that much other music is performed at professional and amateur levels, to have organisations of both kinds devoted to the same specific repertoire is a rare and interesting phenomenon. Nick Sales, a tenor who has moved between amateur and professional spheres in performing Gilbert and Sullivan, noted this as an appealing feature of the repertoire during an interview at the festival:

> I think the accessibility is a major factor, because it's something you *can* do –
> you can watch a performance tonight of *The Mikado*, and in six months time
> you can be on stage with your Gilbert and Sullivan society wherever, and
> you could be Nanki-Poo or the Mikado or whatever. I think the accessibility
> is a massive, massive part of it.

Whether consciously or not, the two strands of Gilbert and Sullivan performance operate in relation to one another: the professionals performing in the knowledge that their audiences are internally singing along with them, and the amateurs with an awareness of the long tradition of D'Oyly Carte performances.

The competitive aspect of the Buxton Festival reflects this sense of heritage, whereby performances are adjudicated by a D'Oyly Carte veteran, and there is an award for the 'most traditional performance' but no equivalent prize for innovation. This decision is sympathetic to the audience's wariness of productions which deviate too far from established performance practice, a topic hotly debated in discussions during the festival and through related publications after the event. Jean Dufty, reporting on the 2001 festival in the *Gilbert and Sullivan News* later that year, stated that 'it is difficult to improve on the masters, who were geniuses of production as well as words and music'; but even while emphasising the pedigree of performances faithful to the first productions of the Savoy operas, the same reviewer showed enthusiasm for a more modern interpretation:

> I loved Southampton's modern *HMS Pinafore* on a Starship, as did most people I spoke to. I do not always like updated versions, but consider that this one demonstrated that if you update really well, consistently and to some purpose and think it all through so that it makes sense, it can be really good. Gilbert observed human nature so well that much of his writing applies to people in any age or situation.[3]

Audience members contribute to the ethos of the Buxton Festival and the preservation of the Savoy operas through their enthusiasm for the repertoire and general inclination towards high-quality, traditional productions. Amateurs, professionals and audience members work together within this already clearly defined genre to construct a shared understanding of what is desirable in performance, so strengthening further the community of Gilbert and Sullivan enthusiasts.

The sociologist Robert Stebbins has written of the differences between amateur and professional approaches to performance activities, noting that the distinction is not necessarily in quality, but in the role of the activity in individuals' lives. He notes that 'whereas professionals must specialize to succeed, amateurs need not'[4] – another sphere in which Gilbert and Sullivan performance is unusual, since it provides a defined repertoire within which amateur and professional singers alike may choose to focus their activities almost exclusively. At Buxton, the veteran members of the D'Oyly Carte Company demonstrate their lifelong commitment to the genre, amateur performers might come from societies which perform little else, and the festival itself is the main musical event of the year for some audience members. A level of hierarchy is maintained through the presence of the festival's own professional Gilbert and Sullivan Opera Company, which occupies the weekend performance slots in the festival and is not subject to an adjudicator's critique. Despite the widely shared knowledge of the Buxton Festival clientèle, therefore, there is respect for the greater experience and authority of professional performers, past and present, and a strong sense of tradition and the desire to maintain performing standards. This 'fun', 'accessible' repertoire brings with it rigorous standards and volubly expressed opinions – this is indeed the 'serious leisure' of which Stebbins writes, whereby amateur commitment is reinforced through a drive to attain the high standards of professional performances.[5]

Experiencing Gilbert and Sullivan: the view from the stage

In order to understand the experience of performing Gilbert and Sullivan, performing groups from the third week of the 2001 festival were surveyed through questionnaires and group interviews as part of a wider project on musical participation.[6] Questionnaires were sent in advance of the festival, and forty-one returns received from across four performing groups. These were followed up with interviews during the festival week, and together offered insight on performers' experiences of the festival, membership of their performing society, and the Gilbert and Sullivan repertoire.

Performers at the festival were principally loyal to their own performing group, seeing the festival as one aspect of their annual cycle of rehearsals and productions, offering the opportunity to perform in a well-equipped venue and monitor their standard of performance against other amateur groups. Performers were less likely than audience members to get involved in the 'Fringe' aspects of the festival, or even to watch performances by other groups, but nonetheless welcomed the focus and intensity of the festival and the sense of being with like-minded people:

> Well if part of your aspiration is to do something well – and to get the warmth, the applause, the buzz, the feedback you get from doing something well – if you take that a little stage further, and you look at doing that for Gilbert and Sullivan, well then as there's a festival in Buxton that is geared to Gilbert and Sullivan, and primarily attended by aficionados of G & S, you want to go there and see how good you really are in relation to others.
>
> (Member of ERCMS, August 2001)

The performing societies approached the festival with varying levels of seriousness: for some it was 'a holiday for the society, a bonding thing' (ERCMS), while others felt the pressure to maintain competitive success:

> Being a local society and champions seems to put a bigger pressure on us to participate. It's great to be able to say we're champions, but it does get to be a slog sometimes.
>
> (Member of Derby Gilbert & Sullivan Society, questionnaire response)

One society – Nene Opera – had been formed the previous year specifically to perform at Buxton, and valued its opportunities to 'celebrate with other enthusiasts' and provide a 'keener edge' through the adjudications and comparisons with other groups. Whilst winning awards and having fun were by no means mutually exclusive, each society appeared to have reached a consensus about which was the more important, so that a shared ethos of sociability or seriousness prevailed in rehearsals and during the festival. Some anonymised descriptions of rehearsals help to illustrate the range of approaches:

> Socialising with friends, singing and practising – talking to friends when other scenes are being practised.
> Disciplined meaningful effort; attention to detail; happy bunch of people pulling on the same rope in the same direction.
> Good humour, great sounds, mutually supportive company.

Enjoyment and achievement are closely intertwined in these accounts of rehearsals, where each society appears to have found a pattern of working which suits their members and achieves the desired result.

Performing groups are known to work best when members share similar aims and ambitions,[7] and the societies performing in Buxton appear to be clear examples of effective groups, where members feel that their contributions to a shared goal are recognised and supported. For some groups, the Gilbert and Sullivan repertoire was integral to their motivation to perform, offering soloists 'a good range of characterisation to develop acting skills' as well as featuring 'good chorus involvement in every show' (Derby G & S). The operas were seen as providing 'good tunes, humorous dialogue/plot, great fun', which in turn contributed to 'happy rehearsals and show week' (Nene). Societies which performed a greater variety of music emphasised more the musical qualities of the Savoy operas, and noted the particular pleasures of performing staged works as opposed to concerts:

> It's a funny thing, because once you've done a show – and people say will you join the society, and so eventually you have to go in – it almost is like a drug, once you do one show. You can feel the warmth coming from the audience, you can feel the adrenalin – it is actually a drug. People when they join they tend to stay; through marriages, through everything. Nobody can actually define what that is ... When you walk out from the curtain and the lights come on, and the audience are looking at *you* when they'd pass you in the street normally – there's kind of a five minutes of fame thing.
> (Member of ERCMS, August 2001)

From this society, too, came one of the rare negative reflections on staged performing – the difficulties of continuing into later life:

> I looked at myself one day when I was about forty and I just thought 'Oh no, stop', and that was it. I just decided that there were so many other things I could do, all these things where you're not in the spotlight, backstage and all.
> (Member of ERCMS, August 2001)

The Savoy operas are particularly unforgiving to women in this respect: at forty, the singer quoted above felt too old to be in the chorus, and diverted her attention to backstage support – a route that has historically afforded older women a sustainable and respected role in amateur musical societies.[8] While D'Cruz's interviews with long-standing members of amateur groups suggested that some women felt empowered by the element of the 'grotesque' in Gilbert's ageing contralto characters (see Chapter 12 in this volume for further discussion), the interviewee quoted above was more fearful of appearing ridiculous on stage. Benson Chamley, a long-standing props-maker and manager at the festival, noted the longer-term implications of an ageing cast and audience:

> It's a dying situation, because the people who followed the original D'Oyly Carte and in fact were themselves Gilbert and Sullivan fans, are all getting older, and there comes a time when in fact you can't perform on stage because you physically can't bob up and down like a policeman or you don't look like a lovesick maiden either when you're 50 years old. So everybody's getting older, and the young people, despite [the] efforts [of the festival organisers], there aren't the amount of young people available who are interested in doing that.   (Interview with Benson Chamley, August 2001)

Some D'Oyly Carte veterans, including those present at the festival, have continued performing well into their eighties, achieving this longevity by building on established reputations. For amateurs, it is perhaps harder to age gracefully on stage, and the competition for solo roles may mean a decline in audition success for older performers.

Involving young people in musical activities is a problem by no means exclusive to Gilbert and Sullivan: audiences at a chamber music series in Sheffield expressed similar concerns about rejuvenating their membership and sharing their musical enthusiasms with the next generation.[9] The Savoy opera repertoire does bring its own challenges though, as the Victorian values of the plot become more remote from social norms; and they suffer too from their marginal place in the musical canon.[10] While these factors are of little importance to those who choose to participate – and indeed were hardly mentioned at Buxton – they contribute to a tight-knit sense of community amongst those who defend and enjoy the repertoire; and conversely risk excluding those who feel more ambivalent towards it. With the repertoire sometimes described as 'best appreciated in performance',[11] performing societies have a strong role to play in nurturing younger enthusiasts. However, concern about the preservation of the Savoy operas was more frequently expressed in the Buxton audience than by those on stage.

Supporting Gilbert and Sullivan: the view from the audience

Audience members at the 2001 festival were surveyed through question-naires distributed by front of house staff during the final week of perfor-mances. One-hundred-and-seventy-two responses were received, and these were supplemented through ethnographic observation, including atten-dance at performances and informal conversations during the cabaret nights held after every show.

For audience members, the Buxton Festival was a chance to enjoy familiar repertoire in high-quality performance, as well as making and renewing friendships within a like-minded community. Connections with the performers were surprisingly limited: only 8 per cent of respondents knew some of the performers, while greater numbers were attracted by the festival (29 per cent) and the repertoire (34 per cent). Performing societies at Buxton seemed not to bring established audiences with them, though previous award-winning groups attracted a loyal following amongst festival-goers. Audience members, of whom the majority attended up to three shows, planned their attendance according to repertoire, reputation and convenience:

> Different every year until seen them all, then repeat the process – hope to attend more next year.
> Enjoy them all, but choose particular shows and attend in that week.
> Always attend the professional performances. Then select others if we have not seen them for a while or if they have a 'novelty' value e.g. youth production, *Cox and Box* sung in Estonian.
> One pro, one with friends in, one haven't seen before.

Apart from the minority who attend 'All of them, regardless', audience mem-bers seemed to seek a balance of familiarity and variety in their choices, being keen to see rarely performed works, but also welcoming new productions of the central repertoire. A small number also related their listening to their own past or current performing activities:

> I like to see shows which my own society will be performing soon.
> *Iolanthe* – nostalgia for schooldays.

Very few audience members described themselves as 'first timers', confirm-ing the general impression that the Buxton audience is knowledgeable, experienced and committed to the repertoire. This fact generates in turn a sense of intensity and enthusiasm that is valued by many, leading to 'good camaraderie and friendship' through 'a coming together of like-minded people, determined to enjoy themselves'. One respondent summarised the festival as 'a wonderful gathering of people, talents, opinions and most of all, united enthusiasm and love of G & S worldwide'.

As well as noting their own enjoyment at attending the festival, some audience members felt a sense of responsibility to supporting an event which helped to 'keep G & S alive and well', so contributing to the preservation of a particular aspect of English culture:

> Enjoyable and interesting to compare different interpretations, and a wonderful way to keep alive our cultural heritage.
> Good fun and the revival of an important part of English cultural and musical tradition.

The notion of the Savoy operas as endangered cultural heritage was entwined with personal memories of childhood listening, such that the repertoire was 'filled with nostalgia for performers and performances encountered with my parents'. But even while audience members, the majority of whom were over fifty, enjoyed 'a trip down memory lane', they expressed concerns about the absence of younger Gilbert and Sullivan enthusiasts, suggesting that 'high-profile advertising might bring in younger audiences'.

Younger performers are already featured at the festival in a separate 'youth production', but some audience members felt that this still offered insufficient opportunities for new talent to develop. It is notoriously difficult to bring minority groups into an established homogeneous audience, and so like many classical music audiences Buxton lacked racial diversity as well as a broad age profile.[12] The festival organisers had responded to this challenge with the launch of a youth initiative, aiming to produce teachers' packs and rescored versions of the operas for children's voices, in recognition that the traditional methods of introducing young people to Gilbert and Sullivan were no longer working:

> We've got to get more and more schools, youth establishments, education authorities, putting it back into schools, because our generation will not have been brought up on it, unlike our parents' generation, who were part of church societies or whatever, and it's been handed down from generation to generation.   (Interview with Neil Smith, festival organiser, August 2001)

This strategy seems a more promising one for the future of the Savoy repertoire than the audience's rather idealistic view that better advertising would bring in younger people to watch established amateur groups. Either way, the Buxton ethos is one of wanting to share enthusiasms and broaden the impact of the repertoire, without compromising the high standards and shared knowledge that make the festival so enjoyable for those who currently attend. One audience member expressed a hope that the festival would stay '"open" to new people and companies', and so reflected the anxiety that surrounds any attempt at audience expansion; how to preserve the character of an event while increasing its membership and demographic.

Another strong factor in the audience's enjoyment of the festival was the appropriateness of the venue, described by one as 'the right place in which G & S should be performed'. Buxton Opera House is a proscenium arch theatre, designed by Frank Matcham and opened in 1903. Amongst its many ornate decorations are two panels, either side of the stage: in one is the name of Mozart, in the other the name of Sullivan – confirming the views of many of the audience that this theatre has long been thought of as a fitting venue for Savoy opera performances. The theatre underwent restoration in the 1970s, after a period of closure, and again in the late 1990s, such that recent improvements will have been evident to regular attendees at the 2001 festival. Audience members commented on the ambience of the theatre, in some cases favouring its intimacy as a 900-seater venue over larger theatres in their home cities. The quality of the performances and the suitability of the venue were closely linked for several respondents:

> An excellent venue to see high class G & S productions in a beautiful area of the country.
> Excellent entertainment in a superb location and setting. Great theatre with the ambience that lends itself to the occasion.

The opera house has the advantage of providing opportunities to mingle with other audience members both in the bars inside and, weather permitting, in the open square at the front of the building. Although its age renders parts of the opera house inaccessible to wheelchairs, provision for disabled access is carefully detailed on the opera house website, and no difficulties in that respect were mentioned in the questionnaire responses. Overall, the venue appears to be held in high affection, its Peak District location adding to its holiday appeal. Perhaps, too, there is a sense in which the genteel, semi-rural location is appropriate to the period genre being celebrated there: the Edwardian setting complementing the Victorian repertoire to create a world untroubled by too many contemporary concerns.

Understanding a self-contained musical world

The Buxton Festival serves as one example of the ways in which the Savoy operas are interpreted, experienced and enjoyed by performers and audience members. The festival is a celebration of the repertoire, which in turn encompasses a campaigning role as the audiences and organisers, in particular, seek to bring new participants into their community. Gilbert and Sullivan is recognised as being 'a genre under threat', associated with past

18 Buxton Opera House.[13]

glories and an older generation, and even while audience members enjoy the nostalgia of the festival, they express concern about whether this can be sustained. Performers are notably less anxious about such matters, perhaps because the very existence of their performing groups means that they are already making a positive contribution to continuing the Gilbert and Sullivan tradition. Their involvement in the comic operas is necessarily more practical, and the works are appreciated for the opportunities they afford for the display and development of performing skills. For all concerned, the Savoy operas bring the security of a nostalgic, predictable plotline, and the challenge and satisfaction of achieving high-quality performance. Performers and audience members are able to occupy a self-contained musical world, and while some may venture outside it, most are fiercely loyal and will defend and promote the Gilbert and Sullivan canon with enthusiasm.

Empirical research with performers and audience members has rarely taken Gilbert and Sullivan as its subject, a choice made here because of the impassioned views about musical participation that were likely to result from a group committed to a relatively marginalised genre. Research of this kind can shed light on the ways in which the repertoire is used and interpreted – and could be taken further by considering the views of new-comers to the repertoire, perhaps less steeped in its tradition and able to assess more objectively its contemporary reception. Studies of Gilbert and Sullivan enthusiasts, in turn, contribute to a wider understanding of how musical behaviour impacts upon people's lives. Performers and audiences are shown here to be gaining personal and social benefit from sharing well-loved and familiar repertoire with like-minded friends, as well as developing musical skills and insights and helping to preserve a valued aspect of English cultural heritage.

The Savoy operas have generated a distinctive sub-culture amongst classical music enthusiasts, within which the repertoire and its traditions are highly respected, and their promotion to the next generation is seen as a social responsibility. There are few other genres of music that are so clearly defined and self-contained: jazz audiences, for instance, have equally passionate but more widely varied affiliations to their shared music, and while chamber music listeners may return repeatedly to particular composers, they usually explore a wider repertoire within which their favourite is set in context, rather than expressing the fierce loyalty of the Gilbert and Sullivan fan. Perhaps there is a certain defensiveness in the love of a repertoire historically located 'outside the main galleries' of classical music[14] that causes Gilbert and Sullivan aficionados to be so single-mindedly devoted? The operas offer a link to the 'stability and predictability' of an earlier age,[15] and an escape to an ordered world of 'topsy-turvy' logic. For the participants whose experiences are reported here, the annual pilgrimage to Buxton brings high-quality music amongst friends in a congenial setting – a situation which perfectly captures the appeal and spirit of the operas for those who attend.

14 'How great thy charm, thy sway how excellent!' Tracing Gilbert and Sullivan's legacy in the American musical

RAYMOND KNAPP

Tracing artistic legacy and ancestry is always a complex affair, and must ultimately depend more on persuasive example and argument than on an abundance of hard evidence. In the case of Gilbert and Sullivan and the American musical, there can be no real question that the influence of the former on the latter was profound, especially with *HMS Pinafore* (1878) coming so soon after *The Black Crook* (1866). The huge success of *HMS Pinafore* and its successors in America – then and since, in adaptations and repertoire – provided both motive and opportunity. Moreover, there is ample testimony, especially from lyricists, regarding the formative impact of Gilbert and Sullivan on important contributors to the American musical.[1] But a broadly based, direct connection is nevertheless hard to argue in the face of stark differences in sensibility. The earnest optimism and elaborate choreography and stage effects typical of the American musical from its late nineteenth-century origins through its twentieth-century maturity seem quite distinct from the wry topsy-turvydom of Gilbert and Sullivan, and the differences multiply quickly upon fuller consideration.[2]

There are, to be sure, more than a few incontrovertible homages. George M. Cohan's 'Captain of the ten day boat' (*Little Johnny Jones*, 1904) is a direct parody of 'Captain of the Pinafore'. George and Ira Gershwin's *Strike Up the Band!* (1927), *Of Thee I Sing* (1931; the first musical to win a Pulitzer Prize) and the latter's sequel, *Let 'em Eat Cake* (1933), follow the larger Savoy tradition in offering full-scale political satires that are both oblique and ridiculous enough in their particulars not to offend, with songs such as 'The illegitimate daughter' (from *Of Thee I Sing*) to reinforce the connection to Gilbert and Sullivan. Kurt Weill and Ira Gershwin's 'Circus dream' (*Lady in the Dark*, 1941) re-creates the situation of *Trial by Jury* within a gendered inversion, along the way incorporating several verbal borrowings, a musical reference to *The Mikado*, a patter song ('Tschaikowsky'), and a forced-rhyme reference, *à la* minstrelsy, to 'Gilbert and Sellivant'.[3] Stephen Schwartz's 'War is a science' (*Pippin*, 1973), in combining patter and satire within an explanatory song, is a clear allusion. And the British Admiral in Stephen

Sondheim's 'Please hello' (*Pacific Overtures*, 1976) delivers an extended pastiche Gilbert and Sullivan patter song, even more intricately rhymed than Gilbert's, and rivalled in recent decades only by the 'Witch's rap' and Amy's mostly unrhymed contribution to 'Getting married today', in Sondheim's *Into the Woods* (1987) and *Company* (1970), respectively.

But these homages are striking in part for being somewhat exceptional, and they in any case point to some discomfiting circumstances. Cohan's parody is a barb pointed directly at England's pretensions, nautical and otherwise, well in line with the extravagant American partisanship of the show – hardly the Anglophilia that might be expected to accompany a tribute to Gilbert and Sullivan. Both Schwartz and Sondheim have claimed not to care much for Gilbert and Sullivan. And Ira Gershwin's unabashed admiration for Gilbert has probably abetted the consignment of most of his work for the musical stage to the sidelines of theatrical history. However much a Gilbertian poetic dexterity enriches his individual lyrics, this dimension comes across, on stage, as a rather precious verbal cleverness that undermines whatever inclination audiences may have to take any of it very seriously. Thus have *Of Thee I Sing* and 'Circus dream' (especially 'Tschaikowsky' in the latter, Danny Kaye's quintessential 'speciality number') come to be regarded as little more than charming relics, notwithstanding recent ardent partisanship on behalf of *Lady in the Dark*.[4] And that judgement applies, more broadly, to Broadway's overall take on Gilbert and Sullivan, at least post-*Oklahoma!* (Richard Rodgers and Oscar Hammerstein II, 1943), after which overt references to specific stylistic features of their work tend either to come across as shtick or to form the basis for pastiche.

Nevertheless, there are truly central contributions that Gilbert and Sullivan have made to the American musical, not least because they helped establish a market in America for book-based musical comedy and set many of its standard features, however murky the precise lineage for some of these may be. Their preference for the two-act format, though shared by many other relevant precursors, may well be decisive, coming as it did with considerable trappings, including a first act framed by an establishing number and a finale that sets the drama's central problem in relief, a tendency towards 'second-act problems', and the device of employing the reprise to reinforce the musical's potential for dramatic reconsideration and transformation. All these and many other structural features typical of their operas persist as Broadway conventions. Other features sometimes cited include their reliance on the chorus to amplify the central love story (a feature particularly gratifying to amateur performance groups), and their penchant for colourful array in scenery and costume[5] – although these features, too, have many precedents, and their latter-day echoes in the American musical range widely regarding how credibly they may be traced to the Savoy in particular.

Because of the undeniable but somewhat indistinct nature of Gilbert and Sullivan's lasting influence on the American musical, it seems somewhat beside the point to present an extended, detailed argument for it here. Most people either need no convincing or will remain sceptics no matter how many specific examples might be listed in evidence. Moreover, the prospect of creating such a list in competition with Bradley, Wren and others – not to mention online resources such as IMDB, Wikipedia and The Gilbert and Sullivan Archive (see websites listed in the Bibliography) – is daunting, not because the task would be so very difficult, but because it would devolve too quickly into mere fandom.

What makes better sense is to focus on legacy rather than influence. By identifying particular features prominent in Gilbert and Sullivan's operas, for example, and by tracing some of their latter-day developments and man-ifestations, one may – without aspiring to comprehensiveness – celebrate and illuminate both the English parent and its somewhat unruly Ameri-can progeny. Four broad topics seem conducive to such an approach, each occupying its own sphere and raising its own order of questions regarding legacy. The first two involve general approaches to writing songs for the stage: first, the broad issue of setting English texts for the stage, for which Gilbert and Sullivan set an extraordinary standard, and second, more nar-rowly, a particular type of number that was developed (if not invented) by them and became a mainstay of Broadway: the combination song. A third topic addresses the many useful tropes and models of representation Gilbert and Sullivan helped establish for the American stage, by creating modes of Englishness that were, in reception, sometimes significantly out of alignment with their original English contexts. A brief consideration of a broader issue, flowing in part from this cultural distancing, will then conclude this exploration: how legacy functions for a repertoire that refuses either to die or to relinquish its essential separateness, a question that will return to the specific problems already raised regarding pastiche and homage.

Transforming the patter of poetic feet

The strong tendency among scholars and commentators to look upon Gilbert as the creative and comic genius of the pair, and thus the more influential, masks what may be the more seminal contribution of Sullivan. Even those – such as Sondheim – who are more irritated than pleased by Gilbert's ditties have had to respond to the fact that Sullivan made those ditties matter far more than they might have done in lesser hands, in the process raising a standard of musical text-setting for Broadway that has, despite the occasional lapse, continued to this day – thanks, indeed, in the latter decades especially to Sondheim and a very few others, and despite the incursion of a rather different lyric standard brought into play with rock. To pass muster on Broadway, especially during the heyday of Tin Pan Alley and the so-called 'Golden Age', and for those since who have attempted to extend the tradition, the music of a song must make the words *count*, and derive its rationale therefrom, however much it may also contribute more abstractly, as music. And the American musical has Sullivan's work with Gilbert, more than anything else, to thank for establishing that standard.

In a pioneering study of Sullivan's approach to text-setting, Robert Fink details the craft that Sullivan brought to the task of setting Gilbert's words, showing in particular how the most startlingly original of their songs owe much more to Sullivan's inventive approach to rhythm than to Gilbert, who was rather too attached to simple strings of iambs and anapaests.[6] Thus, Sullivan's setting of 'Three little maids' from *The Mikado* turns 'So PLEASE you, SIR, we MUCH reGRET . . .' into the giddy and impudent 'So pleaseyousirwemuch reGRET . . .', an example of what Fink calls 'sprung rhythm' (a poetic term that originates with Gerard Manley Hopkins, 1844– 89, used here to mean a deployment of musical rhythm that runs somewhat counter to the given poetic rhythm). In Fink's analysis, sprung rhythm combines with Sullivan's careful deployment of his musical erudition (especially regarding counterpoint and harmony) within a generally simpler song idiom, so as to create character-driven settings that come across as 'natural', that is, straightforwardly serving the lyric. While Sullivan's settings do in fact serve the lyric, enhancing rather than overwhelming Gilbert's wit and occasional eloquence, the effect of simplicity is, as Fink shows, hard won, and is dependably and sufficiently beguiling so that one scarcely notices how much the result diverges from what a more traditionally 'natural' approach to text-setting might produce (despite the nearly universal belief among aficionados that Gilbert's words are the cause of which Sullivan's music is the effect).

This tension between following poetic declamation and finding a complex sung rhythm – that is, a musico-poetic rhythm shaped by not only metrical stresses, but also vocal leaps, harmonic urgency and other means – which will seem expressive of both character and situation, drives much of what is most characteristic of Broadway at its best. The melody of Cole Porter's 'All through the night' (*Anything Goes*, 1934), for example, retains for the most part the dactyls of the lyric, breaking – with the lyric – only at the end of each eight-bar phrase. But a larger, 'sprung' rhythm also brings additional stress to key words, emphasising, in the first half of the song, 'to me' (upward leap, returning to the tonic with the first phrase's closing iamb), 'You' (upward leap at the beginning of a subphrase) and 'ecstasy' (sudden harmonic shift on the second phrase's closing iamb):

> All through the night, I delight in your love,
> All through the night, you're so close TO ME.
> All through the night, from a height far above,
> YOU and your love bring me ECSTASY.

The manipulation of the paired upward leaps is particularly striking because each of them follows, at a different point in its phrase, an extended chromatic descent, recalling Grosvenor's entrance in the first-act finale of *Patience*, where he similarly drifts downward chromatically before leaping upwards (on 'mind's'):

> I'm a broken-hearted troubadour, whose MIND'S aesthetic . . .

Moreover, although the characters in the two shows are quite different from each other, the rationales for their chromatic descents are nearly identical, expressing romantic obsession as their beloveds prepare to marry inappropriately, with a strict adherence to metrical accent in both cases further reinforcing that sense of obsession. In both cases, further, the musical declamation is revelatory, immediately alerting the assembled crowd of Grosvenor's 'difference' on the one hand, and, on the other, alerting us to the depths of feeling that will sustain Billy Crocker's quest to secure Hope Harcourt, within a private moment at odds with his generally cheerful outward demeanour.

Similar examples are legion, and each one highly individual; there is room here to consider two more. The extended, low-register 'My' that opens the chorus of 'My funny Valentine' (Rodgers and Hart, *Babes in Arms*, 1937) embraces all the mockery to follow within the warmth of a deeply personal possessive. Between 'My' and 'Valentine', the intervening 'funny' is nearly eclipsed, rhythmically, so that this hint at the mockery to come is de-emphasised, grounded within an intense and overriding affection. Moreover, the conversion from what might have been set as simple iambs gives added urgency to 'Valentine', as well, owing specifically to the shift from anapaest to iamb in the converted rhythm of the opening phrase (from 'My FUNny VALenTINE' to 'MY funny VALenTINE').

In converting 'Happily ever after' to its replacement number, 'Being alive' (*Company*, 1970), Sondheim retained the opening lyric, but with a new emphasis. Without violating the anapaests of this lyric, he displaces the emphasis from *what* happens when you join with another, to the *person* to whom you join. Thus,

> Someone to HOLD you too CLOSE,
> Someone to HURT you too DEEP...

becomes – in a slower tempo that takes the time to linger over the first word –

> SOMEone to hold you too CLOSE,
> SOMEone to hurt you too DEEP...

Besides shifting away from the incursive and damaging aspects of the projected relationship, to a more ambivalent acknowledgement of the human connection (of SOMEone CLOSE and DEEP), the recast lines also set up different rhythmic consequences, when the syntax of the song shifts. In 'Happily ever after', with its emphasis on verbs, the offending but unstressed subject is simply removed: in order to avoid being hurt, 'someone', as if inevitably, becomes 'no one'. But in 'Being alive', with its emphasis on the encroaching subject, it is the verb that shifts, crucially, from the infinitive to the imperative:

> SOMEbody need me too MUCH,
> SOMEbody know me too WELL...

(To gauge how effectively the reset opening lines act as a pivot, try singing 'No one to hold you too close' to the melody of 'Being alive', or 'Somebody need me too much' to the melody of 'Happily ever after'!)

Sullivan's deployment of musical style as an indicator of (sometimes hidden) character finds significant echo in the American musical, which key examples from *HMS Pinafore*, along with two sharply contrasting sets of examples from American musicals, will serve to illustrate. When Ralph makes his entrance in *HMS Pinafore* singing 'The nightingale' in an elevated style befitting his (still undisclosed) nobility of birth, and, later, when the Captain sings 'Fair moon', in dramatic parallel but in a much simpler style, we are immediately amused by the class-based inversions. But the music turns out to be right about them, thus arguing implicitly that class and societal hierarchies are inborn. Similarly, when the sailors attempt to sing the glee Sir Joseph has written for them ('A British tar'), they discover its counterpoint to be somewhat ungainly. Whether this is meant to indicate the limited musical skills of the crew or of the ostensible composer may be irrelevant; Sir Joseph and the crew are alike in aspiring to a refinement beyond their birth class. Equally telling, though, is the sailors' mode of recovery: with the rousing hornpipe conclusion, they return to secure musical footing.

On Broadway, Sondheim has been the most adept at this kind of character setting, although Hammerstein (with both Jerome Kern and Rodgers), Cy Coleman, Dorothy Fields, Alan Jay Lerner and Frederick Loewe, Frank Loesser, Cole Porter and myriad others tend strongly towards this specific level and type of sophistication. In *A Little Night Music* (Sondheim, 1973), for example, Carl-Magnus, singing a pompous imperial polonaise as befits his being both a count and an officer ('In praise of women'), seems incapable of sorting out possibilities that his rival, Fredrik Egerman, would have dispensed in a few lines of patter in his earlier, lawyerly 'Now'. But Fredrik, despite his elocution and grasp of intricately plotted logic, is no more able than Carl-Magnus to align his world and his desires equably; indeed, more than just his penchant for patter connects him to Gilbert, who, trained as a lawyer, often seems in his shows to strangle genuine feeling within the twisting fibres of intricate verbal logic.

A curious parallel between 'A British tar' and 'Tradition' (*Fiddler on the Roof*, Jerry Bock and Sheldon Harnick, 1964) provides a convenient segue into the next section. Perhaps the most remarkable thing about 'Tradition', as a combination song, is that it does not actually work; however compatible the four perspectives may be, even musically, they – fathers, mothers, sons, daughters – sing together in complete discord until the end, when they come together on the word 'Tradition' with a conviction as great as *HMS Pinafore*'s sailors' in their concluding hornpipe. Even this latter-day indulgence in contrapuntal chaos, which may be seen as grossly exaggerating Sullivan's thorny counterpoint in 'A British tar', has been upstaged by Sondheim, whose 'Please hello' (*Pacific Overtures*, 1976) degenerates even more extremely – even though chaperoned by Gilbert and Sullivan in the guise of the patter-singing British Admiral – before finding its own word of agreement in 'détente'.

Combination songs

According to Stephen Banfield 'Gilbert and Sullivan patented the contrapuntal double chorus – of lovesick maidens versus dragoons in *Patience*, peers versus fairies in *Iolanthe* – and this topic survives as late as *West Side Story* with the Jets and the Sharks'.[7] It has been a problem naming the thing that may be the most distinctive link – apart from the patter song – between the Savoy and Broadway. The most common designation is 'double chorus', which works for many examples in their operas, but not all (not for those involving solo or duet forces, for example, or involving more than two simultaneously presented tunes). Moreover, the term applies to any full gathering of the cast in song ('contrapuntal' does help here, but not enough), and serves even less well to describe many Broadway derivatives. The old term 'quodlibet' has often been used to describe the device – but inappropriately, since it not only is technically wrong, but also seems to indicate a kind of elevation (didn't Bach write them?) while actually indicating the reverse, denoting a kind of musical joke entailing the often inappropriate combination of familiar tunes.

The term 'combination song', while somewhat prosaic, has the merit of clearly describing the compositional device involved: introducing two or more songs separately and then joining them together in counterpoint, whatever the vocal forces involved or the dramatic setting. Within this broader rubric, Banfield's assertion (quoted just above) may be not only endorsed, but also expanded: Sullivan and Gilbert did indeed lay claim to the device in a major way, and it was then picked up and developed further in the American musical. From this perspective, *West Side Story*'s 'Tonight' (Leonard Bernstein and Sondheim, 1957) – which uses the device to prolong a *tableau* of intensifying expectation prior to the show's central dramatic events, as seen from multiple perspectives – represents only one particular line of development, with latter-day applications ranging from *Les Misérables*'s 'One day more' (Claude-Michel Schönberg and Alain Boublil, 1980), to *South Park: Bigger Longer & Uncut*'s 'La Resistance / Tomorrow Night' (Trey Parker and Marc Shaiman, 1999) and *Once More, with Feeling*'s 'Walk through the fire' (episode 107 of *Buffy the Vampire Slayer*, Joss Whedon, 2001).

Sullivan first tried his hand at a combination song in *The Zoo* (Sullivan and Bolton Rowe (B. C. Stephenson), 1875), and offered another sample two years later in *The Sorcerer*, setting the inner passion and outer reserve of Sir Marmaduke and Lady Sangazure in reciprocal apposition. But its effective première for Americans, in *HMS Pinafore* (1878), may have been Sullivan's inspiration, since Gilbert does not indicate that the sailors sing 'We sail the ocean blue' against Sir Joseph's female relatives' 'Gaily tripping'. With this number, establishing both difference and compatibility between the two groups, one familiar dramatic rationale for the device was set, yet the two combination songs from *The Pirates of Penzance* (1879) mark two separate departures in this regard. In the first, Mabel and Frederic sing a love duet ('Did ever maiden wake') while the remaining daughters of Major-General Stanley chatter on about the weather ('How beautifully blue the sky'), creating an effect of background and foreground, which are then overlaid. But early in the second act we find an important precursor for the 'Tonight' – 'One day more' line of development, when the daughters' 'Go ye heroes' combines with the policemen's 'When the foeman bares his steel' to effect a climax through contrasting perspectives.

Many of the combination songs to follow (for they quickly became a Gilbert and Sullivan staple) derive from these; for example, *Patience* (1881) pits the dragoons' 'Now is not this ridiculous' against the maidens' 'In a doleful train', echoing with more dramatic opposition the situation in *HMS Pinafore*; this is also the rationale for *Ruddigore*'s 'Welcome gentry' / 'When thoroughly tired' (1887). But *The Mikado* (1885) further enriches the possibilities of the type by offering three distinct perspectives at once, in the male trio in Act I. In this extraordinary number, Pooh-Bah's ponderous 'I am so proud' and Ko-Ko's skittish 'My brain it teems' (both in B minor) are set against Pish-Tush's cheerful 'I heard one day' (in D major and skipping triplets), creating an opposition that must be resolved dramatically even though the counterpoint works beautifully as it is; hence the concluding homophonic patter 'To sit in solemn silence' in B major. Gilbert and Sullivan's more seriously toned *Yeomen of the Guard* (1888), like *Pirates of Penzance*, offers two combination songs, except that here they are coordinated dramatically. Both involve the Tower Warders, and work as a pair to dramatise their fall from grace in allowing a prisoner to escape. Thus, their self-pride merges easily with the crowd's adoration early on ('Tower Warders' / 'In the autumn of our life'), but Act II opens with that crowd heaping shame on them ('Night has spread her pall once more'), in a number that culminates in a combination of this chorus with the Warders' bitter self-castigation, based on Dame Carruthers's stinging taunt, 'Warders are ye? Whom do ye ward?' All of these applications have significant echoes in the American musical.

Perhaps the most familiar type finds compatibility in contrast, well in accord with the American musical's penchant for assimilationist plots. Leonard Bernstein's *Candide* (1956) originally included 'Venice Gavotte' (lyrics by Dorothy Parker and Richard Wilbur) as a kind of novelty number of musically compatible contrasts, which Sondheim rewrote to function as part of an opening establishing sequence for the 1974 revival ('Life Is happiness indeed'). *The Music Man* (Meredith Willson, 1957) offers several examples of this type, mostly expressing either compatibility or the potential for community (the overlapping melodies of 'Seventy-six trombones' and 'Goodnight my someone'; 'Lida Rose' and 'Will I ever tell you'; and – although the combination never found a place in the show itself – 'My white knight' and 'The sadder but wiser girl'), and also includes one of the foreground–background variety, when 'Pick-a-little, talk-a-little' becomes the background for the School Board's 'Goodnight ladies'. Deriving most directly from Gilbert and Sullivan's model, the operetta spoof *Little Mary Sunshine* offers the delightful tripartite 'Playing croquet' / 'Swinging' / 'How do you do?' (Rick Besoyan, 1959). A few years later, Irving Berlin added 'An old-fashioned wedding' to the 1966 revival of *Annie Get Your Gun* – a combination song that perhaps violates the established sensibilities of Annie and Frank, but extends their separate musical personae as established in 'The girl I marry' and 'I got the sun in the morning', while setting up the hilarious simultaneity of Annie's 'Love and honor, yes, but *not* obey' with Frank's 'You'll vow to love and honor and obey'.[8] As indicated at the end of the previous section, this type, in inversion, has also been used to underscore incompatibilities within apparent alignments, as in 'Tradition' (*Fiddler on the Roof*) and 'Please hello' (*Pacific Overtures*).

Somewhat rarer is the type of combination song that presents contrasting perspectives (except of the *tableau* variety already discussed), in part because this type generally requires some kind of local resolution. Here, Sondheim provides the most impressive examples. In 'Getting married today' (in which resolution comes after the song, despite the reiterated 'Amen' that enforces closure), Amy's inner turmoil churns out a mostly unrhymed patter, as comic hysteria, that will combine with Paul's and the choir's pious devotion. In 'Now / Later / Soon' (*A Little Night Music*), each component song is strikingly individual, expressing the character of its singer. First, the lawyer Fredrik considers a variety of means for seducing his virgin wife, enumerating in volleys of sporadic patter a series of nested As and Bs while his wife babbles seeming nonsense, until he finally opts for an afternoon nap. While he sleeps, his son, caught between his libido and Martin Luther, broods into his cello, taking his theme from Anne's admonition, 'Later'. And Anne, having managed each male in turn, is alluringly both maternal and girlish in 'Soon', a quasi-lullaby in which she shifts keys and tempo capriciously, and gracefully negotiates whimsically intricate rhythms. When the three songs come together, they do mesh, for a time – allowing for Fredrik's drowsier pace, since he's singing in his sleep. But as the song continues, through force of will and gentle persuasion, it is Anne's song that the others bend to, unable to resist submerging their own identities into hers (a setup for Anne's imminent fall: in his sleep, Fredrik's final sung word is not 'Anne', as before, but 'Desirée'). In its hierarchically conceived use of the combination-song principle, Sondheim recalls another model predating Gilbert and Sullivan: the opening duet in Mozart's *Le nozze di Figaro* (1786), in which Figaro's counting first provides Susanna's more lyrical song with a bass line, before he acquiesces completely and simply joins her in parallel harmony.

Images of Englishness: sailors and pirates, closets and imperialists

Gilbert and Sullivan's American successes were extremely productive, thematically, providing Americans with a full slate of useful – and durable – musical images of Englishness. To this end, it hardly mattered that these images were originally intended as parodies. Gilbertian parody took on its own life on the American stage, as a kind of archness that would eventually merge into camp, which freed Broadway to adopt those satirical images as perhaps exaggerated, but nevertheless essential features of Englishness. Thus the effeminised, well-turned-out sailors in *HMS Pinafore*, Bunthorne in *Patience*, and the pairing of peers with fairies in *Iolanthe*, all helped establish and reinforce a familiar trope on the American stage: that Englishness, in a male, is indistinguishable from homosexuality. And *HMS Pinafore*, *The Pirates of Penzance* and *The Yeomen of the Guard* – and in different ways, *The Mikado* and significant elements in *Ruddigore* and *Utopia Limited* (notwithstanding the latter's relative lack of success) – drew important attention to England's history of imperialism, providing a vehicle for both pride and ridicule so delicately nuanced that you could not always tell the one from the other.

Both of these thematic tropes, in large part because of their satirical bases, allowed Americans to view England in a comically demeaning light while at the same time appreciating the creative wit that lay behind it all – and celebrating that wit, too, as essentially English in character. *HMS Pinafore*'s satire points to the folly of disrupting societal hierarchies, yet it could all too easily be read – and surely was by Americans – as tweaking such hierarchies and those who invest in them, in favour of an egalitarianism more in sympathy with America values.[9] That Penzance's pirates could suddenly turn out to be noblemen may play as a final ludicrous joke in the show (funny in part because of its basis in history, most notoriously with regard to Henry Morgan and Francis Drake in England, among others, and Jean Lafitte in America), but the humour in *The Pirates of Penzance* stems more broadly from the cowardice and ineffectuality of all the male characters, police and pirates alike, a running joke that continues *HMS Pinafore*'s emasculation of the very symbol of England's (male) pride, the 'Queen's Navee', and looks forward to Richard Dauntless in *Ruddigore*. Bunthorne was both an example of a 'type' – and after Oscar Wilde's tour, Americans knew that type well – and exemplary of a tendency that might be discerned in Englishmen more generally. The ridicule of English traditions and traditional sites of English authority – nearly everywhere you look in the shows, but especially in *HMS Pinafore*, *The Pirates of Penzance*, *Iolanthe*, *Ruddigore*, *The Mikado*, and *The Yeomen of the Guard* – was irresistibly delicious for an America still relatively young but increasingly less in thrall to its main parental figure, England.

But probably more important than having these tropes available as markers for 'English' were the collateral uses that could be made of them in practice. This may be most obvious in the case of the gay/English trope. Within the theatrical world of Broadway, in which shows for more than a century after Gilbert and Sullivan played simultaneously (and mainly) to heterosexuals and closeted gay males, Gilbert and Sullivan's effeminising satirical strategies helped establish a 'beard' for obviously gay characters. Being 'English', or more generally Bunthornesque – that is, poetic, decadent, a bit too precious, or otherwise effete – offered the homosexual male character a protective cloak of deniability that gay men in the audience could easily see through.

Two examples are especially relevant here. Sir Evelyn Oakleigh in Cole Porter's *Anything Goes* (1934) is an obvious touchstone for this trope, especially since he is surrounded in the show by many other tokens of a gay sensibility, such as the nightclub diva Reno Sweeney (especially had Ethel Merman been willing to sing 'Kate the Great'), the homosocial pairing of Billy and his ineffectual gangster sidekick, and a number of dress-up disguises for the stowaways, including cute sailor outfits.[10] The latter forges an even more direct link to Gilbert and Sullivan's *HMS Pinafore*, since, with the shipboard setting, and with Billy actually dressed like Ralph and later consigned to the equivalent of a 'dungeon cell', the parallels between the romantic triangles in the two shows become all the more obvious.

But equally revealing is the treatment of Henry Higgins in Lerner and Loewe's *My Fair Lady* (1956). Most Americans were so accustomed by then to accepting the English 'beard' for homosexuality (and, perhaps also, so invested in the Cinderella story, and distracted by the fact that this particular beard was created by an Englishman to begin with), that they managed not to notice the closeted significance of much pointed dialogue and situational business in the show (especially in 'A hymn to him' and 'The rain in Spain').[11] Yet, the tropes are all in place. Like Oakleigh (and Harrison Howell in Porter's *Kiss Me, Kate*), Higgins is unmusical, a trait that often undermines the potential for heterosexual coupling in musicals. And he, no less than Billy's sailor suit and situation in *Anything Goes*, recalls Gilbert and Sullivan fairly specifically; indeed, his comic rants are not only quasi-Gilbertian in concept, but also in execution, since in Rex Harrison's definitive creation of the role, he recalls even more specifically the tradition, in performance, for Gilbert's most 'sexless' (read, heterosexually challenged) male characters to speak-sing their songs.

The presence of imperialist tropes in Gilbert and Sullivan, both celebrating and poking fun at English institutions and England's relationship to other nations, has left a similarly ambivalent residue in the American musical. The most striking cases are probably those shows by Rodgers and Hammerstein, post-World War II, that treat subjects related to imperialism (war, exoticism, interracial dynamics): *South Pacific* (1949), *The King and I* (1951), *Flower Drum Song* (1958) and *The Sound of Music* (1959). Each of these is driven by a strong sense of social responsibility, yet none sufficiently complicates its asserted truths, and – surely related to this – each carries a sense of smug superiority that reveals an unconsciously imperialist mindset. This is especially true regarding *The King and I* and *The Sound of Music*, with their gross distortions of history.[12] In some ways these shows, in their very earnestness, stand distinctly apart from Gilbert and Sullivan (except perhaps from *Yeomen*'s more serious questioning of tradition and its potential for abuse). Yet, despite this, *The King and I* owes much to *The Mikado*, even if Rodgers did not follow Sullivan's example of grounding the music in something authentically of the culture being represented.[13] The most important connection may concern the lesson *The Mikado* takes from minstrelsy, of masking the self as Other in order to critique the former and claim an allegiance (of sorts) to the latter. There is a useful conflation in the show, similar in kind to the casting of Julie Andrews in *The Sound of Music*,[14] between English and American, perspectives that merge for audiences however much the show tries to keep them separate. And it is this tension that provides a substitute for the balance between pride and ridicule that underwrites the distinctive tone of Gilbert and Sullivan at their best.

Even more than *The King and I*, *Pacific Overtures* owes much to *The Mikado*, and Gilbert and Sullivan more generally, yet it, too, has trouble establishing a point of balance, with its perspective weighing decidedly in favour of earnest critique; in this respect it recalls 'War Is a Science' in *Pippin*. But its most effective comedy number, 'Please Hello', reduces the scary trappings of imperialism to a colourful musical revue, aping Sousa and the Savoy in turn. And it is here that Sondheim comes closest to Gilbert and Sullivan, not because of the direct homage of the British Admiral's patter, but rather because he employs a basic strategy of the Savoy operas. In the very act of placing judges, sailors, captains, admirals, pirates, major-generals, police, pretentious poets, peers, etc., on the musical stage, making them sing and dance for our entertainment, Sullivan and Gilbert achieved a critical balance between ridicule and celebration, and so were able to engage Britain critically while holding securely on to England.

Living legacies and pastiche

One of the difficulties in tracing legacy in this case is that the parent simply refuses to die ('But you don't go . . .'). The works by Sullivan and Gilbert are still in the repertoire, and so have never become the fertiliser for future American musicals that most American shows before *Show Boat* (Kern and Hammerstein, 1927) were to become. Neither has there been even a strand within the complex development of English-language musical theatre that seems directly descended from their works. The American musical,

19 The American Aspect: Groucho Marx as Ko-Ko in an American television production of *The Mikado* (1960).

in particular, simply has too many 'parents' for one to claim definitively that a particular trait stems from Gilbert and Sullivan. It will thus always be extremely clear just how different American musicals are from Savoy operas, and allusions to the latter – in the form of homages and pastiche – will, as noted, withstand absorption, always pointing outward to their source. It is this dimension that gives some credibility to Gayden Wren's pronouncement that Gilbert and Sullivan were 'in terms of theatre history, an evolutionary dead end'.[15] Within the higher orders, that is what it means to survive more or less intact within the evolutionary paradigm (as, say, with *Homo sapiens*, another evolutionary dead end); implicit in Wren's claim is the disputable notion that their work stands not only apart from, but also above, later Broadway, as an elevated species of comic opera that has no direct descendants.

Yet, there are significant dimensions that, owing to their lack of specificity, have seemed capable of a sustained development across the continuing divide between the Savoy and Broadway. Those identified and briefly explored here – text-setting, combination songs, and themes regarding Englishness, closeted homosexuality and imperialism – seem especially ripe for further thoughtful consideration. But the first task is to dispel some of the clutter, including most of the instances of specific indebtedness that are usually cited as proof of a vital connection, but which too often distract us from looking for deeper and more active linkages.

15 'See how the Fates their gifts allot': the reception of productions and translations in continental Europe

JANA POLIANOVSKAIA

The chronicle of Savoy opera in non-English-speaking countries is an entertaining story of flops and successes, of traditions and prejudices, of copyright conflicts, of translations and adaptations, of creativeness and routine.

The first and most important impulse towards the dissemination of Savoy opera in continental Europe came from the guest tours of the D'Oyly Carte Company. At three different times in 1886 and 1887 Richard D'Oyly Carte had his companies crossing the Channel to play certain of the operas in different centres in Europe, including Vienna and Berlin, Amsterdam and Copenhagen.

The success of the Savoy operas at home quickly came to the attention of continental theatre agents, who were always ready for novelties. Most did not want to pay for expensive stage rights and were always on the lookout for a bargain, and in this regard international copyright law worked in their favour. At that time in Great Britain there were no legal grounds to secure a dramatist's or, especially, a composer's rights outside his own country and, consequently, to prevent unauthorised production of theatre works. On 5 December 1887 the important Berne International Union for the Defence of Literature and Art Works came into force, but the number of countries to sign at first was quite small and there were notable absentees: Austria-Hungary, Holland, Russia, Denmark and Sweden. Theatres and publishing houses in these countries could continue doing as they pleased: no convention, no infringement.

This absence of international agreement thwarted the attempts of Arthur Sullivan and his agents to prevent unauthorised productions of *The Mikado* in Hungarian in Budapest (10 December 1886), in Swedish in Stockholm (24 November 1888 and 22 January 1890), in Croatian in Zagreb (24 February 1892), in Danish in Copenhagen (13 March 1892), in Russian in St Petersburg (10 June 1887), in Dutch in Amsterdam (February 1889) and in German in Prague (10 March 1889).

The composer responded to this problem in his usual manner: he delegated his rights to the Leipzig publishers Bote & Bock (1885) and also applied to his publisher Chappell, who founded a new music-publishing house, Bosworth (in 1889), with the express intent of securing the rights for Savoy opera in Europe.

The driving force behind the international success of Savoy opera was *The Mikado*. Its London triumph caused such a stir that it led Savoy operas both new and old to be staged and translated. Historically, *The Mikado* remained the most popular and most frequently performed of the works by Sullivan and Gilbert, which later meant that, to cite Adolf Aber, 'for most people this composer is only known as the author of the operetta *Der Mikado*'[1] – in this he joins the august company of Bizet (*Carmen*), Mascagni (*Cavalleria rusticana*), Leoncavallo (*Pagliacci*) and Saint-Saëns (*Samson et Dalila*).

Foreign audiences did not have long to wait before they could enjoy performances of Savoy opera in their own languages. Its greatest and most long-lasting success was achieved in German-speaking areas, especially in Germany itself, where a certain continuity of production existed. In other European countries the operas were staged only sporadically, mostly as single enterprises.

Traditionally the performance of comic opera outside its country of origin demands translation. The question arises of how to translate, and, who is to be the translator? 'To carry humour over into another country, another language, is difficult enough. Wit, however, gets irredeemably lost',[2] stated the director of Basle Theatres. No one would describe the task of translating Gilbert's texts, with their complicated rhymes and metres, as an easy one. But, according to Audrey Williamson, these difficulties 'have been overcome in the case of *The Mikado* in many countries, at least to the satisfaction of the local inhabitants'.[3] The truth stands somewhere between. There were 'satisfactory' translations (one might better choose the word 'adaptation'); there were even sensitive, witty and successful ones. But there were also many cases when operas by Sullivan and Gilbert were denied success as a result of a bad translation. The translators were mostly non-specialists – at best librettists, at worst actors or theatre agents – and were always working under the gun, borrowing the clichés. Consequently, these translations became obsolete much faster than the original text.

German-speaking area

One of the countries where the Savoy operas had the greatest success was Germany. There was no other non-English-speaking country, which took to them so enthusiastically. Arthur Sullivan was known in Germany a long time before the worldwide success of *The Mikado*. The Gilbert and Sullivan era began in June 1886, when one of D'Oyly Carte's touring companies brought

20 Box office success in German-language productions: *The Mikado* in the Swiss city of Basle.

the English version of this opera to the Continent, starting in Berlin (using *Trial by Jury* as a curtain-raiser). It enjoyed enormous success, including the presence of high-society members: 'The company of Mr D'Oyly Carte enjoys an ensemble, such as we've never seen in Berlin';[4] so that 'everybody will have to see *The Mikado*'.[5] A German business manager, Dr C. Carlotta (Siegfried Ehrenberg), organised the tour on Carte's behalf and looked after Sullivan's professional interests in Germany and neighbouring countries. He also produced translations for bilingual librettos, where they were printed line-by-line with the English original: *Trial by Jury*, *HMS Pinafore* – according to his statement an 'as exact and literal as possible reproduction of the original' – *The Mikado* and *Patience*. From 9 April 1887 the D'Oyly Carte troupe was again in Germany and performed *The Mikado* in Berlin, Vienna, Munich, Leipzig, Dresden and Breslau (now Wrocław).

The Vienna performance of *The Mikado* took place at the Carltheater on 1 September 1886. The eminent critic Eduard Hanslick was present and generous in his praise. However, he could not, he writes, have believed that such a piece, awash with local hints and specific English jokes, could be doing well with German audiences; but it was, and he attributes the success to the genuine core of comedy in the plot, music and performance.[6]

In translation *The Mikado* was even more successful. The D'Oyly Carte troupe had scarcely packed their suitcases, when work on a German translation began. In a relatively short time there were two. The first, by Zell and Genée – both well-known librettists – was published in Berlin by B. Bernstein (from 1887 Sullivan's continental agent) and in Leipzig by Robert Forberg. Sullivan found it 'much the best in all the lyrical portions'[7] but preferred the dialogue of the second version, translated by Carlotta. He wanted to have both versions combined, but in the end the 'official' D'Oyly Carte English–German libretto was published by Chappell in London and H. Cranz in Vienna under the name of Carlotta. Gilbert was unable to speak German and left the evaluation of translations and financial agreements completely to Sullivan.

The Friedrich-Wilhelmstädtisches Theater in Berlin made use of the Zell–Genée version which had already proved its worth in Vienna, reaching its hundredth performance on 27 May 1894, and continued to be used as the standard version until the 1920s. In Berlin it was also a particularly successful production, where the two-hundredth performance took place on 30 December 1891. Later Adolf Weissmann wrote: 'Like *Die Fledermaus*, which eliminated the prejudice that operetta desecrates the opera house, so now Arthur Sullivan's burlesque *Mikado* was received with much honour and aroused a big response'.[8]

Thus *The Mikado* established the reputation of Savoy opera in Germany. Its melodies soon found a place in the programmes of German and Austrian orchestras, and hence to an increasing interest on the Continent in further works by Gilbert and Sullivan. The latest, but also some earlier, Savoy operas were translated and performed in Vienna and Berlin. However, the German adapters, and more so the music publishers, rarely protected Sullivan's interests. As early as 7 January 1889, in a letter to Bernstein, the composer expressed his fury concerning the German vocal scores of *The Mikado*: 'I find both the finales altered in a most outrageous and unmusicianly manner'.[9] Insulting for both authors was a production at the Carltheater on 2 February 1889 of *The Yeomen of the Guard* under the guise of *Capitän Wilson*. As was usual in unauthorised productions, it was orchestrated from the vocal score by Julius Stern, with text adapted by Victor Leon and Carl Lindau, and published by Weinberger. According to the letter of protest which Sullivan sent to the *Neue Freie Presse* in Vienna, this version had five additional numbers falsely ascribed to him – announced as 'specially composed'.[10] This adaptation was apparently made in accordance with local taste: additional waltz numbers in both acts, which although considered as indispensable for Viennese performance, have little congruence with the plot.

Sullivan's protest, which was reported in the *Era*, brought no real results. Taking advantage of the absence of any international agreement the Theater an der Wien[11] began work on *The Pirates of Penzance* (premièred on 1 March 1889) without Sullivan's authority, and in the same way used their own orchestration of the published vocal score. Zell and Genée translated this unauthorised *Pirates*, 'a decidedly unsporting gesture in Sullivan's eyes'.[12] It was an ongoing story. During a short trip to Vienna in April 1889 Sullivan received a telephone call from Zell (the pseudonym of Camillo Walzel). A short entry in the composer's diary reveals that Sullivan used the opportunity to vent his anger about the behaviour of both librettists with regard to the *Pirates* production.[13]

On 25 December 1889, with the sanction of the composer but not in his presence, *The Yeomen of the Guard* (in this German version *Der Königsgardist*) became the next Sullivan opera to be staged in Germany and in German – once again in a Zell–Genée translation. It was at the Kroll-Oper in Berlin, where the D'Oyly Carte Company had given their original versions of *HMS Pinafore* and *Patience* two years before. The vocal score of *Yeomen*, published by Bosworth in Leipzig, reveals many alterations: 'When our gallant Norman foes', for instance, is transferred from Dame Carruthers to Sergeant Meryll, and the patter trio from *Ruddigore* is integrated into the second act. Only one of the insertions – Meryll's solo song in Act I, removed from the original production – has Sullivan's authority, though, as Arthur Jacobs supposes, 'it will have been too late for the opening night'.[14] Unfortunately this production did not arouse much interest and was cancelled. The same fate befell *The Gondoliers*, staged as *Die Gondoliere* on 20 September 1890 in the Theater an der Wien (Vienna) in a version by Zell and Genée.

Beside these performances there were many others, mainly of *The Mikado*, in cities such as Munich, Leipzig, Dresden, Breslau, Baden-Baden and Bremen. German producers could no longer imagine their repertoire without *Der Mikado*, which was a mixed blessing for the latter.

Up until the First World War the aforementioned operas, and in particular, *The Mikado*, remained in the repertoire of many theatres. A 1912 issue of the journal *Musik für Alle*, wholly devoted to *The Mikado*, was evidence of its popularity. It consisted of a selection of musical numbers and an article, in which the editor placed the work among the classics of operetta.

Table 15.1 *Performances in German-speaking areas, 1886–1914*[a]

Date	Title	Translator	Place, theatre
1882 [GP]	Amor an Bord (Pinafore)	Ernst Dohm	Berlin, Friedrich-Wilhelmstädtisches Theater
2 June 1886	Mikado*		Berlin, Wallner-Theater
14 June 1886	Im Schwurgericht (Trial)*		Berlin, Wallner-Theater
1 Aug. 1886	Im Schwurgericht (Trial)*		Leipzig, Altes Theater
1–27 Sept. 1886	Mikado*		Vienna, Carl-Schulze-Theater
14 Sept. 1886	Im Schwurgericht (Trial)*		Vienna, Carl-Schulze-Theater
26 Dec. 1886	Der Miezekado (parody)	O. Ewald / F. Beier	Kassel
30 April 1887	Patience, oder Dragoner und Dichter*		Berlin, Kroll-Oper
28 May 1887	Patience, oder Dragoner und Dichter*		Vienna, Carl-Schulze-Theater
2 July 1887	Patience, oder Dragoner und Dichter*		Leipzig, Altes Theater
26 Nov. 1887	HMS Pinafore*		Berlin, Kroll-Oper
21 Dec. 1887	Der Miezekado (parody)	O. Ewald / F. Beier	Berlin, Wallner-Theater
1887–95	Der Mikado	(?)	Zurich, Aktientheater
28 Jan. 1888	HMS Pinafore*		Hamburg, Thalia-Theater (?)
2 March 1888	Mikado	Zell / Genée	Vienna, Theater an der Wien
6 Dec. 1888 [GP]	Mikado	Zell / Genée	Berlin, Friedrich-Wilhelmstädtisches Theater
2 Feb. 1889	Capitän Wilson (Yeomen)	Leon / Lindau	Vienna, Carltheater
1 March 1889	Piraten von Penzance	Zell / Genée	Vienna, Theater an der Wien
25 Dec. 1889 [GP]	Königsgardist (Yeomen)	Zell / Genée	Berlin, Kroll-Oper
1889	Mikado	(?)	Hamburg, Carl Schulze-Theater
20 Sept. 1890	Gondoliere	Zell / Genée	Vienna, Theater an der Wien
20 Dec. 1890 [GP]	Gondoliere	Zell / Genée	Berlin, Friedrich-Wilhelmstädtisches Theater
1890	Mikado	E. Olesnitsky (in Ukrainian)	Lvov, Russka Besida Theater
1 Oct. 1892 [GP]	Die Liebe vor Gericht (Trial)	(?)	Berlin, Alexanderplatz-Theater
7 Dec. 1892	Mikado	(?)	Basel, Stadttheater
11 Oct. 1893	Der Königsgardist (Yeomen)	Zell / Genée	Mannheim, Nationaltheater
1893	Mikado	E. Olesnitsky (in Ukrainian)	Lvov, Russka Besida Theater
20 May 1896 [GP]	Grossherzog (Grand Duke)	(?)	Berlin, Theater unter den Linden
28 April 1898	Mikado	(?)	Munich, Gärtnerplatztheater
29 Jan. 1899	Mikado	Children's performance	Vienna, Theatre in der Josefstadt
10 June 1900	Mikado	(?)	Berlin, Königliches Opernhaus[b]
20 April 1901	Princess Ida	(?)	Meran, Amateur production
5 Oct. 1901	Brautpaar vor Gericht (Trial)	Carl Lindau	Vienna, Danzers Orpheum
1902 / 3	Mikado	(?)	Leipzig, Opernhaus[c]
20 Feb. 1903	Mikado	(?)	Mannheim, Nationaltheater
1903–26	Mikado	(?)	Weimar, Court Theatre
c. 1904 [GP]	Patience, oder Liebe und Secession	Rudolph Schanzer	Berlin
8 March 1909	Die Gondoliere	(?)	Mannheim, Nationaltheater
10 Dec. 1909	Mikado	Zell / Genée	Vienna, Volksoper
1912	Mikado	(?)	Munich, Künstlertheater
14 Nov. 1913	Mikado	(?)	Berlin, Theatre on Nollendorf Square

[a] Guest tour performances of D'Oyly Carte Company are marked with '*'. GP – German première.

[b] This production, unusual for the Royal Opera House, came into existence 'on royal demand' due to William I's admiration for Sullivan.

[c] Performed by an opera troupe under the great Arthur Nikisch. Bruno Walter mentioned in his memoires that he had been allowed to conduct *The Mikado* only after he 'had proved the capability for a light touch in operas such as Auber's *Fra Diavolo*, Lortzing's *Zar und Zimmermann* as well as Mozart's works'. See Walter, *Thema und Variationen*, p. 183.

Unfortunately the popularity of the Savoy operas did not endure. After 1914 the 'new reach' made considerable gains with the operetta-going public, which wanted to see a show in the new Paris vogue: 'piquancy, frivolities and legs, legs, legs!'[15] It became clear that one could not play *The Mikado* in its original form and have a success. As a result the first decades of the twentieth century witnessed the freest adaptations (one example is the Berlin production of 1927, in which the second act opened on a naked Yum-Yum bathing). This period produced the first recordings in German[16] – several songs as well as a short version of *Der Mikado* with about fifteen to twenty minutes of music.[17]

But their popularity continued to decrease, and hit rock bottom under Nazi rule: as the creations of an enemy state the Savoy operas were no longer staged (*Die Piraten* of 1936 in Dusseldorf is an exception). A new generation looked for a different type of expression and had no time for the 'old-fashioned' style of Savoy opera; it was no longer acceptable to be 'unsophisticated enough to enjoy the music and the fun pure and simple'.[18]

The post-war period saw the appearance of no fewer than five complete German translations (and accordingly productions) but only of *The Mikado* – by Kurd E. Heyne (Basle, 1944), O. E. Deutsch (Cologne, 1959), A. Assmann and W. Brandin (Vienna, 1962), Dieter Bachmann (Zurich, 1984) and Stefan Trossbach (Hamburg, *c.* 1985). Translations of other Savoy operas could be counted on the fingers of one hand and once put aside did not find further favour (see Table 15.2).

These modern productions deliver a very mixed bag of conceptions and artistic presentations. Some do not go beyond 'museum interpretation' or old German operetta stereotypes. A Dortmund staging of the *Pirates of Penzance* opted for a musical adaptation, changed libretto and instrumentation, mounted a huge publicity campaign and achieved a capacity audience ('Entertainment pure and perfect').[19] *The Mikado* in Freiburg (1990) and Giessen (1995) and *Princess Ida* in Hagen (1986) had good ideas and professional translations, but their authors were under the misapprehension that mediocre singers and superficial study of the score would be sufficient for a Savoy opera. *The Mikado* in the Zurich Playhouse (1984) became the apogee of voicelessness, with a female Mikado thrown in. A *Gondoliers* production in Dusseldorf (2005) employed an English production team, but their concept – a parody of the British amateur theatre – was not understood by the German public. Being English is not in itself a qualification for a proper reading or an appropriate interpretation of Sullivan's stage works.

The custom practised by many mid-sized and small theatres of ordering a new translation for each production, thereby reducing the cost and avoiding copyright issues, has had a negative effect on the reception of Savoy opera. The quality often leaves a lot to be desired, and the tunes do not remain

Table 15.2 *German-language productions 1914–2009*[a]

Date	Title	Translator	Place, theatre
1926	*Mikado*	(?)	Munich, Nationaltheater
1927	*Mikado*	(?)	Darmstadt, Landestheater
1 Sept. 1927	*Mikado*	(?)	Berlin, Grosses Schauspielhaus
23 March 1928 (7)	*Mikado*	Couplets: Paul Schwarz	Hamburg, Stadttheater
1 Dec. 1936 [GP]	*Piraten*	Franz Adam Beyerlein	Dusseldorf, Operettenhaus
11 May 1944	*Mikado*	Kurd E. Heyne	Basel, Stadttheater
18 Oct. 1949	*Gondolieri*	Otto Maag	Basel, Stadttheater
May 1950	*Gondolieri*	Otto Maag	Freiburg
1959	*Mikado*	Otto Erich Deutsch	Cologne
1962	*Mikado*	Arno Assmann/ W. Brandin	Vienna, Volksoper
23 April 1967	*Gondolieri*	Helmut Bez, Jiirgen Degenhardt	Leipzig, Kleines Haus Dreilinden
8 Oct. 1972	*Gaukler von London* (*Yeomen*)	Charles Lewinsky	Kassel, Staatstheater
26 May 1974	*Matrosenliebe* (*HMS Pinafore*)	Charles Lewinsky	Kassel, Staatstheater
29 June 1975	*Mikado*	(?)	Heidelberg, Stadttheater
c. 1983	*HMS Knitterbüx oder Die Seemannsbraut* (*HMS Pinafore*)	Stefan Trossbach	Hamburg, Ascot-Musiktheater
10 Dec. 1983	*Mikado*	(?)	Radebeul
28 March 1984	*Piraten! Piraten!*	Herbert Kreppel	Hildesheim
1984	*Piraten*	Klaus Straube	Lüneburg, Stadttheater
28 June 1984 [GP]	*Iolanthe, Oder Die Hochzeit der Fee*	H.-J. Genzel	Berlin, Komische Oper
1984	*Mikado*	Dieter Bachmann	Zurich, Schauspielhaus
(?)	*Piraten! Piraten!*	Herbert Kreppel	Hannover, Theater am Aegi
c. 1985	*Mikado oder Tumult in Titipu*	Stefan Trossbach	Hamburg, Ascot-Musiktheater
28 June 1985	*Mikado*	Kahl	Dessau
20 Dec. 1986 [GP]	*Prinzessin Ida*	Stefan Trossbach	Hagen, Stadttheater
1987	*Mikado*	Kahl	Plauen, Stadttheater
1987	*Mikado*	Kahl	Neustrelitz, Friedrich-Wolf-Theater
10 Feb. 1990	*Mikado oder Tumult in Titipu*	Stefan Trossbach	Freiburg, Stadttheater
March 1994	*Mikado*	Klaus Straube	Hof, Stadttheater
May 1994	*Piraten*	Klaus Straube	Dortmund, Stadttheater
	Matronsliebe		Detmold, Landestheater
4 Feb. 1995	*Der Mikado oder Tumult in Titipu*	Stefan Trossbach	Giessen, Stadttheater
16 June 1996	*Piraten von Panzance*	Peter Zeug (after the Broadway production of New York Shakespeare Festival)	Berlin, Theater des Westens
19 Jan. 2001	*Patience, oder Damen, Dichter & Dragoner*	Birgit Casaretto and Stephan Kogelschatz	Mettmann, Konrad-Heresbacher Gymnasium Semi-professional staged orchestral version with Classicats Musik Leertaste Theater from Dusseldorf
23 July 2001	*Mikado* (German/English)	Project group	Musikprojekt am Gymnasium Parsberg (amateur)
4 May 2002	*Piraten von Panzance oder Sklave der Pflicht*	English/German (L. Greiffenhagen and B. von Leoprechting)	Vienna, Volksoper
6 Oct. 2002	*Mikado*	(?)	Stassfurt, Salzlandtheater Production of the Music Institute (Hannover?)

(*cont.*)

Table 15.2 *(cont.)*

Date	Title	Translator	Place, theatre
9 Nov. 2002	*Mikado*	(?)	Ballenstedt, Schlosstheater Production of the Music Institute (Hannover?)
21–5 Jan. 2003	*Iolanthe, or Lords in Flight* (*in English*)		Oldenburger Universitatstheater OUT (staged amateur performance)
14–15 June 2003	*Heirat vor Gericht* (*Trial*)	Meinhard Saremba	Concert performances and broadcast at the *Westdeutscher Rundfunk* in Cologne and Bad Ems
23 June 2003	*HMS Pinafore* Original (?)		Basel, Universität. The English Seminar Choir (amateur)
Sept. 2003	*Mikado*	D. Rave/N. Steinkrauss	Berlin, Saalbau Neukölln
1–5 Jan. 2004	*HMS Pinafore* Original (?)		Theater Regensburg (concert performance)
5 March 2004	*Mikado, oder: Ein Tag in Titipu* (Three-ladies version)	Ch. and K. Schwertsik	Graz, Orpheum
Sept./Oct. 2004 and Sept. 2005 [GP]	*Ruddigore*	Meinhard Saremba	Kiel, Ernst-Barlach-Gymnasium (staged amateur performance with school orchestra)
14–23 Oct. 2005	*Piraten von Panzance*	B. von Leoprechting and L. Greiffenhagen	Berlin, Neukölln. Vocal-Concertisten-Ensemble (semi-professional)
17, 19–20 Nov. 2005	*Schwurgericht* (*Trial*)		Wiesbaden, Staatstheater / Junge Oper Rhein-Main
Dec. 2005	*Gondoliers*	English/German (P. Hutchinson)	Dusseldorf, Die Deutsche Oper am Rhein
19 Jan. 2006 [GP]	*Cox & Box*	A. Bisowski	Berlin, Neuköllner Oper
6, 8 Jan. 2007	*Gondoliers* Original (?)		Wiener Kammeroper
11 March 2007	*The Pirates of Penzance* Original (?)		Munster-Hiltrup, Schulmusiktheater at Kardinal-von-Galen-Gymnasium (amateur)
29 Sept. 2007	*HMS Pinafore* Original		Frankfurt am Main, German-American Community Choir (amateur)
Dec. 2007 – March 2008	*Mikado*		Sursee (Schweiz), Stadttheater
15 May 2009	*Die Piraten von Panzance*	Inge Greiffenhagen and Beltina von Leoprechting	Munich, Gärtnerplatztheater
June 2009	*Patience*		English Freiburg, Hochschule für Musik

[a] For the list of German-Language productions in Table 15.2 I have made use of information in Saremba's biography of Sullivan; Obrist, 'Der Mikado' and Wedel, 'Die Savoy Operas von W. S. Gilbert und A. Sullivan', together with press and Internet sources.

in the audience's ears. These translations are so specifically tailored for the individual productions that they cannot be used by other theatres. Reviews are mainly tepid – 'A curate's egg',[20] '"Sailor's love", without approval'[21] – are typical – and at most they praise the commitment of local artists. The reviews in *Opernwelt* of the *Pirates of Penzance* productions at the Dortmund Stadttheater[22] and Vienna Volksoper[23] are exceptional.

Russian Empire and Soviet Union

According to the saying, all roads lead to Rome, but since the Italians hardly cared for Rossini's friend and heir, Sullivan, the most direct route from the comic opera premières of Vienna, Berlin and Paris led to Russian operetta theatre. Russian stage-directors endowed their foreign novelties with new energy and luxury. The transfer of European operettas to Russia was either the result of personal contact in the musical theatre world, the outcome of trips abroad by Russian nationals, or the offerings of famous foreign operetta companies on tour.[24] It is significant that all the Savoy operas went to Russia not directly from England but via Vienna, Berlin and Paris: the sister of the famous Russian stage-director Konstantin Stanislavsky saw *The Mikado* in Paris and Vienna, which led to the Alekseev Circle production; both *The Mikado* and *The Yeomen of the Guard*, given at the Imperial Mikhailovsky Theatre in St Petersburg, were modelled exactly after the Berlin productions; the Russian version of *The Yeomen of the Guard* was a copy of *Capitän Wilson*, the unauthorised Vienna production; the translation of *The Gondoliers* was made from the German version by Zell and Genée.

It is worth mentioning the very first, though amateur, Russian version of *The Mikado* – one of the first staging attempts by Konstantin Alekseev (the future Stanislavsky). The young artists translated it into Russian themselves – one of the first ever translations. Many years after, Stanislavsky remembered the occasion:

> For all the winter our house became a Japanese corner. The family of Japanese acrobats . . . taught us all of their customs . . . Korovin's scenery, the Japanese costumes, and the original music attracted the public's attention. Some enthusiastic reviews and letters appeared. We didn't expect such a success and couldn't imagine it![25]

The Alekseev Circle's production cleverly imitated the outward appearance of the original *Mikado*, but they were probably not aware enough 'to spot the "comic mask" under which a satirical piece in a Japanese setting contains not a single shaft aimed at Japan'.[26]

A felicitous version of *The Mikado*, one that ran for a long time, was produced in 1887 by A. Nikolayev and S. Ukolov. Its title was *The Mikado's Son*, and not without good reason: there is no Mikado among the characters. He is replaced by the Shogoon, the chief commander, since a sovereign was not allowed to appear on stage in a comical work. Most of the characters' names were changed, to Russian equivalent – Dai-Na-Chay (i.e., 'Tip me') or Coo-Kish ('to cock a snook'), for instance. In the Russian 'little list', one can find 'persons who like to borrow money', 'lawyers who sell their clients by accepting bribes', 'wine-sellers who sell tap-water with the label "Our own bottling"', etc.

It was a poor translation that hampered the success of the Russian version of *The Yeomen of the Guard*.[27] 'The music of *Captain Wilson*... is quite original and partly beautiful... The public demanded the repeat of some items, being bored during the dialogue, translated by a hack.'[28]

At this time Russian theatre had a unique feature: the imperial theatre consisted of Russian, German and French troupes. The latter two gave performances accordingly in German and French. In 1887, at the time when Savoy opera came to Russia, the German troupe was already eighty years old and had a stable audience, consisting of Russian Germans (more than 80,000 in St Petersburg alone) and educated Russians with an excellent command of German. Accordingly, the German-language Savoy opera productions – *Der Mikado* and *Der Königsgardist* – appeared only one or two days after the Berlin ones. Indeed, *Der Mikado* was long perceived as a 'German operetta'.

Both performances received numerous reviews in the Russian and German-speaking press of St Petersburg. A dispute arose between block-headed journalists, who expected to find Japanese music in *The Mikado* ('the composer knows Japanese music apparently as little as his public, which looks for it in his music'),[29] and educated critics, who praised Sullivan: 'This is really catching music, which escapes from the common ways of operetta... in ensembles Sullivan is free from the bad form of modern operetta, overloaded with opera effects'.[30] The German *Mikado* bandwagon was soon rolling in Reval, Brno, Prague, Budapest, Trieste, Bucharest, Riga, Basel and Helsinki.

However, these translations were not the end of *The Mikado*'s Russian story. In the Soviet epoch this opera was destined to become a basis for the training of 'a new actor' – one aspect of experimentation in the post-Revolution theatre. The actor had to develop not only the usual emotional technique but also body plasticity and rhythm. Paradoxically the production at the Berezil theatre seems to have been the most faithful to Gilbert's conception among all Russian performances.

Other European countries

The success of Savoy opera in other European countries was less impressive. In most of the countries mentioned below, Sullivan remained known almost exclusively as the composer of *The Mikado*. And even these productions were not as successful as those in Germany. The Brussels production of 23 December 1889, for instance, in a translation by Maurice Kufferath, was a failure. Sullivan was anxious that there should be a French adaptation, but found *The Mikado* to be 'not to French taste'. He was prepared to accept great liberty in adaptation, excluding only the idea of the part of

Table 15.3 *Productions in the Russian Empire / Soviet Union / Russia (1887–2001)*

Date	Russian / German title	Translator / Language	Place
18 April 1887	Mikado	V. S. Alekseev / Russian	Moscow, Alekseev Circle
10 June 1887	Syn Mikado, ili odin den' v Titipu (Mikado's Son, or One Day in Titipu)	S. Ukolov, A. Nikolaev / Russian	St Petersburg, Setov Theatre and Garden
8 Oct. 1887	Syn Mikado, ili odin den' v Titipu (The Mikado's Son, or One Day in Titipu)	S. Ukolov, A. Nikolaev / Russian	Kiev, Bergonier Theatre
7 Dec. 1888	Der Mikado	C. Zell, R. Genée / German	St Petersburg, Emperor Mikhailovsky Theatre
27 Dec. 1889	Der Königsgardist (Yeomen)	C. Zell, R. Genée / German	St Petersburg, Emperor Mikhailovsky Theatre
23 Sept. 1891	Gondoliers	G. Arbenin (from German) / Russian	St Petersburg, Maly Theatre
11 Nov. 1891	Captain Wilson (Yeomen)	? / Russian	St Petersburg, Maly Theatre
8 June 1896	Syn Mikado, ili odin den' v Yaponii (The Mikado's Son, or One Day in Japan)	S. Ukolov, A. Nikolaev / Russian	St Petersburg, Arcadia
21 Oct. 1896	Gondol'ery (Gondoliers)	G. Arbenin (from German) / Russian	St Petersburg, Maly Theatre
21 Jan. 1897	Syn Mikado, ili odin den' v Titipu (The Mikado's Son, or One Day in Titipu)	S. Ukolov, A. Nikolaev / Russian	Moscow, Shelaputin Theatre
28 Nov. 1900	Mikado	C. Zell, R. Genée / German	St Petersburg, Aquarium. Guest tour by Viennese Carlstheater
29 May 1908	Koldun, Hi Eliksir Lyubvi (Sorcerer, or, the Love Potion)	V. Travsky, P. Borodin / Russian	St Petersburg, Theatre of the Comic Opera and Operetta
4 May 1929	Mikado	M. Iogansen, O. Vishnya / Ukrainian	Kiev, Guest tour by Theatre Berezil
1988	Mikado	A. A. Orelovich / Russian	Odessa, Operetta Theatre
2 Oct. 1996	Sud Prisyaznyh (Trial by Jury)	Yu. Dimitrin / Russian	St Petersburg, Maly Philharmonic Hall
30 April 1998	Sud Prisyaznyh (Trial by Jury)	Yu. Dimitrin / Russian	St Petersburg, Bolshoi Philharmonic Hall
2001 (2)	Sud Prisyaznyh (Trial by Jury)	Yu. Dimitrin / Russian	St Petersburg, Children's Opera Theatre

Nanki-Poo being performed by a woman: 'Artistically it is wrong, and I dislike it very much'.[31] The composer even directed his secretary to send some ballet music, most likely *Thespis* or another early work of his own, to liven up the Brussels production, but negotiations with French and Belgian theatrical managements broke down.

The Brussels flop frightened Armand Silvestre, the translator of a planned production in Paris to such an extent that he wormed his way out of an agreement with Sullivan. Since then Paris, the nineteenth-century cultural centre of Europe, has never witnessed a Sullivan opera. Only much later was *Le Mikado ou La ville de Titipou* – a translation by Tony Mayer for an RTF broadcast in 1965 – used for subsequent productions in France: in 1992 at the Grand Theatre de Tours and on tours with its troupe; these were still going strong in 2004 (for example at the Municipal Theatre of Metz), and in 1995 in St Etienne (some parts of the show remained in English for more British *couleur*). The most recent French *Mikado* had its première on 29 December 2001 in Rennes under the baton of Gildas Pungier, making use of the original English in nine numbers.

There is an Italian translation of *The Mikado* by Gustavo Macchi (1899), which seems to have been performed between 1899 and 1901 in Rome, Palermo, Naples, Venice and Cremona. But at the time when the D'Oyly Carte Company performed *The Mikado* in Rome's Teatro Olimpico in November 1974 it was once more new to the Italian audience – warmly received and positively reviewed. In addition, there have been professional productions in Spain and Estonia, a film in Hungary, TV broadcasts in Switzerland, Spain (in Catalan) and Germany, audio recordings in Germany (for instance, *Die Piraten* with Arleen Auger and Martha Mödl (1968)) and Spain and, of course, many amateur productions (in Brussels, Geneva, Bilbao, Guardamar, Kiel, Utrecht, Jonzac, Basel and others).

Studying the different productions of the nineteenth and twentieth centuries one sees that some were triumphant, others had no success at all. This varied not merely with the quality of the music or libretto, but with such obstacles to appreciation as the political situation, contemporary fashion and public taste, the translation or adaptation chosen, and the proficiency and personality of the artists (actors or singers) and stage directors (see Chapter 4 in this volume for further discussion).

The stereotypical approach to Savoy opera in modern times has had grave consequences. Theatre-goers and performers on the Continent do not take the work seriously and do not do it justice. They refuse to recognise Arthur Sullivan's music as anything other than entertainment, believing it not to be worthy of deeper consideration.

Contemporary practice shows that *The Mikado* is not the only Gilbert and Sullivan opera to awaken interest among theatre-goers, or to achieve success. But the Savoy Operas still await a new assessment and genuine appreciation in non-English speaking countries.

PART IV

Into the twenty-first century

16 Adventures in musical detection: scholarship, editions, productions and the future of the Savoy operas

DAVID RUSSELL HULME

Pursuing post-graduate research into the comic operas of Arthur Sullivan was, in 1975, considered in some academic quarters as frivolous, if not virtually a contradiction of terms. I was fortunate, however, in having been delivered into safe hands. The Professor of Music at the University College of Wales at Aberystwyth, Ian Parrott, was himself a pioneering Sullivan scholar – a perceptive article by him on Sullivan had appeared in *Music and Letters* as early as 1942. With the additional support of Sullivan's biographer, Percy Young, one of the department's external examiners, a provisional title was accepted for a PhD thesis: 'The Theatre Music of Arthur Sullivan'. Broadened beyond the comic operas so that it could include the music written for the (respectable) Shakespeare plays, the subject was accepted.

Investigation

To get inside the music, though, it was essential to study it in full score. These had been published for some of the Shakespearean music, such as *The Tempest*, *Henry VIII* and *The Merchant of Venice*, and for *Ivanhoe*. Copies, however, were collectors' rarities; but rarer still were the three comic opera full scores published in Germany during Sullivan's lifetime: the Bosworth editions of *The Mikado* and the Zell and Genée adaptation of *The Yeomen of the Guard* (*Der Königsgardist*), and Litolff's German version of *HMS Pinafore* (*Amor an Bord*). Examining these required a trip to the British Library. Fortunately, however, the university library had acquired a copy of the facsimile of the autograph full score of *The Mikado* issued by Gregg International Publishers Limited in 1968. Beautifully produced, this was to have been followed by a facsimile of the *Iolanthe* autograph with a preface by Ian Parrott but, alas, this never appeared.

The Gregg score of *The Mikado* revealed a great deal about the creative evolution of the musical and verbal texts. Of course, the autograph itself had long been available for study at the Royal Academy of Music, to where it had been bequeathed in Sullivan's will, but the facsimile uncovered the secrets of this unique document for everyone to see. Clearly the autograph manuscripts were essential reading. Not only were they, in some cases, the only full scores available for study of the orchestration; but study of their alterations and adjustments provided important insights into how the works were fine-tuned for performance.

By the 1970s, textual research was an established branch of both musical and literary scholarship; and, of course, bibliographical analysis was very much tied in with this. Critical and Urtext editions, embracing the works not only of major composers but also often relatively obscure ones, became a major commitment for many musical scholars and publishers in the second part of the twentieth century. But all this earnest endeavour had, so far, largely bypassed Arthur Sullivan. Roger Harris had settled most of the issues relating to authorship of the overtures to Sullivan's collaborations with Gilbert in a paper presented at the University of Kansas in 1970; an essay by Max Morris sharpened curiosity about the deleted music from *Ruddigore* that survived in the autograph score. However, such writing about the musical texts was rare. Gilbert had fared somewhat better. Townley Searle (*A Bibliography of Sir William Schwenck [sic] Gilbert*) and Reginald Allen (*The First Night Gilbert and Sullivan*) produced substantial bibliographical studies – although their work is no longer regarded as reliable and the basis for much of Allen's writing on first-night librettos was later proved to be unsound. Among other studies, Terence Rees's brilliant investigative work on the text of *Thespis* in the early 1960s still stands out nearly fifty years later.

Finding the sources

For many years, inaccessibility discouraged study of Sullivan's autograph manuscripts. The composer's will bequeathed some of these to individuals – *The Pirates of Penzance* to François Cellier, *Ruddigore* to W. S. Gilbert, *Iolanthe* to Richard D'Oyly Carte. A few others passed to appropriate establishments – as well as *The Mikado* score left to the Royal Academy of Music, *The Yeomen of the Guard* autograph was inherited by the Royal College of Music. However, the bulk of the manuscripts remained within the Sullivan family. Access to the scores could be difficult or impossible to obtain; so, for many years, only the autographs of *The Mikado* and *Yeomen* were readily available for study. In 1966 the situation changed dramatically. On Monday 13 June, the Sullivan family's collection went under the hammer at a Sotheby and Co. auction in London. A fund-raising appeal had enabled the autograph full scores of *Patience* and *The Gondoliers* to be purchased for the British Library and *Princess Ida* for the Bodleian Library, Oxford. The autograph of *The Pirates of Penzance* was acquired by the Pierpont

Morgan Library in New York, but the bulk of the collection was dispersed into private hands on both sides of the Atlantic. Because some new owners chose to remain frustratingly anonymous, several scores effectively disappeared from view – it was only a few years ago that the autographs of *The Rose of Persia* and *The Beauty Stone* reappeared in the estate of a deceased collector who had always maintained he did not have them! (Released from captivity, they are now happily housed in the Bodleian Library, Oxford.) However, private owners could also be generous. Terence Rees had attended the Sotheby's sale mainly in the hope of buying the autograph of *The Zoo*, a forgotten work which he had recently brought back to the stage. In the event, not only did he succeed in purchasing *The Zoo* but also the autograph scores of several non-Gilbert operas and other Sullivan works.

Although the manuscript sale sent some scores into mysterious inaccessibility, and placed others on the other side of the Atlantic, it made the position for British scholars generally better. As a number of scores privately purchased at Sotheby's found their way into institutional libraries, matters improved further. New interest began to stir in Sullivan's non-Gilbert comic operas and other neglected works. Fired by his newly expanded collection, Terence Rees was a prime mover in revivals of several of these and the performances were an exciting part of a growing interest in the composer, stimulated, to a significant degree, by the newly formed Sir Arthur Sullivan Society. After a forty-year involvement with them, Terence Rees donated his important Sullivan manuscripts to the British Library in 2006.

Discussing autograph scores

The Society's fledgling magazine presented an opportunity to experiment with writing what was, in the area of Sullivan research, a novel study: a detailed discussion of an autograph score as both a musical and textual source. A two-part article on Sullivan's autograph full score of *Princess Ida*, which I had studied at the Bodleian Library, Oxford, was duly published. The *Ida* manuscript was one of the first I had examined in real detail. Doing so had brought about a realisation of just how much such a document could reveal about the creative processes of both composer and author and about the way in which their works were honed and sharpened for performance. So much had been written about Sullivan, about Gilbert and about their comic operas, yet here was a whole field that had barely been touched. It was a gift for a research student. Writing the article for the Sullivan Society crystallised hitherto cloudy intentions and a revised scheme of research was approved by the university: a study of the autograph manuscripts of Sullivan's operas. If this generic classification suggested any lack of substance, the reference to manuscripts, with their hint of the arcane, would have restored academic confidence. (Today it is correct and proper to refer to the works as 'operas' or 'comic operas', but, at that time, describing them in such a way was considered inappropriate for scholarly purposes.)

Progress was helped greatly by the generous cooperation of Terence Rees and John Wolfson, who allowed me to examine their important private collections. However, access to a number of manuscripts remained initially elusive and many could only be examined in microfilmed copies. Most of these were provided by Roger Harris, who had somehow obtained films of a large number of Sullivan's manuscripts during the 1960s. Although I was eventually to examine directly almost all the scores whose whereabouts were known, Roger Harris's help came at just the right time and enabled submission of a dissertation that might otherwise have floundered because it was simply insufficiently comprehensive.

One of the manuscripts first examined on microfilm was the auto-graph full score of *Ruddigore*. Permission to view the autograph itself was famously difficult to obtain. This only served to increase its fascination, already sharpened by the knowledge that it contained substantial passages of deleted music. But, alas, much of the 'lost' music could not be seen on the film – most of the pages carrying it were either pinned together or pasted over. It was therefore a great day indeed when I arrived at the Savoy Theatre to examine the manuscript itself. I was taken to meet Albert Truelove in his tiny office. Sitting at Sullivan's desk, he chatted about my project before taking me to work on the manuscript in an attic room. Reading through the score, it was as though I could hear *Ruddigore* playing on the stage nearby. The matinée of *Noises Off* hardly intruded. The score was the property of the Savoy Theatre and some years later, changes in the ownership of the theatre and of its assets made the future of the score decidedly uncertain. Access again looked problematic as work began on my critical edition of *Ruddigore* for Oxford University Press. Fortunately Giles Wontner, one-time chairman of the Board of Directors of the Savoy Theatre Limited, took control and the score was made available for further study. All this raised Mr Wontner's interest in the manuscript and eventually he was to set in motion a train of events that led to its acquisition by the British Library in 1999.

Along with the *Ruddigore* autograph, I was shown a manuscript copy of the full score prepared by Sullivan's principal copyist, George Baird. This fascinating document contained pencilled amendments by Geoffrey Toye, who had been responsible for making numerous changes to the orchestra-tion when conducting the work in London in 1920. Not long after examining the manuscripts, I spoke about them at a Sullivan Society Festival in York. Arthur Jacob's biography of Sullivan had recently appeared. In it he praised the 'perfectly timed bell' in 'When the night wind howls'. A small point, perhaps, but it underlined the importance of a basic principle: establishing what a composer actually wrote is a prerequisite of any serious assessment of the music.

Expanding research

Work on the sources had expanded beyond the autographs to take in printed scores, librettos and practically anything that was available, and really seemed to be breaking new ground. But it was good not to be alone. In Britain Michael Walters had been delving into the minutiae of Gilbert's librettos for years, and in the USA Marc Shepherd's investigations were throwing new light on the literary sources. Also across the Atlantic, Frederic Woodbridge Wilson had been working in similar directions to my own – and, reassuringly, reaching compatible conclusions. Successor to Reginald Allen as curator of the Gilbert and Sullivan Collection at the Pierpont Morgan Library, New York, Ric Wilson was uniquely placed and it was a privilege to study sources at the library under his guidance. The New York Public Library also housed a collection of Sullivan material, including full scores and orchestral parts that had mostly come from the D'Oyly Carte American agent. Fragmentary though some of the material was, it yielded valuable new information and highlighted the importance of casting a wide net – as the Sullivan Society found when it tracked down what seemed to be the only available source of orchestral parts for *The Rose of Persia* in Australia, thus making it possible for the work to be recorded for the *BBC Music Magazine* in 1999.

Detailed study of Sullivan's autographs, contemporary copyists' manuscripts, printed scores, orchestral parts, early audio recordings and other sources, not only revealed much about how the composer had fine-tuned his comic operas for performance but also uncovered a good deal about how the works had been altered after his death. For years the view had been widely held that the D'Oyly Carte Opera Company presented Sullivan's music and Gilbert's librettos pretty well exactly as their creators left them. This was simply not the case. It became apparent, however, that establishing an 'authentic' text was hugely problematic. The autograph full scores did not offer a final, settled musical text; neither did the published librettos present the literary text as it was performed in the theatre. The D'Oyly Carte Company had made numerous cuts and other alterations to the fabric of the music, as well as adjustments to the orchestrations, during the earlier part of the last century. However, research revealed that Sullivan, too, authorised a considerable number of changes that are not definitively recorded. Alterations were made to orchestral parts used at the

Savoy that were neither recorded in the full scores nor in other sets of parts. Most of these original sources seem to be lost, so that attempts to establish the origins of textual revisions have proved fraught with difficulties. With the librettos, too, study of prompt books from Gilbert's own productions makes clear that establishing exactly what verbal text was performed is also extremely problematic.

All this added, of course, to the fascination of the subject and provided material for numerous articles in the publications of the Sullivan Society and, occasionally, the pages of *The Savoyard*. Study of the musical sources also illuminated issues relating to Gilbert's literary text. It became obvious that the published librettos did not present the verbal text as it was sung in performance, and that in this respect the musical sources were often more reliable. In particular, the claims of Reginald Allen and others that the libretti sold in the theatre at the first performances presented virtually exact records of what was performed were now proved to be mistaken.

It was becoming increasingly clear how poorly served were both Sullivan and Gilbert by available performing material. In Britain, the source of orchestral material for the comic operas Sullivan had written with Gilbert was the D'Oyly Carte organisation, whose established performing versions were enshrined in the complementary piano-vocal scores and librettos sold by Chappell and Co. The American publisher, Edwin F. Kalmus, issued orchestral parts mostly reproducing D'Oyly Carte material, but with the bonus of full scores – albeit mostly simply extracted from the parts and sometimes very badly presented. (The full score of *Ruddigore* compiled by Tom McCanna is a valiant exception.) Publishers in other countries, such as Schirmer in the USA, issued piano-vocal scores and librettos with the same D'Oyly Carte origins. For years there had been talk of a complete critical edition of the Sullivan and Gilbert comic opera collaborations being prepared by the American publisher, Broude Brothers. In the early 1980s a proof of *Trial by Jury*, the first volume, was circulated but the decade passed and nothing had been issued. An Eulenburg edition of *The Gondoliers*, edited by David Lloyd-Jones, appeared in 1984. Unfortunately editorial involvement did not encompass the libretto; and without the issue of matching orchestral material, its practical impact was necessarily limited. Nevertheless, for a major international publisher to bring out a full score of a Sullivan comic opera was an important step towards recognition of the composer as an international figure. It is unfortunate that from a projected Eulenburg edition of *The Yeomen of the Guard*, edited by Sir Charles Mackerras and David Lloyd-Jones, only the overture was published.

It was disconcerting to realise that Sullivan's comic operas were being performed in versions that were simply not his. Although this was done mostly in innocent ignorance, it was also the case that, in practical terms, there was no real alternative – unless, that is, new performing material was specifically commissioned. There were clearly genuine issues over texts and it seemed to me to be a priority to raise awareness of this situation, especially among those involved in professional productions and recordings – widely looked upon to set standards in every aspect of performance.

Productions

An opportunity arrived with the New Sadler's Wells Opera production of *Ruddigore,* marking the work's centenary in 1987. Of all Sullivan's comic operas written with Gilbert, this had undergone the most extensive unauthorised alteration. Keen to do something special for the centenary, New Sadler's Wells Opera decided to restore the 1887 musical text. It wanted not only to eliminate later, unauthorised, D'Oyly Carte changes but also to reinstate some of the material Sullivan had cut himself. Unfortunately, with only a few weeks to get everything prepared, this was not going to be an exercise in meticulous scholarship. Nevertheless, the musical performing material used probably came nearer to what Sullivan had written than anything anyone had sung or played for a very long time. As well as the 'lost' music included in the stage production, including the *Don Giovanni*-inspired section for Sir Roderic and the Chorus of Ancestors, 'By the curse upon our race', some of Gilbert's excised dialogue was also reinstated. The latter had been published, along with a wealth of other material from pre-production librettos and other sources in *The Annotated Gilbert and Sullivan,* edited by Ian Bradley, issued initially in two volumes by Penguin Books in 1982 and 1984. These detailed commentaries certainly made a valuable contribution to raising awareness of the textual histories of the works.

The textual novelties caused much interest – so much so that even more 'lost' music was included on the audio recording of the production. I continued to work with New Sadler's Wells Opera on subsequent productions of Sullivan comic operas, editing the performing material to bring it closer to something the composer would have known. Later, Bramwell Tovey, music director of the re-established New D'Oyly Carte Opera, and his successors, John Pryce-Jones and John Owen Edwards, proved keen to reassess the performing texts and return to something more authentic. So the editorial work continued, and particularly influenced the company's audio recordings made during the late 1980s and the 1990s. English National Opera commissioned me to put the performing material into more authentic order for its production of *Princess Ida* in 1992. I was also able to advise Welsh National Opera on textual issues when it produced *The Yeomen of the Guard* in 1994. All this was undoubtedly positive. However, the *modus operandi* limited what could be done. There was never much time in which to do the work and the revisions had mostly to be worked in by physically altering the standard orchestral material and vocal scores. My priority was with the differences that would be heard in performances, rather than with minutiae that probably would not. It also became clear very early in my involvement with professional productions, that although conductors and directors might be enthusiastic in principle about following more authentic texts, the familiar corruptions would often remain if they decided these better suited their ideas. One had to be consoled with the thought that at least they had made an informed choice.

Lost numbers

The textual detective work uncovered a considerable quantity of music cut either before the operas' first performances or later. Much of it was fragmentary or in some way incomplete but a significant amount was performable. Bringing this 'lost' material out of obscurity so that it can again be heard has been fascinating and rewarding. Thanks to New Sadler's Wells Opera and, later, the New D'Oyly Carte Company making a point of including deleted numbers as 'bonus tracks' (even when they had not been incorporated into the stage production), it was, at last, possible to hear first-class professional performances of hitherto largely forgotten and unknown material.

The New D'Oyly Carte recording of *The Yeomen of the Guard* included no fewer than three songs discarded after orchestration – an earlier version of 'Is life a boon', and solos for Sargeant Meryl ('A laughing boy') and Shadbolt ('When jealous torments'). The Shadbolt number had not been sung in the company's stage production but Meryl's solo had. Interestingly, this is one of the few instances where Gilbert's rationale for deleting a number is explicitly recorded. It makes a good deal of sense. He was concerned about the comic/serious balance at the opening of the work and felt the song upset this. So should we simply override his decision? Gilbert was, as we know, extremely sensitive to the reception of his new pieces and often made last-minute changes prior to the first night and cuts and alterations afterwards in the light of public and press response. When one remembers that only hours before *The Mikado* was due to open, he had to be dissuaded from cutting 'A more humane Mikado', it is difficult to claim the author always knew best. Yet, an occasional lapse does not mean that his judgement was fundamentally unsound. As for Sullivan's part in all this, there were probably quite a few times when he objected to the cutting of his music, but he had enormous respect for Gilbert's theatrical mastery and ultimately, of course, no changes were made without his agreement.

One justification for reinstating numbers – in all kinds of works, not just Sullivan's – is that circumstances originally responsible for their demise no longer apply. The restoration to *Patience* of the Act I song for the Duke, 'Though men of rank', is sometimes defended on the grounds that it was *probably* cut to avoid offence to the Church, whereas today such hypersensitivity is unnecessary. Even if this was the reason, however, it could be argued that Victorian taste shaped the works and to redefine the parameters of acceptability for our own time distorts and misrepresents them.

As it happens, the Duke's song seems to me to be a happy reinstatement of deleted material – despite the fact that the vocal lines can now only be performed in reconstructed form. The originals having disappeared after the number was cut just prior to the first night, we are left to deduce the vocal parts from the evidence of the extant orchestral score. (Several realisations have been produced; the one I made for the 1994 D'Oyly Carte recording seems to be most widely favoured.)

Incomplete musical sources obstruct the reinstatement of several other deleted numbers. While we have nothing more than a second-violin copy of the 'De Belville' song, cut from *Iolanthe*, we are never going to have a chance to assess the setting in context. More material survives for the duet between the Captain and Josephine, deleted from *HMS Pinafore*, but, in my view, this still awaits convincing reconstruction and, consequently, a fair evaluation. Many more lyrics can be found in pre-production states of the librettos for which we have no music at all. Not all were set, of course, but more than a few were: 'Thy wintry frown' (*The Gondoliers*) and the 'Hymn to the Nobility' (*The Pirates of Penzance*) are just two examples.

However, lack of sources is not always an insurmountable obstacle. In 1996 Peter Mulloy devised a production of *The Pirates of Penzance* that brought in early versions of the dialogue and worked in almost all the extant music (complete or incomplete), adding repeats and the like implied by early versions of the lyrics but mostly never set by Sullivan. The result, a kind of 'Pirates-That-Might-Have-Been', was produced with great success at the Buxton International Gilbert and Sullivan Festival. It was never intended as an 'improvement' to the opera as we know it; yet the experiment did provide interesting insights into the evolution of *Pirates*, especially for an audience well versed in the minutiae of the piece.

When Mulloy was preparing a new production of *The Pirates of Penzance* in 2001 for the Carl Rosa Opera Company, he drew on the experience of his earlier Buxton production and worked various sections apparently performed in early performances at Paignton and/or New York into the

Act II finale – the return of the 'Hail, poetry' music ('Hail, House of Peers'), as well as 'To Queen Victoria's name' and the reprise of the Major-General's Song. I was responsible for the musical reconstructions and conducted many performances of this 'fantasy finale' with the company. Audiences generally enjoyed the novelty of it all – nevertheless, I could appreciate how Sullivan and Gilbert might have thought the hymn-like apostrophes obstructed momentum.

More 'lost' music may well surface in years to come. Generally, though, when composer and author discarded a number it was surely for the best. Of course, it is fascinating to hear the 'out-takes' and occasionally experience them within a stage performance. It was wonderful to hear all the excised music from the Ghost Scene restored at the Buxton Gilbert and Sullivan Festival production of *Ruddigore* in 2005, but the experience also confirmed my view that, in the context of the opera as a whole, the scene really does work better in its revised form.

New editions

The edition of *Ruddigore* used at Buxton was published by Oxford University Press in 2000. As editor, I had set out to present, as accurately as possible, the musical and literary text performed during the original Savoy Theatre production after this had reached a 'settled' state. Material discarded along the way was included in notes and appendices. However, it is this that has caused the most interest. Indeed, almost all the publisher's hirings of the edition have been to performers wishing to include the 'lost' music. Yet, of all Sullivan's comic operas written with Gilbert, *Ruddigore* is the one that has been most altered since the composer's death; so it is revealing to find so little interest in staging a 'cleaned-up' version of the work as determined by composer and librettist. The *Ruddigore* edition was to have been the first of a series, 'The Oxford Savoy Operas', subsequently abandoned. If Oxford University Press had looked to its edition of *Ruddigore* to gauge the interest of performers – especially in the important amateur market – in working with more 'authentic' texts, it would have been sadly disappointed. The reasons are, to some extent, practical. The Chappell and Schirmer vocal scores are on the shelves of singers everywhere; numerous libraries have sets of them. Also, amateur companies – and even some professional ones – often use reduced orchestrations, and these are invariably prepared from the usual corrupt sources.

In 1994 the long-awaited Broude edition of *Trial by Jury* appeared, followed by *HMS Pinafore* in 2003. Meticulously edited and beautifully produced, Sullivan and his librettist could not be better served. With full scores and supporting performing material now available for these works. there is no artistic reason why productions should not take full advantage of these resources. Even if amateur companies have their excuses, professionals making any claim to respect the works they perform can have none.

Other publishers, too, have been busily issuing full scores of Sullivan's comic operas. Since 1999, Dover Press has published full scores of *The Mikado*, *The Pirates of Penzance* and *HMS Pinafore*. Newly typeset by the editors, the quality of their printed presentation is excellent. Care has been taken to resolve many of the anomalies and present a musical text that is generally consistent with itself. Practical though they may be, however, these are far from being scholarly editions. The range of sources consulted is inadequate and, in many places, speculative (albeit often sensible) editorial intervention is not identified. Supporting orchestral material is available from the editors, but my impression is that many conductors use the Dover scores in conjunction with the D'Oyly Carte or Kalmus orchestral parts to which they make whatever adjustments they see fit. This, at least, is progress. Conductors need to work from full scores. Lack of them will always raise barriers – psychological as well as practical – to Sullivan's recognition as a major operatic composer.

These Dover scores were made possible by the ready availability of technology that enables production of material – musical and literary – which looks, to all intents and purposes, as good as publications from the most respected publishing houses – but unfortunately may lack the scholarly credentials of such an imprimatur. On the positive side, however, it does enable publication of excellent editions that would previously have been financially unviable. Roger Harris's fine editions of Sullivan's works are a shining example. So far, the only comic opera full score he has tackled is the Sullivan and Burnand collaboration, *Cox and Box*. Encouragingly, Chandos used this edition for its 2005 recording. Alas, it did not take advantage of the Broude edition for the recording of *Trial by Jury* issued on the same disc.

Outlook

The moves are in the right direction, but it will be a long time before reliable, thoroughly researched editions of all the comic operas are available – and probably much longer still before they are widely accepted by performers. H. C. Robbins Landon's scholarly editions of Haydn have been available for decades, yet many performances still use the old established Breitkopf & Härtel parts – and so it is for many other composers. There is also the issue of familiarity. People are used to the D'Oyly Carte versions of Sullivan's comic operas. Offering something different arouses irrational suspicions. Not only that, a few of the modifications are undeniably effective, and performers are loath to abandon these simply in the name of authenticity. Take the *Ruddigore* overture, for example. Many would rather hear Geoffrey Toye's effective twentieth-century replacement for Hamilton Clarke's rather undistinguished original overture – even though the latter was approved by Sullivan. There is a fine balance to be struck between respecting what the composer wrote or approved and treating the works as embalmed museum exhibits.

It is inevitable that performers will do what they think best for the purposes of the piece as they see it. Years of conducting professional performances across the world with artists dedicated to bringing Sullivan's comic operas alive to the widest audience with respect and affection has taught me this. That said, establishing reliable texts for the comic operas, supported by the fullest information about sources and variants, must continue to be a priority for scholars of both Sullivan and Gilbert. Their works have yet to receive universal recognition as the great comic operas they are. Establishing what composer and librettist actually wrote is a fundamental necessity if this is to happen. Performers will continue to choose this version or that, authentic or dubious; but those choices should and can be informed ones.

21 *The Tables Turned*: An English Christmas pantomime seen through the eyes of the Japanese artist Kru Shan Ki. *Illustrated London News*, 25 December 1880.

Appendix 1   Who wrote the overtures?

Not all Sullivan's operas have overtures. Victorian audiences showed little regard for these orchestral preludes, chatting over and generally paying little attention to them. Sometimes, therefore, when time was short, Sullivan delegated the task of arranging an overture from the music of the opera to others. In some – possibly all – cases he set out his structural and thematic requirements and usually made some alterations to his assistants' work.

For a long time, the question of authorship of several overtures remained unresolved and a number of incorrect attributions were widely accepted. Roger Harris went a good way towards producing a definitive list and my own later researches finally settled the issue in the case of the works marked *.

Overtures by Sullivan: *The Sapphire Necklace, Cox and Box, Iolanthe, Princess Ida, The Yeomen of the Guard, The Gondoliers, Utopia Limited, The Grand Duke.* The overture to *Thespis* is lost. Because, thematically, it seems to have been significantly independent of the opera, it is likely to have been Sullivan's own work.

Alfred Cellier arranged the overtures to *HMS Pinafore* and *The Pirates of Penzance*, and Eugene D'Albert the overture to *Patience**. Hamilton Clarke was responsible for the overtures to *The Mikado, Ruddigore* and *The Sorcerer** – the last having been written for the 1884 revival to replace the 'Graceful Dance' from Sullivan's *Henry VIII* music pressed into service for the original production.

David Russell Hulme

Appendix 2 Stage and choral works by Arthur Sullivan and W. S. Gilbert

Work	Première*	Composer/Librettist
Ages Ago (G)	22 Nov. 1869, Gallery of Illustration	Frederick Clay
Beauty Stone, The (S)	28 May 1898, Savoy Theatre	A. W. Pinero/Comyns Carr
Chieftain, The (S)	12 Dec. 1894, Savoy Theatre	F. C. Burnand
Contrabandista, The (S)	18 Dec. 1867, St George's Hall	F. C. Burnand/Sullivan
Cox and Box (S)	11 May 1867, Adelphi Theatre	F. C. Burnand
Dulcamara! (G)	29 Dec. 1866, Theatre Royal, St James's	Burlesque of Donizetti's *L'elisir d'amore*
Emerald Isle, The (S)	27 April 1901, Savoy Theatre	Basil Hood
Fairy's Dilemma, The (G)	4 May 1904, Garrick Theatre	Edward Rickett
Fallen Fairies (G)	15 Dec. 1909, Savoy Theatre	Edward German
Golden Legend, The (S)	16 Oct. 1886, Leeds	Joseph Bennett
Gondoliers, The	7 Dec. 1889, Savoy Theatre	Gilbert/Sullivan
Grand Duke, The	7 March 1896, Savoy Theatre	Gilbert/Sullivan
Haddon Hall (S)	24 Sept. 1892, Savoy Theatre	Sydney Grundy
His Excellency (G)	27 Oct. 1894, Lyric Theatre	Osmond Carr
HMS Pinafore	25 May 1878, Opéra Comique	Gilbert/Sullivan
Iolanthe	25 Nov. 1882, Savoy Theatre	Gilbert/Sullivan
Ivanhoe (S)	31 Jan. 1891, Royal English Opera	Julian Sturgis
Light of the World, The (S)	27 Aug. 1873, Birmingham	Composer
Martyr of Antioch, The (S)	15 Oct. 1880, Leeds	Henry Hart Milman
Merry Zingara, The (G)	21 March 1867, Royalty Theatre	Burlesque of Balfe's *The Bohemian Girl*
Mikado, The	14 March 1885, Savoy Theatre	Gilbert/Sullivan
Mountebanks, The (G)	4 Jan. 1892, Lyric Theatre	Gilbert/Alfred Cellier
Our Island Home (G)	20 June 1870, Gallery of Illustration	German Reed
Patience	23 April 1881, Opéra Comique	Gilbert/Sullivan
Pirates of Penzance, The	30 Dec. 1879, Royal Bijou-Theatre, Paignton	Gilbert/Sullivan
Pretty Druidess, The (G)	19 June 1869, Charing Cross Theatre	Burlesque of Bellini's *Norma*
Princess Ida	5 Jan. 1884, Savoy Theatre	Gilbert/Sullivan
Princess Toto (G)	24 June 1876, Theatre Royal, Nottingham	Frederick Clay
Prodigal Son, The (S)	8 Sep. 1869, Worcester	Composer
Robert the Devil (G)	21 Dec. 1868, Gaiety Theatre	Burlesque of Meyerbeer's *Robert le Diable*
Rose of Persia, The (S)	29 Nov. 1899, Savoy Theatre	Basil Hood
Ruddigore	22 Jan. 1887, Savoy Theatre	Gilbert/Sullivan
Sensation Novel, A (G)	30 Jan. 1871, Gallery of Illustration	Frederick Clay
Sorcerer, The	17 Nov. 1877, Opéra Comique	Gilbert/Sullivan
Thespis (G & S)	26 Dec. 1871, Gaiety Theatre	Lost
Topsy-Turvydom (G)	21 March 1874, Criterion Theatre	Alfred Cellier
Trial by Jury	25 March 1875, Royalty Theatre	Gilbert/Sullivan
Utopia Limited	7 Oct. 1893, Savoy Theatre	Gilbert/Sullivan
Vivandière, La (G)	17 June 1867, St James's Hall, Liverpool	Burlesque of Donizetti's *La fille du Régiment*
Yeomen of the Guard, The	3 Oct. 1888, Savoy Theatre	Gilbert/Sullivan
Zoo, The (S)	5 June 1875, St James's Theatre	B. C. Stephenson

* Place of production London, except where otherwise stated.

Appendix 3 Modern editions of works by Arthur Sullivan and W. S. Gilbert

Works by Arthur Sullivan

Full score

The Contrabandista, edited by Robin Gordon-Powell
The Prodigal Son, edited by Robin Gordon-Powell
Ivanhoe, edited by Robin Gordon-Powell
Kenilworth, edited by Robin Gordon-Powell
The Foresters, edited by Robin Gordon-Powell
On Shore and Sea, edited by Robin Gordon-Powell

Published by The Amber Ring
9 Killieser Avenue
London SW2 4NU
e-mail: robin@amber-ring.co.uk

Vocal score

The Golden Legend
Cox and Box
The Zoo
Haddon Hall (also full score)
The Chieftain

Published by R. Clyde
6 Whitelands Avenue
Chorleywood
Rickmansworth
Herts WD3 5RD
e-mail: r.clyde@dial.pipex.com

The Light of the World, edited by Raymond J. Walker
Cramer Music
23 Garrick Street
London WC2E 9RY

Works by Gilbert and Sullivan

Trial by Jury, edited by Steven Ledbetter
The Sorcerer, edited by Steven Ledbetter
HMS Pinafore, edited by Percy M. Young
The Pirates of Penzance, edited by Bruce I. Miller and Marc Shepherd
Patience, edited by Percy M. Young and Bruce I. Miller
Iolanthe, edited by Gerald Hendrie and Dinah Barsham
Princess Ida, edited by Richard Sherr
The Mikado, edited by Ronald Broude

All the above published by Broude Brothers Limited
141 White Oaks Road, PO Box 547
Williamstown, MA 01267-0547, USA
e-mail: broude@sover.net

Ruddigore, edited by David Russell Hulme
Published by Oxford University Press
www.oup.co.uk/music

The Gondoliers, edited by David Lloyd-Jones
Edition Eulenburg no. 927.
London: Eulenburg, 1984.

Appendix 4 Sullivan's archetypes of English opera

Influences:	Catalyst I: French one-act *operettes* and *Opéra bouffe*		Catalyst II: Early nineteenth-century British opera (Balfe–Wallace type)
Archetype	Ancient world comedy	Topsyturvydom	National topic with realistic plot
Composition	*Thespis* (1871)	*Cox and Box* (1866) *The Zoo* (1875)	*The Sapphire Necklace or the False Heiress* (1862–64) *The Pirates of Penzance* (1879)

National English (comic) opera
German Spieloper (Mozart-Lortzing type)
Italian *opera buffa* (Rossini type)
French *opéra comique* (Auber–Gounod type)

Exotic/Mediterranean	Imaginary societies	Comic-supernatural	Social comedy
The Contrabandista (1867) rev. as *The Chieftain* (1894)	*Princess Ida* (1884)	*The Sorcerer* (1877)	*Trial by Jury* (1875)
The Mikado (1885)	*Utopia Limited* (1893)	*Iolanthe* (1883)	*HMS Pinafore* (1878)
The Gondoliers (1889)	*The Grand Duke* (1896)	*Ruddigore* (1887)	*Patience* (1881)
The Rose of Persia (1899)			

'The opera of the future is a compromise' (Sullivan):
French style (Berlioz, Meyerbeer)
Italian style (Rossini, Donizetti, Verdi)
German style (Weber, Cornelius, Wagner)

Semi-staged dramas
Models:
Handel, Liszt, Berlioz
(concert, but also staged)

Lyric-romantic	Historic-romantic (English icons)	Legends (biblical, secular)
The Yeomen of the Guard (1888)	*Ivanhoe* (1891)	*The Prodigal Son* (1869)
The Beauty Stone (1898)	*Haddon Hall* (1892)	*The Martyr of Antioch* (1880)
The Emerald Isle (1900)		*The Golden Legend* (1886)

Notes

1 Savoy opera and its discontents

1 Moody, *Illegitimate Theatre*, p. 10.

2 Kinservik, *Disciplining Satire*, chapter 2.

3 *The Times*, 21 and 25 September 1809.

4 Baker, *The London Stage*, vol. 2, p. 3.

5 O'Hara, *Midas*, p. ii.

6 Davis and Emeljanow, *Reflecting the Audience*, p. 273.

7 Morley, *Journal of a London Playgoer*, p. 17.

8 Mathews, *Life of Charles James Mathews*, vol. 2, p. 76. Vestris's last stage manager was T. W. Robertson (1829–71), whom Gilbert claimed as his mentor.

9 Mathews, *Life of Charles James Mathews*, vol. 2, pp. 105–6.

10 Roy, *Plays by James Robinson Planché*, pp. 9–10.

11 *Ibid.*, pp. 29–30.

12 Preface to *The Dragon of Wantley* (1737), quoted in White, *The Rise of English Opera*, p. 70. Carey's classic *Chrononhotonthologos* (1734) saw production at the Gaiety as late as 1880.

13 Roy, *Plays by James Robinson Planché*, p. 16.

14 *Ibid.*, p. 29.

15 New Strand Theatre: *Alcestis* by Frank Talfourd (1828–62); review in *The Times*, 5 July 1850.

16 Royalty Theatre, 29 September 1863.

17 Morley, *Journal of a London Playgoer*, pp. 6–7. *The Times* review (30 September 1863) is altogether more appreciative.

18 It was Byron, not Gilbert, who invented the exchanged baby joke. LORD LEVERET: 'I was old in crime e'en when but an infant in months. I was your foster-brother; in the absence of the nurse – my mother – I crept into your cradle, having previously flung you out. Forgive me, for I was but two months old, and youth will have its fling'. *Village Virtue, or The Libertine Lord and the Damsel of Daisy Farm – A Domestic Drama of Thrilling Interest*. In Byron, *Sensation Dramas for the Back Drawing Room*, p. 42.

19 See, for example, 'Getting Up A Pantomime', in *London Society* (January 1868), pp. 50–1.

20 *The Orchestra*, 7 October 1880; See also Archer, *Real Conversations*, pp. 117–20.

21 *The Sporting Times*, 2 December 1882.

22 Archer, *Real Conversations*, p. 117.

23 Sullivan and Flower, *Sir Arthur Sullivan*, p. 131. We may note in passing that the conclusion of *Iolanthe* ('Everyone is now a fairy') represents the point at which in pantomime the cast would be transformed into the characters of the Harlequinade.

24 Clinton-Baddeley, *The Burlesque Tradition*, p. 115.

25 Widow Twankey, as Widow Twankay, makes her first appearance in Byron's *Aladdin, or The Wonderful Scamp* (Strand Theatre, 1 April 1861).

26 Baily, *The Gilbert and Sullivan Book*, p. 125.

27 *The Era*, 4 November 1877.

28 Dark and Grey, *W. S. Gilbert*, pp. 167, 211–12.

29 Booth, *Theatre in the Victorian Age*, p. 107.

30 W. S. Gilbert, letter to *The Daily Telegraph*, 4 May 1907.

31 Quiller-Couch, *Studies in Literature*, p. 231.

32 Jacobs, *Arthur Sullivan*, p. 196.

33 Sullivan and Flower, *Sir Arthur Sullivan*, p. 140.

34 *Ibid.*, p. 141.

35 *Ibid.*, p. 142.

36 Jacobs, *Arthur Sullivan*, p. 199.

37 *The Theatre* (1 April 1885), pp. 186–7.

38 Jacobs, *Arthur Sullivan*, p. 220.

39 *San Francisco Daily Chronicle*, 22 July 1885.

40 As a character of burlesque Rose Maybud, the virtuous foundling, should harbour a secret passion for whisky or ambitions as a ballet dancer; Robin Oakapple, the bashful young farmer, should pine for his lost life of insurance fraud and vampirism – he should certainly kidnap Rose at the end of the first act. The chorus of Bucks and Blades should be despised by the professional bridesmaids as being insufficiently steeped in infamy. In the second act Dame Hannah, the bold maiden aunt, should lead the bridesmaids in an heroic attempt to rescue Rose from the clutches of the evil baronet, only to find that being in the clutches of an evil baronet was precisely the realisation of her fondest dreams. The ghosts should certainly be frightened of Robin.

41 The lyrics of 'Only Roses' might have been disposed of by Gilbert after excision from *The Pirates of Penzance*. The sentiments are as appropriate to Ruth as they are to Margaret.

42 Watson, *A Sporting and Dramatic Career*, p. 85.

43 When a *Ruddigore* revival was suggested in 1909, Gilbert proposed to 'cut a good deal of the heavy ghost music in Act 2' (Pearson, *Gilbert, His Life and Strife*, p. 255).

44 *Saturday Review*, 29 January 1887.

45 Sullivan and Flower, *Sir Arthur Sullivan*, pp. 170–1.

46 *Ibid.*, p. 173.

47 Jacobs, *Arthur Sullivan*, p. 270.

48 'Mr Gilbert tells some anecdotes'; *Daily Mail*, 30 October 1906.

49 Sullivan and Flower, *Sir Arthur Sullivan*, p. 184.

50 *Ibid.*, pp. 185–6.

51 *Ibid.*, p. 187.

52 *Ibid.*, p. 188.

53 Jacobs, *Arthur Sullivan*, p. 294.

54 *Ibid.*

55 W. S. Gilbert, affidavit made in the course of the Carpet Quarrel. Public Record Office, Affidavits in Chancery, J4/3875/1936.

56 Diary entry for 6 May 1890.

57 Richard D'Oyly Carte, letter to the *Pall Mall Gazette*, 5 December 1891.

58 Gilbert, *Original Plays*, vol. 3, p. 374.

59 *Ibid.*, vol. 3, p. 87.

60 Reply to Sir George Alexander, given in response to a request for incidental music, quoted in the *Musical Times*, 50/792 (1 February 1909), p. 116.

2 Identity crisis and the search for English opera

1 One of them, *Quite an Adventure* (1881), was composed by Solomon.

2 *The Times*, 1 July 1891.

3 *San Francisco Daily Chronicle*, 22 July 1885.

4 Facsimile letter in Cellier and Bridgeman, *Gilbert, Sullivan and D'Oyly Carte*, facing p. 300.

5 In his autobiography Henry Wood recalls how disappointed and hurt Sullivan was when he found the audience talked through the overture to *The Yeomen of the Guard*. 'I shall never take the trouble to write another', he told me. 'Next time I shall get you or Ernest Ford to score a medley of the tunes.' Wood, *My Life of Music*, p. 39.

6 Tillett, 'Jane Annie', in Eden (ed.), *Utopia Limited*, p. 5.

7 *Jane Annie* was at least notable in that one of its minor characters, Greg, was assigned to the music hall artist Walter Passmore. Passmore made such a success that a special part – Tarara – was written by Gilbert for him in *Utopia Limited*, and he became the theatre's star turn for the next ten years. Selwyn Tillett (*ibid.*, pp. 20–1) suggests that a key strand in the plot of *Jane Annie* found its way into *Utopia Limited*:

Barrie's Proctor and his two Bulldogs bear more than a passing resemblance to Gilbert's King Paramount and his Public Exploders.

8 Sullivan's diary entry for 13 May 1893.

9 Pearson, *Gilbert, His Life and Strife*, p. 179.

10 Tillett, 'Mirette', in Eden (ed.), *Mirette and His Majesty*, p. 3.

11 Gilbert's letter to Mrs Bram Stoker, in Ainger, *Gilbert and Sullivan*, p. 360.

12 The ultimate source of the *Grand Duke* libretto is *A Duke in Difficulties*, a play by Tom Taylor produced at the Haymarket Theatre on 6 March 1861.

13 Reviewing Stanford's *Eden* in *The World*, 14 October 1891.

14 Mackenzie wrote a detailed and penetrating essay on Sullivan's music for the prestigious *Internationalen Musikgesellschaft*.

15 Mackenzie, *A Musician's Narrative*, pp. 201–2.

16 *The Entr'acte*, 6 March 1897.

17 'A Chat with Sir Arthur Sullivan', *The Daily Mail* (17 May 1898), p. 3.

18 Sullivan's diary entry, December 1897; Sullivan and Flower, *Sir Arthur Sullivan*, p. 245.

19 'The New Musical Drama at the Savoy – What Sir Arthur Sullivan Says', *The Daily News* (25 May 1898), p. 3.

20 *Ibid.*

21 Young, *Sir Arthur Sullivan*, pp. 255–6.

22 Hood provided the book not only for *The Rose of Persia* and its successor *The Emerald Isle*, but also for *Merrie England* (1902) and *A Princess of Kensington* (1903), both with music by Edward German.

23 Sullivan's diary entry for 24 November 1899.

24 Gänzl, *The British Musical Theatre*, vol. 1, p. 718.

3 Resituating Gilbert and Sullivan

1 See Brewer, *The Pleasures of the Imagination*, pp. 56ff.

2 *The Spectator*, 21 March 1711. Addison, speaking of Italian opera of his day, is reflecting a broader eighteenth-century reservation concerning the aesthetic standing of music, but whereas in Germany attitudes would change markedly in the years around 1800, England would only slowly move to this new aesthetic.

3 Sullivan, 'About Music', address given to Birmingham and Midlands Institute, 19 October 1888, reproduced in Lawrence, *Arthur Sullivan*, pp. 261–87.

4 See Temperley, *The Lost Chord*, chapter 1.

5 At Covent Garden in the 1860s and through his work as editor of Boosey's 'Royal Edition' scores, Sullivan was exposed to major repertoire works by Auber, Balfe, Beethoven, Bellini,

Donizetti, Flotow, Gounod, Meyerbeer, Mozart, Nicolai, Rossini, Verdi, Wagner and Weber.

6 Zedlitz, 'Sir Arthur Sullivan', p. 170.

7 Mackenzie, 'The Life-Work of Arthur Sullivan', p. 544.

8 Rogers, *Memories of a Musical Career*, p. 168.

9 Obvious jesting is relatively lacking from this scene, with the possible exception of the repetitions Sullivan gives to Gilbert's almost interminable catalogue of insults 'Coward, poltroon, shaker, squeamer . . .', the music getting stuck on a G major chord for four and a half bars before both it and the action can move on, and the tongue-in-cheek reference to *Hamlet* Act I, scene 5 ('Alas, poor ghost!', etc.) a few bars later.

10 Hughes, *The Music of Arthur Sullivan*, p. 55.

11 Letter to Gilbert, 2 April 1884, in Sullivan and Flower, *Sir Arthur Sullivan*, p. 140.

12 *San Francisco Daily Chronicle*, 22 July 1885.

13 Zedlitz, 'Sir Arthur Sullivan', p. 169.

14 See chapter 8 in this volume.

15 Mackenzie, 'The Life-Work of Arthur Sullivan', pp. 539–40.

16 Paraphrasing a similar argument made by Richard Taruskin on behalf of Tchaikovsky (*Defining Russia Musically*, p. 307).

17 Robert Papperitz, for instance, a teacher at Leipzig, claimed that the young Sullivan had more natural talent than Brahms. See Midgley, *My 70 Years Musical Memories*, pp. 21–2.

18 Young, *Sir Arthur Sullivan*, p. 70; see further Taylor, '*The Lost Chord*: Sentimentality, Sincerity, and the Search for "Emotional Depth" in 19th-Century Music'.

19 Dunhill, *Sullivan's Comic Operas*, p. 81. Another example is the Act I finale to *The Mikado*, which exhibits strong echoes of 1850s Verdi. Sullivan's work loses nothing by the comparison, and indeed in melody, harmonic colour and orchestration might have something over the latter's works of this period. Here, as on occasion elsewhere, the boundary between parody and pastiche becomes blurred.

20 Eden, 'The Unperson of English Music'.

21 Quoted in Hibbert, *Gilbert and Sullivan and their Victorian World*, p. 167.

22 Fuller-Maitland, 'Sir Arthur Sullivan', *Cornhill*, March 1901, pp. 300–9.

23 Maclean, 'Sullivan as a National Style-Builder', p. 89.

24 Stradling and Hughes, 'Sir Arthur Sullivan's Crime', in *The English Musical Renaissance*, pp. 186–91. Also see Burton, 'See How the Fates: Sullivan Reassessed', and Saremba, 'In the Purgatory of Tradition'.

25 While still engaged in composition Sullivan played 'Ho Jolly Jenkin' to the conductor, Ernest Ford: 'When he had finished I remarked, "Sir Arthur, why, it will be an immense success," and he replied, somewhat with a sigh, "Yes, I think it would; but it won't do. I can hear them now saying 'redolent of the Savoy'".' Ford, *A Short History of Music in England*, pp. 234–5.

26 Cannadine, 'Gilbert and Sullivan: The Making and Un-making of a British "Tradition"'. Even during their lifetime Gilbert would note that he and Sullivan had become 'as much an institution as Westminster Abbey' (letter of 1888, quoted in Sullivan and Flower, *Sir Arthur Sullivan*, p. 175).

27 *The Daily Telegraph*, 25 May 1939.

28 Quoted in Hughes, *The Music of Arthur Sullivan*, p. 150.

29 Vaughan Williams, *Nationalism in Music and Other Essays*, p. 3.

30 Day, *Englishness in Music*, p. 150.

31 Parrott, 'Arthur Sullivan (1842–1900)', p. 203.

4 'We sing as one individual'?

1 Reich (ed.), *Gustav Mahler*, p. 47.

2 *The Strand Magazine* (1891), quoted in *The Savoyard* (September 1966), p. 9.

3 *San Francisco Daily Chronicle*, 22 July 1885, quoted in Jacobs, *Arthur Sullivan*, pp. 222–3.

4 *The Strand Magazine* (1891), quoted in *The Savoyard* (September 1966), p. 9.

5 Wickes: 'The Texts for *The Mikado* & *The Yeomen of the Guard*'.

6 See Appia, *Die Musik und die Inszenierung*; Craig, *The Art of the Theatre* (1905 and 1911); Craig, *Towards a New Theatre*.

7 See Percy Fitzgerald, *Savoy Operas*; S. Adair Fitzgerald, *The Story of the Savoy Opera*; Godwin (1926); Cox-Ife, *W. S. Gilbert*; Hayter, *Gilbert and Sullivan*; Broude, 'Satire'; Fischler, *Modified Rapture*; Ffinch, *Gilbert and Sullivan*; Crowther, *Contradiction*; Wren, *Ingenious Paradox*; and others.

8 See Emmerson, *Arthur Darling*, and Wolfson, *Sullivan and the Scott Russells*. Sullivan dedicated *Twilight* for piano solo and the song 'O fair dove, O fond dove' to her. Rachel Scott Russell (1845–82) translated Berlioz's *Mémoires* into English (1884).

9 See Stradling and Hughes, *English Musical Renaissance*.

10 Lert, *Mozart auf dem Theater*. In the late twentieth century Willaschek's *Mozart-Theater: vom 'Idomeneo' bis zur 'Zauberflöte'* can be regarded as a modern equivalent. Both result from productions in major opera houses, so they offer the perspective of the musicologist *and* the opera producer.

11 See, for example, Brian Jones, 'The Sword that Never Fell', pp. 22–5.
12 Quoted in Joslin, 'A Substructure of Gilbert's Plots', p. 154.
13 *Punch* 1926, quoted in the programme booklet of the English National Opera: *The Mikado* (1986).
14 Raeithel, *Geschichte der nordamerikanischen Kultur*, vol. 3, p. 381.
15 According to Kuykendall ('English Ceremonial Style', pp. 119 ff.) Sullivan partially created the English ceremonial march which was developed further by the following generation.
16 See Schmook and Busch, *Kunst*, pp. 670–1, and Saremba, *Arthur Sullivan*, pp. 127–8.
17 See Darlington, 'G. and S. without the Addicts'.
18 See Saremba, 'In the Purgatory of Tradition', pp. 33–71, and Stradling and Hughes, *English Musical Renaissance*.
19 Dunhill, *Sullivan's Comic Operas*, p. 38.
20 Mackenzie, *A Musician's Narrative*, p. 205.
21 E. J. Dent, editorial revision to Streatfeild, *The Opera*, p. 379.
22 See 'Warten auf Sullivan' in Saremba, *Arthur Sullivan*, pp. 279–85. English translation by Tony Obrist in the *Sir Arthur Sullivan Society Magazine*, 39 (Summer 1994), pp. 9–13.
23 Saremba, *Arthur Sullivan*, pp. 281–2; trans. pp. 10–11.
24 Dan H. Lawrence (ed.), *Shaw's Music*, p. 174.
25 Jacobs, *Arthur Sullivan*, p. 116; Saremba, 'Ein Weites Feld'.
26 Osborne, *Rossini*, chapter 18.
27 Klein, *Thirty Years of Musical Life in London*, p. 196.
28 Sullivan conducted the *Meistersinger* overture in the same concert at which he conducted Saint-Saëns in Beethoven's Fourth Piano Concerto. *The Musical Times*, 1 June 1886. He conducted the Prize Song from *Die Meistersinger* on 22 April 1885. *The Times*, 24 April 1885.
29 Chantler, *E. T. A. Hoffmann's Musical Aesthetics*.
30 Berger, 'Retrospects', p. 548.
31 An *opéra comique* is characterised by spoken passages, like *Carmen*, and it is not necessarily funny. An *opéra-bouffe* corresponds to comic or light opera. French *opérettes* were one-act works on a modest scale.
32 Mozart's *The Magic Flute* had its first London performance in 1811 (and in New York in 1833); *The Abduction from the Seraglio* was played in London in 1827 (and in New York in 1860). Lortzing's *Zar und Zimmermann* (*Czar and Carpenter*) had been premièred in 1837 in Leipzig and played in New York (1857) and

London (at the Gaiety Theatre in April 1870 under the title *Peter The Shipwright*); his *Der Wildschütz* (*The Poacher*) premièred in 1842 in Leipzig, was performed in Milwaukee (1853), New York (1859) and at London's Drury Lane Theatre (1895); *Der Waffenschmied* (*The Armourer*), premièred in 1846 in Vienna, and went to New York in 1867 (Seeger, *Das große Lexikon der Oper*). While the main venue for (Italian) opera was Covent Garden, other London theatres frequently entertained French or German companies. For example there was a season of 'German *opéra-bouffe*' in November 1871. The problem is that these performances have been forgotten because they did not feature big-name stars.
33 Lawrence, *Sir Arthur Sullivan*, p. 286.
34 Bradley, *Annotated Gilbert and Sullivan*, vol. 1, p. 106.
35 *Pall Mall Gazette*, 5 December 1889.
36 Jacobs, *Arthur Sullivan*, p. 288.
37 See Saremba, 'Arthur Sullivan', in *MGG*.
38 Listen to the CD 'The Anna Russell Album', Sony MDK 47252.
39 *The Saturday Musical Review* (24 May 1879), p. 333; quoted in Sullivan and Flower, *Sir Arthur Sullivan*, pp. 74–5.
40 Letter from Sullivan to Bote & Bock, 15 January 1887. Published with kind permission of the archive of the Deutsche Staatsbibliothek, Berlin in *Sullivan-Journal, Magazin der Deutschen Sullivan-Gesellschaft*, no. 1, June 2009.
41 Sullivan's diary, Berlin, 8–9 June 1900.
42 See Lawrence, *Sir Arthur Sullivan*, pp. 226–7.
43 The Prime Minister, Gladstone, earned about £7,500 per year, the Brontë's father, a vicar, earned £200, an accountant in a bank about £100. Jessie Bond, one of the most prominent cast members of the Savoy ensemble, got her first contract at £3 a week (later she received £30 a week in *The Gondoliers*); most workers had to live on less than £2 a week. The average living costs for middle-class London were about £145; society expected that other members of the family would provide living expenses.
44 See Saremba, 'In the Purgatory of Tradition'.
45 Standard works are Istel, *Das Libretto*; Smith, *The Tenth Muse*; Gier, *Das Libretto*.
46 'From Minerva House – 1962: G or S?' *Musical Opinion* (January 1962), p. 197–8.
47 Ellis, *The Bab Ballads*, pp. 280–1.
48 See Fitzgerald, 'Sullivan's Friendship with Dickens', *Gilbert and Sullivan News*, p. 15; and Saremba, 'Brother Sir Arthur Sullivan', pp. 14–19.
49 Bradley, *Annotated Gilbert and Sullivan*, vol. 1, p. 340.

50 Both versions sung by David Fieldsend can be heard on Sullivan, *The Yeomen of the Guard*, New D'Oyly Carte Opera Company, conductor: John Owen Edwards, Sony S2K 58901.
51 Bradbury, 'Music and Musicians'.
52 Williamson, *Gilbert and Sullivan Opera*, p. 283.
53 Dark and Grey, *W. S. Gilbert*, p. 144.

5 The operas in context
1 Jacobs, *Arthur Sullivan*, p. 250.
2 Arthur Sullivan, *Marmion* Overture, full score, ed. Robin Gordon-Powell (London: The Amber Ring, 2003), p. vii.
3 See the Appendix: The orchestration of Sullivan's major works.
4 Philips 434 916–2, cond. Marriner, track 4.
5 Philips 464 916–2, cond. Marriner, track 1.
6 Nikolai Rimsky-Korsakov's *Principles of Orchestration* was published posthumously (by his son-in-law Maximillian Steinberg) in 1912 (New York: Dover Publications, Inc., 1964, pp. 49–50).
7 Philips 434 916–2, cond. Marriner, track 7.
8 Review in *The Musical Times*, 27/52 (1 June 1886), p. 335.
9 Goldman, *Harmony in Western Music*, pp. 155–6.
10 EMI 0777 7 64406 2 0, cond. Sargent, disc 1, track 11.
11 Symposium 1289, cond. Balcombe, track 3.

6 The librettos in context
1 Bulwer, *Fables in Song*. See Dölvers, *Fables*, pp. 91–113.
2 Dölvers, *Fables*, p. 154.
3 Wren, *A Most Ingenious Paradox*, p. 109.
4 A fitting quotation from Shakespeare, *Othello*, III, iii, 90.
5 Jenkins, 'Swinburne, Robert Buchanan, and W. S. Gilbert'. Jenkins finds, like Isaac Goldberg before him, 'a touch of Swinburne in Grosvenor' (p. 373) and thinks that 'Gilbert inserted several subtly disguised private jokes on this subject (i.e. sado-masochism) into *Patience*' (p. 370).
6 Saremba, *Arthur Sullivan*, p. 164.
7 Grzbek has proposed the translation 'primary' for 'einfach' in André Jolles's influential study *Einfache Formen* (Halle: Niemeyer, 1930). Grzbek, 'Invariant Meaning Structures in Texts', p. 350.
8 Perry, *Aesopica*, vol. 1, p. ix.
9 La Fontaine, 'Fable X,6, L'Araignée et l'Hirondelle'. *Œuvres complètes*, p. 50.
10 Perry, *Aesopica*, vol. 1, 'Asinus ad Lyram' (no. 542), 'Vulpes et umbra lunae' (no. 669), 'Mus Matrimonium Quaerens' (no. 619).
11 Gardner, *Lewis Carroll*, p. 134.

12 Skipsey, 'The Bee and the Rose'.
13 See note 1.
14 Harlan, *Owen Meredith*, p. 204.
15 Stevenson, 'Lord Lytton's *Fables in Song*', pp. 191–5.
16 Buchanan's devastating doggerel appeared in *St Paul's Magazine*, August 1872.
17 Bausinger, 'Die moralischen Tiere', p. 242.
18 Carnes, *Fable Scholarship*, pp. xv and 379. See also Thompson, *Motif Index of Folk Literature*.
19 Perry, *Aesopica*, vol. 1 ('Jackdaw and Pigeons', no. 129).
20 *Ibid.* ('Fox and Grapes', no. 15).
21 i.e. 'strike her sails'.
22 Wren, *A most Ingenious Paradox*, p. 188.
23 For the following see Dölvers, *Fables*, pp. 58–66.
24 'Amaranthus et Rosa', Perry, *Aesopica*, vol. 1 (no. 369). A contemporary definition of society verse was given by W. D. Adams in his collection *Songs of Society from Anne to Victoria* (London: Pickering, 1880), p. xiii.
25 Bulwer, *Fables in Song*, vol. 1, p. 48.
26 P. B. Marston, 'The Rose and the Wind', in Miles, *The Poets and the Poetry of the Nineteenth Century*, vol. 7, p. 324.
27 Saremba, *Arthur Sullivan*, p. 350 and p. 316 n. 383.
28 Temperley, 'The English Romantic Opera', p. 299. 'Amorous in effect', *ibid*. Further details in Disher, *Victorian Song*.
29 Temperley, 'The English Romantic Opera', p. 301.
30 I am quoting and paraphrasing Wren, *A Most Ingenious Paradox*, p. 188.
31 Gilbert, *The Bab Ballads*, pp. 536–8.
32 'Swarm': [+ multiple], 'alone': [– multiple].
33 These examples are further discussed in Dölvers, *Fables*, pp. 91–104.
34 'His size anent' i.e. 'concerning his size'. Gilbert, *The Bab Ballads*, pp. 138–42.
35 Aristotle, 'Prior Analytics', 25: 'Every demonstration will proceed through three terms and no more'. *The Complete Works of Aristotle*, vol. 1, p. 66.

7 'This particularly rapid, unintelligible patter'
Many thanks to David Eden, Andrew Miller, Ivan Kreilkamp and Peter Bailey for their advice and assistance.
1 W. S. Gilbert, draft of a speech, Gilbert Papers, vol. 18, fol. 119, British Library, Add. MS 49306. For more on humour in music, see Burnham, 'Haydn and Humor'. Gilbert and Sullivan criticism often concerns itself with the biographical relationship between Gilbert and Sullivan and emphasises their conflict, using the

operas to illuminate the interpersonal or the intrapersonal to illuminate the operas. I would like to bracket this discussion and consider the patter songs as words and music together producing an effect, regardless of how the words and music came about.

2 The idea of a third type of meaning in song, beyond words or music, was inspired by Matthew Head, 'Plenary session II: Critical Language and Methodology', given at the conference *Words and Notes in the Nineteenth Century*, Stewart House, London, 3 July 2007.

3 'Patter Song', *Grove Music Online*, ed. L. Macy, www.grovemusic.com.

4 Maitland, 'Patter Song' (1880).

5 *Ibid.*

6 Maitland, 'Patter-Song' (1907), p. 654.

7 Maitland, 'Patter-Song' (1880).

8 For more on music hall patter, see Vicinus, *The Industrial Muse*, pp. 238–85; Bailey, *Popular Culture and Performance in the Victorian City*.

9 Maitland, 'Patter-Song' (1880).

10 Mathews, 'Patter Versus Clatter', in Booth (ed.), *English Plays of the Nineteenth Century*, pp. 125–6.

11 St James's Theatre, 9 July 1864. Review in *The Times*, 11 July 1864. This work contains a scene in which Margeurite sues Faust for breach of promise, receiving £2,000 in damages, thanks to 'an impartial jury'.

12 Joseph Knight, 'Grain, Richard Corney (1844–1895)', rev. Nilanjana Banerji, *Oxford Dictionary of National Biography*, www.oxforddnb.com/view/article/11232 (accessed 24 July 2007); Peter H. Hansen, 'Smith, Albert Richard (1816–1860)', *Oxford Dictionary of National Biography*, www.oxforddnb.com/view/article/25768 (accessed 24 July 2007).

13 'Royal Italian Opera', *The Times*, 12 May 1856; see also 'Music', *The Times*, 21 June 1858.

14 See Grout and Hermine, *A Short History of Opera*, pp. 272–98; Platoff, 'The Buffa Aria in Mozart's Vienna'.

15 More familiarly known as *Orlando Paladino* (1782).

16 Maitland, 'Patter-Song' (1880).

17 Grossmith, *A Society Clown*, p. 95.

18 Including *Thespis* and *Trial by Jury*.

19 See Grossmith, *A Society Clown*; Grossmith, *Piano and I*; Naylor, *Gaiety and George Grossmith*.

20 *Liverpool Review*, 19 February 1887, in cutting-book 'Ruddigore 1886–87', D'Oyly Carte Collection, Theatre Museum, London.

21 Grossmith, *A Society Clown*, p. 38.

22 'At the Theatre', *Modern Truth*, 29 January 1887, in cutting-book 'Ruddigore 1886–87',

D'Oyly Carte Collection, Theatre Museum, London.

23 See Grossmith, *Piano and I*, p. 72 and *passim*.

24 Grossmith, *A Juvenile Party*, pp. 3, 7.

25 For extemporising, see Bradley, *The Complete Annotated Gilbert and Sullivan*. For reports on rehearsals and accuracy, see Grossmith, *A Society Clown*, pp. 101–2.

26 'Patter', *OED Online*, http://dictionary.oed.com/entrance.dtl.

27 *Ibid.*

28 'The Only Jones', *Judy*, 2 February 1887, in cutting-book 'Ruddigore 1886–87', D'Oyly Carte Collection, Theatre Museum, London.

29 W. S. Gilbert and Arthur Sullivan, *Ruddigore* (London: Chappell, [1911?]), p. 126.

30 W. S. Gilbert and Arthur Sullivan, *Iolanthe* (London: J. M. Stoddart, 1882), p. 125.

31 This song was cut in the first few weeks of production; for the text, see Bradley (ed.), *Complete Annotated*, p. 732; for the score, see W. S. Gilbert and Arthur Sullivan, *Ruddigore*, ed. David Russell Hulme (Oxford: Oxford University Press, 2000), pp. 289–92.

8 Standing still and moving forward
A version of this essay first appeared in *Comparative Drama*, 22/1 (Spring 1988), pp. 1–16.

1 *Haddon Hall*'s initial run was greater, incidentally, than that of *Thespis* (64), *Trial by Jury* (131), *The Sorcerer* (175) and *The Grand Duke* (123), and was in the same bracket as *Utopia Limited* (245), *Princess Ida* (246) and *Ruddigore* (288).

2 Jane Stedman, '"So far we haven't quite solved the plot . . .": Sullivan's Other Librettists' (paper delivered at a conference entitled 19th Century Musical Theatre in English, New York City, June 1985). I quote from the abstract of this paper.

3 Shaw, *Music in London, 1890–94*, pp. 150–4. Shaw devoted a substantial part of his column of 28 September 1892 to a discussion of *Haddon Hall*.

4 Nigel Burton, 'Opera: 1865–1914', in Temperley, *Athlone History of Music*, p. 339.

5 The terms used here to discuss aspects of dramatic representation derive from the work of Bernard Beckerman, whose *Dynamics of Drama* was a comprehensive theory of dramatic structure.

6 Beckerman, 'Historic and Iconic Time', p. 48.

7 Beckerman, *Theatrical Presentation*, chapter 3.

8 Beckerman, 'Historic and Iconic Time', p. 48.

9 Shaw, *Music in London*, p. 151.

10 Beckerman, 'Historic and Iconic Time', p. 48.

11 See Michael Hurd, 'Glees, Madrigals and Partsongs', in Temperley, *Athlone History of Music*, pp. 242–65.

12 *Ibid.*, pp. 254–63.

13 Shaw, *Music in London*, p. 154.

14 That this quality found a response in early audiences cannot be doubted, as the following excerpt from the *Sunday Times* of 25 September 1892 reveals: 'An English story with a fine healthy English tone, set to music essentially English in idea, form, and character, *Haddon Hall* . . . is one of those happy combinations of national qualities that can never appeal in vain to popular audiences. It breathes at every point the true racial spirit.'

15 For Sullivan's deference to conventional social behaviour, for example in the matter of his liaison with Fanny Ronalds, see Jacobs, *Arthur Sullivan*, pp. 86–7.

16 See *ibid.*, p. 275.

17 Beckerman, 'Historic and Iconic Time', p. 48.

18 *Ibid.*, p. 52.

19 'However little the critics thought of my libretto, I have the satisfaction of knowing that it pleased my collaborator. He never tired of telling me what a pleasure it was to him to set my words.' Sydney Grundy, facsimile letter in Cellier and Bridgeman, *Gilbert, Sullivan and D'Oyly Carte*, facing p. 300.

20 See Beckerman, 'The Sword on the Wall'.

9 Musical contexts I

1 For example, Taylor, *The Indebtedness of Handel*.

2 Reynolds, *Motives for Allusion*, p. 6.

3 Hughes, *The Music of Arthur Sullivan*, p. 154.

4 *Ibid.*, p. 155.

5 Wilson and Lloyd, *Gilbert & Sullivan*, p. 58.

6 Beckerman, 'The Sword on the Wall'.

7 Maclean, 'Sullivan as National Style-Builder', p. 98; Champion, 'Sullivan's Innocent Cribs'; Williamson, *Gilbert and Sullivan Opera*, p. 62.

8 Burrows, 'Some Aspects', p. 148.

9 Hughes, *The Music of Arthur Sullivan*, p. 152.

10 For an argument for why 'D'un pensiero' specifically was the model, see Jacobs, *Arthur Sullivan*, p. 94.

11 A starting point is Powers, '"La solita forma"'.

12 See, for example, Fischler, 'Gilbert and Donizetti'.

13 Parrott, 'Arthur Sullivan (1842–1900)', p. 209.

14 Jacobs, *Arthur Sullivan*, p. 114.

15 Young, *Sir Arthur Sullivan*, p. 210.

16 Quoted in *Ruddigore*, ed. D. R. Hulme (Oxford: Oxford University Press, 2000), p. ix.

17 Temperley, 'Mendelssohn's Influence on English Music'.

18 Letter dated 30 August [1863] reproduced in Allen, *Sir Arthur Sullivan*, p. 51.

19 For example, Williamson, *Gilbert and Sullivan Opera*, p. 113; Wren, *A Most Ingenious Paradox*, p. 123.

20 Kuykendall, 'The English Ceremonial Style', pp. 171–82; see also Scott, 'English National Identity', pp. 140–1.

21 Quoted in Lawrence, *Sir Arthur Sullivan*, p. 45.

10 Musical contexts II

1 *San Francisco Daily Chronicle*, 22 July 1885.

2 Prefatory argument to *The Light of the World* in Sullivan, *Light of the World*.

3 Hugo, quoted in Gerhard, *Urbanization of Opera*, p. 168.

4 See M. Yates, 'Contrast and Unity in the Score of *Ivanhoe*', in Eden (ed.), *Sullivan's Ivanhoe*, pp. 29–53.

5 *Strand Magazine* (July/December 1897), p. 653.

6 Barrington, *Rutland Barrington*, pp. 56–7.

7 Sullivan's approach at this point foreshadows a similar response by Britten in *Albert Herring*, where a ridiculous situation – the assumed death of Albert – gives rise to a serious chorus, the threnody.

8 'The composition of a light or comic opera where I must appear to be in a chronic state of high spirits, and write in a light, tuneful vein throughout, with the constant fear of the commonplace or the banal before me, is no easy task.' Arthur Sullivan, interview in the *Daily News* (25 May 1898), p. 3.

9 Hughes, *The Music of Arthur Sullivan*, p. 21. The 'delightful trembling' evident throughout is not, however, unique to *The Mikado*. The Eastern Maidens of *The Martyr of Antioch* are equally beautiful.

10 Day, *Englishness In Music*, p. 146.

11 Mitchell, *The Paradox of Gloriana*, in Banks (ed.), *Britten's Gloriana*, p. 67.

12 Diary entry, 3 October 1888, in Sullivan and Flower, *Sir Arthur Sullivan*, p. 181.

13 Burton, 'Opera, 1865–1914', in Temperley, *The Athlone History of Music*, p. 333.

14 In *Ivanhoe* (Act II, scene 3) Ulrica is given a very different kind of spinning song, imbued with the dark forbidding atmosphere of Torquilstone.

15 Sullivan's own analysis of this song appears in Lawrence, *Sir Arthur Sullivan*, pp. 224–5.

16 Nietszche, *The Will to Power*, trans. Kaufman and Hollingdale, p. 435.

17 Westrup, 'An Eminent Victorian', p. 389.

18 It is regrettable that Sullivan's intended effect is destroyed by conductors who either continue in the same tempo, or faster, and also ignore the four-bar repeat.

19 See, for example, the confessions of the comedienne Jo Brand, who played the Sergeant of Police in a Carl Rosa production of *The Pirates of Penzance*. *Daily Telegraph* (30 January 2008), p. 29.

12 Amateur tenors and choruses in public

1 Young, *A Century of Service*, p. 3.

2 Typescript account of the conception and birth of the G & S Fellowship by H. W. Bickle, made available by Pauline Smith, the Fellowship's archivist.

3 Conversation in Philadelphia, November 2003.

4 D'Cruz, 'Dainty Little Fairies', p. 351.

5 *Ibid.*, p. 362.

6 *New York Times*, 13 August 2000. CDs privately produced by the company.

7 Research carried out among members of St Andrews University G & S Society, 2005. Further details can be found in Bradley, *Oh Joy!*, p. 153.

13 Champions and afficionados

1 Pitts, '"Everybody wants to be Pavarotti"'.

2 The original D'Oyly Carte Opera Company, officially founded in August 1879, ceased performing in 1982. The Sadler's Wells Opera Company, the later English National Opera, and the Welsh National Opera were able to perform the operas after the expiry of copyright from 1961 onwards. The Birmingham-based New D'Oyly Carte Company (1988–2003) brought fresh impulses with a new generation of performers and an accurate reading of the original scores – integrating lost music, using critical editions etc. – which can still be heard in their recordings.

3 Dufty, 'Review'.

4 Stebbins, *Amateurs*, p. 39.

5 *Ibid.*, p. 9.

6 Pitts, *Valuing Musical Participation*.

7 Murninghan and Conlon, 'Dynamics'.

8 D'Cruz, 'Dainty Little Fairies', p. 352.

9 See Pitts, 'What Makes an Audience' and Pitts and Spencer, 'Loyalty'.

10 Stradling and Hughes, *The English Musical Renaissance*, p. 225.

11 Wren, *A Most Ingenious Paradox*, p. ix.

12 Cf. Kolb, 'The Effect of Generational Change'.

13 The billboard advertises a performance of *Why Smith Left Home* (1912), a farce by G. H. Broadhurst.

14 Stradling and Hughes, *The English Musical Renaissance*, p. 225.

15 Wren, *A Most Ingenious Paradox*, p. 296.

14 'How great thy charm, thy sway how excellent!'

1 Bargainnier, 'W. S. Gilbert and American Musical Theatre'; Bradley, *Oh Joy!*, pp. 5–8; Wren, *A Most Ingenious Paradox*, pp. 197–311.

2 Wren, *A Most Ingenious Paradox*, pp. 191–7.

3 mcclung, 'Life after George'; mcclung, *Lady in the Dark*, pp. 75–7.

4 Knapp, *The American Musical*, pp. 266–73; mcclung, *Lady in the Dark*.

5 Bradley, *Oh Joy!*, pp. 3–9.

6 Fink, 'Rhythm and Text Setting in *The Mikado*'.

7 Banfield, 'Popular Musical Theatre', pp. 295–6.

8 Knapp, *The American Musical and the Performance*, pp. 214–15.

9 Knapp, *The American Musical and the Formation*, pp. 34–46.

10 *Ibid.*, pp. 88–99.

11 See Knapp, *The American Musical and the Performance*, pp. 284–93.

12 Knapp, *The American Musical and the Formation*, pp. 230–9 and 261–8.

13 Beckerman, 'The Sword on the Wall'.

14 Knapp, *The American Musical and the Formation*, p. 238.

15 Wren, *A Most Ingenious Paradox*, p. 294.

15 'See how the Fates their gifts allot'

1 Aber, *Die Musik im Schauspiel-Geschichtliches und Asthetisches*, p. 55.

2 Quoted in Obrist, 'Der Mikado'.

3 Williamson, *Gilbert and Sullivan Opera*, p. 283.

4 'Berliner Presse', *Vossische Zeitung*, 6 June 1886.

5 *Norddeutsche Allgemeine Zeitung*, 6 June 1886.

6 See Hanslick, *Musikalisches Skizzenbuch*, pp. 288–95.

7 Jacobs, *Arthur Sullivan*, p. 255.

8 Weissmann, *Berlin als Musikstadt*, p. 402; translations by the author unless otherwise stated.

9 Jacobs, *Arthur Sullivan*, p. 284.

10 *Birmingham Daily Post*, 13 February 1889.

11 Arthur Jacobs contradicts Alfred Loewenberg at this point. Jacobs, *Arthur Sullivan*, p. 285, mentions the *Carltheater* under this date.

12 Jacobs, *Arthur Sullivan*, p. 285.

13 See *ibid.*, p. 292.

14 *Ibid.*, p. 309.

15 Keller, *Die Operette*, p. 144.

16 Late 1920s or early 1930s by Electrola and HMV (labels of the Grammophon Company).

17 A surprising discovery of a connection between Savoy opera and Bertolt Brecht's plays has been made by Michael Morley. In his article 'Archetypes or Readymades?', Morley mentions associations with *The Mikado* in Brecht's *Der Gute Mensch von Sezuan* and *Der kaukasische Kreidekreis*. Morley found the information about Brecht's (and also Weill's) interest in Gilbert and Sullivan – a planned adaptation of *Pinafore* (around 1948).

18 Obrist, 'Der Mikado', p. 4.

19 'Bunte Seemänner', *Wochenkurier*, 8 February 1994.

20 *Rhein-Neckar-Zeitung*, 1 July 1975.

21 *Landwirtschaftlicher Wochenblatt*, 2 June 1974.

22 Review by K. Leymann, *Opernwelt* (1994), p. 33.

23 Review by K. Kalchschmid, *Opernwelt* (2002), p. 44.

24 See Polianovskaia, '"The Gaiety" in St-Petersburg' and 'The English Operetta and Musical Comedy in German Guest Performances'.

25 K. Stanislavsky, *Complete Works*, 8 vols. (Moscow: Iskusstvo, 1954), vol. 1, p. 82; Obrist, 'Der Mikado', p. l.

26 Obrist, 'Der Mikado', p. 1.

27 Translator unknown.

28 *Peterburgskaya gazeta*, 13 November 1891.

29 *Peterburgskaya gazeta*, 10 December 1888.

30 'Deutsches Theater', *Beiblatt der Leertaste SPb. Zeitung*, 9 (21) December 1888.

31 Jacobs, *Arthur Sullivan*, p. 310.

Bibliography and further reading

Aber, Adolf, *Die Musik im Schauspiel Geschichtliches und Ästhetisches*. Leipzig: Beck Verlag, 1926.

Adams, W. Davenport, *A Book of Burlesque*. London: Henry & Co., 1891.

Adams, W. D. (ed.), *Songs of Society from Anne to Victoria*. London: Pickering, 1880.

Ainger, Michael, *Gilbert and Sullivan: A Dual Biography*. Oxford: Oxford University Press, 2002.

Allen, R. (ed.), *Sir Arthur Sullivan: Composer and Personage*. New York: Pierpont Morgan Library, 1975.

Anderson, R., *Elgar in Manuscript*. Portland: Amadeus Press, 1990.

Appia, Adolph, *Die Musik und die Inszenierung*. Munich: F. Bruckmann, 1899.

Archer, William, *Real Conversations*. London: Heinemann, 1904.

Aristotle, *The Complete Works of Aristotle*, The Revised Oxford Translation, ed. J. Barnes, vol. 1. Princeton: Princeton University Press, 1984.

Ayre, Leslie, *The Gilbert & Sullivan Companion*. London: W. H. Allen, 1972; Pan Books, 1974.

Bailey, Peter, *Popular Culture and Performance in the Victorian City*. Cambridge: Cambridge University Press, 1998.

Baily, Leslie, *The Gilbert and Sullivan Book*. London: Cassell, 1952; new edn 1966.

Baker, H. Barton, *The London Stage: Its History and Traditions from 1576 to 1888*. 2 vols. London: W. H. Allen & Co., 1889.

Banfield, Stephen, 'Popular Musical Theatre (and Film)', in *The Cambridge Companion to Twentieth-Century Opera*, ed. Mervyn Cooke. Cambridge: Cambridge University Press, 2005.

Banks, Paul (ed.), *Britten's Gloriana*. Woodbridge: The Boydell Press, 1993.

Bargainnier, Earl F., 'W. S. Gilbert and American Musical Theatre', *Journal of Popular Culture*, 12 (Winter, 1978).

Barrington, Rutland, *Rutland Barrington by Himself*. London: Grant Richards, 1908.

Bausinger, H., 'Die moralischen Tiere', *Universitas*, 45 (1990), pp. 241–51.

Becker, Heinz (ed.), *Die 'Couleur locale' in der Oper des 19. Jahrhunderts*. Regensburg: Gustav Bosse Verlag, 1976.

Beckerman, Bernard. *Dynamics of Drama*. New York: Drama Book Specialists, 1979.
'Historic and Iconic Time in Late Tudor Drama', in Kenneth Muir *et al.* (eds.), *Shakespeare, Man of the Theatre*. Newark: University of Delaware Press, 1983.
Theatrical Presentation: Performer, Audience and Act, ed. Gloria Beckerman and William Coco. London: Routledge, 1990.
'The Sword on the Wall: Japanese Elements and their Significance in *The Mikado*', *Musical Quarterly*, 73 (1989), pp. 303–19.

Beckerman, Michael, 'Arthur Sullivan, Haddon Hall, and the Iconic Mode', *Comparative Drama*, 22 (1988), pp. 1–18.

Benford, Harry, *The Gilbert and Sullivan Lexicon*. Ann Arbor: Sarah Jennings Press, 1991.

Berger, Francesco, 'Retrospects', *Musical Opinion* (March 1929).

Berman, Leon E. A., 'Gilbert's First Night Anxiety', *The Psychoanalytic Quarterly*, 45 (1976), pp. 110–27.

Bond, Jessie, *The Life and Reminiscences of Jessie Bond*. London: John Lane, The Bodley Head, 1930.

Booth, Michael R., *Theatre in the Victorian Age*. Cambridge: Cambridge University Press, 1991.

(ed.), *English Plays of the Nineteenth Century*, vol. 4: *Farces*. Oxford: Oxford University Press, 1973.

Bourjo, Richard, 'Gilbert and Hardy', *Sir Arthur Sullivan Society Magazine*, 26 (Spring 1988), pp. 8–11.

Boyer, R. D., 'The Directorial Practice of W. S. Gilbert', unpublished diss., Ohio State University 1970.

Bradbury, Ernest, 'Sullivan's Comic Operas', *Yorkshire Post*, 13 January 1962.

Bradley, Ian, *Oh Joy! Oh Rapture! The Enduring Phenomenon of Gilbert and Sullivan*. Oxford: Oxford University Press, 2005.

Bradley, Ian (ed.), *The Annotated Gilbert and Sullivan*. 2 vols. London: Penguin, 1984.

The Complete Gilbert and Sullivan. Oxford: Oxford University Press, 2006.

Brahms, Caryl, *Gilbert and Sullivan: Lost Chords and Dischords*. London: Weidenfeld and Nicholson, 1975.

Brenner, Arthur E., 'The Fantasies of W. S. Gilbert', *The Psychoanalytic Quarterly*, 21 (April 1952), pp. 337–401.

Brewer, John, *The Pleasures of the Imagination: English Culture in the Eighteenth Century*. London: Harper Collins, 1997.

Broude, Ronald, 'Satire and Sentiment in *The Yeomen of the Guard*', in *Studies in the History of Music*, vol. 2, *Music and Drama*. New York: Broude Brothers Ltd, 1988, pp. 194–214.

Browne, Edith A., *W. S. Gilbert*. London: John Lane, 1907.

Bulwer, E. A., Earl of Lytton, *Fables in Song*. 2 vols. Edinburgh: Blackwood, 1874.

Burnham, Scott, 'Haydn and Humor', in *The Cambridge Companion to Haydn*, ed. Caryl Clark (Cambridge: Cambridge University Press, 2005), pp. 61–76.

Burrows, D., 'Some Aspects of the Influence of Handel's Music on the English Musician Arthur Sullivan (1842–1900)', *Händel-Jahrbuch* (1998), pp. 148–71.

Burton, Nigel, 'See How the Fates: Sullivan Reassessed', *The Musical Times*, 141 (2000), pp. 15–22.

'*The Yeomen of the Guard*: Apogee of a Style', *Musical Times*, 128 (1988), pp. 656–9.

Byron, Henry J., *Sensation Dramas for the Back Drawing Room*. London: Thomas Hailes Lacy, n.d. [1864].

Cannadine, David, 'Gilbert and Sullivan: The Making and Un-making of a British "Tradition"', in Roy Porter (ed.), *Myths of the English*. Cambridge: Polity Press, 1992.

Carnes, P., *Fable Scholarship: An Annotated Bibliography*. New York and London: Garland, 1985.

Cellier, François and Cunningham Bridgeman, *Gilbert, Sullivan and D'Oyly Carte*. London: Pitman, 1914; 2nd edn 1927.

Champion, T., 'Sullivan's Innocent Cribs', *Gilbert & Sullivan Journal*, 1/3 (October 1925), p. 7.

Chantler, Abigail, *E. T. A. Hoffmann's Musical Aesthetics*. Aldershot: Ashgate, 2006.

Clinton-Baddeley, V. C., *The Burlesque Tradition in the English Theatre after 1660*. London: Methuen & Co., 1952.

Cox-Ife, William, *W. S. Gilbert: Stage Director*. London: Dennis Dobson, 1978.

Craig, Edward Gordon, *The Art of the Theatre*. Edinburgh and London: T. N. Foulis, 1905; rev. edn London: Mercury Books, 1911.

Towards a New Theatre. London and Toronto: J. M. Dent and Sons, 1913.

Crane, W. and W. J. Linton, *The Baby's Own Aesop. Being the Fables Condensed in Rhyme. With Portable Morals Pictorially Pointed out by Walter Crane*. London: Warne, 1887.

Crowther, Andrew, *Contradiction Contradicted: The Plays of W. S. Gilbert*. Madison: Fairleigh Dickenson University Press, 2000.

D'Cruz, S., 'Dainty Little Fairies: Women, Gender and the Savoy Operas', *Women's History Review*, 9/2 (2000), pp. 345–67.

Dahlhaus, Carl, *Nineteenth-Century Music*, trans. J. Bradford Robinson. Berkeley and Los Angeles: University of California Press, 1989.

Dark, Sidney and Rowland Grey, *W. S. Gilbert: His Life and Letters*. London: Methuen and Co., 1923.

Darlington, William Aubrey, 'G. and S. Without the Addicts', *The Daily Telegraph*, 22 January 1962.

The World of Gilbert and Sullivan. New York, 1950.

Davis, Jim and Victor Emeljanow, *Reflecting the Audience: London Theatregoing 1840–1880*. Hatfield: University of Hertfordshire Press, 2001.

Day, James, *Englishness in Music from Elizabethan Times to Elgar, Tippett and Britten*. London: Thames Publishing, 1999.

Disher, M. W., *Victorian Song*. London: Phoenix, 1955.

Dixon, Geoffrey, '"I copied all the letters in a big, round hand": Indexing W. S. Gilbert', *W. S. Gilbert Society Journal*, 1/6 (1990), pp. 178–82.

The Gilbert & Sullivan Concordance: A Word Index to W. S. Gilbert's Libretti to the 14 Savoy Operas. 2 vols. New York: Garland Press, 1987.

The Gilbert & Sullivan Photofinder: An Index to Published Illustrations of Savoy Opera. Ayr: Rhosearn Press, 1995.

Index to the Sir Arthur Sullivan Society Magazine, Nos. 1–40, 1977–1995. (G. Dixon, 93, Carcluie Crescent, Ayr, 1995).

The Gilbert and Sullivan Journal 56-year Index. Ayr: Rhosearn Press, 1996.

The Gilbert and Sullivan Sorting System: A Classification Scheme for Use with the Materials of G. & S. Studies. Ayr: Rhosearn Press, 2001.

Sullivan's Diaries: An Index to Sir Arthur Sullivan's Diary, 1876–1900. Ayr: Rhosearn Press, 2007.

The Gilbert & Sullivan Fact Finder: An Index to 5 Major Journals. Ayr: Rhosearn Press: in preparation.

Dölvers, Horst, *Fables Less and Less Fabulous: English Fables and Parables of the Nineteenth Century and their Illustrations.* Newark: University of Delaware Press, 1997.

Dufty, J., 'Review of the Eighth International Gilbert and Sullivan Festival, Buxton, August 2001', *Gilbert and Sullivan News*, 3/3 (Autumn/Winter 2001), p. 8.

Dunhill, Thomas, *Sullivan's Comic Operas: A Critical Appreciation.* London: Edward Arnold & Co., 1928.

Eden, David, *Gilbert and Sullivan: The Creative Conflict.* Fairleigh Dickinson, 1986.
  'The Unperson of British Music', lecture given at the Sullivan Society Conference at Calver in May 1992, www.sullivan-forschung.de.
  W. S. Gilbert: Appearance and Reality. Saffron Walden, 2005.

Eden, David (ed.), Commemorative Booklets, for the Sir Arthur Sullivan Society, published in Coventry: *Princess Ida* (1984); *The Mikado* (1985); *Ruddigore* (1987); *Ivanhoe* (1991); *Haddon Hall* (1992); *Utopia Limited* (1993); *The Chieftain* (1994); *King Arthur* (1995); *The Ballets of Sir Arthur Sullivan* (1995); *Mirette/His Majesty* (1996); *The Grand Duke* (1996).
  Sullivan's Ivanhoe. Saffron Walden, 2007.

Ehrlich, Cyril, *Harmonious Alliance: A History of the Performing Rights Society.* Oxford: Oxford University Press, 1989.

Eimermacher, K., P. Grzybek and Georg Witte (eds.), *Issues in Slavic Literary and Cultural Theory.* Bochum: Brockmeyer, 1989.

Ellis, James (ed.), *The Bab Ballads by W. S. Gilbert.* Cambridge, Mass.: Belknap, 1970.

Emmerson, George S., *Arthur Darling: The Romance of Arthur Sullivan and Rachel Scott.* London, Ont.: Galt House, 1980.

Feggetter, Graeme, 'Suicide in Opera', in *Opera* (February 1988), pp. 172–8.

Ffinch, Michael, *Gilbert and Sullivan.* London: Weidenfeld & Nicolson, 1992.

Fink, Robert, 'Rhythm and Text Setting in *The Mikado*', *19th Century Music*, 14/1 (Summer 1990), pp. 31–47.

Fischler, A., 'Gilbert and Donizetti', *Opera Quarterly*, 2 (1994), pp. 29–42.
  Modified Rapture: Comedy in W. S. Gilbert's Savoy Operas. Charlottesville: University Press of Virginia, 1991.

Fitzgerald, Percy, *The Savoy Operas and the Savoyards.* London: Chatto & Windus, 1894.

Fitzgerald, S. Adair, *The Story of the Savoy Opera.* London: Stanley Paul, 1924.
  'Sullivan's Friendship with Dickens', *The Gilbert and Sullivan Journal*, 2 (July 1925); reprinted in *Gilbert and Sullivan News*, 4/3 (Autumn/Winter 2007).

Ford, Ernest, *A Short History of Music in England.* London: Sampson, Low, Marston & Co., 1912.

Gänzl, Kurt, *The British Musical Theatre*, vol. 1: *1865–1914*. London: Macmillan, 1986.

Gardner, M. (ed.), *Lewis Carroll: The Annotated Alice*, rev. edn. Harmondsworth: Penguin Books, 1970.

Gay, Peter, *The Naked Heart.* New York and London: W. W. Norton, 1995.

Schnitzler's Century: The Making of Middle-Class Culture 1815–1914. New York: W. W. Norton, 2001.

The Tender Passion. New York: Oxford University Press, 1986.

Gelfert, Hans-Dietrich, *Max und Monty: Kleine Geschichte des deutschen und englischen Humors*. Munich: C. H. Beck, 1998.

Gerhard, Anselm, *The Urbanization of Opera: Music Theater in Paris in the Nineteenth Century*, trans. Arnold Whittall. Chicago: University of Chicago Press, 2000.

Gier, Albert, *Das Libretto: Theorie und Geschichte*. Frankfurt and Leipzig: Insel Verlag, 2000.

Gilbert, W. S., *Original Plays*, 4 Series. London: Chatto and Windus, 1915.

Godwin, A. H., *Gilbert and Sullivan*. London: J. M. Dent & Sons, 1926.

Goldberg, Isaac (ed.), *New and Original Extravaganzas*. Boston: J. W. Luce & Co., 1931.

The Story of Gilbert and Sullivan. New York: AMS Press, 1928.

Goldman, Richard Franko, *Harmony in Western Music*. New York: W. W. Norton, 1965.

Goodman, Andrew, *Gilbert and Sullivan at Law*. London: Fairleigh Dickinson University Press, 1983.

Gilbert and Sullivan's London. Tunbridge Wells: Spellmount Limited, 1988.

Gould, Stephen Jay, 'The True Embodiment of Everything That's Excellent', in *I Have Landed*. New York: Harmony, 2002; German trans. Sebastian Vogel in S. J. Gould, *Das Ende vom Anfang der Naturgeschichte*. Frankfurt, 2005, pp. 99–124.

Grossmith, George, *A Society Clown*. Bristol: J. W. Arrowsmith, 1888.

Piano and I. Bristol: J. W. Arrowsmith, 1919.

A Juvenile Party. London: J. Bath, [1881].

Grout, Donald Jay and Hermine Weigel Williams, *A Short History of Opera*. New York: Columbia University Press, 2003.

Grzbek, P., 'Invariant Meaning Structures in Texts: Proverb and Fable', in K. P. Eimermacher, P. Grzbek and George Witte (eds.), *Issues in Slavic Literary and Cultural Theory*. Bochum: Brockmeyer, 1989.

Hamilton, Edith, 'W. S. Gilbert: A Mid-Victorian Aristophanes', *Theatre Arts Monthly* (October 1927).

Hanslick, E., *Musikalisches Skizzenbuch. Die Moderne Oper*, 2nd edn, vol. 4. Berlin: Allgemeiner Verein für Deutsche Literatur, 1888.

Harlan, A. B., *Owen Meredith: A Critical Biography of Robert, First Earl of Lytton*. New York: Columbia University Press, 1946.

Hayter, Charles, *Gilbert and Sullivan*. Basingstoke: Macmillan, 1987.

Helyar, James (ed.), *Gilbert and Sullivan: Papers Presented at the International Conference in May 1970*. Kansas City: University of Kansas Publications, 1971.

Hibbert, Christopher, *Gilbert and Sullivan and their Victorian World*. New York: American Heritage, 1976.

Hodnett, E., *Francis Barlow, First Master of English Book Illustration*. London: The Scolar Press, 1978.

Honolka, Kurt, *Opernübersetzungen: Zur Geschichte der Verdeutschung musiktheatralischer Texte*. Wilhelmshaven: Noetzel Verlag, 1978.

Hughes, Gervase, *The Music of Arthur Sullivan*. London: Macmillan, 1960.

Hughes, Meirion (ed.), *The English Musical Renaissance and the Press 1850–1914: Watchmen of Music*. Aldershot: Ashgate, 2002.

Hulme, David, 'The Operettas of Sir Arthur Sullivan: A Study of Available Autograph Full Scores'. Ph.D. diss., University of Wales, 1986.

Istel, E., *Das Libretto*. Berlin and Leipzig: Schuster & Loeffler, 1914.

Jacobs, Arthur, *Arthur Sullivan: A Victorian Musician*, 2nd edn. Aldershot: The Scolar Press, 1992.

    Henry Wood: Maker of the Proms. London: Methuen, 1994.

Jenkins, W. D., 'Swinburne, Robert Buchanan, and W. S. Gilbert: The Pain Was All But a Pleasure', *Studies in Philology*, 69 (1972), pp. 369–87.

Jolles, André, *Einfache Formen*. Halle: Niemeyer, 1930.

Jones, Brian, *Lytton: Gilbert and Sullivan's Jester*. London: Basingstoke Books Ltd, 2005.

    'The Sword that Never Fell', *W. S. Gilbert Journal*, 1/1 (1985), pp. 22–5.

Jones, John Bush, 'Gilbertian Humor: Pulling Together a Definition', *Victorian Newsletter*, 33 (1968), pp. 28–31.

Jones, John Bush (ed.), *W. S. Gilbert: A Century of Scholarship and Commentary*. New York: New York University Press, 1970.

Joseph, Tony, *George Grossmith*. Bristol: By the author, 1982.

    The D'Oyly Carte Opera Company 1875–1982: An Unofficial History. Bristol: Bunthorne Books, 1994.

Joslin, Peter, 'A Substructure of Gilbert's Plots', *W. S. Gilbert Journal*, 1/6 (1990), pp. 184–7.

Keller, O., *Die Operette*. Leipzig, Vienna and New York: Stein-Verlag, 1926.

Kinservik, Matthew J., *Disciplining Satire: The Censorship of Satiric Comedy on the Eighteenth-Century London Stage*. Lewisburg: Bucknell University Press, 2003.

Klein, Herman, *Thirty Years of Musical Life in London: 1870–1900*. London: Heinemann, 1903.

Knapp, Raymond, *The American Musical and the Formation of National Identity*. Princeton: Princeton University Press, 2005.

    The American Musical and the Performance of Personal Identity. Princeton: Princeton University Press, 2006.

Kolb, B. M. 'The Effect of Generational Change on Classical Music Concert Attendance and Orchestras' Responses in the UK and US', *Cultural Trends*, 41 (2001), pp. 1–35.

Kuykendall, James Brooks, 'The English Ceremonial Style c. 1887–1937 and its Aftermath', Ph.D. diss., Cornell University 2005.

La Fontaine, J. de, *Œuvres complètes*, ed. R. Groos and J. Schiffrin, vol. 1. Paris: Gallimard, 1954.

Lawrence, Arthur, *Sir Arthur Sullivan: Life Story, Letters, and Reminiscences*. Chicago: Herbert S. Stone, 1899; London: James Bowden, 1899; rpt. New York: Haskell House Publishers, 1973.

Lawrence, Elwood P., 'The Happy Land: W. S. Gilbert as Political Satirist', *Victorian Studies*, 15 (1971), pp. 161–83.

Leigh, Mike, *Topsy-Turvy*. London: Faber & Faber, 1999.

Lert, Ernst, *Mozart auf dem Theater*. Berlin: Schuster & Loeffler, 1918; 3rd and 4th edns, Berlin, 1921; trans. as *Mozart on the Stage*, London: Calder and Boyars, 1972.

Liebman, Arthur M., 'The Works of W. S. Gilbert: A Study of their Aristophanic Elements and their Relationship to the Development of the Nineteenth and Twentieth Century British Theatre', Ph.D. diss., New York University 1971.

Loewenberg, A., *Annals of Opera 1597–1940*. Totowa, NJ: Rowman and Little Field, 1978.

Mackenzie, Sir Alexander C., *A Musician's Narrative*. London: Cassell & Co., 1927.

'The Life-Work of Arthur Sullivan', *Sammelbände der Internationalen Musikgesellschaft*, 3 (1902), pp. 539–64.

Mackie, David, *Arthur Sullivan and The Royal Society of Musicians of Great Britain*. London: The Royal Society of Musicians of Great Britain, 2005.

Maclean, Charles, 'Sullivan as a National Style-Builder', *Proceedings of the [Royal] Musical Association*, 28 (1902), pp. 89–104.

Maitland, John A. Fuller, 'Sir Arthur Sullivan', *Cornhill Magazine* (March 1901), 300–9.

'Patter Song', *A Dictionary of Music and Musicians*, ed. George Grove. London: Macmillan, 1880, vol. 2, p. 673; 2nd edn (1907), vol. 3, p. 654.

Mathews, Charles, *The Life of Charles James Mathews*, ed. Charles Dickens. 2 vols. London: Macmillan, 1879.

mcclung, bruce d., *Lady in the Dark: Biography of a Musical*. Oxford: Oxford University Press, 2007.

'Life after George: The Genesis of *Lady in the Dark*'s Circus Dream', *Kurt Weill Newsletter*, 14 (Fall 1996), pp. 4–8.

McFarlane, Gavin, *Copyright: The Development and Exercise of the Performing Right*. London: John Offord Publications Ltd, 1980.

Midgley, Samuel, *My 70 Years' Musical Memories 1860–1930*. London: Novello, 1934.

Miles, A. H. (ed.), *The Poets and the Poetry of the Nineteenth Century*, vol. 5. London: Routledge, 1905.

Mitchell, Donald, *The Paradox of Gloriana: Simple and Difficult*. Aldeburgh Studies 1993.

Mitchell, Jerome, 'Sullivan's *Ivanhoe*', in *The Walter Scott Operas*. Tuscaloosa: University of Alabama Press, 1977.

Moody, Jane, *Illegitimate Theatre in London 1770–1840*. Cambridge: Cambridge University Press, 2000.

Morley, Henry, *Journal of a London Playgoer 1851–1866*. London: Routledge & Sons, 1866.

Morley, Michael, 'Archetypes or Readymades? A Consideration of Some Moments at Death's Door in Three Brecht Dramas', *Brecht und der Tod – The Brecht Yearbook*, 32 (2007), pp. 57–67.

Murninghan, J. K. and D. E. Conlon, 'The Dynamics of Intense Work Groups: A Study of British String Quartets', *Administrative Science Quarterly*, 36 (1991), pp. 165–86.

Naylor, Stanley, *Gaiety and George Grossmith*. London: Stanley Paul, 1913.

Nelson, John C., 'Tonal and Structural Design in the Finales of the Savoy Operas, with Some Suggestions as to Derivation', *Indiana Theory Review*, 12 (1992), pp. 1–22.

Nettel, Reginald, *The Orchestra in England*. London: Jonathan Cape, 1946.

Nietzsche, Friedrich, *The Will to Power*, trans. Walter Kaufman and R. J. Hollingdale. London: Weidenfeld and Nicolson, 1968.

O'Hara, Kane, *Midas: An English Burletta (1766)*. Los Angeles: University of California Press, 1974.

Obrist, T., 'Der Mikado – Il Mikado – Le Mikado', in Eden (ed.), *The Mikado* (1985), pp. 1–6.

Orel, Harold, *Gilbert and Sullivan: Interviews and Recollections*. London: University of Iowa Press, 1995.

Osborne, Richard, *Rossini*. London: J. M. Dent and Sons, 1986.

Parrott, Ian, 'Arthur Sullivan (1842–1900)', *Music and Letters*, 23 (1942), pp. 202–10.

Peacock, Alan and Ronald Weir, *The Composer in the Market Place*. London: Faber Music, 1975.

Pearson, Hesketh, *Gilbert: His Life and Strife*. London: Methuen, 1957.

Perry, B. E., *Aesopica*, vol. 1. Urbana: University of Illinois Press, 1952.

Pfister, Manfred and Bernd Schulte-Middelich, *Die 'Nineties' – Das englische Fin de siècle zwischen Dekadenz und Sozialkritik*. Munich: Francke Verlag, 1983.

Pitts, Stephanie, '"Everybody Wants to be Pavarotti": The Experience of Music for Performers and Audience at a Gilbert and Sullivan Festival', *Journal of the Royal Musical Association*, 129/1 (2004), pp. 143–60.

   Valuing Musical Participation. Aldershot: Ashgate, 2005.

   'What Makes an Audience? Investigating the Roles and Experiences of Listeners at a Chamber Music Festival', *Music and Letters*, 86/2 (2005), pp. 257–69.

Pitts, S. E. and C. P. Spencer, 'Loyalty and Longevity in Audience Listening: Investigating Experiences of Attendance at a Chamber Music Festival', *Music and Letters*, 89/2 (2008), pp. 227–38.

Platoff, John, 'The Buffa Aria in Mozart's Vienna', *Cambridge Opera Journal*, 2/2 (1990), pp. 99–120.

Plumb, Philip W., 'The Bab Ballads, a Publishing Account', *W. S. Gilbert Society Journal*, 1/2 (Autumn 1985), pp. 58–62.

   'The Dramatic Works of W. S. Gilbert', *W. S. Gilbert Society Journal*, 1/1 (Spring 1985), pp. 26–31.

   'Gilbert's Contributions to Periodicals', *W. S. Gilbert Society Journal*, 1/3 (Spring 1986), pp. 68–77; 1/4 (Autumn 1986), pp. 100–3.

Polianovskaia, J., 'English Operetta and Musical Comedy In Russian Translations and Adaptations', *Musique et théâtralité dans les îles Britanniques, Centre d'Étude des Textes et Traductions (CETT)*, 7 (2005), pp. 175–90.

   '"The Gaiety" in St. Petersburg', *Daly's British Musical Theatre of the Victorian and Edwardian Eras*, 2 (2003), pp. 30–4.

   'The English Operetta and Musical Comedy in German Guest Performances in St. Petersburg', *Musikgeschichte in Mittel- und Osteuropa. Mitteilungen der internationalen Arbeitsgemeinschaft an der Universität Leipzig*, 8 (2002), pp. 140–6.

Powers, H., '"La solita forma", and "The Uses of Convention"', *Acta Musicologica*, 59 (1989), pp. 65–90.

Quiller-Couch, Arthur, *Studies in Literature*, 3rd series. Cambridge: Cambridge University Press, 1929.

Raeithel, Gert, *Geschichte der nordamerikanischen Kultur*, vol. 3. Weinheim: Parkland, 1989.

Reich, Willi (ed.), *Gustav Mahler: Im eigenen Wort – Im Wort der Freunde*. Zurich: Atlantis Verlag, 1958.

Reynolds, C., *Motives for Allusion: Context and Content in Nineteenth-Century Music*. Cambridge, Mass.: Harvard University Press, 2003.

Rogers, Clara, *Memories of a Musical Career*. Boston: Little, Brown, 1919.

Rognoni, Luigi, 'Komischer Realismus und romantischer Subjektivismus bei Rossini', *Oper 1972*, pp. 70–8.

Rowell, George, 'Gilbert and Pinero: Two Flights of Fancy', *W. S. Gilbert Journal*, 1/6 (1990), pp. 164–8.

  The Victorian Theatre: A Survey. Oxford: Oxford University Press, 1956.

  (ed.), *Plays by W. S. Gilbert*. Cambridge: Cambridge University Press, 1982.

Roy, Donald, *Plays by James Robinson Planché*. Cambridge: Cambridge University Press, 1986.

Russell, D., *Popular Music in England 1840–1914: A Social History*. Manchester: Manchester University Press, 1988.

Samson, Jim (ed.), *Man and Music*, vol. 7: *The Late Romantic Era*. London: Macmillan, 1991.

Saremba, M., 'Arthur Sullivan', *MGG*.

  'Arthur Sullivan', in *Metzlers Komponistenlexikon*. Stuttgart and Weimar: Metzler Verlag, 2003.

  'Arthur Sullivan: Die Unperson der britischen Musik', in *Elgar, Britten & Co.: Eine Geschichte der britischen Musik in zwölf Portraits*. Zurich and St Gallen: Edition Musik & Theater, 1994.

  Arthur Sullivan: Ein Komponistenleben im viktorianischen England. Wilhelmshaven: Noetzel Verlag, 1993.

  'Brother Sir Arthur Sullivan: Sullivan and Freemasonry', *Sir Arthur Sullivan Society Magazine*, 61 (Winter 2005), pp. 14–19.

  'Ein weites Feld: Über Rossini und Sullivan', in *La Gazetta*, Zeitschrift der Deutschen Rossini Gesellschaft, vol. 17. Leipzig: Leipziger Universitätsverlag, 2008.

  'Gilbert & Sullivan als komische Oper statt Operette – Plädoyer für eine Neubewertung' (paper given at a conference in Vienna 1999, see www.sullivan-forschung.de).

  'In the Purgatory of Tradition: Arthur Sullivan and the English Musical Renaissance', in Christa Brüstle and Guido Held (eds.), *Music as a Bridge: German–British Musical Relationships*. Hildesheim: Olms, 2005, pp. 33–71.

  'Sir Arthur and Mr Sullivan: Von Lust und Last mit dem Komischen (Zum 100. Todestag von Arthur Sullivan)', *Opernwelt* (November 2000), pp. 18–25.

'W. S. Gilbert', *MGG*.

Saunders, Ernest, '*Oberon* and *Zar und Zimmermann*', *Musical Quarterly*, 40/4 (October 1954), pp. 521–32.

Saxe Wyndham, H., *Arthur Sullivan*. London: Kegan Paul, 1926.

Schmook, P. and W. Busch, *Kunst: Die Geschichte ihrer Funktionen*. Weinheim and Berlin: Quadriga/Beltz, 1987.

Scott, D., 'English National Identity and the Comic Operas of Gilbert and Sullivan', in Bennett Zon and Peter Horton (eds.), *Nineteenth-Century British Music Studies*, vol. 3. Aldershot: Ashgate, 2003, pp. 137–52.

Seeger, Horst, *Das große Lexikon der Oper*. Berlin: Henschel Verlag, 1978.

Seeley, Peter, 'Who was Helen Lenoir', *The Savoyard*, 21/2 (September 1982), pp. 16–18.

Shaw, George Bernard, *Music in London, 1890–94*. London: Constable, 1949.

Silverman, Richard, 'Longfellow, Liszt and Sullivan', *The Musical Review*, 36 (1975).

Skipsey, J., 'The Bee and the Rose', in A. H. Miles (ed.), *The Poets and the Poetry of the Nineteenth Century*, vol. 5. London: Routledge, 1905, p. 571.

Smith, P. J., *The Tenth Muse*. London: A. A. Knopf, 1970.

Stanford, C. V., *Studies and Memories*. London: Constable, 1908.

Stanislavsky, K., *Complete Works*. 8 vols. Moscow: Iskusstvo, 1954.

Stebbins, R., *Amateurs, Professionals and Serious Leisure*. Montreal: McGill-Queen's University Press, 1992.

Stedman, Jane, 'From Dame to Woman: W. S. Gilbert and Theatrical Transvestism', *Victorian Studies*, 14 (September 1970), pp. 27–46.
  W. S. Gilbert: A Classical Victorian and his Theatre. Oxford: Oxford University Press, 1996.
  'W. S. Gilbert: His Comic Techniques and their Development', Ph.D. diss., University of Chicago 1956.

Stedman, Jane (ed.), *Gilbert Before Sullivan: Six Comic Plays*. Chicago: University of Chicago Press, 1967.

Stephens, John Russell, *The Censorship of English Drama 1824–1901*. Cambridge: Cambridge University Press, 1980.

Stevenson, R. L., 'Lord Lytton's *Fables in Song*', in *Works*, vol. 20, ed. E. Gosse. Pentland Edition. London: Cassell, 1907.

Stradling, Robert and Meirion Hughes, *The English Musical Renaissance 1860–1940: Construction and Deconstruction*. London: Routledge, 1993.
  The English Musical Renaissance 1840–1940: Constructing a National Music, 2nd edn. Manchester: Manchester University Press, 2001.

Streatfeild, R. A., *The Opera: A Sketch of the Development of Opera*. London: Nimmo, 1897.

Strong, Jonathan, 'The Musical Gilbert: Without Sullivan', *W. S. Gilbert Society Journal*, 1/2 (Autumn 1985), pp. 36–9.

Subotnik, Rose Rosengard, 'Lortzing and the German Romantics: A Dialectical Assessment', *Musical Quarterly*, 57/2 (April 1976), pp. 241–64.

Sullivan, Arthur, 'About Music', address given to Birmingham and Midland Institute, 19 October 1888, reproduced in Arthur Lawrence, *Arthur Sullivan: Life*

Story, Letters and Reminiscences, pp. 261–87, German trans. in Saremba, *Arthur Sullivan*, pp. 328–38.

Interview, *The Musical World*, 24 January 1885.

Interview, *San Francisco Daily Chronicle*, 22 July 1885.

Interview, *Pall Mall Gazette*, 5 December 1889.

Sullivan, Herbert and Newman Flower, *Sir Arthur Sullivan: His Life, Letters & Diaries*. London: Cassell & Co., 1927 (2/1950).

Sutton, Max Keith, *W. S. Gilbert*. Boston: Twayne, 1975.

Taruskin, Richard, 'Chaikovsky and the Human', in *Defining Russia Musically: Historical and Hermeneutical Essays*. Princeton: Princeton University Press, 1997.

Taylor, Benedict, 'The Lost Chord: Sentimentality, Sincerity, and the Search for "Emotional Depth" in 19th-Century Music', *International Review of Aesthetics and Sociology of Music*, 40/1 (2009).

Taylor, S. *The Indebtedness of Handel to Works by Other Composers: A Presentation of the Evidence*. Cambridge: Cambridge University Press, 1906.

Temperley, N., 'The English Romantic Opera', *Victorian Studies*, 9 (1966), pp. 293–301.

    The Lost Chord. Bloomington and Indianapolis: Indiana University Press, 1989.

    'Mendelssohn's Influence on English Music', *Music & Letters*, 43 (1962), pp. 224–33.

Temperley, Nicholas (ed.), *The Athlone History of Music in Britain*, vol 5: *The Romantic Age 1800–1914*. London: Athlone Press, 1981.

Thompson, S., *Motif Index of Folk Literature*. Bloomington, Ind.: Indiana University Press, 1955.

Tillett, L. S., 'Jane Annie', in D. J. Eden (ed.), *Utopia Limited: A Centenary Review of the Year 1893*. Coventry: Sir Arthur Sullivan Society, 1993.

    'Mirette', in D. J. Eden (ed.), *Mirette* and *His Majesty: A Study of Two Savoy Operas*. Coventry: Sir Arthur Sullivan Society, 1996.

Vaughan Williams, Ralph, *Nationalism in Music and Other Essays*. Oxford: Oxford University Press, 1972.

Vicinus, Martha, *The Industrial Muse: A Study of Nineteenth-Century British Working-Class Literature*. New York: Barnes and Noble Books, 1974.

Vinogradskaya, I., *Life and Art of K. S. Stanislavsky: Chronicle*, 4 vols. Moscow: VTO, 1971.

Walter, Bruno, *Thema und Variationen: Erinnerungen und Gedanken*. Frankfurt: S. Fischer Verlag, 1950.

Walvin, James, *Victorian Values*. London: Andre Deutsch, 1987.

Watson, Alfred E. T., *A Sporting and Dramatic Career*. London: Macmillan, 1918.

Wedel, Michaela, 'Die Savoy Operas von W.S. Gilbert und A. Sullivan: Übersetzungsproblematik und Rezeptionsgeschichte in Deutschland unter besonderer Berücksichtigung des Mikado', Unpublished diss., Mannheim 1994.

Weissmann, A., *Berlin als Musikstadt*. Berlin: Schuster & Loeffler, 1911.

Westrup, Jack, 'An Eminent Victorian', *The Listener*, 13 March 1941.

White, Eric Walter, *The Rise of English Opera*. London: John Lehmann, 1951.

Willaschek, Wolfgang, *Mozart-Theater: vom 'Idomeneo' bis zur 'Zauberflöte'*. Stuttgart and Weimar: Metzler Verlag, 1995.

Williamson, Audrey, *Gilbert and Sullivan Opera: A New Assessment*. London: Rockliff, 1953; 2nd edn. London: Marion Boyars Inc., 1982.

Wilson, Fredric Woodbridge, 'The W. S. Gilbert Papers in The British Library', *W. S. Gilbert Society Journal*, 1/4 (Autumn 1986), pp. 105–19.

Wilson, Glenn, 'The Behaviour Therapy of W. S. Gilbert', *The Sir Arthur Sullivan Society Magazine*, 23 (Autumn 1986), pp. 10–14.

Wilson, R. and F. Lloyd, *Gilbert & Sullivan: The Official D'Oyly Carte Picture History*. New York: Knopf, 1984.

Wolfson, John, *Final Curtain: The Last Gilbert and Sullivan Operas*. London: Chappell, 1976.

  Sullivan and the Scott Russells. Chichester: Packard Publishing Ltd, 1984.

Wood, Henry J., My *Life of Music*. London: Gollancz, 1938.

Wren, Gayden, *A Most Ingenious Paradox: The Art of Gilbert & Sullivan*. Oxford: Oxford University Press, 2001.

Yates, Martin, 'Musical Unity in the *Yeomen* Score', in Eden (ed.), *The Yeomen of the Guard and Macbeth* (1988), pp. 22–34.

Young, G. M., *Victorian England: Portrait of an Age*. London: Oxford University Press, 1977.

Young, J. A., *A Century of Service: The National Operatic and Dramatic Association*. London: NODA, 1997.

Young, Percy M., *A History of British Music*. London: Benn, 1967.

  Sir Arthur Sullivan. London: J. M. Dent & Sons, 1971.

Zedlitz, M. A. von, 'Sir Arthur Sullivan' (Interviews with Eminent Musicians No. 3), in *The Strand Musical Magazine*, 1 (January–June 1895), pp. 169–74.

Websites

Sullivan research: www.sullivan-forschung.de

The Gilbert and Sullivan Archive: http://math.boisestate.edu/GaS/

Sir Arthur Sullivan Society: www.sirarthursullivansociety.uk.org

Magazines

Sir Arthur Sullivan Society Magazine

W. S. Gilbert Society Magazine

Gilbert and Sullivan Journal

Original sources: Sullivan

Sullivan's diaries can be found in the Pierpont Morgan Library, New York (1876–80) and in The Beinecke Rare Book and Manuscript Library, Yale University Library (1881–1900).

For details see Geoffrey Dixon: *Sullivan's Diaries: An Index to Sir Arthur Sullivan's Diary, 1876–1900*. Ayr: Rhosearn Press, 2007.

Current location of Sullivan's manuscript full scores

The Beauty Stone Oxford, Bodleian Library

The Chieftain London, British Library

The Contrabandista London, British Library
Cox and Box New York, Pierpont Morgan Library
The Emerald Isle London, British Library
The Golden Legend London, Royal College of Music
The Gondoliers London, British Library
The Grand Duke New York, collection John Wolfson
Haddon Hall London, British Library
HMS Pinafore New York, Pierpont Morgan Library
Iolanthe London, D'Oyly Carte Opera Trustees
Ivanhoe New York, Wolfson Foundation
The Light of the World Oxford, Oxford University Faculty of Music
The Martyr of Antioch London, Royal Academy of Music
The Mikado London, Royal Academy of Music
Patience London, British Library
The Pirates of Penzance New York, Pierpont Morgan Library
Princess Ida Oxford, Bodleian Library
The Prodigal Son London, private collection
The Rose of Persia Oxford, Bodleian Library
Ruddigore London, British Library
The Sorcerer New York, Wolfson Foundation
Trial by Jury New York, Pierpont Morgan Library
Utopia Limited Lost
The Yeomen of the Guard London, Royal College of Music
The Zoo London, British Library
A facsimile of the *Mikado* autograph was published by Gregg International
   Publishers Limited, Farnborough, Hampshire, 1968.

Original sources: Gilbert
Gilbert's correspondence, diaries, plays and librettos (drafts, manuscripts,
   typescripts, prompt-books etc.) can be found in the British Library, London.
For a detailed list, see 'The W. S. Gilbert Papers in The British Library', *W. S. Gilbert
   Society Journal*, 1/4 (Autumn 1986), 106–19.

Index

Cambridge Companions to Music

Topics

The Cambridge Companion to Ballet
Edited by Marion Kant

The Cambridge Companion to Blues and Gospel Music
Edited by Allan Moore

The Cambridge Companion to the Concerto
Edited by Simon P. Keefe

The Cambridge Companion to Conducting
Edited by José Antonio Bowen

The Cambridge Companion to Eighteenth-Century Music
Edited by Anthony R. DelDonna and Pierpaolo Polzonetti

The Cambridge Companion to Electronic Music
Edited by Nick Collins and Julio D'Escriván

The Cambridge Companion to Grand Opera
Edited by David Charlton

The Cambridge Companion to Jazz
Edited by Mervyn Cooke and David Horn

The Cambridge Companion to the Lied
Edited by James Parsons

The Cambridge Companion to Medieval Music
Edited by Mark Everist

The Cambridge Companion to the Musical, second edition
Edited by William Everett and Paul Laird

The Cambridge Companion to the Orchestra
Edited by Colin Lawson

The Cambridge Companion to Pop and Rock
Edited by Simon Frith, Will Straw and John Street

The Cambridge Companion to Recorded Music
Edited by Eric Clarke, Nicholas Cook, Daniel Leech-Wilkinson and John Rink

The Cambridge Companion to the String Quartet
Edited by Robin Stowell

The Cambridge Companion to Twentieth-Century Opera
Edited by Mervyn Cooke

Composers

The Cambridge Companion to Bach
Edited by John Butt

The Cambridge Companion to Bartók
Edited by Amanda Bayley

The Cambridge Companion to the Beatles
Edited by Kenneth Womack

The Cambridge Companion to Beethoven
Edited by Glenn Stanley

The Cambridge Companion to Berg
Edited by Anthony Pople

The Cambridge Companion to Berlioz
Edited by Peter Bloom